D0138875

Five Per Cent Philanthropy

Five Per Cent Philanthropy

An account of housing in urban areas
between 1840 and 1914

John Nelson Tarn

Cambridge
at the University Press · 1973

Published by the Syndics of the Cambridge University Press
Bentley House, 200 Euston Road, London NWI 2DB
American Branch: 32 East 57th Street, New York, N.Y.10022

© Cambridge University Press 1973

Library of Congress Catalogue Card Number: 77-186253

ISBN: 0 521 08506 3

Printed in Great Britain by
Alden & Mowbray Ltd
at the Alden Press, Oxford

for my father
and to the memory of my mother

Acknowledgements

I should like to thank the Managers, Secretaries and Surveyors of the many housing trusts and companies mentioned in this book; the town clerks, city architects, planning offices and librarians in many of the towns and cities I have referred to. They have all answered many questions and provided me with a great deal of information, maps and plans.

I should also like to thank Professor Jack Napper who first turned my attention to urban problems long before they were so popular a subject, Professor Sir Leslie Martin who guided the early stages of the work when I was a research student, and Sir John Summerson and Sir Niklaus Pevsner who gave encouragement and gently persuaded me that a thesis was not a book. To them all I owe a great deal, although they bear no responsibility for the view I hold.

The final stages of the work were carried out with a grant from the Historical Architectural Research Trust Fund of the Royal Institute of British Architects: to them I owe a very real debt for their practical help.

The illustrations in this book are reproduced by kind permission of the following:

Illustrated London News, Figs. 3.1, 3.4, 3.6, 4.1, 4.2, 4.3a, 4.6a, 6.7; *The Builder*, Figs. 1.2, 2.3, 3.3, 4.24, 4.25, 4.26, 4.32, 6.6b, 6.8b, 6.9a,b, 6.10a,b, 6.11b, 9.5a; Henry Roberts, *The Dwellings of the Labouring Classes*, Figs. 1.1a, 2.1a,b, 2.8, 2.10a, 3.2; Prices (Bromborough) Ltd, Figs. 9.2a,b; Palatinate Engraving Co., Fig. 4.29; Aerofilms, Figs. 3.9, 9.16c, 9.18a; Ebenezer Howard, *Garden Cities of Tomorrow*, Figs. 9.15a,b,c; James Hole, *Homes of the Working Classes*, Figs. 4.12a, 8.5a, 8.6a,b, 8.8a,b, 8.10a,b; 1830 Housing Society, Figs. 2.6a,b, 2.7; C. J. Stewart (for the L.C.C.) *The Housing Question in London*, Figs. 6.2, 8.1a,b, 8.2; Paul Marsh and *The Architect*, Fig. 9.1; Bournville Village Trust, Fig. 9.13a; Joseph Rowntree Memorial Trust, Fig. 9.17a; Bedford Park, Fig. 9.10; Mrs S. Coddington, Fig. 3.10; Birmingham Public Libraries (Local Studies Library), Fig. 6.6c; The Controller of Her Majesty's Stationery Office for the Ordnance Survey, Figs. 3.11b,c, 4.15a, 6.3a, 6.4b, 9.10, 9.12b, 9.13b, 9.17b, 9.19c, 9.20; Plans in Figs. 4.3b, 4.6b, 4.13a,b, 4.15b, 6.14, 6.16b, 9.14 were prepared by Mrs S. Coddington from drawings belonging to various Trusts and Companies. All other illustrations are by the author.

J.N.T.
April 1973

Contents

List of Illustrations

Introduction

This book sets out to examine the growth of working class housing in this country during the nineteenth century. Its purpose is twofold: first to make some attempt to expound the complex philosophy behind the developing housing movement, and secondly, to set against this the history of the buildings which were constructed specifically to house the poor. It is an attempt to explain why housing policies formulated early this century took the form that they did. Thus, indirectly, I am seeking to analyse why people are often today so unwilling to accept what architects and planners, because of their historical attitudes, seek to impose upon them.

It is frequently assumed that somewhere in the middle of the nineteenth century the industrial town suddenly 'happened' and that ever since we have been struggling to restore the mythical conditions of a more gracious, supposedly healthier, happier and more stable age. True, we have been struggling ever since we became aware that there were such problems and with what result you may see by examining any great industrial city. It is a fallacy, however, to believe that these conditions suddenly came into existence at some fixed point in history. The industrial town had been growing for several generations and a glance at the chronology of technological invention in the eighteenth, or at the population statistics during the early decades of the nineteenth century will show that the roots of the revolution go back much further than our awareness of the social problems which they produced would suggest.[1]

We must remember, too, that in England before the industrial revolution, change of any kind had been relatively slow, so that the structure of society was able to assimilate it without undue difficulty and there had grown up a philosophical outlook on life which was deeply entrenched. This was enshrined in the doctrine of *laissez-faire*, the idea that events would take care of themselves if allowed to do so and that interference of any kind, particularly paternalistic interference by government, was as undesirable as it was unnecessary.

On this basis, the industrial town was allowed to grow, while society as a whole accepted the changes as inevitable; it was believed that such problems as might become apparent would be solved by mutual consent or they would in the end somehow miraculously disappear as they had always seemed to do in the past. But this time it was not to be so. The problems of too many people living too close together without adequate supplies of the basic necessities of life defied this old order, and the inherent complacency of society was shaken as never before by the outbreak of cholera and typhoid, diseases which did not appear to respect class or district and which scourged the country from the thirties onwards until the worst evils of the town were finally removed by concerted popular action and civic initiative. By then, the old order was broken down.

Many people speculated upon the cause of the new evils, and at the same time they were obliged to recognise that urbanity was no longer necessarily a term of delight – the town was now patently not a pleasant place in which to live. That was the price of progress. England led the industrial revolution, its towns were larger and uglier than those of any other country, they were filled with great mills and factories belching forth acrid smoke and fumes, each employing vast and ever-growing armies of people who had been drifting in from the country for several generations in search of work; people who believed that in the towns there were better prospects for the future than under the old agrarian order of the rural areas. Now, for the first time, they constituted a separate recognisable and articulate class, living together in well defined ghettos either newly run up by speculative builders around the gates of the works, or in old courts taken over and over-occupied as the old owners foresook the central areas for the pleasanter suburbs.

The eighteenth century idea of the town as a place of urban elegance was gone, the town was now seen as squalid and monotonous, a great amorphous area of tangled building, unplanned and unloved, pushing the countryside further and further away so that it was an effort to reach it, a place for outings on holidays and fine summer Sundays. The country was soon held in high regard; it was better than the town, it represented all that was seen to be worthwhile in life: to leave the town was like escaping hell itself. The significance of this growing hatred of urbanism and all it stood for is important because it is the root cause of the popularity of the garden city movement later in the century.

By mid-century, then, the town was a symbol of hopelessness, of grinding poverty, ill health, disease and dirt, of inadequate water supplies, non-existent drainage and the absence of scavenging. This was how it appeared to those forced to live there, while those who could afford to, established themselves in villas in the suburbs where they could enjoy the wealth that could be made out of the squalid town without exposing their families from day to day to its physical problems. When we first read of the problems of health and housing it is at that point when society has been obliged to give them proper consideration, although in reality we are concerned only with the magnitude of a problem which had long existed. It is rather like assuming today that we do not have a traffic problem until the traffic ceases to move, because it is only then that we are obliged to count the cost of failing to plan for it. So it was with the problem of physical growth in towns a century ago.

Attempts to find the machinery and the method by which the industrial town might be changed are symptoms of the crisis which was recognised to exist first between 1830 and 1840, and at that point it is fair to say that the whole historical attitude to the town was reversed. The industrial town now fast assumed a predatory quality; people were afraid of the physical problems it engendered, afraid too of the uncontrollable mob, learning to speak with a unified voice through their first attempts at combination.[2] In addition, there was from time to time a growing feeling of guilt which was a new reaction to such a situation. Had it been right for so long to treat the working classes, men, women and children, as sub-human fodder for the great machines, a class of person without feeling or any right to basic human dignity? Many began to feel uneasy about the way in which they had achieved their wealth and it was not only the fear of revolution, politically, but the rise of a queasy Christian conscience which caused some of them to feel a moral obligation to interest themselves in welfare work of various kinds and to indulge in paternalistic interference initially of the mildest variety, although of the utmost significance.[3]

There was another important aspect of this discovery of the industrial town. Once the ugliness and the cruelty was realised, those who could run away from it not only decamped into the suburbs, but at the same time took refuge in a romantic intellectual movement which in architecture took the form of stylistic eclecticism and especially a delight in the revival of Gothic forms. The escape, as young Pugin so clearly explained, was to a medieval catholic utopia somewhere in the 14th century.[4] What better way could there be of removing the stigma of the industrial age than to recreate the architecture of the idyllic medieval past which he and many others like him began to romanticise and indeed to revive for the nouveau riche and the church? The nineteenth century town is littered with artistic aberrations, seriously exotic buildings by the standards of the day, which would be a far better memorial of the Victorian age if they did not represent at the same time the total failure of the architectural profession to come to terms with the real problems of the century. One looks in vain for the great designer in the early working class housing movement and that is another reason why so little is known about housing policies and the men who built our towns. It is a twilight world because there was no room for aesthetic discussion and still less for frills in design. Working class housing was social realism of a new kind.

Perhaps it did not matter whether the architect was involved or not, for there was probably little that he or any one else could have done to change the pattern of events or alter the steadily growing demand for too much accommodation on too little land at too small

a price. The early examples of organised working class housing were regularly described as 'barracky', but none knew how to make them otherwise. Yet if we do not try to understand the pressures which produced this pattern of development we will fail to see why well meaning re-housing developments only added to the ultimate hatred of the town. Model dwellings might be healthy, whereas the slums were not, but visually they were no more beautiful and they only added to the anti-urban view of life which found its outlet in the idealism of Ebenezer Howard at the very end of the century.

Finally, if we are to understand the roots of the housing policies which operate within our own society, as well as the aspirations of the people for whom housing is built, then we must follow step by step the long drawn out battle for basic human rights – the right of a working man to have a living wage and a decent home – and we must try to understand the arguments and prejudice about common ownership and subsidisation which concerned those involved in the housing movement, particularly in the last quarter of the nineteenth century.

Housing is one of the central themes of our own welfare programme, that it is so is the legacy of the Victorian conscience. That curious mixture of social guilt and business acumen which made the Shaftesburys and the Salts the men they were, unique products of one special age. It produced, too, the social and political novels of people so widely differing in background and motive as Dickens and Mrs Gaskell, Kingsley and Disraeli, but who were united in a common concern for the society which the ingenuity of their own age had accidentally created.[5]

Housing is essentially a social problem but it is also inextricably mixed up with a whole range of environmental problems. For this reason the account which follows tries to sort out the issues which led to the formulation of a housing policy, against the tangled background of political, social, economic and legal pressures of nineteenth century England. It is, in the end, the account of how council housing, as we understand it, was born out of that curious Victorian private enterprise housing movement which was so often then called 'five per cent philanthropy' that I have chosen to use it as the title of this whole work.

I

The slum exposed: housing, public health and parliament before 1855

Chadwick and the movement for reform

If one was asked to choose a single figure who stood for the new attitude to health and housing problems at the beginning of Queen Victoria's reign, it would most certainly be Edwin Chadwick, the first Secretary of the Poor Law Board.[1] A controversial figure by any standards, he devoted much of his energy to the problems of public health during a long and often stormy career which, particularly in the early years, kept him constantly in the public eye. He was born in 1800, and after studying initially for the legal profession, came under the influence of Jeremy Bentham and the radical political theorists of the late twenties and early thirties. As a person he seems to have been unattractive; a crushing bore, overbearing, and at times quite unreasonable in the tenacious way he held to a point of view in which he personally had faith. These faults led to his inability to work with committees and boards, and thus eventually to personal frustration and disappointment, but although he moved from the full glare of public life during the fifties, many of the views and opinions which he expressed while working for the Poor Law Board were eventually proved right, and before he died at the great age of ninety he had the dubious satisfaction of seeing many of his early proposals accepted and carried out by others.

Chadwick's appointment to the Poor Law Board in 1834 took him temporarily away from the subject of public health while he helped to establish the general administrative pattern of the new Board, which in itself was a significant achievement, but following the renewed epidemics of cholera and typhoid in 1837 and 1838, the Poor Law Commissioners were requested by the government to investigate the condition of towns throughout the country. Thereafter the issues of public health became again of paramount importance to him, linked with the problem of creating adequate machinery such as he had helped to create for the Poor Law Board, to administer the sanitary reforms which were required. The scale of Chadwick's inquiry was quite unprecedented and it took several years of investigation to amass the evidence necessary to write a report. Meanwhile, a Select Committee was set up by the government in 1840 'to inquire into the circumstances affecting the health of the inhabitants of large towns, with a view to improving sanitary arrangements for their benefits'. The Committee's Report, dated 17 July 1840, recommended a General Building Act, a Sewage Act, and it suggested that large towns should have permanent boards of health with inspectors to enforce sanitary regulations. The other contentious issues, concerned with burial grounds, open space, lodging houses, the provision of baths and the cleansing of streets, were all recommended for further study. The work of the Select Committee was totally eclipsed, however, by the publication two years later, on 9 July 1842, of the Poor Law Board's *Report on the Sanitary Conditions of the Labouring Population and on the Means of its Improvement*, although it was signed by George Nicholls, George Cornewall Lewis, and Edmund Head Walker the Commissioners, it was almost entirely the work of their Secretary, Edwin Chadwick.

He was able to make use of the network of boards of guardians which covered the country and to each of them had been sent detailed questionnaires about local conditions. The wealth of information which was returned for Chadwick to edit was reinforced by personal eye-witness accounts provided by the Board's own doctors, Arnott, Kay and Southwood Smith. Chadwick himself inspected parts of London and visited Edinburgh, Glasgow, Manchester, Leeds and Macclesfield.

The Report was an epoch-making document, novel, thorough and seemingly incontrovertible. It begins with a description of the general conditions which prevailed in a country where, Chadwick claimed, more died each year from preventable diseases than had been killed at the battle of Waterloo. The cause of this, he wrote, was atmospheric impurity, which in turn varied with the quality of the water supply and the nature of the drainage:

In the manufacturing towns of England, most of which have enlarged with great rapidity, the additions have been made without regard to either the personal comfort of the inhabitants or the necessities which congregation requires. To build the largest number of cottages on the smallest allowable space seems to have been the original view of the speculators, and the having the houses up and tenanted, the *ne plus ultra* of their desires. Thus neighbourhoods have arisen in which there is neither water nor out-offices, nor any conveniences for the absolute domestic wants of the occupiers. But more than this, the land has been disposed of in so many small lots, to petty proprietors, who have subsequently built at pleasure, both as to outward form and inward ideas, that the street presents all sorts of incongruities in the architecture...[2]

There were parts of London where water was purchased by the pailful and others where it was necessary to walk a quarter of a mile to the nearest tap. The Report stressed the need for an adequate water supply, since this was necessary for a water-borne drainage system, which was advocated by John Roe and strongly supported by Chadwick.

Chadwick found little evidence of organised working class housing, except for a few scattered examples in the country, provided by benevolent aristocratic landowners:

In the manufacturing districts, the tenements erected by building clubs and by speculating builders of the class of workmen, are frequently the subject of complaint, as being the least substantial and the most destitute of proper accommodation...[3]

He extolled the virtue of organised model housebuilding either on a philanthropic basis or commercially, from both the health and the social point of view.

There was, of course, already in existence the rather curious social experiment of Robert Owen at New Lanark, where substantial housing had been built as part of the development of a new community. The Report also cites an example on a more humble scale at Catrine in Ayrshire, where the Buchanan family had laid out a small estate and offered financial help for their workers to build houses. A further example was mentioned at some flax mills at Cupar in Fife but these were all the investigators were able to find.

An interesting theoretical contribution on this subject, which is worthy of mention, was made by the well known architect, Sydney Smirke, who wrote:

I propose that there should be erected buildings, in various parts of the suburbs, consisting of perhaps 50 or 60 rooms, high, airy, dry, well ventilated, light and warm, comfortably fitted up, fireproof, abundantly supplied with water and thoroughly drained...[4]

The section of the Report concerned with the contemporary legislative position was one of its most important, showing up a diversity of unrelated bodies responsible for water supply, drainage and other public services. It pointed out that the existing building acts were largely confined to stipulating fire precautions and that they paid little or no attention to spatial controls. No provision was made for the operation of legal powers outside the jurisdiction of the local building surveyor or the commissioners of sewers, and it was common for speculative builders to develop suburban estates unimpeded by any form of control. Thomas Cubitt, the London contractor, recommended that future legislation should be uniformly and skilfully administered, so that the speculative builder was not encouraged to build outside the town, to the detriment of the working classes. This was easy enough to recommend but difficult to put into practice. Chadwick went further than this and recommended that builders should be obliged to submit plans of their developments for approval by local authorities and that the indiscriminate development of land outside the jurisdiction of authority should be prevented. In effect he was seeking the powers contained in twentieth century town planning legislations, and the same kind of nation-wide administrative network as existed for the Poor Law Commission.

The Report was a massive condemnation of contemporary society; but it was a personal appraisal, and it showed Chadwick's particular bias towards the creation of the proper machinery for administrating bye-laws and controls, with local boards working under a central authority. In this he was a true disciple of Bentham. He also believed that the creation of additional housing was a secondary matter; more important was the establishment of proper drainage and an adequate, pure water supply. Scientific and engineering remedies seemed to be more important than medical ones and this minimising of the doctor's role was perhaps Chadwick's greatest blind spot, and one which aroused most criticisms.

The Royal Commission on the Health of Towns

However, 1842 was not the most auspicious year for the publication of a report such as this; a year which has been described as the most gloomy in the century, notable for unemployment, and for the economic depression which followed a series of disastrous harvests.[5] There was the recurring fear of a working class revolt, although Chartism was even then a declining force, a fact which was not obvious, however, at that time. Public interest rose and fell, in a fickle way, with the incidence of cholera. The prospect of swift political action was also negligible, for parliament was preoccupied with other matters, particularly the vexing agrarian problems which led to the repeal of the corn laws in 1846. Nor was a polemical report expressing the views of one man, in reality, sufficient evidence for legislation. Despite the scale of the enquiry and the honesty of purpose with which it was carried out, it did not, and indeed it could not, have the authority of a parliamentary enquiry. Its critics regarded it, cynically, as inflammatory and biased.

If major reforms were not yet possible, significant measures which reflect a growing concern for the working classes did reach the statute book, such as the Coal Mines Act of 1842 and the Factory Act passed two years later, both aimed at improving the working conditions of the poor, and preventing the exploitation of children. The inspiration for them was Lord Ashley, afterwards the 7th Earl of Shaftesbury, one of the curious new generation of evangelical tory churchmen who were filled with a deep and abiding sense of social responsibility. Ashley was to play a not insignificant part in the housing movement itself.

A third measure which, it will be remembered, had been suggested by the 1840 Select Committee, was a Building Act, and while no national measure reached the statute book, this proposal led to the passing of the Metropolitan Building Act in 1844, based on an abortive bill first presented to parliament in 1841.

Chadwick's report for the Poor Law Board might not have been an impartial document, but the sheer weight of evidence which it unearthed and laid before a rather unwilling public could hardly be ignored. It was now imperative that its validity should be tested and in 1843 the Government set up a Royal Commission on the Health of Towns. Much of the evidence about existing conditions which it heard from medical men and building surveyors reinforced what Chadwick had found. Following his example the Commissioners again sent out questionnaires and followed them up with personal visits to a group of towns which had grown rapidly and possessed a death rate rather higher than average.

The Commissioners found evidence of laxity in public administration nearly everywhere. Towns which possessed local acts did not use them, drainage and water supplies were hopelessly inadequate, housing developments were uncontrolled and there was overcrowding everywhere.

An interim report, together with much of the evidence, appeared in 1844 and the final report on 3 February 1845. This contained the findings and recommendations of the Commissioners. An important section, from our point of view, dealt with building regulations. There was little control, they said, over the width of streets and the provision of open space, and builders constructed defective property whenever there was the absence of restraint – which was frequently – and they built to high densities. The Commissioners, therefore, recommended that local authorities should be empowered to raise money in order to purchase property which would permit streets to be widened and courts opened to the fresh air. But the well established principle of back to back housing did not receive the condemnation which was its due:

The mere provision that an open space shall be left at the back, as well as the front of a house affords little security for a due supply of fresh air in the interior, while the addition of another outer wall, besides enhancing the cost of the building, increases the surface exposed to the damp and cold, which readily penetrates through the scantily constructed walls of inferior houses.[6]

They were thus unwilling to suggest any fundamental amendment of the existing law on this point:

With the view therefore of ensuring better external ventilation, we recommend that courts and alleys be not built of less width than twenty feet, and that they have an opening of not less than ten feet from the ground upwards at each end; the width of the court being in proportion to the height of the houses.[7]

On the whole the Report suggested the strengthening of legal and administrative procedures rather than the introduction of novelties. For example, the vexed question of cellar dwellings, which the Commissioners might well have wished to see abolished, were not condemned – no doubt because of the disastrous effect upon overcrowding that would have resulted – rather the Commissioners sought to bring them inside the control of the law so that a minimum standard might be established.

Chadwick's views on drainage were endorsed by their recommendation that water-borne systems should be adopted; and altogether the two massive volumes vindicate, in an official and impartial way, many of the findings of the Poor Law Board. By 1845, then, the whole sordid story of the growth of industrial England had been exposed and committed to cold print in the pages of parliamentary papers, for all who cared to read them. They make a massive and revolting indictment of the *laissez-faire* philosophers of the older generation. But it took many years for the evils of health and housing to be rectified, and it required the

reversal of many prized social theories. It was one thing to expose the evils of existing towns; quite another to cure them.

The growth of public concern

The climate of public opinion in the early forties contained none of the radical elements which were to assert themselves later in the century in the attempts to try and solve the housing problem by centralised, authoritarian methods. The growth of public concern – by which I really mean the growth of tangible activity – was at first a matter for private individuals. This was the only way that the newly fledged social conscience, brought up against a strictly *laissez-faire* background, was able to conceive its role in relation to these helpless myriad masses pent up in the towns so luridly described in the quiet pages of the blue books. It is largely the history of aristocratic interest, fostered by a sense of guilt which was peculiarly Victorian and it created a kind of benevolent paternalism which was entirely new in English urban society.

The development of the first organised housing will be discussed later: that was the most useful and practical outcome of the revelations at the beginning of the decade, but there were other events which in their small way built up to create a definite trend.

The foundations of the model housing movement were soundly laid during the years between 1845 and 1850. Its progress was by no means straightforward; but the point had been well made that the community as a whole could aid the working classes in a practical way by supporting the construction of model dwellings which were subsequently carefully managed. Already it was clear that the building of similar tenement blocks would not be commercially profitable and it was this aspect, particularly, which nearly halted the housing movement after 1850.

The sense of public responsibility grew in other ways, however, during the forties.

In 1844 the Health of Towns Association was founded:

for the purpose of diffusing amongst the people the information obtained by recent enquiries, as to physical and moral evils that result from the present defective sewerage, drainage, supply of water, air and light, and the construction of dwelling houses; and also for the purpose of assisting the legislature to carry into practical operation any effectual and general measures of relief, by preparing the public mind for the change.[8]

The central committee of the Association included men of such differing political persuasions as Disraeli, lords Normanby and Morpeth, and John Manners. That same year an Association for Promoting Cleanliness Amongst the Poor was set up to promote the establishment of public baths and wash-houses, and Chadwick tried, unsuccessfully, to form a Town Improvements Company.[9] Another highly significant event, although of a rather different nature, was the foundation of a new magazine, *The Builder*, at the end of 1842, and the appointment soon afterwards of an architect, George Godwin, as its editor. During the next forty years, he made the magazine a forum for opinions and reports on housing and sanitary reforms, constantly using its pages to expose existing conditions throughout the country and to publicise improvements and new buildings. By his tenacity, the problems of the poor were brought constantly before the eyes of an often unwilling public; *The Builder* was a major force in the history of the following decades, and its editor one of the great influences in the housing movement. Its pages week by week are amongst the chief sources of information on the subject.[10]

London's problems gradually became more specialised as the century advanced. Partly this was because of its unprecedented size, for it had become far larger than any city previously known in English history; but also because it remained a great magnet throughout the century, continuously attracting people from all over the country. The great provincial towns were faced with rather different problems of growth. They were not so much concerned with the pressure of overcrowding due to the sheer size of the town, although overcrowding due to poverty was a very real problem, as with the problem of sudden and very rapid expansion. Small country towns found themselves within a single generation large amorphous industrial cities. If the origins of the problems were different the conditions which existed were no less serious: as Chadwick has shown, the state of many great industrial cities was often appalling. Administrative procedures were frequently so embryonic, if existent at all, that they were quite incapable of coping with such sudden growth. Many towns had obtained local Acts specifically for the purposes of water supply or drainage. The possession of an Act did not mean that it was enforced, and most councils or boards of guardians were unwilling to undertake schemes which would place a burden on the rates, thus endangering their own popularity.[11]

The large quantities of housing which were built at this time usually resulted from speculative developments, many of which were totally uncontrolled, so that reports of jerry-building, of inadequate or non-existent drainage and water supplies, were common; and as a result the epidemics spread by these defects were numerous and often more virulent in the new suburbs around provincial towns than in the metropolis. There were occasional examples of public concern, although, as a general rule, the metropolis led the way at this time, while the provincial towns lagged behind. The early development of building legislation at Liverpool was a positive step in one direction, it was unique in its scope and in its intention at that time.[12] There were also reports during the decade of the foundation of various societies, for example the Suffolk Society for Bettering the Condition of the Labouring Classes in 1844,[13] and the Hereford Cottage Association two years later.[14] The Leeds Friendly Loan Society held its first meeting in 1845,[15] and there were

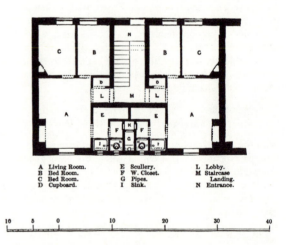

A Living Room.   E Scullery.   L Lobby.
B Bed Room.   F W. Closet.   M Staircase
C Bed Room.   G Pipes.   Landing.
D Cupboard.   I Sink.   N Entrance.

1.1 *Tenements built by the Birkenhead Dock Company in 1847, probably the first working class flats to be built in this country; the architect was C. E. Lang*

reports of meetings concerned with working class dwellings from places as far apart as Dorsetshire, Inverness and Macclesfield.[16] That they did little at first except pass pious resolutions is not important: they reflected interest and concern and this was significant.

Certain towns were beginning to take an interest in model dwellings, and the foundation of small organisations very often dates from this decade. The first recorded building venture was at Birkenhead, where the problems of the dockers must have been acute for the town had grown from a population of 200 in 1821 – a mere village – to 20,000 in 1847.[17] As *The Builder* put it, 'The Birkenhead Dock Company have viewed the matter broadly: they have taken into consideration not merely profit and loss, but the comfort of the inmates and the welfare of their neighbours...'[18] Various designs had been submitted and that of a London architect, Charles E. Lang, was accepted by the Company and submitted to Lord Ashley's Society for comment. A special sub-committee was set up, which included Henry Roberts, the London housing architect and Becket Denison, the Leeds housing expert, a man well known in the north for his interest and knowledge of housing problems. Their report was not very favourable; they complained that while the buildings were four storeys high there was only 18 ft. between blocks; that the bedrooms were too small and insufficient in number for families with children of both sexes.[19] However, despite these adverse comments, the blocks were built and completed in 1845, and therefore they were the first multi-storey tenements in the country. As such, they attracted a good deal of attention:

These workmen's dwellings then: what are they? One hardly knows at the first glance what to think of them. They are so totally unlike anything of the kind to which we are accustomed, that a standard of comparison is not easily suggested. They are not rows of cottages containing two or three rooms each, fronted and backed by gardens. They are not scattered cottages, speckling a valley or the side of a hill, like so many of our pretty, old English villages. On approaching nearer them, along one of the wide roads which will one day form a chief street of Birkenhead, they appear more like houses for the upper class of society; and we feel puzzled how to associate them with the requirements and limited wants of a working population. If we look at the front and end elevations, there is, it must be owned, something altogether out of the usual order of things in respect to workmen's dwellings.[20]

Perhaps as a result of what was at the time a novel scheme, a similar venture was shortly afterwards begun across the Mersey in Liverpool, where a block of dwellings with balcony access was built in Kent Terrace.[21]

The other west coast town which received many of the Irish poor was Glasgow, and here activity was continuous from the forties onwards, first building work and later legislative measures. The Glasgow

Association for Establishing Lodging Houses for the Working Classes opened a converted lodging house in Mitchell Street during 1847. The architect was James Wylson, and he seems to have shown considerable ingenuity of a somewhat dubious nature in effecting economies: the building consisted of a ground floor with the usual communal facilities and above, four floors of dormitories with a variety of accommodation for single men and women as well as for families. For economy these were 'fitted up with two tiers of berths, after the manner of passengers' cabins on ship-board, excepting that the upper and lower berths are entered at opposite sides; thus, though rendering more standing room necessary, accomplishing the complete separation which is essential in houses of this description'.[22]

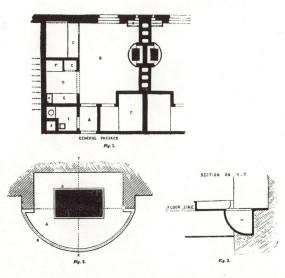

1.2 *Lumsden's Model Dwellings for the Working Classes, Glasgow, 1847, designed as minimum self-contained flats by James Wylson*

The following year Wylson designed a completely new building containing family dwellings alone, which was paid for by a Mr. Lumsden.[23] It was situated in New City Road, and was four storeys in height, containing 31 tenements. Access was by means of a common stair leading to a central corridor on each floor. Each tenement had a small entrance lobby off which was the closet, a living room with a fireplace, window and cupboard, and two bed recesses, one at the back against the passage wall, and the other in the opposite corner against an outside wall but without windows. Between the bed recess and the closet on the inside wall was a scullery, with a sink, larder, dust shaft and coal box. The dwelling was in a sense complete, since all the essential amenities were to be found inside its four walls, but Wylson made no attempt to achieve the standards adopted in London, and his dwellings were basically single rooms with one window and a number of internal partitions.

Wylson converted another lodging house, this time

in Greendyke Street, to replace the Mitchell Street establishment, which turned out to be very uneconomical to run and was abandoned when the lease ran out. The new house seems to have been very similar in its arrangements, and indeed much of the furniture was taken from Mitchell Street. This building was a success and the association was able to purchase further property in Carrick Street during the next decade.[24]

A parallel organisation, the Edinburgh Lodging House Association, was founded in 1841. Only two lodging houses were open by the end of the decade, however, and both were conversions; the first, opened in 1844, in West Port, housed seventy men, and the second followed three years later in Rattray's Close, Cowgate, for eight men. In 1849 a hotel was converted in Merchant Street for a further seventy-six men. Edinburgh lagged behind Glasgow in the provision of new buildings and it was not until the end of 1850 that there was any mention of such ventures, or indeed of any provision for family dwellings. Lord Ashley

visited both Edinburgh and Glasgow during that year, and we know that he addressed an Edinburgh association on the subject of lodging houses.[25] In the same report which recorded this in *The Labourer's Friend* the writer noted that the association proposed to erect a block of forty family dwellings behind John Knox House in Nether Bow. Thereafter the rate of building seems to have increased. In Leith Walk Pilrig Buildings was built at the expense of a group of gentlemen for whom Patrick Wilson was architect. There were 44 dwellings, the first completed in 1850, and the rest the following year. They were arranged in three two-storey blocks around an open space with the entrances to the first floor flats on the opposite side to those for the ground floor, each approached through its own small garden. Accommodation varied, although no flats had fewer than two rooms, and they were all self-contained with a scullery and closet, gas and water supplies.

1.3 *Chalmers Buildings, Edinburgh, 1855; a tenement block based on the Scottish 'land'. Patrick Wilson architect*

Wilson also designed a tenement block in Fountain-bridge, known as Chalmers Buildings. The proposed block near John Knox House was completed in 1851 and named, appropriately, Ashley House. It consisted of three traditional 'lands' four and five storeys in height with three flats on each floor. Again they were self-contained, designed and built by a local firm of contractors, W. Beattie & Sons. They built a similar block in the Pleasance soon after and another in Beaumont Place. Thereafter there seems to have been a lull in building activity in Edinburgh until later in the decade.[26]

This was the scale of activity, and these were the towns where it took place. There are doubtless other places where local gentlemen undertook perhaps the construction of a single lodging house, but the important fact was the small scale of the work although it is important to note as well that the pattern of activity was established by 1850.

The growth of building legislation

Well meaning individuals struggled to do what they could; and when they built they tried to follow the sanitary advice of Chadwick and his disciples while at the same time they took care usually to employ an architect and a reputable contractor so that the buildings were as soundly and healthily constructed as contemporary knowledge knew how to make them. This was entirely laudable, but what of the speculative builder, concerned with profit and dealing with poor people and those of modest means often urgently in need of a home, ignorant of the ways of builders and unable to pick or choose the kind of homes they would like? They were at the mercy of the speculator and nothing short of stringent legal sanctions would prevent the annual construction of more and yet more potential slums.[27] For this reason a major part of any history of 19th century housing must contain an account of the acquisition of local restrictive powers and the growth of national legislation at first permissive, only later coercive, but aiming from the forties onward to provide a minimum standard of building, planning and sanitation. The 1840 Select Committee plaintively reported:

There is no building Act to enforce the dwellings of these workmen being properly constructed; no drainage Act to enforce their being efficiently drained; no general or local regulation to enforce the commonest provision for cleanliness and comfort.[28]

That referred to London, which was by tradition excluded from any national legislation; but it could have been written of any great industrial city, for, like Topsy, they grew and few cared to ask exactly how. That is, until cholera attacked without regard for class or district and then concern was shown – at least while the epidemic lasted, for fear is always a prime moving force.

In London local government revolved fundamentally around two organisations; the new Poor Law Boards of Guardians, and the older Commissioners of Sewers. Both were local, independent and often in the case of the Commissioners of Sewers entirely unrelated bodies; in London there were numerous, quite separate, sewer systems as a result. In addition there were usually a whole series of petty commissions, set up as a result of local Acts relating to water supplies, gas, scavenging and street lighting, for example. Without exception, they caused local rivalries, they duplicated and multiplied services causing extravagance, waste and boundless incompetence. The Metropolitan Paving Act, for example, was obtained in 1817 and by mid-century there were 84 paving boards, no less than 19 operating within one parish! In Lambeth, street lighting was controlled by 9 separate organisations. Such bodies were usually either self-electing or elected for life; they appointed officials, often at very good salaries and took every care that they themselves were never out of pocket.[29]

Urban legislation, then, was ill-conceived, unco-ordinated and well-nigh useless at the time of the Poor Law Board's enquiries. There were, however, two interesting attempts to remedy the situation early in the decade, the first at Liverpool where the problems of Irish immigrants intensified the slum conditions; the second as might be expected in metropolitan London itself.

Dr Playfair described the method of building common in Liverpool in a document appended to the Royal Commission Report of 1845:

...the soil is subdivided into a multitude of holdings, and a man runs a new street, generally as narrow as he possibly can, through a field, not only to save the greater expense of soughing and paving, which, in the first instance falls upon himself, but also that he may have a greater quantity of land to dispose of. The new owner continues the street, if it suits him but he is not obliged to do so, and the consequence is the growth of narrow thoroughfares, the erection of mean edifices, the utter neglect of proper sewerage, the inattention to ventilation, and the train of evils which is so much to be deplored, is the natural consequence.[30]

These were the conditions in about 1840; then the corporation obtained in 1842 'an Act for the Promotion of the Health of the Inhabitants of the Borough of Liverpool and the Regulation of Building in the said Borough' and for the first time an attempt was made to control the nature of developments as yet unbuilt; previously building legislation had usually dealt with alterations and additions to existing streets and had made no attempt to control the spatial qualities of speculation. The minimum width of a street with carriageways was fixed as 24 ft. and without at 15 ft., courts were also to be at least 15 ft. wide, although their entrances might be as narrow as 5 ft. if the height of the buildings inside did not exceed 10 ft. There were regulations for the provision of privies and the size of windows and an important clause requiring an open area of a least 108 sq. ft. in front of all ground floor rooms.

Samuel Holme told the Royal Commission[31] that the magistrates strictly enforced the Act – which was rare at that time – but its practical effectiveness was less than one might have hoped. Another witness, James Aspinall, pointed to loop-holes:

We have found that 15 feet at the entrance of a court is not sufficiently large if it is confined to the entrance, and I am sorry to say that in most of our courts there is merely an entrance; in many cases they merely put an entrance of 15 ft. and then the rows of houses go up in a wedge shape, branched like a tree....
The entrance is 15 ft. wide, but they evade the Act by making a great many branches, and have only one entrance – it is evading the spirit of the Act.[32]

The evasion of the spirit was a symptom of the ruth-lessness of the speculator and of the problems which faced those attempting to rectify the problems of housing.

In London the first steps came as a direct result of the 1840 Select Committee's recommendations. An abortive bill was introduced in 1841, but it did not reach the statute book until 1844 as the Metropolitan Building Act.[33] Primarily it was still concerned with the prevention of fire, as had been the 18th century legislation. Property was divided into classes and there were careful regulations for the thickness of walls in relation to use and height. There were elementary and ineffective drainage clauses, for example, a house built within 100 ft. of a sewer was required to connect its drains into that sewer, but at the same time an intermediate cesspool was permitted, provided it was airtight and so long as it eventually overflowed into the sewer! The sewer itself, having a minimum section of 9 ins. was to be constructed of brick, tile, stone or slate, set in mortar or cement and laid to a minimum fall of $\frac{1}{2}$ in. in 10 ft.

The most important provisions in the new Act were concerned with space about buildings. All new streets were to be not less than 40 ft. wide, and should any building fronting the street exceed 40 ft. in height, then the width was to be not less than the height of that building. Alleys and mews which did not have carriageways were placed in a different cate-gory: they were not to be constructed less than 20 ft. in width, and when the buildings fronting onto them were more than 25 ft. high, the width again must be equal to the height. There were to be two entrances to an alley, both the full width and one, at least, the full height. In addition there was, for the first time, a curious provision about open space at the rear of all dwellings, which is best quoted in full:

Every house hereafter built or rebuilt must have an enclosed back yard or open space of at the least one square, exclusive of any building thereon, unless all the rooms of such house can be lighted and ventilated from the street, or from an

area of the extent of at the least three quarters of a square, above the level of the second storey, into which the owner of the house to be rebuilt is entitled to open windows for every room adjoining thereto. And if any house already built be hereafter rebuilt – then, unless all the rooms of such house can be lighted and ventilated from the street, or from an area of the extent of at the least three quarters of a square, into which the owner of the house to be built is entitled to open windows for every room adjoining thereto, there must be above the level of the floor of the third storey an open space of at least three quarters of a square.[34]

There were also regulations for that contemporary iniquity, the cellar dwellings, requiring an open area in front of its window of certain minimum area. The requirements of the Act look strict on paper, but they were impossible to enforce without the proper machinery and officers recommended in the Poor Law Board Report, and they were, of course, inoperative outside the boundary of the metropolitan area. The legal requirements were minimal, in reality, and loop-holes were soon found; for example, it was discovered that it was possible to build a shop in the front garden of a house without any impediment, and there was nothing to prevent the haphazard development of back land.[35]

The Public Health Act of 1848

Following the publication of the Poor Law Board Report of 1842, and the Royal Commission Report of 1845, the Peel administration introduced a Bill that same session to legislate for their findings, but when Peel soon afterwards resigned, the Bill was abandoned. In the government which Lord John Russell then formed, a staunch supporter of Chadwick, Lord Morpeth, was appointed First Commissioner of Woods and Forests, and he it was who introduced the next Bill concerned with health. This was on 30 March, 1847. It made provision for a central Board of Health presided over by five commissioners, and a network of local boards rather like the Poor Law Board organisation. The Bill showed evidence of hasty preparation, and it contained a large number of clauses borrowed from other Acts, notably the Clauses Consolidation Acts which had originally been designed to facilitate the preparation of private Acts of Parliament prepared by local authorities. The Bill had a stormy passage, and objections were raised especially to the principle of central administration and the inclusion of metropolitan London. On 8 July, the government withdrew the Bill and Morpeth contented himself with the appointment of a Metropolitan Sanitary Com-mission to investigate the organisation and adminis-tration of drainage and refuse disposal in London. The Commission made three reports which showed up the diversity of responsible authorities and the total lack of organisation. As a result, an Act was passed abolishing the existing commissions of sewers and setting up a single unified body, the Metropolitan

Commission of Sewers. A second Act was passed making similar, although independent, provision for the City of London.[36]

The following year, on 10 February, Morpeth introduced a revised Public Health Bill, which in his own words was intended to have the following effect:

It will be imperative upon the local administrative bodies – To hold meetings for the transaction of business; to appoint a surveyor; to appoint an inspector of nuisances; to procure a map of their district; to make public sewers; to substitute sufficient sewers in case old ones be discontinued; to require owners or occupiers to provide house-drains; to cleanse and water streets; to appoint or contract with scavengers; to cleanse, cover, or fill up offensive ditches;...to provide sufficient supply of water for drainage, public and private, and for domestic use. The permissive powers to be granted to the local administrative bodies...to make house-drains upon default of owner and occupier; to require that new buildings be altered, &c., in case of building upon improper levels; to alter drains, privies, water closets, and cesspools, built contrary to the Act; to make bye-laws with respect to the removal of filth, and the emptying of privies &c.; to whitewash and purify houses after notice; to require that certain furnaces be made to consume their own smoke;...to pave streets, &c.; to provide places for public recreation; to purchase and maintain waterworks.[37]

The battle for its passage was as great as in the previous year, for public opinion was not yet fully behind the need for reform and the voices of 'self-interest' were loud in their opposition to centralised administration. While the Bill was being debated the following passage appeared in *The Economist* well illustrating the strength of the opposition:

In our condition, suffering and evil are nature's admonitions; they cannot be got rid of; and the *impatient attempts of benevolence* to banish them from the world by legislation, before benevolence has learnt their object and their end, have always been more productive of more evil than good.[38]

The Bill, however, became law as the Public Health Act, 1848, but in what Chadwick, with his strong belief in central administration, believed to be a much diluted form. Nevertheless, it established the organisation necessary for the initial control of health, with a General Board of Health – initially appointed for a five year term – and a network of local authorities. In towns, power was vested in the council, but where no council existed, a separate local Board of Health was created. Attached to each board was an inspector of nuisances and a surveyor; also, but this unfortunately was not compulsory, the authority might appoint a medical officer. Each board was given power to make regulations requiring all new houses to have adequate drainage and sanitary accommodation; it could undertake to supply water and construct sewers, under certain conditions, and for this purpose it might levy a rate or obtain a mortgage. But the powers were permissive, and few councils were likely to undertake large scale works which would place a burden on the rates. The central Board could only interfere upon the

petition of one tenth of the ratepayers, or when the death rate rose above 23 persons per 1,000 of the population: circumstances which were unlikely to occur frequently.

The Bill had been debated with the ominous signs that cholera was again in Europe and a second Act was rushed through parliament that same session because of the threat of a further outbreak in this country. It was known as the Nuisance Removal and Diseases Prevention Act, and all the clauses dealing with cholera which were originally intended for the main Health Act were relegated to it.

The Public Health Act excluded the City of London and the metropolitan area; but the City corporation was an enlightened body and was fortunately able to use the powers contained in the City Sewers Act to reorganise its sanitary administration, and subsequently they appointed Dr. John Simon as Medical Officer of Health.[39] He it was who began the regular collection and analysis of statistical information concerning public health, some of which was already becoming available through the office of the Registrar General, and particularly through the efforts of the Registrar General himself, Major George Graham, who held office from 1842 to 1879, and William Farr, the Compiler of Abstracts in the same department. Simon was able to call upon the medical officers of the local networks of Poor Law Boards within the City, and from them obtain the statistics of the weekly incidence of fever. This information enabled him to pin-point areas where disease and epidemics were particularly rampant, and with the assistance of inspectors of nuisances and Orders in Council requiring nuisances to be abated, Simon was able to make remarkable improvements in drainage and water supply and also in the gradual removal of cesspools. The City Sewers Act was renewed and made permanent in 1851 and this Act contained for the first time provision for the registration and regulation of tenement houses.

The lesson which the work in the City taught at that time was that a responsible authority could usually find in the existing legislation the means for controlling the conditions within its administrative area. On the whole willingness was more important than actual legal power at this time. But the emphasis was upon local responsibility, for no government was yet able to provide a coercive central authority; and this, in retrospect, was the great weakness of the situation in the years immediately after 1848.

The Public Health Act of 1848 is now regarded as the first major step in the reform of our sanitary legislation, but when it was passed Chadwick thought that it did less than justice to the problems which it set out to solve: he believed that the government had given way to those who so violently opposed central administration. In this he was doubtless right, but it would probably not have been possible for any government to move at the speed Chadwick would have desired because public opinion was quite unprepared for such violently radical changes at the first attempt: 'The subtle all-pervading influence of vested rights was too powerful for any such reforms to be attempted.'[40]

The Act nevertheless established the organisation necessary at least in theory to control health; there was a central General Board, appointed initially for five years with special powers to bring the sanitary provisions of the Act into operation and establish local health authorities to carry them into effect. In existing municipalities power was vested in the town council, but where there was no such authority an entirely new Local Board of Health could be created. Attached to each health authority was to be an inspector of nuisances, a surveyor and, at the discretion of the local authority, a medical officer. The Local Board could make regulations requiring that all new houses should have proper drainage and adequate sanitary accommodation, it could undertake to supply water, under certain conditions, to construct sewers, and to defray the expenses involved; there were provisions for a special rate to be levied or, alternatively, the Board might take out a mortgage.

On paper this seemed a comprehensive and all-embracing measure and were it passed today it would doubtless be so in fact: local government has changed considerably during the course of a century. But in 1848 it left too much responsibility in the hands of the local councillors and rate-payers and far too many of its provisions were permissive. For example, the original Bill made provision for the General Board to bring the Act into operation, in any town, upon petition by one fiftieth of the rate-payers; as it became law this was increased to one tenth, too large a proportion of the middle class frequently to vote an organisation into being which would inevitably increase the rates and would have wide powers of inspection, powers to compel house owners to construct proper drains, powers to ensure a proper supply of water, powers to control the removal and disposal of rubbish, powers even to provide places of recreation. All things which would have spelt out vast expenditure, and it was difficult as yet to convince the rate-payers that it was in their own interest that every town should be a safe place in which to live and work. On the other hand, once a local Board was established, the General Board was powerless to coerce them into activity, they could choose how to act, or indeed whether to act at all.

The relation of the Act to housing problems was important, although indirect: the growth of a sanitary administration, however slow, would lead to the establishment ultimately of control over speculation as well as to proposals for slum clearance; it would, in the end, raise the environmental standards of industrial towns; but above all, it would provide a framework for the efficient operation of building bye-laws and thus the whole machinery of the housing movement. Finally, it would lead to council-built, council-owned and council-managed housing.

The Royal Commission, in its Report of 1845, recommended individual towns to obtain private legislation in order to control their sanitary condition and after 1847 they were greatly facilitated by the Town Improvement Clauses Act, which provided a series of model clauses for inclusion as a whole or in part in private local Acts, largely in order to give some degree of uniformity to local legislation. There were similar Acts for clauses concerned, for example, with gasworks, waterworks, cemeteries and the police. Despite these aids local legislation at this stage played little part in the growth of the sanitary and housing movements and the reasons, often the result of parsimonious self-interest, have already been discussed. Liverpool obtained a private Act in 1846 which reinforced its Building Act, obtained four years earlier, and extended the legal controls over the building of courts. The implication of this was that a corporation could find the means of controlling its development if it had the desire to do so. If all this seems commonplace today, in 1848 the procedure was novel and the measures taken seemingly as high-handed as they were sometimes effective. If the City of London could be made healthier within the legislative climate of the forties and fifties, then there was no reason why other places should not do likewise, had there been the civic or popular desire for reform. Much of the early history of housing and public health is concerned with the contribution of individuals or small groups who, in their own towns, were able to arouse enthusiastic and responsible activity through their personal dynamism. The general consensus of public opinion remained too lethargic – it would be over-charitable to call it more than this – to allow any nationwide concern for these matters until about 1875.

The General Board of Health

The Public Health Act nevertheless established a new kind of central authority, the General Board of Health, with an initial life of five years. It consisted of three members, Lord Morpeth, the ex-officio member by virtue of his government post as First Commissioner of Woods and Forests, Lord Ashley and Chadwick. Two years later a fourth member, with special medical qualifications, was added in the person of Dr. Southwood Smith, an eminent doctor with experience in housing matters and a man largely in sympathy with Chadwick. The Board had no ministerial head and its relationship with the government of the day was rather different from that of a normal department of state. Chadwick was temperamentally unable to work with anyone for long, few could keep up with his voracity for work and although all went well at first, his pathological distrust of the medical profession sometimes strained relations even with Southwood Smith, and when Morpeth was replaced by Lord Seymour – a man quite unsympathetic to Chadwick – the affairs of the

Board degenerated into a battle of personalities, which was at once sad and unseemly.[41]

The circumstances surrounding the establishment of the General Board in 1848 made it sufficiently remarkable that a central authority should be set up at all. In many ways its teeth were drawn at birth and as has already been pointed out apart from a petition by one tenth of the rate-payers, the only other time the Board could interfere in local affairs was when the death rate rose above 23 persons per 1,000. Once the General Board had established a Local Board it still possessed no authority to force it to take action, and although certain officers were bound to be appointed there was no power to compel the appointment of a medical officer. Similarly, the General Board had no powers to appoint permanent officers or inspectors for its own purposes, and was consequently obliged to take advice from professional men who might afterwards offer themselves to carry out the work they had first suggested!

The Board did possess more extensive executive powers under the Nuisance Removal and Disease Prevention Act of 1848, the Act to which many of the clauses relating to epidemics, contained in the original bill of 1847, were hastily relegated. These were invoked first soon after the Act became law and again in 1853-4, both times to deal with major outbreaks of cholera. Each time the Board worked with commendable speed, providing regulations, circulars containing advice, and inspectors; and each time it found the local authorities dilatory and obstructive. At the height of the epidemics Chadwick more or less assumed complete control in London, sewers were flushed as never before, unwittingly pouring forth disease into the Thames from whence the water supply for the city was drawn. So Chadwick was defeating his own objective, but if he was guilty of helping to spread cholera, it was more through ignorance than his latent distrust of medical advice; he was never unwilling to take the action he thought necessary within the limits of his own knowledge and indeed that of contemporary science; he was never guilty of the criminal neglect practised by most local authorities who frequently were unwilling to do anything which might reduce the incidence of cholera because of its financial implications.

In times of crisis Chadwick proved that through herculean effort a central authority could make some impression upon the tangled mass of local obstruction and opposition. Between epidemics the General Board seemed ineffective, it gradually sank in public esteem as it became more and more identified with Chadwick, the polemical individual, but the saga of its short but tumultuous life is no part of the housing movement so does not concern us here. For one reason or another all Chadwick's attempts to secure his principle objective, a unified administration for London, were doomed to failure; the Royal Commission on London, over which he had presided in 1847, failed to secure a unified sewerage system for the metropolis and the Sewer Commission which ultimately resulted took its advice on sewer construction from Robert Stephenson, the railway engineer, because, it was said, of his knowledge of tunnel construction! Similarly, the two reports on 'Extra-mural Sepulture', gruesome documents on burial practice in London, which lead to Chadwick's Interment Act of 1850 – described by one modern critic as 'an extraordinary amalgam of religion and Benthamism'[42] – aimed at breaking down the petty systems of local administration. The Act failed to work and was repealed two years later, doing insufferable harm to Chadwick's reputation.

Thirdly, he tried to secure the unification of water undertakings, producing in 1850 a 'Report on the Supply of Water to the Metropolis' which recommended a joint commission to administer water supplies and drainage disposal. The Metropolitan Water Supply Act of 1852 was the result, a mild affair by comparison with the radical proposals contained in the report. It gave the existing companies five years to remove their intake points from the lower reaches of the Thames to places above Teddington Lock. The Southwark Company was still drawing its supply from a point near Hungerford Bridge during the cholera epidemic of 1853 with quite disastrous effects for the community it served.

These, then, were the great public battles in which the General Board, through Chadwick, was involved: it would be difficult to imagine a series of events with such unfortunate consequences. At the same time the Board made a positive contribution to knowledge in a much less dramatic way, collecting and sifting information, evolving statistics which were to become part of the background to later health administration. By 1853 the Board had been asked to apply the provisions of the Public Health Act in 284 towns and legally defined districts, and it had done so in 182 of them. As a result, in 126 of these, survey work had been undertaken, in 70 plans for improved water and drainage supplies had been prepared, and in 31 of these they had been approved and mortgages sanctioned.[43] On the whole, the Local Boards had more success than the General Board in London, perhaps it was a question of personalities, or as one of Chadwick's biographers suggests, because of the novelty of the procedure.

It should be emphasised that the degree of success was relatively small by comparison with the scale of the problem. Many towns still went to the expense of obtaining a private Act since this prevented the General Board applying the powers contained in the Public Health Act, and the reason was usually a selfish one: to show outwardly that they had taken suitable action whilst ensuring that once obtained they need do little more. Newcastle upon Tyne was such a town, yet when cholera broke out on 1 September 1853, it reigned with unparalleled fury; despite this, several years later *The Builder* was still able

1.4   *Terraced cottage flats in Newcastle*

to describe the town as one of the most insanitary in the country.[44] It is interesting also that Newcastle was slow to take part in the housing movement and examples of private action were extremely rare.

When the position of the General Board was reviewed at the end of the first five years of its life in 1854, it was proposed in parliament that it should be renewed and this became the signal for a violent attack upon its structure, upon its members and upon Chadwick in particular. Before the Bill was read a second time Palmerston had secured the resignation of all the members in an attempt to placate the critics, but this was not enough, and in an unexpected division the government was defeated and the Bill thrown out. However, later that year the Board was reconstituted, but its life hung by a thread since it was to be renewed annually, and under the terms of the Public Health Act of 1858 it ceased to exist.

The sad thing was that Chadwick was right about many of the issues for which he fought so ardently – even if hot-headedly – before 1854. A central authority for the country as a whole was a necessary institution and so, too, was a unified administration for metropolitan London. Perhaps it was some small consolation that during the rest of a very long life, the remaining part of it outside public office, he was able to see all his work carried into fruition but, alas, by others; though this last must have been difficult to bear.

Sir John Simon, whose first appointment as medical officer for the City of London was one small result of Chadwick's work for the Royal Commission on London, later wrote in retrospect of Chadwick's achievements and this shows, I think, that the defeat of 1854 was more apparent than real:

> Mr Chadwick, beyond any man of his time, knew what large fresh additions of human misery were accruing day by day under the then almost universal prevalence of sanitary neglect; and the indignation which he was entitled to feel at the spectacle of so much needless human suffering is a not ignoble excuse for such signs of over-eagerness as he may have shown.[45]

Lord Ashley and the restraint of overcrowding

Throughout the difficult years of the existence of the General Board of Health, one of Chadwick's staunchest supporters had been Lord Ashley who, whatever he might have thought and felt about the events of these years, never seems to have lost faith in the principles for which his querulous colleague was fighting. Ashley's role in early Victorian society is one of the strangest in all English history, and one which perhaps no peer of the realm could have contemplated at any other time. His concern for the well-being of the poor was a deep and abiding part of his evangelical conscience and his achievements were surprisingly numerous, the Factory Act, and the Mines Act testify to this early in the forties; so does his part in the construction of model dwellings which will be discussed in the next chapter.

Another outcome of his interests was a series of measures concerned with the regulation of overcrowing in public lodging houses. In 1851 Ashley introduced his Common Lodging House Bill; he was able to quote evidence of the need for such a measure from an account by a city missionary:

On my district is a house containing eight rooms, which are all let separately to individuals who furnish and relet them. The parlour measures 18 ft. by 10 ft. Beds are arranged on each side of the room, composed of straw, shavings, rags, &c. In this one room slept, on the night previous to my inquiry, 27 male and female adults, 31 children, and two or three dogs, making in all 58 human beings breathing the contaminated atmosphere of a close room. In the top room of the same house, measuring 12 ft. by 10 ft. there are six beds, and, on the same night, there slept in them 32 human beings, all breathing the pestiferous air of a hole not fit to keep swine in. The beds are so close together that, when let down on the floor, there is no room to pass between them; and they who sleep in the beds furthest from the door can, consequently, only get into them by crawling over the beds which are nearer the door. In one district alone there are 270 such rooms.[46]

It would have been possible to find many accounts similar to this, and Ashley was in a good position to know the real situation at that time through his work with Chadwick and the General Board of Health. He was against leaving this matter in the hands of private enterprise:

Private speculation was very much confined to the construction of the smallest houses, of the lowest possible description, because it was out of those the most inordinate profits could be made.[47]

Sir George Grey, the Home Secretary, was not so easily convinced and he spoke for the traditional English attitude:

But, after all, it was not to the Government, it was rather to the efforts of individuals, and associations of individuals, that they must look for real and general improvement among the great body of the people.[48]

But Ashley got his way and parliament passed a remarkably positive measure, the Common Lodging House Act, which gave extensive powers of supervision to the Metropolitan Police in London and to local authorities elsewhere in the country. Furthermore, the Act was obligatory, unlike the Public Health Act which was adoptive, although it did only refer to common lodging houses and gave no powers of control in cases of overcrowding in private houses. Within these limits, however, it was successful, and it was proof indeed that, given adequate power and a firm directive, local authorities were able to mitigate some of the social evils of the day.

At the same time Lord Ashley introduced a second measure, which became the Labouring Classes Lodging

1.5 *A back lane and rear staircase for the Newcastle flats*

Houses Act in 1851. Whereas the first Act aimed at improving the standard of existing lodging houses, the second was concerned to increase the amount of accommodation available. In several important ways it differed from the Common Lodging Houses Act, which it was designed deliberately to complement; it was adoptive, and it was intended that it should enable local authorities and similar bodies to acquire lodging houses. Private companies were expressly excluded from its provisions doubtless because their inclusion might have laid the Act open to commercial profiteering. There were powers to enable local authorities to borrow money, either to purchase existing buildings or to build new ones; powers enabling them to levy a rate as an alternative means of finance and powers for the appropriation of special land. In fact, little use was made of this measure, again because of its permissive nature, but it is important to realise that Ashley established the principle of a local authority itself erecting buildings should it desire to do so as early as 1851.

The General Board of Health issued a set of bye-laws for lodging houses in 1852, and in December of that year Captain Hay, of the Metropolitan Police, produced 'a most authentic and business-like report'[49] on the work of inspection and the remedial measures which had been taken up to that time in London. Here was proof of the efficacy of Ashley's work; 'Of all the sanitary measures recently conceived, the principal if not the only one immediately productive of much practical good, has been the Common Lodging Houses Act.'[50] Hay, in his report, asked for increased legal powers and Ashley, now the Earl of Shaftesbury and a member of the House of Lords – inspired by the success of the Act – sought during 1853 to strengthen its provisions, while at the same time attempting to steer a delicate course which would avoid tampering too much with the popular concept of personal liberty:

The maxim that 'every man's house is his castle' is a very good one, till it interferes with health, the peace, the comfort, the property, and the lives of the neighbourhood. When that is the case we beg to interpose the still older, still more universal, and we hope equally English maxim, *Salus populi suprema lex est*, for we cannot conceive what laws and society are made for, if it shall be the sacred right of any man occupying a tenement in a crowded locality to convert it into an ambuscade or rather a battery against the lives and property of his neighbours.[51]

The new Act cleared up various practical difficulties and Captain Hay was able to report the greater efficiency with which he was now able to carry out his work.[52]

Shaftesbury tried again in 1860 to break down the barriers of personal liberty in the interests of the community when he attempted to secure the right of inspection to private houses let out room by room, but parliament would have none of it, and the Bill was defeated.

Within their limited field of operation, the Lodging Houses Acts remained effective. In 1857, for example, the General Board of Health was able to remark upon the sanitary and moral improvement which had taken place in the lodging houses of the provinces, as well as in London, since 1851: buildings which were once the reproach of society were fast becoming an example to it.

This was perhaps the one ray of hope in an otherwise rather gloomy situation. By the middle of the decade, despite the work of the last ten years, various organisations, of which *The Labourers' Friend* was typical, were calling for stronger measures in both health and housing:

These, remember, are matters in which the poor cannot help themselves...The Building Act must be remodelled: selfish men must no longer be *permitted* to erect whole streets of disease. The Public Health Act must be amended, extended, and made compulsory: our most ignorant towns require it most, yet by these it is most commonly rejected.[53]

2
Victorian philanthropy I:
the first housing societies

The housing movement grew out of the exposition of the industrial town described in the previous chapter; it represents the tangible outcome of the parliamentary reforms and the pressure in society for a new kind of social responsibility which I have described as the essence of early Victorian thought.

The exact nature which this action should take was decided by two societies which successfully turned the rather incoherent sympathy of one small section of the nation into practical help for those who suffered as a result of industrial progress. They decided to experiment with the construction of various kinds of housing, and they set an example which was followed by other people with similar inclinations. The two organisations which will be discussed next were both founded early in the forties during the first traumatic official enquiries into urban conditions. One was a public company in all but name, seeking to invest with limited profit in the working class housing movement, yet keeping well clear of the normal speculative builder's approach; the other was an exemplary society, setting out to show the alternative housing systems and to provide an example for others to follow. In the event neither built a great deal, and the public company failed to attract enough investors for it to expand freely. By comparison with the great organisations which flourished later in the century, their work was negligible, but the quantity of their work bore no relation to its impact; these two organisations were pioneering a new kind of housing and pointing the way for future practical interest in the problems of the poor.

The Society for Improving the Condition of the Labouring Classes

The Society for Improving the Conditions of the Labouring Classes was founded on 11 May 1844, but although new in name, it grew out of The Labourers' Friend Society, which was an older organisation concerned primarily with agricultural labourers. *The Labourers' Friend* magazine, which began publication in 1834, was the official organ of the original society and later, in a revised form, also of S.I.C.L.C. It is here that reference was made to the earlier society founded by Sir Thomas Bernard 'which although it existed at a time of comparative tranquility as regards the agitation of questions connected with the labouring classes, and confined itself to the publication of tracts, nevertheless produced very considerable effects'.[1] William Bardwell who wrote about the Society in 1853 mentioned a Society of this name founded in 1827 by George Law, Bishop of Bath and Wells, and several other gentlemen.[2] They purchased a site at Shooter's Hill in Kent, and there built six pairs of model cottages for agricultural workers, these were subsequently illustrated in Loudon's *Encyclopaedia of Cottage and Villa Architecture*,[3] and Bardwell reproduced a plan and perspective from this well known nineteenth-century work.[4]

The Society seems to have pursued its quiet policy of example in agricultural districts, interesting itself especially in the allotment movement, until a group of gentlemen, of whom Lord Ashley and Dr. Southwood Smith were prominent, called a meeting at Willis' Rooms, St James' on 11 May 1844, and succeeded in gaining sufficient support for the Society to change its name and widen its interests, especially in connection with the metropolis.[5]

Three modes of effecting great benefits for the working classes have been particularly pointed out. These are:

    I By endeavouring to introduce the Allotment System into some parish in the neighbourhood of London, to such an extent as materially to reduce, if not entirely eradicate, the pauperism heretofore existing in the place;...

    II By raising, either in the metropolis or near it, a planned dwelling, or cottages, for a certain number of poor families; so contrived as to unite comfort with economy...

    III One other point is that of well-conducted LOAN FUNDS...[6]

The meeting ultimately agreed that the following means were the most suitable for them to adopt to achieve this kind of assistance:

1st.   By arranging and executing plans as models, for the improvement of the dwellings of the Poor, both in the metropolis and in the manufacturing and agricultural districts; and by establishing in some localities, convenient for general observation, the Field-Garden and Cottage Allotment System, and also Loan Societies, upon sound principles, and so superintending the working and reporting the results of both, as to make them available as models for more extended adoption.

2ndly. By the formation of country, parochial and district associations, acting upon uniform plans and rules.

3rdly. By correspondence with clergymen, magistrates, landed proprietors and others, disposed to render assistance in their respective localities, either individually or as members of local associations.[7]

These, in fact, became embodied in the 'Plans and Objects of the Society'.

The Society set out with the intention of being exemplary, and its Charter, obtained in 1850, limited the dividend each year to 4 per cent. This was an important policy decision since it inevitably affected the popularity of the society so far as financial investment was concerned: Victorian investors required a much greater return than this and elsewhere they could command it, so that support was limited in reality to those disposed to philanthropy. Chadwick urged them to reconsider their attitude to finance at the outset, and was himself unwilling to support the society because it was to his mind vaguely charitable. He suggested that the limitation upon profits should be removed, in order: 'to place the proceedings on a commercial principle simply, as being really the most benevolent in its ultimate operation to the working classes'[8] and it was the failure to do this, more than anything else, which finally limited the actual work of the Society.

The patronage of the Queen was transferred from the original Society to the new one, and in July 1844 *The Labourers' Friend* announced that three sub-committees had been set up to deal with cottage allotments, dwellings and loan funds.[9] They were already looking for a site on which to build their first model houses in the metropolis, and after careful searching, one was found that autumn near Gray's Inn Road; by the end of the year work was in progress on the demolition of the existing property and the erection of new buildings. These were the Model Dwellings in Lower Road, Pentonville.[10]

This scheme was the first attempt in the metropolis to provide the working class with some kind of new and appropriate housing, specially designed for the purpose, and it was the first time that an architect had lent his skill to such a humble work. The Bagnigge Wells scheme, as it was popularly called, was a landmark in the history of housing and in the relationship between the architect and the community. It marked the beginning of the end of a *laissez-faire* attitude to the problems associated with the poor and indeed the whole development of towns.

The site of the Society's first venture was by no means ideal, as their architect, Henry Roberts, pointed out:

...the Society proceeded to build...on the only eligible site of ground then offered, and which they had some difficulty in securing, owing to the adverse feeling of the parties who apprehended injury to their property from the vicinity of what they regarded as likely to prove a sort of nondescript pile of pauper buildings.

The form of the site, and the unfavourable nature of the foundation for a lofty building, being newly-made ground, in some degree influenced its appropriation to a double row of two-storey houses, facing each other, and on three distinct plans, to accommodate in the whole twenty-three families,

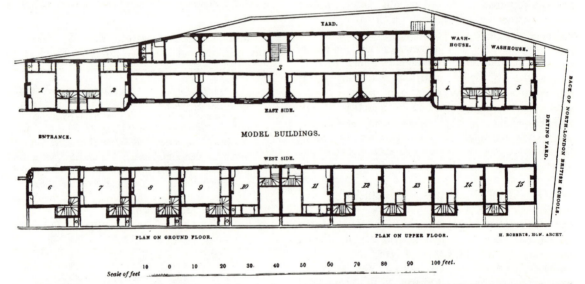

2.1 *The Bagnigge Wells estate of S.I.C.L.C.; their first development in 1844. Henry Roberts architect*

and thirty single females. In their arrangement, the main object has been to combine every point essential to the health, comfort and moral habits of the industrious classes and their families, particular attention being paid to *ventilation, drainage, and an ample supply of water*.[11]

This was Roberts' first attempt at a housing scheme and it marked the beginning of a close relationship between him and the Society. He was responsible for all the buildings erected by S.I.C.L.C., each of which was intended as an example, or 'model', so there is little repetition in their work; in every way he was a real pioneer of housing design, the father of the whole working class housing movement. The Bagnigge Wells building showed how much there remained to be learnt about housing the poor. Roberts and his Society did not really know what was required of them and for the most part they built to the same pattern as any other speculating builder might have done. The difference was that they built soundly, cleanly and

with attention to sanitation and ventilation; but they did not create a new environment. The problem of providing as many separate homes as was possible, on a very limited site and with little capital expenditure, influenced the Society so strongly that they departed from an ideal solution and indulged in rather disastrous economies of space. They overbuilt and reduced the accommodation to a bare minimum; both of these trends became characteristic of working class housing later in the century. The actual planning of the dwelling was immature, which showed the difficulties of designing on a miniature scale and the disadvantages under which Roberts was labouring. All this was evident to contemporary critics, not least to Godwin, the editor of *The Builder*, who was not slow to point out that the two parallel rows of cottages looked grim, that they were too close together and had entirely inadequate yards at their rear.[12]

The scheme provided three kinds of accommodation; first, two-storey houses divided into flats, each with two rooms; secondly, complete houses, each with a living room containing a bed recess, a scullery, two bedrooms on the first floor and a small yard at the rear; and thirdly, a lodging house for widows, which provided each of them with a separate room. The scheme seems to have been very tentative; only one row of nine houses was proceeded with at first, and when this proved a success, the parallel row of flatted houses and the lodging house were added, so that the whole street was not finally completed until the spring of 1846; the little estate was open to view from 23 to 28 March of that year.[13]

The practical steps which the original meeting of 11 May 1844 had proposed in connection with the provision of dwellings, then, were quickly taken up and were successful; the other two objectives, however, were not to have similar success. Difficulties were at once experienced in the search for land in the metropolis on which to plan allotments, and the loans committee were unable to see any way of obtaining or administering a loan fund. These early difficulties were to continue, and although a limited number of allotments were laid out, the idea of loans never materialised and the society concentrated on its exemplary building works.

By this time the health and sanitary movement was fast approaching its first great climax: the Royal Commission on the Health of Towns reported in 1844 and again in 1845 and in the following years the final form of the long-awaited Health Act was established. The other important housing society, the Metropolitan Association, now several years old, had at last started to build, in Old St. Pancras Road, and the two Societies rapidly became the focus of housing reform.[14] The work of S.I.C.L.C. now became less tentative and they were very active during 1846, concentrating their attention on the development of lodging houses. The first scheme was for a completely new building to provide accommodation for men and boys in St. Giles:

It is on behalf of this large, much neglected and deserving class, and with a view of showing how they may be rescued from the discomfort and contamination to which they are at present (through no fault of their own) so injuriously subjected, that the Committee propose erecting a Model Lodging-House in St. Giles's.[15]

It was completed in the following year, to the designs of Henry Roberts, in time for the Annual Meeting to be held in its Common Room. The block was five storeys in height, in addition to a basement which contained washing and cooking facilities. In the centre was the main stair with a common room and steward's flat, one on either side of it, on the ground floor; each of the floors above was divided into two dormitories, and these in turn were divided into cubicles, 8 ft. 9 ins. × 4 ft. 3 ins.–4 ft. 9 ins. There was also a washroom with six basins on each floor, but there was only one W.C. for every twenty-five people. The site again was a difficult one, and the building was so tightly planned that it was impossible to have windows at the rear except for the staircase. Once more this led to criticism of the arrangements for ventilation and the adverse comments about the rather cramped conditions under which the lodgers slept, each in his tiny cubicle, since about one half were entirely without direct natural light and air.[16]

The Society was also experimenting at this period with conversions; it had obtained small properties in Charles Street and King Street which were converted into lodging houses, and both buildings proved successful and, of course, alteration work was much less expensive than completely new buildings. It was only a partial solution and the limitations of the converted lodging houses were recognised from the start:

...however valuable as an experiment, and calculated as a stimulant to produce highly beneficial results, the houses in Charles Street cannot be considered as the model of what a lodging-house ought to be.[17]

2.2 *The Model Lodging House for Men. George Street, 1847. Henry Roberts architect; a fully developed lodging house for S.I.C.L.C.*

During 1849 the Society opened a further converted lodging-house for women in Hatton Garden, but demand for this kind of accommodation was slight and the building was closed soon after 1850. It was used by the Emigration Fund Committee for three years, and on its return to the Society it was reopened in 1855 as a lodging house for men, this time with more success.

The Society had more ambitious plans for erecting a new building on the principle of a tenement-block for families, perhaps in emulation of a similar building which the Metropolitan Association were then completing, and this scheme was to prove their most important single contribution to the housing movement. Early in 1848 an appeal was made for funds with which to build the new block; but in June, at the annual meeting, presided over that year by Prince Albert himself, the money had not been raised because, it was said, of the distress in Ireland during the previous year. During the next year sufficient money was eventually subscribed, but further difficulties were now experienced in finding a site, and it was not until the annual meeting of 1849 that the Society could report that work had actually started, and then the design was made public.[18] Roberts has written at considerable length about this building in his book *The Dwellings of the Labouring Classes*, and because of the importance attached to it, the arguments which preceded his final solution are of unusual importance.

The question of lodging a large number of families in one lofty pile of building has been the subject of much discussion, and in reference to it the most contradictory opinions were stated before the Health-of-Towns' Commission. Some thought it the best adapted and most economical plan to provide in one house, with a common staircase and internal passages, sufficient rooms for lodging a considerable number of families, giving them the use of a kitchen, wash-house and other necessary conveniences, in common; others objected that such an arrangement would lead to endless contentions; and be attended with much evil in cases of contagious disease.

It must be obvious that in many localities where labourers' dwellings are indispensable, it is impossible to provide them with isolated and altogether independent tenements; and therefore, though modified by local and other circumstances, it will be found the general practice in Great Britain, as well as in the large towns on the Continent, for several families of the working class to reside in one house.

The important point, then, for consideration, is, in what manner can the advantages of this economical arrangement be retained without the serious practical evils which have been referred to?

In providing for the accommodation of a large number of families in one pile of building, a leading feature of the plan should be the preservation of the domestic privacy and independence of each distinct family, and the disconnexion of their apartments, so as effectually to prevent the communication of contagious disease. This is accomplished in the model houses for families in Streatham Street, Bloomsbury, by dispensing altogether with separate staircases, and other internal communications between the different storeys, and by adopting one common open staircase leading into galleries or corridors, open on one side to a spacious quadrangle, and on the other side having the outer doors of the several tenements, the rooms of which are protected from draught by a small entrance lobby.[19]

Roberts was also influenced by the effect of the window tax, which was still in force when the block was designed, and he argued that the balcony was in fact an elevated street so that each tenement, with its independent access from this 'street', was in reality a separate dwelling. This view was not shared by the authorities, and the building was at first assessed for window tax; but the Society appealed against this decision, Roberts' interpretation was accepted and the appeal upheld. Shortly afterwards the tax was repealed and subsequently the Streatham Street building was exempted from the House Tax which replaced it. During 1850 a further incentive came with the repeal of the brick tax, which had amounted to some £300 on the Streatham Street scheme.

The 'Model Houses for Families' at Streatham Street were important for other reasons than merely for the legal precedents which they created. They set a standard of accommodation which was well in advance of contemporary practice, and perhaps because the standard was lavish, in relation to the rents which the poor could pay, the building was not very profitable. This did not mean that the scheme cost the society more than they had expected, nor that they failed to realise the rents they decided to charge, which varied from 4s. to 7s. per week; rather, it was an example of their social policy to provide the best accommodation at the least rent compatible with their desire to make a limited profit.[20] Two points emerge from this; first the rents were not small by comparison with those then prevailing for a slum tenement, and this limited the value of the building to one particular social class, the artizan. Secondly, the Society had under-estimated the financial return necessary to secure popularity and encourage commercial investment, which was an important reason why their exemplary principle failed to encourage large scale developments on similar lines. There was no rush by investors or speculators to build family tenements such as the society had ardently hoped and expected. The sharp rise in prices, which took place during the decade, made it quite impossible to build more family dwellings of this type, except as non-profit-making ventures. The initiative then passed from the hands of the social philanthropists to those of business men, and with this came a reversal of Ashley's philosophy: that the dwelling was the first step in the improvement of the individual.

Fortunately the 'Model Houses for Families' in Streatham Street still survive, alone amongst the Society's early properties, and it is still possible to see them very much as they originally appeared. This is important because the building marked an epoch; establishing, and indeed perfecting a new build-

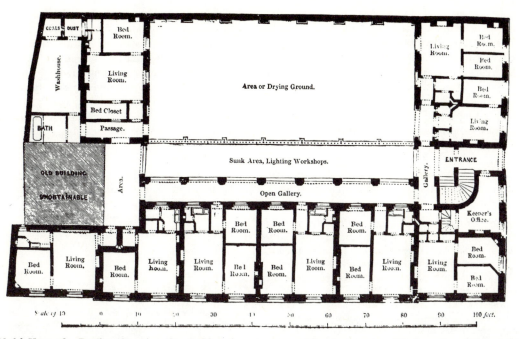

2.3 *Model Houses for Families, Streatham Street, Bloomsbury, S.I.C.L.C., 1850. Henry Roberts architect; probably the most important early model housing of the self-contained flat pattern*

ing type at the first attempt: it therefore provides a useful comparison with later work. The layout was controlled by existing site conditions and the buildings form three sides of a court; the fourth consisted of existing property. The access galleries were all on the courtyard side, so that the main façades to the street present a simple rhythm of windows, relieved only by the main entrance to the court. The quality of the architecture is pleasing, the proportions good and the whole building refreshingly free from superfluous decoration; in architectural terms it was excelled only very rarely during the second half of the century. The

external façades are a modified version of the traditional London domestic style with simple, well proportioned, classical sash windows; the internal façades have a series of great brick archways, carrying the wrought iron access balconies, which act as a fine foil for the mass of brickwork. This part of the scheme seems particularly successful; Roberts managed to keep

2.4 & 2.5 *Streatham Street, Bloomsbury*

the scale human, and he successfully avoided any appearance of grimness. Each dwelling is approached from one of the galleries and has a small lobby leading to the living room and also to one of the bedrooms. Off the living room, which overlooks the street, is a second bedroom, a cupboard and a scullery with a separate W.C., which is properly ventilated. The planning is simple and direct, showing little evidence of previous clumsiness, and it resembles the small modern flat more closely than much of the work which immediately followed it.

The building was completed in the spring of 1850, and it was open to view on 20 May, when it attracted much attention:

...a plain, but handsome and massive, building of very considerable size...suited for the accommodation of large numbers of the families of the artizan and journeyman class, with all requisite conveniences for household life complete in each dwelling, with a perfect system of ventilation and drainage – managed on the newest and most approved principles – the building arrangements being wonderfully compact, and the rents at which wholesome, airy, and convenient premises can thus be let, lower than the average sums paid for the airless, lightless and fetid rooms in which are lodged so great a proportion of the operative classes of London and of England.[21]

Meanwhile, in 1849 there had been a further outbreak of cholera, and when it finally died away there was a National Day of Thanksgiving. On this day, the Bishop of London had recommended in an encyclical to his diocese, that the collections taken at the services should be given to the Society in order to further its work. A sum of £5,300 was raised – about half the cost estimated for a new block of buildings – and the Society raised the remainder so that it could purchase a second site in Grays Inn Road. Roberts prepared designs for a new block of family dwellings with additional special accommodation for single needlewomen, who earned a very small income at that time. He used this scheme to show how the disadvantages of the enclosed common stair could be obviated, and he provided different solutions in the two separate four storey blocks. One version was arranged with a pair of two-roomed tenements on each floor, the other with three, each of three rooms. There was accommodation for 128 single women, each sharing a room off a common corridor; an old building adjoining was converted into a communal wash-house.[22]

Model cottages at the Great Exhibition

The next scheme with which the Society was connected was probably the most famous of all its ventures; but, curiously, it is now never associated with it, nor with Roberts, and it is always linked instead with the name of the Prince Consort. S.I.C.L.C. was very interested in taking part at the Great Exhibition of 1851, so that its work might be brought to the notice of a much wider public; in addition to the usual exhibits such as drawings, perspectives and models, it wished to erect a complete building which would illustrate the latest ideas on the design and construction of healthy working class dwellings. The authorities for the Exhibition were very unwilling to allow such a large scale exhibit, and they refused the Society permission to build; but the Prince Consort, who was still their President, seemed to have approved and, as well as obtaining a reversal of the official policy, he bore all the expense of constructing the houses, and for this reason the building has always been known as The Prince Consort's Model Cottages. The design represents the logical development of Roberts' earlier thoughts, and it is possible to see the building development from the ideas in his published essay on *The Dwellings of the Labouring Classes*.[23]

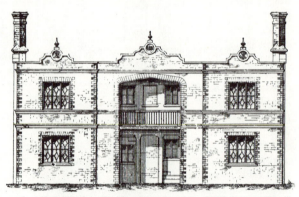

2.6 *'Model Houses for Families erected by HRH Prince Albert' at the Great Exhibition of 1851; designed by Roberts and instigated by S.I.C.L.C., they provided the model for Waterlow's early work with the Improved Industrial Dwellings Company*

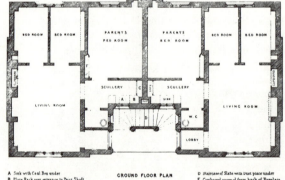

A Sink with Coal Box under
B Plate Rack over entrance to Dust Shaft
C Meat Safe ventilated through hollow bricks

GROUND FLOOR PLAN

D Staircase of Slate with Dust place under
E Cupboard warmed from back of Fireplace
F Linen Closet in this recess

The building was erected in the grounds of the Cavalry Barracks in Hyde Park, and provided accommodation for four families, two on each floor; but the design was in reality two 'cells' which could be repeated vertically, so that one stair might serve perhaps eight families, and it could be joined linearly to an indefinite number of similar units.[24] It was a prototype. One of the most interesting features of the scheme was the arrangement of the stair; it was recessed into the building but completely open to the air, with a small access balcony in front of it, serving the pair of flats on the upper floor. It was one of

Roberts' most useful innovations, since it provided a compromise between the long external gallery and the totally enclosed staircase access systems. Sydney Waterlow used the design as the basis of the work of The Improved Industrial Dwellings Company, and it was also the inspiration for several other buildings erected during the latter half of the century.

The Exhibition cottages established a standard of accommodation which Roberts and the Society thought should constitute a norm. They stipulated a minimum of three bedrooms, because this allowed a separated bedroom for the children of each sex as well as for the parents. The actual arrangement of the plan is curious: Roberts thought for some reason that it was desirable to have one bedroom cut off from the main living area, and he chose to plan it off the scullery. Otherwise the design displayed his customary facility in organising a group of very small units.

It is important to remember that each dwelling was complete with its own scullery, closet, water supply, fireplace and dust shaft: it was an independent dwelling in all respects, and this was the ideal which the Society constantly advocated in urban as well as rural housing. Nor did the exemplary qualities cease with the general planning; equal care was lavished upon a system of ventilation, and upon the quality of the materials, all carefully chosen for their durability and hygienic qualities. The rooms were of a reasonable shape and size, each with a separate window, so that, in all respects the houses were as perfect as Roberts knew how to make them.

The Society for Improving the Condition of the Labouring Classes after 1851

The publicity which these houses gave to the Society seems to have been considerable: there was a steady flow of requests for advice and for copies of their plans during the succeeding years, not only from enquirers in this country but also from abroad.[25] In many ways, however, the Exhibition Houses were the culmination of the Society's activities: it had now provided model versions of all the different types of accommodation then required by the working class and its work was in a sense complete. Its example did not attract investment to other commercial societies on any great scale, which was always a disappointment, and as it never intended itself to build on a repetitive plan it had really completed its work. Lord Shaftesbury soon became accustomed to admit at the annual meetings that there was little fresh to report; for example in 1853 the annual report referred to 'comparative inertness and inactivity',[26] and the Society contented itself more and more with reports on the work done by other companies and societies in the country at large; inspired largely, it claims, by its own shining example; and this indeed was probably true.

There was another factor which at least initially retarded progress in the years immediately after 1851;

this was the ill-health of the honorary architect, Henry Roberts, who was obliged to journey to France and Italy, and was prevented from taking any active part in the current work at London. From time to time he would send reports of continental housing activities, and mention the advice he had been able to give to those attempting to build for the poor in foreign places; but his personal initiative in England, which to a large extent had been responsible for the important contributions that S.I.C.L.C. were able to make, was now at an end.[27]

Various economic factors, including the Crimean War, had contributed to the rising cost of building during the fifties and by the middle of the decade the Society was less keen to start building again.[28] It is not surprising then, that their next venture was again a conversion, this time of a complete existing court. In a sense this, too, was a pioneer work for it attempted to strike at the very roots of the slum problem, but it carried with it a sense of compromise for in reality it was only a palliative. The ideas which prompted this new course of action were symptomatic of a new phase in housing philosophy; one in which the ideal, represented by the Streatham Street building, was slowly given up in the face of a two-fold pressure: first of cost, and secondly the need to provide sanitary homes in increasing quantity, as quickly as possible, and in a way which was an economic and commercial proposition.

It took some considerable time to find a suitable court in which to carry out this experiment, and it was not until the autumn of 1854 that Wild Court in Drury Lane was acquired. On November 8 Lord Shaftesbury conducted a party of noblemen and representatives of the press over the court, so that they might see it in all its filth and squalor before conversion began.[29] The visit, and the Society's proposals, were subsequently reported at great length in the daily press, and also in Dickens' *Household Words* under the title of the 'Conversion of a Heathen Court'.[30] The conversion proved satisfactory and Dickens was able to write by contrast of 'Wild Court Tamed',[31] later in 1855. Consequently the Society was able to raise money for two other similar conversions; the first, Clark's Buildings, St Giles, the other Tyndall's Building, Gray's Inn Road.

A branch of the Society was formed at Tunbridge Wells during 1847; it built a group of cottages, and it possessed a lodging house.[32] The only other scheme worthy of note was more comprehensive and much later in date. It consisted of a court, surrounded on three sides by dwellings built at Hull in 1862 to the designs of Henry M. Eyton.[33] The buildings were two and three storeys in height and provided separate tenements for 32 families. Eyton also altered some property in Seven Dials which the Society obtained in 1872, but apart from this solitary and very minor scheme there was no further work.

The importance of the Society for Improving

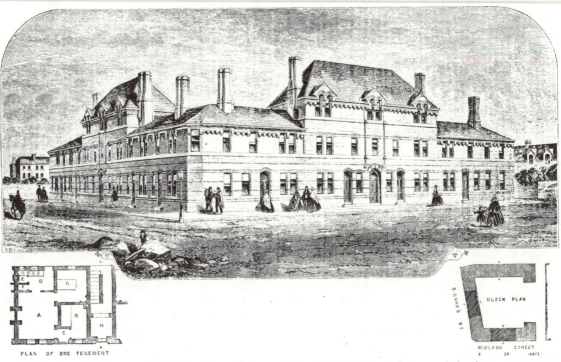

2.7   *S.I.C.L.C., a development at Hull in 1862. Henry M. Eyton architect ; this was the Society's only provincial venture*

the Condition of the Labouring Classes lay quite clearly in the work which it was able to undertake during the first ten years of its existence, for this was the period during which it contributed fresh ideas and developed new building types. It undertook practical research of great value, but it had little sense of the need for organised housing on a large and repetitive scale. It was content to make its own demonstration that working class housing of various designs was a commercial possibility, and with this done it regarded its task as completed. These were limited terms of reference, but it cannot be denied that within them, the Society achieved considerable success.

The Metropolitan Association for Improving the Dwellings of the Industrious Classes

The Metropolitan Association for Improving the Dwellings of the Industrious Classes was in fact the earliest of the societies founded for the purpose of building houses; it was founded at a public meeting held on 15 September 1841, presided over by the Rev. Henry Taylor, Rector of Spitalfields. This meeting resolved:

That an association be formed for the purpose of providing the labouring man with an increase of the comforts and conveniences of life, with full compensation to the capitalist. That the first object of the association be to erect, rent, or purchase suitable buildings, to be let in compartments, at a moderate weekly rent.

That the second object of the association be to erect, rent, or purchase dormitories for the reception of nightly lodgers.

That the third object of the association be to erect, rent, or purchase small tenements for families, to be let at a moderate weekly rent.[34]

Unlike its near contemporary S.I.C.L.C., it set out to build dwellings as a sound commercial proposition and to build in quantity in order to solve a housing shortage, not merely to set an example for others to follow; but after its foundation in 1841 the Metropolitan Association remained inactive for four years whilst it raised capital amounting to £20,000, and for this reason it is treated here after S.I.C.L.C. In 1845 it obtained a royal charter, which was an expensive but necessary business, since it was then the only means of limiting the liability of the shareholders in proportion to their investment. The charter fixed the maximum rate of

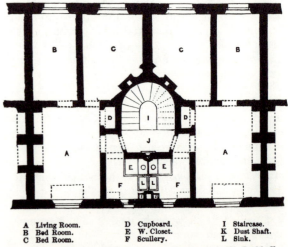

A	Living Room.	D	Cupboard.	I	Staircase.
B	Bed Room.	E	W. Closet.	K	Dust Shaft.
C	Bed Room.	F	Scullery.	L	Sink.

2.8   *Family Houses in Old St Pancras Road, 1848. W. B. Moffatt architect ; built by the Metropolitan Association*

interest at 5 per cent and provided that any surplus should first go towards the provision of a guarantee fund of £15,000, and afterwards to the furtherance of the society's objectives. The first annual meeting took place in 1847, when there were definite plans to build a block of family dwellings on a site opposite the church in Old St Pancras Road.[35] It was an ambitious scheme for a first project, consisting of twenty-one tenements of two rooms, and ninety of three, each with a sink, a supply of water and a refuse chute. The architect was W. B. Moffatt, and the work was completed the following year.[36] Less original than the Streatham Street Model Dwellings, which followed soon after, they also had the disadvantage of being liable for the window tax because of the enclosed staircases, and the Association was obliged to pay the House Tax on its buildings until as late as 1867 when it obtained special exemption.[37] Roberts has this to say about the St Pancras scheme in his survey of housing developments:

These buildings...present an extended and imposing front of about 226 feet, with advancing wings, and are five storeys high. The sub-division into distinct double-houses, with a central stone staircase to each, is similar to that of the Birkenhead building.[38]

it would be used by the tenants of the adjoining family dwellings, when it necessitated a markedly higher rent for the lodgers.[41] The building was 'U' shaped, four floors in height, excluding a basement. The ground floor contained the communal rooms; kitchen, library, coffee room, reading room, living accommodation for the superintendent and the cook, and various offices; while on the floors above dormitories were placed in each of the long wings, and the lavatories and washing facilities in the central link-block. The open space between the blocks was completely filled at ground level by a coffee room, which had a steeply pitched glazed roof. The block of dwellings were started in 1849 and completed the following year. This building was four storeys high and was placed parallel to one of the wings of the lodging house, but with a small return-block to the main street, thus forming a second court in reality, this time free of all building at ground level. The character, like that of Roberts' Streatham Street building, was simple and rather classical; there was no attempt to create special architectural effect except for some very restrained modelling on the main façade of the lodging house, and the building again bore the imprint of a traditional London vernacular

2.9 *The Artizan's Home, Spicer Street, 1849. William Beck architect; part of the Metropolitan Association's ambitious estate*

They seem to have been successful, for the Association immediately proposed a second and equally ambitious scheme on a site in Spicer Street, Spitalfields. During 1848, rather unusually, a competition was held for the design of a lodging house to accommodate 300 men, and dwellings for 40 families. William Beck sent in the successful scheme, despite the fact that his lodging house only accommodated 234 men instead of the stipulated 300.[39] Work must have proceeded quickly after the results of the competition became known since the lodging house was completed by the end of 1849.[40]

It was more elaborate than the George Street establishment built by S.I.C.L.C., and Roberts wondered whether the more lavish communal accommodation could be justified, despite the intention that

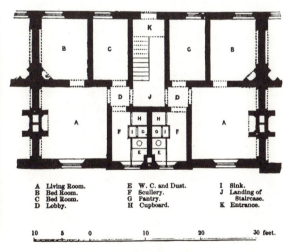

A	Living Room.	E	W. C. and Dust.	I	Sink.
B	Bed Room.	F	Scullery.	J	Landing of
C	Bed Room.	G	Pantry.		Staircase.
D	Lobby.	H	Cupboard.	K	Entrance.

2.10 *Tenements at the Spicer Street Estate, built in 1850*

style. The planning of the dwellings, which were all self contained, and arranged off staircases, accepted the same kind of standards as those adopted by S.I.C.L.C., and most of the tenements were of three rooms, only a few of two, and there were none, significantly, with only one room. This, then, can be taken as fairly representative of the views which were currently acceptable amongst the earliest reformers, but it should be noticed that there was no unanimity about the system of access, the Metropolitan Association sticking to enclosed staircases and S.I.C.L.C. to galleries or external stairs.

The Association also acquired some further property in Mile End New Town at this time, which it converted and repaired; these were two cottage schemes, both small in scale, that in Pelham Street housed twelve families, and that in Pleasant Row nine. In addition, a lodging house in Compton Street for 128 single men was taken over from the vicar of St Anne's, Soho.[42]

By 1852 the success and failure of the various schemes was becoming apparent, and could be measured financially; it was evident by that time to the Metropolitan Association, as well as to S.I.C.L.C., that lodging houses were not as remunerative as family dwellings, and the annual meeting of 1852 decided, therefore, to confine future work to the construction of tenements. A scheme was evolved for a building to contain 108 families in tenements of up to four rooms in addition to sculleries, but there was a note of financial concern in the following year, similar to that voiced by S.I.C.L.C: tenders suggested that the average cost of a set of rooms would be £215, which contrasted unfavourably with a sum of £160 when the Old St Pancras Road building was erected. The work was postponed, and at the following annual meeting the committee were only able to declare a dividend of $1\frac{1}{2}$ per cent. Half the rooms in the Artizan's Home at Spicer Street were then empty; and there had been trouble at Soho chambers, when the superintendent and 40 lodgers had walked out and started a rival, although short lived, establishment.[43] The Artizan's Home proved unsuccessful over a long period, and in 1869 the company decided to convert it into family dwellings, despite the considerable expense which such a radical change in function involved; the coffee room was pulled down, an open court created, and galleries were added on the outside to give access to the new tenements. After this the building proved much more popular.[44]

The Metropolitan Association had one great advantage over S.I.C.L.C., it was properly organised for continuous expansion and it was prepared to establish branches in the provinces. Soon after 1850 there were affiliated associations at Brighton, Newcastle, Dudley, Ramsgate, Southampton and Torquay.[45] More followed later in the decade, and their first flush of enthusiasm, although often short-lived and unproductive, served to keep the parent body alert and vital, by contrast with S.I.C.L.C. which began to decline at this period. A

return of less than 2 per cent was not likely to encourage investment, and in order to raise more money the parent Association made vigorous efforts to restore its position. A public meeting was called during February 1854, when the following resolution was passed:

That very many of the sanitary and social evils which affect the condition of the labouring classes have been proved to be attributable to the insufficient and inferior accommodation afforded by the habitation at present within their command, and the removal of so serious an obstacle to the advancement of their moral and physical welfare is therefore an object of extreme importance...

That this object has been attained to a remarkable degree by the operation of the metropolitan societies for improving the dwellings of the industrious classes, as shown by the results of sanitary improvement recently published by Dr Southwood Smith, the average rate of mortality in the improved dwellings erected by the Metropolitan Association not being one-third that of the metropolis generally, while the rate of infant mortality in the same dwellings is little more than one fifth...

That improved dwellings can only be extensively and permanently established on terms affording a fair remuneration to the capitalist; and that this object can most readily be effected through the instrumentality and extended operations of the Metropolitan Association for Improving the Dwellings of the Industrious Classes, in which the liability of the shareholders is limited to the amount of their shares.[46]

The result of this meeting was very gratifying; there was a public response from the city which raised £15,275. This enabled the Association to continue its

2.11 *Ingestre Buildings, Golden Square, started by Viscount Ingestre in 1854 and bought by the Metropolitan Association*

2.12 *Ingestre Buildings, Golden Square*

work: and, as *The Builder* pointed out, the case for model dwellings was a sound one.[47] Dr Southwood Smith's report dealing with the technical effect of sanitary improvements, which was published in 1854, made this clear. In it he wrote: 'The conviction has become equally strong, that whatever improvement is effected in the physical condition of the people is conductive to a corresponding elevation in their intellectual and social state.'[48]

With this new source of finance the Association was able to extend its work, and during 1854 it acquired two sets of property belonging to the General Society for Improving the Dwellings of the Working Classes, which had been founded in 1852 by Viscount Ingestre; the first was an uncompleted block in New Street, Golden Square, intended for sixty families, which was finished by the Association, and opened the following December. The second, a minor property in Queen's Place, Fashion Street, Dockhead, consisting of five double cottages each with four rooms, had already been converted by Ingestre.[49] The other properties of the Metropolitan Association were also making better financial return now, and it is good to note an atmosphere of reasonable prosperity and expectancy about the 1854 report.

The views of Charles Gatliff on housing the poor

As part of this general campaign to inspire confidence in the housing movement, the Secretary of the Association, Charles Gatliff, published his *Practical*

Suggestions on Improved Dwellings for the Industrious Classes. He emphasised the need to erect buildings near to the work-place of the labourer, and the need for building upwards, in order to counteract the high price of land:

The position of such dwellings with reference to the locality of employment being of primary importance, the object of the following table is to show, among other things, that, by constructing them, where practicable, on the plan adopted in some instances by the Metropolitan Association – viz., lofty buildings with large open courtyards attached for safe recreation – workmen may reside in a healthy and comfortable manner in the immediate vicinity of their work, notwithstanding the high price of land upon which the dwellings may be built…

…in re-building the houses in Pelham Street and Pleasant Row, more than four times the number of Improved Dwellings can be erected on the same quantity of land as is at present occupied by 23 four-roomed cottages, which suggests the inquiry how far the working population now living in cottages in the suburbs, or in lofty houses in more crowded districts, and frequently ejected to make way for new streets of other improvements, and those employed about Railway Termini and Stations, at many of which new towns are springing up, can be accommodated in the Improved Dwellings occupying the same or a less superficial area (including the courtyards attached for safe recreation), and that in the immediate vicinity of their work; while the adoption of such an arrangement of the Dwellings would improve as much the architectural appearance as the sanitary state of large towns: and the increased labouring power and other advantages secured to the working man would enable him to pay the requisite rent to insure such a dividend as would be satisfactory to the shareholder, independent of the diminution in the poor rates and crime which both landlord and tenant would be instrumental in effecting: nor would such rent be more than at present paid for far inferior accommodation.

From the construction and arrangement of Dwellings on the plan before alluded to both the natural and artificial ventilation is better than in cottage property, which, in crowded districts will almost inevitably be surrounded by higher buildings, whereby the air is excluded from them; while the lofty buildings erected by the Metropolitan Association intercept the higher and purer currents, which thus become distributed in the courtyards formed around for safe recreation...

With a good system of ventilation...money may be economised and rents reduced, as it is not necessary to make rooms so large, and if they are more numerous the superficial area covered will be less and consequently the cost of the whole building diminished.[50]

He went on to point out that too many rooms were not desirable in dwellings where the tenants have but little furniture: he had found that they tended to use a third bedroom as an additional sitting room, while frequently the living room was used as a bedroom for young children. After discussing certain details of the internal planning and ventilation, he returned to the problems of external space standards:

However advisable it may be to preserve large courtyards where land can be had, still, as this may not always be attainable, *any separate block may be erected with very many advantages wherever the requisite space for it alone occurs*; though another advantage in arranging Dwellings round a courtyard is, the protection gained by the entrances to them being made from it, whereby the expense and trouble attendant on street doors is saved.[51] [The italics are Gatliff's.]

The pamphlet concluded with a series of plans to illustrate the ideas which Gatliff had expressed, both in the disposition of rooms within the dwelling and for the relation of these blocks to one another. There was an interesting scheme, for example, with galleries at the second and fourth floors, from which individual stairs led up to flats on the third and fifth floors respectively: this was especially designed to avoid the House Tax, just as several years earlier, Roberts had evolved the gallery principle for each floor.

This pamphlet provided a useful contrast between the attitude of the Metropolitan Association and that of S.I.C.L.C. towards the middle of the decade. The era of experiment was over by the time Gatliff wrote his tract, and it was increasingly evident that the two principal societies would be unable to attract large scale commercial investment for their work if they continued with their current policies. Gatliff's pamphlet tried to popularise the movement and expand the work of the Association; he was worried by the problem of how to build a reasonable volume of

property, with sound accommodation, while at the same time making the venture pay a good return. Therefore, he was obliged to look for economies which would make his buildings more remunerative and his Association attractive to a typical mid-Victorian investor.

But this was only one side of the problem: Lord Shaftesbury's beautiful theory that a good dwelling improved the occupant was now questioned, probably for the first time from within the housing movement; there was an increasingly practical and realistic outlook, no doubt because it suited the economic argument so well, and was it not also true that the poor had not the means even to furnish a tenement so large as a model dwelling? Gatliff, then, stood for a point of view which became more common after 1860. The principles underlying the dwellings which Roberts built in Streatham Street, and all that they represented, were soon to be abandoned in the face of economic *and* social pressure: on the one hand was the typical Victorian commercial philanthropist and on the other the social realist: but both were afraid of *losing* money.

The later work of the Metropolitan Association

The work of the Association, however, continued to develop for a while following the fresh endeavours of 1854: Albion Buildings, Bartholomew Close, Aldersgate Street were purchased early in 1855, and a new building was finished and occupied in December at Nelson Street, Bermondsey, designed by Charles Lee, who was described the previous year as the Association's architect.[52] The original charter was also extended that year to allow branches of the Association to be formed in all parts of the country which were independent of the parent body but titularly affiliated to it, and this helped to overcome the objections previously raised concerning central interference in local affairs. Most of the new work, however, was executed by branches already in existence. A branch had been formed at Dudley in the spring of 1854 and designs made for a group of cottages, laid out around grassed courts.[53] On 17 May 1854 a public meeting was held at Liverpool to found another branch, and a local gentleman subscribed £5,000 before the end of the proceedings. The Brighton branch was already several years old, and had built its first model dwellings in Church Street during 1852, and followed them with a second block two years later. A lodging house was opened by the Torquay branch in 1855,[54] for fifty single men; and an association was formed at Bristol, the Mayor taking the chair at the inaugural meeting, when he expressed his regret that he had been unable to persuade the City Council to take up the cause of housing as a civic duty.[55]

The London Association, meanwhile, rather surprisingly turned its attention to cottage properties, a mode of building which was fairly rare amongst the housing societies during this period. It is difficult to conjecture the reasons for this decision, especially in view of Gatliff's previous observations, and also bearing in mind the growing economic pressure upon the Association to build high. It is possible that they were influenced by the preponderance of cottage property in Mile End New Town to which the Londoner was by choice addicted, preferring the way of life in an individual house to that in high buildings. Another reason may have been the unpopularity of the Artizan's Home, which was a high building, but its unpopularity seems to have been due to its function as a lodging house, rather than its height. The first group of cottages to be built were in Albert Street, Spitalfields, adjacent to the Artizan's Home. They were, in fact, cottage flats, a housing type much more common in the north of England than in London. The buildings were of two storeys, arranged in two parallel rows which were separated by a small pedestrian walk and little gardens. Each of the 33 flats consisted of two rooms and a large scullery, and they all had individual front doors. The group was completed during 1858, and six years later the Association built another terrace nearby, for 36 families, which were of a similar design except for eight larger flats which had an extra room. These were known as Victoria Cottages.[56]

While the Association was building Victoria Cottages it also began a much more ambitious scheme known as Alexandra Cottages, at Beckenham in Kent – the first really suburban venture of a housing society. The cottages were built in pairs like the modern semi-detached house, each pair occupying a plot some 40 feet wide and 90 feet deep. It was a lavish layout by the standards of that day, made possible because the land had belonged to the Duke of Westminster, who on this occasion, and again some years later, aided the society by granting them very favourable purchase terms. The first sixteen cottages were completed in 1866, and two years later there were about seventy pairs; a few more were built soon after this bringing the total number of cottages to 164.[57] They were a more ambitious venture than Albert and Victoria cottages in Mile End New Town; each of the Beckenham cottages having two or three bedrooms. The Association made it their policy from the outset to let the cottages to men who worked in London, despite the fact that they did not at first obtain special concessionary railway fares for that purpose. The venture seems to have been very successful since it paid a handsome interest of nearly 7 per cent from the outset, but the Association did not repeat the experiment, because the directors thought quite rightly that their proper sphere of activity was in the central areas where the problem was the most difficult, and the least capable of private, speculative, solution.

It was with block dwellings, then, that the Association was most closely linked in its later developments, as it had been in its earlier years; the group of cottage schemes were merely an interesting experiment in what was otherwise very much a central London society.

2.13 *Victoria Cottages, Spicer Street, added to the estate in 1864*

3.1   *Columbia Square, Bethnal Green*

3

The housing scene 1851–62

The new societies

Of new societies during the fifties there is less to say than during the preceding decade, or during the sixties. In London, Viscount Ingestre was responsible for the formation of the General Society for Improving the Dwellings of the Labouring Classes in June 1851. The 'Objects of the Society' show quite clearly the kind of problem the early societies were attempting to solve:

1 To improve existing dwellings in densely-populated districts.
2 To destroy the system of subletting, by which both the real owner and the tenant suffer, the latter most severely, by the exactions of the middleman.
3 To enable the tenant, by small weekly payments, to have the use of, and ultimately to become the possessor of, furniture, at a cheap rate.
4 To alter the system of nightly lodgings, by which at present the middleman derives the sole profit. This society to be self-supporting.
5 The society, whilst carrying out these objects, desires to show, by periodical statements of its expenditure and receipts, that it offers as safe an investment as those companies whose avowed object is return of capital; so that, by its system of collecting rents and management, landlords would improve their properties without risk.[1]

A site was purchased and cleared in 1852, and the following year the foundations were laid for a block of tenements to house 64 families, designed by Charles Lee.[2] The Company was anxious to proceed on a proper commercial basis and the annual report for 1852–3 outlined the policy which they hoped to pursue when the building was completed:

...the society is anxious to impress upon the public that these buildings will be let out to the working man at a rate which will remunerate the outlay. It will be our endeavour to show that capital may find employment in the erection of similar buildings, and a fair interest will be yielded in the shape of rent, and yet that the working man may occupy three rooms for a little more than he now pays for one which is unfitted for human dwelling.[3]

Thereafter, however, the Company seems to have been beset by financial troubles and the following year the Metropolitan Association bought the property together with a small group of cottages which the Company possessed at Dockhead. The dwellings were completed, but the Company was at an end, the victim of the conditions which came to militate against such ventures during the decade.[4]

There were only a few more new societies; in Lambeth a Dwellings Improvement Committee had been formed after the 1848 cholera outbreak and in the next decade a dwellings company was formed, which began to build in 1857.[5] There was a society in Hampstead, another on a small scale in Marylebone founded under a royal charter, and a society in Kensington formed after the 1856 Act limiting the liability of company shareholders.[6] The last foundations during the decade were the Strand Buildings Company, and the Dwelling-house Improvement Company both dating from 1857.[7] Apart from these, which were concerned with housing alone, there was the Metropolitan Sanitary Association, which existed for the dissemination of knowledge in its chosen field.[8]

In 1852 Henry Roberts designed a group of cottages

3.2 *Housing built by the Windsor Royal Society for Improving the Condition of the Working Classes, 1852. Henry Roberts architect*

for 40 families and a lodging house for 50 single men for The Windsor Royal Society for Improving the Condition of the Working Classes, which was founded that year under the patronage of the Queen and Prince Albert. This, of course, was not an urban scheme, since the site chosen was situated in Windsor Great Park, but Roberts used his exhibition plan for some of the cottages.[9] The buildings were laid out as though in a street and all of them were two-storeys high. Two years later the little estate was extended by the well known and fashionable Victorian architect S. S. Teulon, probably because Roberts had by then become a sick man and left England for a warmer climate.[10] The lodging house quickly proved unsuccessful and was closed in 1855,[11] but the remaining houses were popular and remained in the Society's possession until 1872 when they were sold to Richardson Gardner, who owned much cottage property in Windsor.[12]

Private ventures

One of the first privately built schemes was in New Street Mews, Dorset Square, where a Mr Harton built a small block of dwellings for eighteen families in 1850, and there was another in Grosvenor Mews built two years later by John Newson to the design of Roberts.[13]

In Lambeth, the Duchy of Cornwall attempted to set an example as well as a standard, by building its own version of a block of tenements in 1855; and, as befitted an agency which was not obliged to rely upon the whims of investors, it provided accommodation of the 'ideal' standard, and there were tenements with up to three bedrooms. On the ground floor were shops, and rather oddly, the living accommodation for their tenants was in the basement. Each separate dwelling was provided with its own scullery and closet, which was considered very satisfactory, if rather Utopian by that time.[14]

The army, too, had built a lodging house in Victoria Street for the families of soldiers stationed in London, which attracted considerable attention;[15] and in 1857 Miss Burdett Coutts started perhaps the most famous and certainly the most ambitious private development, known as Columbia Square in Bethnal Green, to be undertaken up to that time.[16] The square, which was demolished and replaced by a modern housing development soon after 1960 was an important step in the history of working class housing. It was physically grim, despite the lack of commercial motive in its construction, and this goes some way to reinforce the argument that those interested in housing at this time were concerned with the health issues to the exclusion of nearly all others. The estate was designed by Henry Darbishire an architect who subsequently built all the early estates for the Peabody Trustees. So it can be argued that Columbia Square was, in effect, a trial run for a whole programme of housing and the appearance of the buildings was to influence the popular view of organised housing for many years to come.

There were four five-storey blocks formally sited around a central open space. The sets of rooms were arranged off central spine corridors and they shared lavatories and washing facilities. The attic floor was used either for laundries or covered areas for drying clothes and for children's play space on wet days. All of these features were subsequently developed in the Peabody estates. The first block was completed in 1859 the last in 1862;[17] then Miss Burdett Coutts decided to add a more magnificent gesture, a new covered market. For this Darbishire produced a French Gothic design which was as incongruous as it was fantastic. Whereas the Square was hardly worthy of the name architecture, the Market was an essay in entirely misplaced grandiloquence. The hall itself was modelled on the Sainte Chapelle in Paris: it formed the

3.3   *Housing built by the Duchy of Cornwall in Vauxhall Row, Lambeth, 1855. Hunt and Stephenson architects*

SCALE OF   FEET.

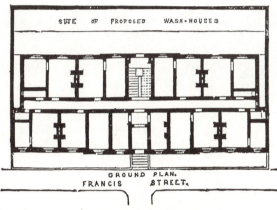

3.4   *Victoria Lodging House, built for the Army in 1854*

3.5   *Columbia Square, Bethnal Green, 1857–60, built by Miss Burdett Coutts. Henry Darbishire architect; this was the precursor of Darbishire's Peabody designs*

back of a rectangular court of buildings which had its main entrance on the opposite side and a cloistered effect on the other two sides with some dwelling accommodation above. The Square was stripped of ornament, the Market Group was loaded with Gothic detail. So much so that it frightened away the stall-holders as well as the customers and it was doomed to failure from the start.[18]

A scheme in direct contrast to this, built in 1855, was Cowley Gardens, Shadwell, erected at the expense of a Mr Hilliard, a barrister, to the design of Roberts' Exhibition houses.[19] The cottages were two storeyed, built of a mellow red brick, arranged in two parallel rows which were separated by the street and a small garden in front of each house, so that the effect was still one of pleasant domestic scale.

The pattern for the housing movement in London was thus established; it consisted either of privately built schemes such as those just described which followed perhaps some well tried precedent or made an aristocratic, ill-informed but well-intentioned, shot in the dark at what might be good for the poor. Or, alternatively, it was the result of a development by a society or company more or less philanthropic in nature. This was still the period of experiment: architectural, social and financial; there was, as yet, no established pattern of development. That was a task for the next decade. But whatever the means of building the motives were the same: a society newly

rich attempting to recompense the people out of whom its wealth was made for the inconvenience – the inhumanity – of their homes and indeed their lives. The haughtily sanctimonius, the earnest evangelical, the apostles of self help, the prophets of socialism: all were motivated by a deep and abiding sense of guilt, of a peculiarly Victorian kind.

The provinces

On the whole, towns outside London were slow to take up the housing cause. It can be argued that in many provincial towns it was unnecessary to provide model housing on central area sites because there was frequently enough speculatively built housing in the suburbs. But such an argument ignores the equally important fact that few working men could either afford to rent such a house or look forward to enough security to start purchasing it. For the artizan – the better-off workman – the prospect became increasingly realistic as the century advanced, but for the rest it remained a

3.6   *Columbia Market, adjacent to Columbia Square, 1865. Henry Darbishire architect; a Victorian folly*

3.7 *Cowley Gardens, privately built by a Mr Hillyard using Roberts' Great Exhibition design*

dream. The journey to work and the sheer physical size of towns was not the only valid criteria for judging the need for central area rehousing.

It is not true, however, that London was alone in fostering the growth of organised, responsible housing, even though because of the magnitude of its problems it became the centre of activity. There was from time to time activity elsewhere, although with the exception of the Metropolitan Association and S.I.C.L.C.'s Hull scheme there was little impetus from London in the development of housing in provincial towns. The Metropolitan Association branches at Brighton, Dudley, Torquay, Bristol and Liverpool all owned property although more frequently it was converted lodging accommodation rather than new housing.[20]

There were independent societies flourishing in several provincial towns, notably at Hastings where a society was founded in 1857, which concentrated first on conversion work, but later commenced building and with sufficient success to form a branch in the metropolis.[21] There were several more, most of them working on a small scale and showing little originality. Mention is made at this time of work in the following towns: Nottingham, Wolverhampton, Worcester, Saffron Walden, Norwich, Hertford, Halifax, Glasgow and Cambridge.[22] This last will serve to show the kind of scheme which was built in a provincial town:

A ricketty and filthy mass of building, called Sharpe's Rookery, at the Falcon-yard, leading from Petty-cury... has been razed by the Rev. John Cooper, the vicar of the parish, [St Andrew the Great] who has made a public carriage-way in lieu of a narrow, low, covered passage, and erected a model lodging-house for sixteen familes, under the title of "Vicar's-buildings", from the designs by Mr R. R. Rowe, architect...The exterior is brick, but moulded

in various forms of divers colours: no particular style of architecture has been adopted...Two open arches lead into the entrance-halls, whence two stone staircases rise to the upper floors: one staircase leads to four suites of apartments, the other to twelve. Each door upon the landings is the front door of a distinct dwelling, consisting of a sitting-room, two bedrooms, scullery, water-closet, sink, coal-place, cupboard and a dust-shoot.[23]

All these developments, however, belonged to the first half of the decade with the exception of that at Hertford, and this was yet another sign of the decline in

3.8 *Vicar's Buildings, Cambridge, built in 1855 by the efforts of the vicar of Great St Andrew's*

active building which took place towards the end of the period. There was also a noticeable change in the nature of housing developments after the passing of the 1856 Limited Liability Act[24] facilitating the formation, amongst many other things, of housing companies and these were often concerned not with model dwellings but with schemes which would permit the artizan eventually to buy his own house. There was in this perhaps also a sign of the growing prosperity of the artizan class; and in the north of England, especially, the co-operative housing movement was becoming increasingly popular,[25] a typical company being that founded at Leeds in 1861.

A committee of gentlemen, well known for their interest in the working-classes, and connected with the building and provident societies of the town, have originated and in-augurated a scheme which, it is hoped, will supply the want which has been so long felt, and, at the same time, enable working-men to become the owners of their own dwelling-houses, at an outlay very slightly exceeding the rent usually given by the better paid of the artizan class.[26]

Capital investment was, therefore, finding a safer outlet in a class which did not require direct support: for those less able, and the model dwellings were supposedly built for them, the prospect of financial support was less certain because it was an increasingly less safe form of investment.

It would be difficult to gather together in one chapter all the varying examples of provincial housing for the poor. The construction of an isolated block of tenements, or a common lodging house, may have intrinsic interest but it rarely had significance. The plain fact was that most towns paid scant attention to over-crowding and housing generally; the pattern of laissez-faire applied equally to housing as to public health. There were certain exceptions, and mention was made in the previous chapter of work started either by private individuals or as a result of civic initiative – that rare thing – in places like Liverpool, Glasgow and Edinburgh during the years after 1840. In all three towns the fifties were characteristically without momentous events, as was largely true of London during the latter part of the decade, and then, in the sixties, there was a veritable renaissance of interest and activity.

For this reason I have chosen to discuss another town, of quite different character, to illustrate the frustration of lethargic local government, the occasional gleams of hope when private individuals managed to stir the community into some sort of activity, and the difficulty with which this work was sustained. The account takes us somewhat beyond the scope of this chapter but it speaks for itself in its entirety and it is typical of the situation in many other towns, particularly in northern England.

The condition of Leeds at the time of the Royal Commission on the Health of Towns had been described by James Smith:

But by far the most unhealthy localities of Leeds are close squares of houses, or yards, as they are called, which have been erected for the accommodation of working people. Some of these, though situated on comparatively high ground, are airless from the enclosed structure, and, being wholly unprovided with any form of under-drainage, or convenience, or arrangements for cleaning, are one mass of damp and filth. In some instances I found cellars, or under-rooms, with from two to six inches of water standing over the floors, and putrid from its stagnation in one case, from receiving the soakage of the slopwater standing in pools in the street adjoining. The ashes, garbage, and filth of all kinds are thrown from the doors and windows of the houses upon the surface of the streets and courts; and in some cases, where a gallery of entrance has been erected for the inhabitants of the second floor, the whole of the slops and filth are thrown over the gallery in front of the houses beneath, and as the ground is often sloping towards the doors of the lower dwellings, they are inundated with water and filth, and the poor inhabitants placed in a miser-able and unhealthy condition. The privies, as usual in such situations, are few in proportion to the number of inhabi-tants. They are open to view from in front and rear, are invariably in a filthy condition, and often remain without the removal of any portion of the filth for six months.[27]

These were, then, comparatively new buildings: houses rushed up in the fever of the industrial revolution, often by unscrupulous men, with no thought for the morrow. The town of Leeds, in a sense, was directly responsible for its own problems in a much more intimate manner than were the citizens of Edinburgh, for example, who were facing a problem of central area deterioration due to prolonged growth and decay.

It was in a part of the town such as has just been described that a private citizen, William Becket Denison, provided his first lodging house for men in 1851.[28] It was a conversion, and accommodated 70 single men. His intention was to set an example, but at the same time he hoped that sufficient investors would be attracted to make the venture profitable. So successful was the scheme, in fact, that the following year provision was made for a further 32 beds, and in 1853 a similar house was opened for women, separated from that for men by the superintendent's house, but this was not a success. There was insufficient demand for the accommodation, which consisted of rooms shared by two lodgers, and those who did make use of it were apparently unmanageable. Within five months it was closed, and converted into a better class house for men, each of whom had a single room, and in this form it was successfully re-opened as the Mechanic's Home.[29] That year, the building was paying $6\frac{1}{4}$ per cent which was an encouraging rate of interest for a venture which was not entirely a commercial proposi-tion.[30]

Denison seems to have been very active in his endeavours to popularise the lodging house movement, and he was always ready to provide information about the social and financial position of his own scheme.[31] The outbreak of war in 1854, however, came as a setback: Denison had planned a further extension to his lodging house, but this had to be postponed. The existing houses were not so well filled, and during the war the scheme was only just able to pay its way. Joe Raistrick, the superintendent, made an inquiry into the reasons for this rapid falling off in membership, only to find that it was due to enlistment in the army; and this, Denison must have been satisfied to find, was typical of the country at large. After the war the Leeds house returned to normal, and in 1857, eleven additional rooms were added to the Mechanic's Home.[32]

This was the conclusion of Denison's practical work; it seemed to have little effect upon the citizens of Leeds, for there are no accounts of similar ventures being started, despite his financial success and the average yearly return of 5 per cent. *The Builder*, in a series of articles dealing with large towns, summed up the conditions of Leeds in 1860 very succinctly: 'Leeds, speaking broadly, is a filthy and ill-contrived town',[33] and it went on to point out that despite great industrial wealth the town had no regard for the plight of the poor: which showed very clearly the fruitlessness of Denison's attempts to arouse public support.

Perhaps it would be impossible to find a town in all England where the house accommodation for the labouring populations has so unequally kept pace with the increase of population as in Leeds.[34]

But Leeds, indeed, as *The Builder* recognised, was a 19th century boom town: in 1801 its population was 53,302; and the figures at the end of each following ten year period were 62,665; 83,943; 123,548; 150,234; 172,270; and it was expected that by 1861 they would have passed the 200,000 mark.[35] The article in *The Builder* seemed to attract considerable attention in the town – which was not surprising considering the vehemence of the attack – but *The Builder* later noted that while certain points were denied, the local press admitted that much was true.[36] Practical results, however, still remained difficult to find, and the only notable benefaction was from one local man who put up the capital to build ten houses, which the tenants were able to buy for very little extra cost in addition to their weekly rent.[37]

This seems to have been the first venture of what became the Leeds Model Cottage Building Committee, referred to earlier, which, during the next few years was to continue its activities as a non-profit-making society, financing itself mainly through a building society, then a relatively new means of raising the necessary capital for housing, and one which developed very rapidly in Yorkshire and Lancashire.[38] The houses in Beeston Terrace, which comprised this first venture, were not intended for the very poor, but they were cheap and soundly built and were followed in 1862 by a second group of eight houses, Albert Terrace at Burley, and by a third of fifteen known as Langham Street, near Wortley, while a fourth in Meadow Lane, a more centrally placed site, was proposed in the following year. These were completed in the spring of 1865, and were quickly followed by a larger venture at Wortley, where houses were offered for sale a year later. The Society then held a public meeting to explain the way in which the poor could buy these houses through a building society, and therefore it seems that they were aiming to provide homes for the less wealthy as well as the more affluent artizan.[39]

These model dwellings were a useful contribution to housing, and the rate of building was increasing as we have just seen, but they were a small contribution in the face of the speculative building which provided the vast majority of homes in the town. There was, of course, no obligation to build decent houses; there were no standards, no regulations; there was apathy to the law, inadequate as it was, and there was little more real concern for its application on the part of the authorities. *The Builder* was not alone in its condemnation of the city and its authorities, for in 1866 James Hole published *The Homes of the Working Classes*, in which he described the town in similar terms to those used six years previously by Godwin. Leeds had already sacrificed itself upon the altar of industrial progress; it had little communal self-respect, and there had been no statistical information until Robert Baker undertook the task between 1833 and 1840. He was instrumental in obtaining the Leeds Improvement Act of 1842, which enforced a general sewage scheme; and the Burial Act, which put an end to intra-mural burials and provided cemeteries outside the town. But there were still no building regulations, and overcrowded conditions were as common in new as in existing properties. Working class housing was as a consequence very badly built because it was subject to no legal control: back-to-back housing was a problem in 1840 when Baker reported, and Hole noted that much of the property then described still existed, only in worse condition: respectable streets in 1840 had become, in 1866, slums; and indeed the back-to-back system was still in vogue:

Hundreds of them are being run up by mere building speculators, who build them not for permanent investment, but for immediate *sale*, and hence put as little material and labour into them as they can. No effectual control or inspection exists to check such proceedings.[40]

If there was no inducement for the builder to provide substantial properties because of the complete lack of proper regulations, there was also every reason why the multiple landlords, into whose hands the majority of these properties would eventually fall, would prefer a cheap job enabling them to charge a relatively small rent and still make an extortionate profit. The reason was the existence of an extraordinary process whereby the landlord could obtain a reduction of fifty per cent in the rating of house property if the annual rental did not exceed £7. 4s. od. The advantages of this provision, known as compounding, are obvious: to the tenant it meant the enticement of a cheap rent; to the landlord, an increased profit because he had built cheaply. Thus another measure designed to aid the poor eventually benefited most that nebulous class of landlords and middlemen who, without social conscience of any sort, made every possible profit out of property which very soon would become a liability to the community.

As we have seen, one of the most serious defects of nineteenth century sanitary and building legislation was that it was permissive and impossible to enforce, since the authority in whom it was vested was often unwilling to operate against its own diverse private interests. Much depended upon the vigilance of the local authority: in Leeds, for example, the local Act permitted proceedings against houses without separate privies, but these were never taken, and so long as back-to-back developments continued to be practised it remained impossible to enforce this particular section of the Act. Despite the provision of sewers after 1842, many houses remained unconnected to them, and when Hole was writing, the Council was applying for additional powers in this matter: 'but the most extensive powers are valueless unless enforced'.[41] This was the root of the trouble; until a council accepted whole-heartedly that sanitary control and building control were necessary, that properly qualified and responsible officials in sufficient number must be employed to enforce these controls as at Glasgow; unless these steps were taken, regulations remained but empty words. Permissive legislation might look very fine on paper; but unless it is implemented, it does not exist in reality.

The sanitary regulations in Leeds were in this sense meaningless, and so too it appears were those for building. The basic stipulation that no street should be less than 30 feet wide was often neglected:

The town is a maze, without plan, order, or arrangement: here a *cul-de-sac*, there a house projected far beyond the general line of building, spoiling what would else have been a decent street...In Leeds every man who lays out land, or builds, does simply what is right *in his own eyes*; if it suits his neighbour, well; if not, so much the worse for his neighbour, and frequently for himself. Opportunities still exist, but are rapidly passing away, for securing *open spaces* for the health and recreation of the inhabitants.[42]

Denison had been an advocate of high building on the flat principle as early as 1852[43] but such a building was not actually built until 1867, and this provides an interesting comparison with many other towns where the idea of horizontally divided tall buildings were usually their first solution to the housing problem. There is, I think, a link between the importance of the building society movement in the Leeds district and the prevalence of the individual house as a unit. The first block dwellings were built by The Leeds Industrial Dwellings Company in Shannon Street to the designs of a local firm, Adams and Kelly. There were shops on the ground floor, and above, three floors of dwellings on the gallery access principle to avoid the house tax. They were much less ambitious than some of the housing schemes which have just been discussed and each flat consisted of only two or three rooms; washing facilities were shared, and *The Builder* complained that there were too few lavatories.[44]

One of the first slightly encouraging signs of a tangible improvement in outlook must have been the competition held in 1873 for the development of the Roundhay Estate, which included provision for a park as well as a housing estate, which was developed in most solutions with detached and semi-detached houses. However, apart from the park, which was an amenity to the town, the housing was for the middle and upper classes. This kind of action was typical of the way in which a number of towns sought to improve their amenities later in the century.[45] If green lungs were desirable, they did little to alleviate the housing problem itself.

Events such as this, however, are no more than signs which to a later generation connote a change in attitude; when viewed in a larger perspective, a national context, they did not denote any marked improvement for the mass of people upon whom the wealth of such towns as Leeds depended. In 1874 The Leeds Social Improvement Society reminded the council of the insanitary condition of the town, and this again showed that there had been no improvement due to civic action since *The Builder*, fourteen years previously, had castigated Leeds in the great surveys of towns.[46] After the 1875 Housing Act was passed the Guardians of the Poor again found it necessary to call attention to the powers which the authorities could use, and the advantages gained by using them, in closing some five hundred cellar dwellings which were still inhabited. They noted, as this account bears witness, the lack of philanthropic action in the town. It was apparently still necessary for Becket Denison and his friends to take similar action to that which they had initiated many years previously. In 1878 they purchased Millgarth Mill in Millgarth Street: W. B. Perkins altered it for them and it was opened as a lodging house with very cheap accommodation in the form of three dormitories for one hundred and eighty people.[47]

Public health and the model dwellings movement

The first model dwellings had an excellent chance of proving themselves soon after they were built; cholera broke out mildly in 1852, and again in late 1853, that time much more seriously. When the great epidemic of 1848, which had hastened the passing of the Public Health Act, was over, the interest in sanitation waned, and most towns did little or nothing to improve their drainage or water supply, and they failed to instigate cleansing activities, especially in the poorer quarters. It is significant that the new outbreak began at Newcastle, a town which had legislated itself out of the national Act and thereafter proceeded to do nothing.[48] But most towns were completely unprepared: in a typical editorial 'How London is prepared for the Cholera', *The Builder*[49] attacked the authorities for their lack of action despite frequent admonitions from its columns. Later, a second editorial[50] on the subject noted with some satisfaction that the earlier comments had eased the path of the local boards of health and made their work less difficult and circumscribed. Many of the model dwellings had been immune from cholera, and presented a marked contrast to the unhealthy districts in which they were usually situated, and Godwin seized upon this factor to point out the effect of good water supply, adequate ventilation and proper drainage. These factors were probably all in part responsible for good health, but no doubt the real reason was that the water supply for many model buildings at that time was taken from the New River Company, one of the few which drew its supply from reasonably pure sources. The advantages to be gained from simple sanitary remedies were again shown by Dr Southwood Smith in a Report published during 1854.[51] In Lambeth Square, for example, where the houses were built with cesspools and brick drains, he found that the death rate fell at once from 55 per 1,000 to 13 when glazed pipe drains and trapped closets were substituted. When the cholera outbreak was over, Palmerston was petitioned for a National Fast Day, but bluntly and typically he refused:

...the best course which the people of this country can pursue, to deserve that the further progress of the cholera should be stayed, will be to employ the interval that will elapse between the present time and the beginning of next spring in planning and executing measures by which those portions of their towns and cities which are inhabited by the poorest classes, and which, from the nature of things, must most need purification and improvement, may be freed from those causes and sources of contagion which, if allowed to remain, will infallibly breed pestilence and be fruitful in death, in spite of all the prayers and fastings of a united but inactive nation.[52]

Advice such as this from high places was much needed, but when it was interpreted by petty local authorities it was seen to imply increases in the rates to pay for the improvements, or the diminution of local power into the hands of a larger health authority or water board. Self help usually, therefore, won the day, and the practical result of this admonition was negligible.[53]

Speculative house building

Speculative work still provided the great bulk of new housing, but there was here also a decline in the rate of building during this period. At Birmingham, for example, the yearly totals of new dwellings erected between 1853 and 1856 were said to be respectively 2,784, 2,219, 1,253 and 803.[54] If quantity fell, quality certainly did not seem to show a corresponding improvement, and uncontrolled speculation was still the most common evil. A lecture by Patrick Allen Fraser, 'On some of the causes which at present retard the Moral and Intellectual Progress of the Working Classes',[55] devoted considerable space and attention to

3.9   *A typical example of monotonous bye-law street housing from the air*

contractual problems and the sharp practices then typical of the building trade. Similarly, J. W. Papworth, lecturing to The Society of Arts, 'On Houses as they were, as they are, and as they ought to be',[56] complained of the competition in the building trade which caused skimping and undercutting, which in its turn was encouraged by the known gullibility of a public who would neither seek nor take the advice of the architectural profession. Papworth went on to describe the changes which had taken place in the nature of speculation: in the last two decades of the eighteenth century it had been common for one member of a building trade to buy a piece of land and arrange with the other trades involved to build the houses, each

3.10   *Speculative housing which became slum property in Birmingham*

3.11 *Back-to-back and Court housing, Broadmarsh, Nottingham*

taking one when completed in lieu of payment. This system, popularly known as 'blood for blood' was iniquitous: in order to make as much profit as possible each trade was naturally encouraged to skimp wherever possible and the resultant building was of the worst kind. Early in the 19th century it became more common for builders to undertake the complete erection of a house, borrowing money from any sources available, and paying their debts according to the sale of the houses. This system became unpopular with the money lender, who frequently found unfinished property in his possession, and it eventually became more difficult for speculating builders to obtain capital. Seeking fresh sources of money, they therefore sought agreements with merchants, who would lend them money on condition that they used their particular materials. This source of money became scarce when the supplier found that the builder habitually misused his materials, and by mid-century active speculation had passed into the hands of the ground landlord:

who lets ground and advances money, in the hope that the speculative builders would put up a good deal more money of their own or other people's in the shape of carcasses on his ground, and by failing would allow him as mortgagee to foreclose and get, at a cheap rate, carcasses to be finished scampishly and sold cheaply.[57]

The landlords were thus deliberately encouraging insecure builders to gamble on housing, in the hope that they would go bankrupt. In this event the landlord would obtain a shell, built at another's expense, which he could then finish as cheaply as possible and sell for a good price, compared with its actual cost, to an unsuspecting artizan. Papworth observed that many houses but recently built were consequently in worse condition than property very much older in date.

The builder required money to erect his houses; but there were other financial problems which faced the artizan who wished to buy. Some loan societies

made working class borrowers pay as much as 22 per cent[58] on the original sum and it was not until the 1866 'Loans Act' that the poor could find less extortionate sources of support.

It was, therefore, unfortunately true that while the new movement for reform in housing conditions in the central areas was making positive if slow progress, the unscrupulous speculative builder or landowner in the suburb was deliberately creating a new slum, dangerous structurally because it was often liable to physical collapse, but worst of all dangerous to health because of his failure to provide adequate drainage and sewerage. Such neglect was criminal, but it was not a punishable crime for there was no law to prevent it. Parts of Canning Town were built in the mid-fifties without proper drainage, and on marshland which was below the level of the river and thus liable to flooding.[59] Godwin found cesspools in Islington which were the cause of ill health, and in Kentish Town epidemic was a frequent visitor because of stagnant pools in the street for which no one took responsibility.[60] Similarly, Henry Mayhew described an area known as Jacob's Island, built around an open sewer, from which the water supply was drawn.[61] Provincial towns were no better, and in a series of articles describing the 'Condition of our Great Cities', which took the form of editorials in *The Builder* during the early sixties, indescribable filth is the chief characteristic from Edinburgh and Glasgow in the North, through Newcastle, and on to Leeds, Manchester and Birmingham.[62] The Medical Officer for Whitechapel could give examples of an 'open space' 2 ft. wide and 50 ft. long which was strictly in accordance with the law but deliberately defying its spirit.[63]

The literature of health and housing

Conditions such as those just outlined were the subject of numerous articles and pamphlets; one of the most effective writers in this decade was George Godwin who, in addition to his pungent editorials for *The Builder*, published two extended works. The first, *London Shadows*, appeared in 1854; in it he described in great detail the homes of the poor, and campaigned against public apathy to the problems and dangers of bad drainage and over-burial. *Town Swamps and Social Bridges*, the second of his works, was published in 1859; here he emphasised that little had been done to improve the great bulk of slum property which had previously been described. In addition, Godwin was able to review the work done by the various housing agencies during the decade, and some of them came in for severe criticism: the rents charged by the Metropolitan Association at Old St Pancras Road were too high for the poor and 'the style, approaches, and staircases are not sufficiently attractive for those who cannot afford so much'. Consequently many tenements were empty. Miss Burdett Coutts' buildings at Columbia Square were too high, he considered, and unsuitable for the type of tenant which she envisaged. For S.I.C.L.C. he had no criticism and much praise, but he was forced to admit that their rate of interest, at $4\frac{1}{2}$ per cent, was discouraging, and he concluded:

If the improved dwellings which have been erected are not remunerative to the builders, or appreciated by those for whom they are intended, it is time to think of some other plan which may supply shelter to a large class that must be cared for.[64]

So far as these alternative solutions were concerned Godwin confined himself to his 'social bridges', rather than to practical alternatives such as new ways to house the poor; about these he was unfortunately reticent. The principle of re-housing was of course included in his list of bridges, the others were juvenile reformatories, ragged schools, infant nurseries and similar institutions; anything in fact which avoided recommending pecuniary aid, which Godwin could not countenance and in this he represented a solid core of Victorian opinion. Education, he saw as the panacea for all ills:

Improve the homes and teach the children and we shall soon lessen the number of the 'dangerous classes' and prevent much suffering and misery, and enable men and women to live out the term of their natural lives, and to play their proper part in increasing the sum of general wealth and general happiness.[65]

and he concluded:

We may dry up many sources of crime by education, and by the same means may lessen the amount of sorrow and lengthen life. Here, surely, are good wages to be had for good work, we may:

DRAIN THE SWAMPS AND INCREASE
THE BRIDGES[66]

Godwin wrote this at the end of the decade and it illustrates his own views on the likely remedies to a great social problem, but he was echoing a more general change in mood. Several years earlier Cobden, at the opening of a Mechanics' Institution at Barnsley, had adopted a similar attitude:

...you can't do anything in social reform but you are met with the question of education. Take the question of sanitary reform. Why do people live in bad cellars, surrounded by filth and disease? You may say it is their poverty, but their poverty comes as much from their ignorance as their vices; and their vices often spring from their ignorance. The great mass of the people don't know what the sanitary laws are; they don't know that ventilation is good health; they don't know that the miasma of an unscavenged street or impure alley is productive of cholera and disease. If they did know these things people would take care that they inhabited better houses...Therefore, when you wish to make them more temperate, and secure moral and sanitary and social improvements among the working classes, education, depend upon it, must be at the bottom of it all.[67]

Cobden assumed that the poor were in possession of the means to improve themselves; but Shaftesbury, in reply, pointed out that, because he must live near his work, the labourer was forced to live in insanitary property, under conditions which were often so terrible that eventually he gave up all hope, and ceased to want to be clean and healthy.

Education in these cases becomes an impossibility. We know it by experience. No one who will walk into some of the scenes that we could show him, would doubt the assertion that it is vain to take a child and train it for three hours, and then send it back for the 21 to witness the practical horrors of these localities. Education, after all, though it must be begun under teachers and masters, is best when completed by a man's own self; no education will ever be so good for the working man as that which he will acquire in the peaceful evenings of a cleanly, decent, suitable home.[68]

Shaftesbury represented a position which was more popular in the early years of the housing movement, particularly before 1850, when the poor were more frequently regarded as oppressed, but nevertheless inherently thrifty and responsible. The later point of view was not necessarily cynical or reactionary; Cobden saw, because experience taught it to be so, that the poor were not necessarily by nature clean or temperate; the frailty of human nature and the sins of ignorance did not automatically correct themselves because the environmental conditions, intemperance or dirt, were removed, nor did a sound system itself create the people to make it effective. The poor, these social realists believed, must be taught the righteousness of clean living: that effort was as worthwhile as it was necessary. There was more than a grain of truth in both schools of thought, but neither possessed the whole truth; one attitude was the natural successor of the other in the social and economic climate of the period.

Other writers were usually concerned with more practical issues in the housing movement. Viscount Ingestre, the earnest young man in the tradition of Shaftesbury, although lacking the strong Evangelical qualities which dominated Shaftesbury's outlook, edited a series of essays under the title of *Meliora: or, Better Times to Come*, which were published in 1852 in order to publicise the work of his housing society, The General Society for Improving the Dwellings of the Labouring Classes. There were contributions by Becket Denison, the great Leeds reformer, on model lodging houses; by Henry Mayhew on dwelling conditions – 'Home is home, be it never so homely'; and Ingestre himself described how his interest in the welfare of the poor had developed when he was only 18 years old, during a potato famine in his native village; and he went on to describe how his new society proposed to help the poor by providing new homes. The next year, following the success of the first book, Ingestre produced a second volume on very similar lines.

William Bardwell's *Healthy Homes* was also published in 1853; in it he reviewed the progress made in the sanitation of the individual house and discussed the typical faults of design and layout then prevalent. His own recommendations laid great stress on the necessity for each house to have proper drainage and for the public sewers to be continuously flushed. He entered the sewer controversy in favour of the man-size, brick-built system, rather than the glazed small pipe sewer, which was advocated by the more advanced sanitarians. His other views are less open to criticism, and his recommendations for the preservation of open space around the metropolis and for the use of church-yards as local open spaces were more far seeing. The work included the inevitable personal solution to the

housing problem; Bardwell proposed a tenement block where each dwelling consisted of a living room, 15 ft. 9 ins. by 11 ft; 2 bedrooms, each 11 ft. 2 ins. by 9 ft; a scullery containing a sink, pantry, coal bin, a slate water cistern and a separate closet: the tenements were thus in the 'ideal' tradition. He gave great attention to his own elaborate system of ventilation, based on an arrangement of flues, which was typical of that period with its inordinate interest in vitiated air and its supposed influence upon health.[69] His proposals for the general layout of the housing were founded upon Roman principles with a grid network of streets: the lateral streets, which were to contain the dwellings, were to be 40 ft. wide with shops at either end, but they were not to be used for traffic, so that the children could play in them with safety. There was also to be a space 40 ft. wide at the rear of each street which was to be laid out with trees and grass. Bardwell ventured too far into the realms of idealism; he took little account of contemporary economic stringencies, which must have made his ideas of much less practical value than he at first intended.

The following year a book with the same title – *Healthy Homes* – was published to make known the activities of the Metropolitan Association, with contributions from Dr Southwood Smith on the origins of the Association;[70] and from Charles Gatliff, its Secretary, dealing with the buildings which had been developed, and giving detailed figures of their cost and the rent charged. His opinions have been discussed already. Again there were a series of plans, some based on existing housing schemes, which were suggested for future use.

Finance was fast becoming the dominant topic, even in literature, and some two years later, in 1856, G. B. Tremenheere devoted nearly all his pamphlet *Dwellings of the Labouring Classes in the Metropolis* to a consideration of the financial implications of the two early societies, drawing attention to the factors such as siting, height, and appearance, which influenced popularity and affected the prosperity of individual buildings. His conclusions were not novel, but they were sound; he wrote that economy in construction and finish, and the removal of the fixed maximum rate of interest, were essential to future prosperity. In addition he recommended that there should be public loans at cheap rates, and he drew attention to the good financial return which could be expected from conversions. Similarly, Arthur Ashpitel and John Which-cord in their essay on *Town Dwellings* published in 1855 recommend public investment in the housing movement, because the benefit of a healthy working class accrued as much to the rich as to the poor. They took a more sanguinary view than others, however, since they believed that the two early societies were financially successful, so they confined their criticisms to lodging houses, of which they thought there were too many, and to the lack of privacy of the common stair and corridor in model dwellings. In place of this system of access they suggested a system of flats off a common stair, rather similar to the Scottish 'land', arranged in five storey blocks planned around a common garden. These flats, with a minimum of three bedrooms, were intended for a superior class of tenant able to pay a rent of 6s. 6d.–15s., which it was believed would bring a return of 8 per cent. For the very poor the authors suggested a block with two-room tenements off external galleries and sharing communal services; but they admit to reservations:

Let it be distinctly understood, we do not approve of two rooms only for a family residence, and we certainly prefer the superior accommodation of a separate water-closet and scullery to every dwelling; but the problem is to construct the best thing that shall compete in economy of cost with the existing objectionable erections, and that done, there would be no doubt of success.[71]

This steady stream of literature shows very clearly that there was no unified approach to the housing problem: it was still a literature of ideas and theories, many of which differed widely in their outlook. What, then, was the position in 1860, at the beginning of the new decade? In all truth it was not encouraging, and there was unusually little activity. Unsatisfactory signs appeared, as we have seen, early in the decade, but they increased latterly. For example, in 1857, when *The Builder* was reviewing the current position in the housing movement,[72] it returned to the problem of a new generation arising amongst the working class, who were not interested in social reform, and some who actively obstructed it, despite the fact that lectures on the basic principles of healthy living were neither unknown nor uncommon. It noted that there was a need to overcome prejudices to new dwelling types. At Tyndall's Buildings, for example, which were bought in part by S.I.C.L.C., the remaining house owners in the court did not co-operate – indeed their tenants had a 'wilful and ignorant contempt for the means of health and comfort'.[73] *The Builder* pointed out the need to overcome prejudice to new dwelling types, but it also again criticised the model dwellings. The rents at the Metropolitan Association's property in St Pancras Road had recently been increased, for example, and in consequence tenements were empty, for this was by no means the first increase in rent, and *The Builder* complained that the property was not sufficiently attractive for tenants who would pay the rent asked. Rents in model dwellings were generally too high, but vacancies might also occur because of dissatisfaction with the accommodation provided; this had happened at S.I.C.L.C.'s Thanksgiving Buildings, where amongst other things there were complaints about the water supply and leaky pipes. The class for whom the model dwellings catered was evidently becoming less easy to please.[74]

During the last two years of the decade only one new society had been formed in London, and the old ones, as we have seen, were not thriving;[75] neither the Metropolitan Association nor S.I.C.L.C. had built

anything of consequence during the previous three or four years, and their profits were declining, which was not encouraging when both were well established. Roberts thought the prospect was gloomy, and he suggested that there should be some measure to assist the working classes to buy their own houses as was possible at Mulhouse,[76] in France, where the Société Mulhousienne des Cités Ouvrières, which was founded in 1853 as a co-operative housing society, was enjoying considerable success, and in an earlier paper he seems to support some kind of action by the state or the local authority, since he quoted approvingly the words of Lord Kinnaird, who had written:

I am inclined to think that the local authorities in large towns (despite the 1851 Act which does not define a lodging house) might be empowered, under proper restrictions, to raise money on the security of the town's property for the purpose of erecting dwellings to be let out to the working classes, in cases where employers cannot, or more frequently will not, undertake the necessary trouble and expense.[77]

In a letter to *The Times* he made it clear that he supported the agitation for obligatory legislation to enforce sanitary measures, and to extend the powers of inspection under the lodging houses Acts.[78]

The end of the decade

What had emerged from the work of the fifties was the knowledge that family dwellings were the most suitable building type since the demand had proved much greater for these than for lodging accommodation. It had become clear, as a result of this demand, that rents must decrease rather than increase if the movement was to benefit a wider and poorer section of the community. This left for the next decade the problems of cheapening the cost of building and of finding some *via media* to the question of housing standards. One was a commercial issue; for obviously it was necessary to make the movement commercially attractive if the housing problem was to be solved numerically without artificial aid. The other problem resolved itself into a social issue centering around the relative merits of education and the model dwelling; whether to improve the poor in their existing homes – or perhaps in a new single room dwelling – or alternatively, whether to provide model dwellings, complete with all the amenities of self contained existence. But these issues were so hedged and circumscribed by economic issues that it rapidly became impossible to disentangle the two attitudes; the later solutions were nothing if not a nicely held balance between sociology and economics.

The decade which had begun in the first flush of enthusiasm ended in stagnation, frustration and inactivity. Fresh initiative was required to show how the seed, which had already been sown by the exemplary societies, could bear fruit in a commercial world.

In other ways it was a decade which underlined the differing qualities which separated the second half of the century so radically from the first. The 1851 census showed for the first time that the greater proportion of the population lived in towns, and this trend was of course to continue and become a dominant feature of English life.[79] The outward sign of urbanisation was the unparalleled growth of towns during the early years of the century. In London this resulted in problems which had not been experienced previously and which were not yet really noticeable in provincial towns: problems concerning transport and commuting, the relation of industry to the worker and his home. It was this rapid growth and its resultant problems which caused *The Times* to comment in 1853:

A kindred calamity is the distance from their occupations at which *many are* compelled to reside. Let anyone visit the outskirts of town and explore those rows of yellow brick, one storey high, of which we may have had *a birds eye view* when a traveller by railway. The most respectable inhabitants of such districts are working men, who are compelled to reside there from the impossibility of finding houseroom in the heart of the town, and near their work. This is the extension of the metropolis which is to some a subject of pride. There is really nothing to rejoice at in an increase of London by perpetual additions to its extent, while vast tracts within its limits may be made available...The remedy is at hand in a proper use of those districts which are at present crowded only because the houses in them are small and paltry, and which, covered with edifices of improved construction and a sufficient height, would supply to a poor and striving class advantages which would eventually be found to be a benefit to those above them.[80]

The Times believed that parliament would be justified in granting special powers to facilitate the erection of such buildings, since it believed that new dwellings would improve the people: 'It is the property of a *good system* to educe the virtues necessary to its success.'[81] This attitude affected the views of a portion of the community, but before the end of the decade that proportion had dwindled and the enthusiasm it reflected had been lost because there had been no successful legal assistance, and no evidence of the great block dwellings which *The Times* foreshadowed. The block dwellings came later, however, but the expansion of towns continued to outstrip the building of cheap tenements, and the system did not improve the people: they had to be educated.

The last factor which should be mentioned before concluding this review of the fifties, and it was an important one, was the effect of the railways. Together with street improvements, the expansion of the railway companies had been responsible during the two previous decades for the demolition of vast areas of

working class housing. Railway work was to go on for many years to come, but already the companies were seen as a possible agency for relieving the pressure on house accommodation in the centre of cities. In 1859 *The Builder* was already commenting on the rapid development of suburban London and particularly, in this article, of housing built at Loughton as a result of cheap fares and new lines developed by the Eastern Counties Railway.[82] Henry Wyldbore Rumsey was scheming to practice J. S. Mill's ideas, again aided by the railways:

The removal of population from the overcrowded to the unoccupied parts of the earth's surface is one of those works of eminent social usefulness which most require, and which at the same time best repay the intervention of government.[83]

Rumsey wished to disperse the town-dwellers to new communities in the country, organised, under state control, where everyone would live in semi-detached cottages of not more than three storeys in height, built at a density of eight houses, or about sixty people, per acre. He believed that industry and amenities would follow the people, but until they did so he was proposing to rely upon cheap fares and an ample train service to transport the workers from their arcadian bliss to work in the doomed city.[84]

The new decade did not bring any immediate change to this gloomy scene of declining interest and activity, which characterised the housing movement in the last years of the fifties. The problems were underlined rather, and the pitiful lack of enthusiasm made more apparent. Nor should one forget an event like the defeat of the referendum on whether or not to drain the Scottish town of Montrose,[85] for it was as typical in its way of this period as was the work of the model housing societies, and it showed the opposition which existed to reform. The slums which had first attracted attention in the forties still remained, new ones had arisen as a result of street improvements and railway demolitions; new ones had actually been built as a result of *laissez-faire*. There were, however, institutions developing to cater for the needs of the poor; schools, clubs and orphanages for example. The housing movement itself was to have an unexpected renewal of life through the aid of two men, both of whom owed their wealth to the great city which was so full of abjectly poor people, living in conditions unfit for animals and still, in 1861, without much hope for the future. Knowing this, as we do, it is possible to say perhaps with more conviction than did Godwin: 'The swamps still abound; but the bridges are building.'[86]

4.1   *Corporation Buildings, Farringdon Road, 1865. Horace Jones*
architect ; built by the City of London and very like Waterlow's work

4
Victorian Philanthropy II:
the great housing organisations founded after 1862

There are several important dates in the development of a housing policy during the last century which, for the historian, seem to have considerable significance and conveniently divide the century into clearly defined phases. The first of these was 1842, the year Chadwick presented his great report on the condition of towns, and within a year or so the two important early housing societies were founded. Twenty years later, in 1862, George Peabody established his Trust Fund which became one of the most successful of all the philanthropic housing organisations discussed in this book and the following year Sidney Waterlow founded a commercial company which was to prove, at last, that working-class housing could produce a workable, if modest return. So the two-pronged attack on the housing problem was carried on, on the same dual basis of philanthropic and commercial responsibility, those uneasy partners who were in possession of all the available ingredients of progress so long as progress was in the hands of private enterprise alone.

Since about 1852 the housing movement had been searching for fresh inspiration, the injection of more money and perhaps also it hoped for the arrival of some dynamic personality willing to face the problems of rising building costs and soaring land values, yet still managing to construct cheap dwellings for the poor in the centre of towns: something which in the late fifties seemed beyond the realms of reasonable possibility. Practical help was forthcoming from Peabody and Waterlow, yet the approach which their two organisations adopted underlined the problems and attitudes which existed at the end of the previous decade. The Peabody Trust accepted that, if it was to house the class of people it set out to house, it must accept the principle of associated dwellings, that is, tenements sharing sculleries and lavatories. They argued that this was a sensible arrangement since it allowed proper supervision of the sanitary arrangements. Waterlow's company, on the other hand, followed the earlier doctrine of the self-contained dwelling, seeking technical economies to equate the additional cost with the rents they wished to charge. One might well have expected the two organisations to have adopted the reverse positions on these questions; that they did not, is only another sign that standards were not necessarily a matter merely of economies in 1862. The philosophy behind decisions such as these was by no means clear-cut, and 1862 does not mark a watershed in anything else but practical activity; the old arguments continued unabated.

The housing movement in 1862: housing standards

The new decade in fact had begun very much as the old one had ended; the ever-present problem of equating cost with desirability, economic criteria with social, loomed as large as ever and a general sense of oppressive inadequacy prevailed because, while the nature of the solution remained elusive, the magnitude of the overcrowding problem increased almost daily.[1] Many of the men who, twenty years before had been filled with the zeal of Young England or the enthusiasm of an Evangelical sanitary reformation, were ageing, discredited or disillusioned. Some, it is true, had great tenacity like Lord Shaftesbury, but many of this group were bewildered by the failure of the movement to gain momentum. One of the few who remained with interest undimmed was Henry Roberts, the original architect to S.I.C.L.C., a sick man, forced to live most of the year in Florence but with his belief in the efficacy of model housing unchanged. His rare visits to London came to be regarded with considerable interest and in 1862 he addressed the Royal Institute of British Architects 'On the Essentials of a Healthy Dwelling and the Extension of its Benefits to the Labouring Population';[2] it was a combination of practical and detailed constructional advice, with an able assessment of the wider contemporary problems. He believed that many had embarked upon the provision of working class housing in complete ignorance of the implications only to find that the financial return was very disappointing. This, Roberts suggested, had been responsible for declining interest and the dearth of practical activities during the latter years of the previous decade. With care, a dividend of $3\frac{1}{2}$ or 4 per cent could be obtained but it required a good knowledge of the planning and building problems involved. Nevertheless, he admitted that housing societies could not hope to attract commercial investment, because a return of that sort was not a good investment by the standards of the day. This was the whole basis of 'philanthropy and 5 per cent': it became a peculiar Victorian habit, a penance for more fulsome success elsewhere. But like all such movements, the numbers willing to make such an alternative gesture were few.

Roberts observed that time had shown family dwellings to be the most useful as well as the most profitable building type, while lodging houses, which had once enjoyed a considerable vogue, were not now very popular and only paid their way when constructed out of converted property. He also pointed to one of the most significant and less creditable factors in housing, the absence of any useful contribution to urban housing theory from the architectural profession. Only two architects of national standing had shown evidence of interest; Sydney Smirke had published his *Suggestions for the Improvement of the Western Parts of the Metropolis* in 1834, and G. G. Scott his *Remarks on Secular and Domestic Architecture* in 1857. Neither work was strictly concerned with working class housing which continued to be designed by very minor architects or builders. Roberts himself was an exception, an architect of no small ability who, by choice, had given up a growing commercial practice, to devote his energies to housing reform. In 1862 he was probably the greatest living authority on the planning and construction of model dwellings.

A few years later, housing was again discussed at the Institute. A paper was read by Professor Robert Kerr, Professor of the Arts of Construction in King's College, London, 'On the Problem of Providing Dwellings for the Poor'.[3] It provoked considerable interest and was regarded by *The Builder* as an important contribution to housing theory.[4] Kerr suggested that the types of dwellings which were currently being built were unsuitable for the kind of working man most in need of accommodation. At the same time, he believed they were uneconomical to the builder. He dismissed the suburban house as unsuitable for the poorer classes; it was merely an expression of the war between ground rents and rail fares. Kerr said that housing must be provided in the central areas and, if this was to be achieved, he thought that the ideal unit of the three-bedroom house should be abandoned and more single room dwellings constructed. This went against the views of the early reformers, who thought it a reactionary point of view, but it was in line with some of the views mentioned at the end of the last chapter and was a point of view which gained ground during the next two decades, justified as we have noted already on the grounds of financial expediency, social realism or an inextricable mixture of both. Kerr was in the vanguard of coherent social realist thought; he was one of the first to make out a precise case in favour of minimum dwellings and the furore which his lecture precipitated showed the reluctance with which many would abandon the higher standards set by men like Roberts and Shaftesbury in the earlier buildings.

Kerr argued that the three-bedroom cottage was not a practical minimum: it was expensive to build and in order to keep the selling price down the rooms were usually reduced in size so that some were quite useless. As a more practical alternative he recommended a series of rooms 20 ft. by 17 ft., linked together to form a 'terrace'; a series of these terraces might be built one above the other with an access balcony 4 ft. wide along one side, and another 8 ft. wide on the other, serving as a back yard. There would be common stairs at either end and lavatories could be grouped together. Elaborate cooking facilities would be dispensed with, since he considered that the poor preferred their own simple ad hoc arrangements, and simple partitions might be erected inside the rooms to provide the privacy which any tenant thought necessary.

The Builder refuted Kerr's argument point by point, believing that any solution which fell below the three bedroom standard was not valid because it defiled the common decencies of family life.[5] But the editor, Godwin, was not able to offer a practical alternative and merely wrote: 'The lower classes of working men may have to pay more than they pay for inferior places at present, and may be able to do so.'[6]

Roberts, on the other hand, while accepting that there was no simple solution to the existing situation, refused to believe that there was any lasting virtue in the reduction of housing standards.[7] He seems to have thought that some kind of state assistance might become necessary – exactly how it might be administered he does not suggest – but such an idea was too radical; society was not ready to accept subsidisation in any form in the sixties.

The discussion on Kerr's paper at the R.I.B.A. showed that the architectural profession had no precise views about housing, but it did make clear that he was not alone in his assessment of the problem. Several members agreed with him wholeheartedly, and many more commented unfavourably on what they called the excessively lavish standards of workmen's accommodation. One member cited the reply which Lord Palmerston was said to have received from a tenant during a visit to a block of dwellings, in answer to a comment that more cupboards might have been provided: the quick answer had been 'True your honour, but we have nothing to put in them'.[8]

The profession seemed to have little conception of the meaning of poverty, it was out of touch with the problem of the poor and it had no idea what kind of housing was either suitable or economically practical. One speaker had the supremely naïve view that 'after all, it resolves itself into the cost of materials and construction – the cheapest materials and the least costly way of using them'.[9] Kerr himself summed up:

The result of the whole discussion therefore, appears to me to be this. The error of all high standards of accommodation has been proved and admitted; but the expediency of keeping to the very lowest standard is not yet so thoroughly acknowledged as I think it must some day be.[10]

The foundation of the Peabody Trust

Discussions such as these were centred around the idea that the poor must be housed by private enterprise in the same way as any other class of people: the builder must expect to make the same kind of profit, and in order for him to do this economies must be made either in the standard of accommodation or the method of constructing it. These were nearly always accepted as the terms of reference at this time for, of course, the whole housing movement had grown up with the central idea that what was required were responsible organisations who would build well and refrain from the malpractices of normal cheap speculation. Apart from S.I.C.L.C., which deliberately set out to provide experimental buildings for others to copy, all the attempts to house the poor had been started as normal commercial companies with the intention of providing the investors with a modest return on their money. In the Victorian scheme of things this was still, in the early sixties, the only foreseeable way of solving the problem.

It must have come as a considerable surprise, then, when a philanthropic trust was established within the housing movement in London:

We have today to announce an act of beneficence unexamplued in its largeness and in the time and manner of the gift.[11]

Thus did *The Times*, in a leading article on 26 March 1862, comment on the publication elsewhere in its columns that day of the correspondence between George Peabody, the wealthy American banker and a group of people he had appointed as trustees of a gift totalling £150,000 which he was proposing to set aside for the benefit of the London poor. There was no specified use for the money, that was for the Trustees to decide, but Shaftesbury had suggested that housing was an urgent need in London and Peabody passed on the suggestion for their consideration.[12]

Peabody had settled in England in 1837 when he was 42 and already a successful merchant in America. Six years later he retired from the American firm of Peabody, Riggs & Company in order to establish himself as merchant and banker in London under the title of George Peabody & Company, a firm which still exists as Morgan, Grenfell & Co, Ltd. Peabody enjoyed prosperity and respectability as his business flourished, and he became noted for his philanthropic works, chiefly in America where he founded institutes, libraries, and schools. In this country he was responsible for financing the American exhibits at the Great Exhibition of 1851 and he supported the American expedition which set out to search for the explorer Sir John Franklin.

The Trust which he created in 1862 was his one strictly English benefaction, but it was a substantial gift, and one to which he added several times until its capital amounted to £500,000. The trustees were business colleagues and friends; J. S. Morgan, his partner; Edward Henry Stanley, 15th Earl of Derby, a prominent politician; Sir James Emerson Tennent the

traveller, politician and author; Sir Curtis Miranda Lampson a fellow American merchant who had become a British subject, and finally the American Ambassador to Great Britain. In his letter establishing the Fund he outlined to these men his intention:

First and foremost amongst them is the limitation of its uses, absolutely and exclusively, to such purposes as may be calculated directly to ameliorate the condition and augment the comforts of the poor, who, either by birth or established residence, form a recognised portion of the population of London.

Secondly, it is my intention that now and for all time there shall be a rigid exclusion from all management of this fund, of any influence calculated to impart to it a character either sectarian as regards religion, or exclusive in relation to local or party politics.

Thirdly, it is my wish that the sole qualification for a participation in the benefits of the fund, shall be an ascertained and continued condition of life, such as brings the individual within the description (in the ordinary sense of the word) of 'the poor' of London; combined with moral character, and good conduct as a member of society.[13]

After considerable discussion the Trustees decided that housing was the one need which best fulfilled all the requirements of the donor:

In postponing other projects...it is not to be supposed that the Trustees ignore their value or question their importance; but a concurrence of circumstances at the moment combine to give pre-eminence to the one above alluded to. In the poorer districts of London the dwellings of the lower classes had been suddenly disturbed by the long pent-up invasion of metropolitan railroads, whose incursions were overthrowing whole streets inhabited by humble and

4.2 *Peabody Buildings, Commercial Road, the first estate of the Trust, 1864. Henry Darbishire architect; this was an experimental design*

industrious labourers and artisans. This dispossessed the population who, unprovided with adequate accommodation elsewhere, were thus driven away into alleys and courts, already inconveniently crowded by their previous inmates; and discomfort and disease were in many instances added to loss of employment and expense.[14]

Peabody made it clear that he approved of their choice by his subsequent gifts.[15] The Trustees themselves decided that from the outset the Trust should be self-perpetuating, so that future generations might gain some benefit, and for this reason all their housing developments showed a modest return. They, too, practised the policy of 'philanthropy and five-per-cent'.

The Trustees did not waste time; in 1863 a site was purchased from the Commissioners of Public Works in Commercial Street, Spitalfields, and shortly afterwards work began on a block of shops and dwellings designed by Henry Darbishire, the architect who had collaborated with Miss Burdett Coutts in the development of Columbia Square.[16] The site was small and rather awkward, situated at the junction of two streets; the main block faced Commercial Street and a shorter wing at a sharp angle to it faced White Lion Street (now Folgate Street); there was a small irregular yard at the rear. The building was four storeys high, incorporating shops on the Commercial Street façade

4.3 *Peabody Square, Islington, 1865; Darbishire's first plan using corridor access to two- and three-room flats with shared kitchens and lavatories at each end*

which had basement storage and living accommodation on the first floor. The remaining floors and all the floors in the side street contained sets of rooms approached off central spine corridors. On the top floor were communal laundries and baths. Most of the flats were of two rooms, although there were a small proportion with only one and a few of three. All shared communal washing facilities and sculleries which were arranged on the landings. Finishes were spartan; all the walls were left unplastered to minimise the risk of vermin and wallpaper was forbidden. The building was opened on 29 February 1864 and the first tenants payed 2s. 6d. for a single room and up to 5s. od. for a set of three.[17]

The building was not really typical of the subsequent work of the Trust, but the precedent for 'associated' flats, that is flats sharing common lavatories and sculleries, was established at Spitalfields and so, too, was the quality of the internal finishes. The Trustees argued that communal lavatories were sensible because they were capable of easy supervision, and as they were well away from the living rooms and bedroom they helped to create a more healthy environment.[18] Doubtless this was true by contrast with the slums where the complex evils of bad sanitation were often the cause of epidemic, but there were other ways of preserving sanitary conditions.

After the successful completion of the experimental Spitalfields estate, the Trustees embarked on an ambitious series of developments which established the pattern for the future work. Four large estates followed during the remaining years of the decade; Peabody Square at Islington, Shadwell, Westminster and Chelsea; they were completed in that order.[19] The Trust was a wealthy organisation, with considerable financial security in contrast to the societies established twenty years previously, and it was able to work on a larger scale, purchasing sites of considerable area, usually rectangular in shape, so that it was possible to build four detached blocks of flats surrounding a central open space which served as a playground and entrance fore-court. The site itself was railed off from the surrounding streets so that the Peabody community was in every sense separate, socially as well as physi-

Feet
0   10   20   30   40   50   60

cally, and this was deliberate. The blocks were either four or five storeys high with a centrally placed staircase in each, leading to spine corridors on every floor and off these opened the sets of rooms. There were no shops in any of the estates after Spitalfields.

The principle organisation in each of these extensive structures is the same. Drainage and ventilation have been insured with the utmost possible care; the instant removal of dust and refuse is effected by means of shafts which descend from every corridor to cellars in the basement, whence it is carted away; the passages are all kept clean and lighted with gas without any cost to the tenants; water from cisterns in the roof is distributed by pipes into every tenement and there are baths free for all who desire to use them. Laundries, with wringing machines and drying lofts, are at the service of every inmate, who is thus relieved from the inconvenience of damp vapours in his apartments and the consequent damage to his furniture and bedding. Every living room or kitchen is abundantly provided with cupboards, shelving, and other conveniences, and each fireplace includes a boiler and oven. But what gratifies the tenant, perhaps, more than any other part of the arrangements, are the ample and airy spaces which serve as playgrounds for their children, where they are always under mother's eyes, and safe from the risk of passing carriages and laden carts.[20]

All these estates still stand, although that at Westminster has been sold and does not now illustrate as well as the others the Trustees' intentions. They seem today memorable primarily for their grimness and physical bulk; a new and depressing characteristic had been added to the model housing movement. The slight touches of decoration which Darbishire permitted himself at the first estate were very soon

banished and the later blocks are severe and unadorned, all the barrack-like qualities of his first essay in housing, Columbia Square, are here underlined. The central doorway is the only relieving feature on the main façade emphasised by a coarsely detailed round arch, while the unglazed openings to the attic drying areas look dark and forbidding. The emphasis was certainly upon sound construction – it seems that it was made a Puritanical virtue – and the white stock bricks have withstood the trials of a century: they look as though they might last for at least another.

The estates have a distinct family resemblance except for the last of the group at Chelsea which was a more densely developed site using a block plan which abandoned the corridor access system in favour of staircases.

The importance of this group of estates built by a new agency was undoubtedly much greater at the time they were built than would now appear. First, because they were so much larger than any previous venture either philanthropic or commercial; secondly, because they set a standard of accommodation and construction which established a definite point of view, although not necessarily one with which everyone would agree; thirdly, because Peabody made his gift at a psychologically sound time when men were looking for fresh inspiration to continue striving for better conditions and when the poor themselves needed to see that someone cared for their wellbeing. The work of the Trust, therefore, stands at the forefront of the next wave of expansion which occupied much of the sixties.

4.4 *Peabody Square, Islington, as it is today*

4.5 *Peabody Square, Chelsea, 1870; a very densely built estate with an experimental plan*

The Chelsea estate was completed in April 1870, and after eight years of work the Trustees might well be said to have established themselves and their policy as an important part of a vastly changed housing scene from that described a decade previously. The Trustees as a building and management organisation brought a degree of respectability to the movement which was without parallel; the nature of their charge was sufficiently high minded to set them apart even from the early organisations like S.I.C.L.C. Their position was unimpeachable; society looked up to them for leadership and action, and on the whole they were to give both in good measure. Their policy was firm and undeviating, they aimed to house the artizan and not the pauper, and there was little chance that the Trust would offer 'a premium for hereditary and continuing poverty',[21] as one alarmist had suggested when Peabody announced his gift. Yet the accommodation they provided was not lavish, but its planning was realistic, although based on principles not approved by everyone.

Why should the Trustees deliberately avoid the problems of extreme poverty; why should they, a philanthropic organisation, expect to make a profit, and choose to accept standards well below the ideal which might have been expected of them? The answer to these questions was simply that, with the best intentions, they believed their greatest and most effective contributions could be made at this particular level in society and with the approach they adopted.

Contemporary criticism may be summed up in the comments made by *The Times* in 1869:

The rooms in the present buildings are too small. A tenement of two rooms, inhabited by a man and his wife and his two children, would contain little more than 2,000 cubic feet, and this space is greatly curtailed by the portion of it that is occupied by furniture and by human beings. If the door between the rooms is closed, the case becomes still worse. Large rooms for families seem to us to be imperatively required. We object, also, to the present walls. They look cold and feel cold, and if dirty, they cannot be washed without disfigurement and much absorption of moisture. They should either be papered or coated with some waterproof coating – such as varnish or Peacock and Buchan's paint – so that the covering might be renewed or cleansed whenever necessary. In the construction of new buildings, moreover, much fuel might be saved the inmates by an arrangement for heating the walls by hot air from a single furnace below. An entrance lobby to each tenement, and a little scullery and sink to each, with a supply of water, would tend to greater privacy, to make each dwelling more complete in itself, and to raise the standard of domestic comfort among the tenants.[22]

In the next group of estates the Trust did increase the size of the rooms in the tenements, but not to any great extent, and they did not change their policy of building associated flats. The most important development was that introduced at Chelsea: of using staircase access as opposed to a corridor system. The advantage was that it reduced the length of the block and made site planning more flexible, particularly on

4.6a *Peabody Square, Blackfriars, 1871, an estate built on cheaper land in south London allowing a more open layout of a new block type*

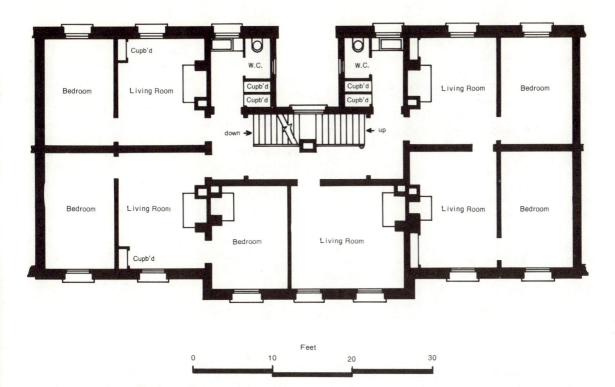

Bedroom	Living Room	Cupb'd	W.C.	W.C.

4.6b Peabody Square, Blackfriars, the plan of a typical staircase unit which shows an increase in space standards upon the first estates

4.6c A detail of the buildings today

large sites, although Chelsea was hardly of sufficient size to develop any of these ideas fully.

The next estate, their first in south London, was larger than anything the Trustees had built previously, and it enabled the new block to be tried out effectively. It was built on a site in Blackfriars Road, formerly the site of the Magdalen Hospital for the Reception of Penitent Prostitutes. Land was cheaper here than in central and east London and the estate is particularly spacious by comparison with any of the earlier work, but especially with the Chelsea estate, and it was possible to plant trees both in front of the buildings and amongst them. The site plan consisted of two courts, one opening from the angle of the other, surrounded by sixteen identical blocks, half detached and the others joined to make 'double blocks'. The overall height of the buildings was reduced to four floors, there was no attic laundry and drying area since laundries were provided in separate buildings this time, and there were baths on the ground floor of each block.

The aspect...is decidedly superior to that of the other establishments erected by the Trustees. The buildings are not so lofty, are more spread about, have trees in front of them next to the high-road and within the quadrangles and are altogether more home-like and less barracky.[23]

Other critics agreed and one added: 'People who have been born and reared in dens into which broad daylight and fresh air never penetrate would in such a place probably feel like bats in the sunshine'.[24] The implication was that they were unsuited to such havens of working-class bliss and would be lost and unhappy, which was what the Trustees also seemed to believe.

The Blackfriars estate was followed by a brief experiment with concrete construction at a small estate in Earl Street, Bermondsey, which did not prove very successful,[25] and then Darbishire reverted to the standard London stock brick as his building material, and varied it only slightly before 1890. Several more estates were built during the seventies, all extensive developments based on the Blackfriars model; Stamford Street was opened in 1875, Southwark Street the next year. The first stage of the terrifying avenue, ultimately stretching to 29 blocks, at Pimlico, was opened in 1876, the second two years later and the final section not until 1888.

By 1875, however, the Trustees were finding it extremely difficult to buy land at prices which they could afford while still building as they would wish and letting their property at unsubsidised rents to artizans. Their problem was solved by a deal with the Metropolitan Board of Works which permitted them to expand their work on a grand scale: this will be discussed in a subsequent chapter.

4.7   *Peabody Estate, Pimlico, 1876–8, the most monotonous of all the nineteenth-century estates*

The Improved Industrial Dwellings Company

Parallel with the development of the Peabody Trust went the growth of a commercial company, founded by another wealthy Londoner, who sought to show that the economic problems which had confronted the housing movement during the late fifties were not incapable of solution, so long as there was a drastic re-appraisal of planning construction. The Improved Industrial Dwellings Company was founded by Sydney Waterlow in 1863. He was born in 1822 the son of a city stationer, and his life story was typical of many successful careers built up at that time.[26] Together with three brothers he was responsible for turning the small family business into the great printing house which still today bears their name. But in addition to his business career Waterlow was interested in politics, and in the social problems of the community in which he lived and worked. He was elected a City Councillor in 1857, and five years later became an Alderman, was knighted in 1867, became Lord Mayor of London in 1872 and two years later entered parliament.

Waterlow built a small block of dwellings during 1863 in Mark Street, Finsbury, known as Langbourne Buildings, the name of the ward which he represented on the Council. The building was evolved, rather than

4.8 *Peabody Estate, Great Wild Street, 1882; an estate completed under the terms of the 1875 Cross Act to a very high density*

4.9 *Peabody Estate, Herbrand Street, 1885*

4.10 *Peabody Estate, Whitecross Street, 1883*

designed, by Waterlow himself in consultation with a builder, Matthew Allen, and their intention was to produce a housing unit which could be easily built and let at a suitable rent to artizans, while at the same time showing a profit of five-per-cent for the owner. By doing this, Waterlow hoped to convince his friends that they might invest their money in a good cause which would pay them a modest yet stable dividend.

The idea for the new building came from Henry Roberts' model cottages built at the 1851 Exhibition, which had always been intended as a prototype capable of vertical and lateral expansion. Waterlow took the single staircase 'unit' and built it up to five floors in height, the practical maximum for 'walk-up' flats in the last century, and eventually he added several units, together making a terrace. The staircase was centrally placed, giving access to an open balcony on each floor, from which two tenements were reached. This much did Waterlow and Allen take from Roberts' design, but the internal planning of the dwellings they worked out for themselves, on the whole with less satisfactory results than if they had adopted Roberts' own plan in its entirety. The main feature which Waterlow wanted to establish was the idea of a self-contained tenement – quite the opposite view from that held by the Peabody Trustees – complete with its own scullery and W.C. But in order that the closets should not constitute a sanitary nuisance, Waterlow positioned them at the end of small, off-shoot-like, projecting wings, so that they would be exposed to the maximum amount of fresh air. But by doing this, many of the other rooms in the tenements were deprived of good daylight and altogether the planning was very curious.

4.11 *Peabody Estate, Whitechapel. A standard entrance-door used after 1875*

There was general approval of the venture, although some criticism of the planning faults just outlined and of the tortuous access stair, features which showed the lack of proper architectural consultation.[27] But there was praise for the carefully thought out construction, for the use of concrete floors, roofs and lintels. Waterlow summed up his intentions at this stage very simply:

All I have endeavoured to show is that capital, expended in the erection of light, cheerful, healthy habitations for the industrial classes in crowded cities, may be made to yield a fair interest on its investment, if care is taken to avoid extravagance in external architectural decoration or loss by large management expenses.[28]

The experiment impressed Waterlow's friends, and at a public meeting held at the Mansion House in June 1863, a public company was inaugurated and funds were soon raised for a series of buildings modelled on those in Mark Street: this was the start of The Improved Industrial Dwellings Company.[29] The first to be completed were Cromwell Buildings, New Southwark Street, which were opened in 1864 and housed 22 families.[30] Then followed a steady stream of developments of increasing size, usually on long narrow sites previously occupied by a terrace of poor quality houses. It was then possible to string out the simple repetitive units to make a new more lofty terrace. Palmerston Buildings, on a site near King's Cross station, were completed in 1866 and were favourably reviewed by *The Times*,[31] which gave a detailed description of the two and three roomed tenements each with a living room containing a cupboard and a range with an oven and a boiler; there was a separate scullery with a sink and water cistern, a small fireplace, a washing-copper and a dust-shoot. Opening off the scullery was a lavatory, much as in the Mark Street prototype.

A more picturesque contemporary account of a smaller estate in Hamilton Row, completed at about the same time as Palmerston Buildings, adds further to the impression made by the early buildings of the Company:

A really cheerful, pleasant-looking pile is that which now replaces the six dirty dwellings of Hamilton Row, Bagnigge Wells. The entrance, with its green gates and newly painted doorways, is not altogether unlike the front of a theatre or place of amusement. A winding staircase in the middle lands you, at every floor, on the corresponding balcony in front, so that in ascending to the flat roof of the building you make a series of public appearances. You have your exits and your entrances, each being on a different stage, till you come upon the last scene of all, which is that same flat roof, arranged to serve the inhabitants of the several floors as a drying ground for clothes. Some of the tenants have only two rooms, and others three, but attached to all of them are closets and wash-houses, making each abode a completely comfortable habitation. The windows open outwardly, like an old-fashioned English lattice, and like the casements of the houses throughout Continental Europe.

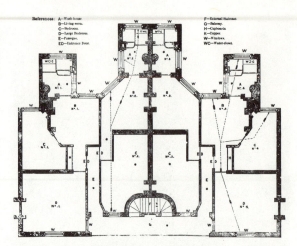

4.12 *Langbourne Buildings, Mark Street, Finsbury, 1863; built by Sidney Waterlow using the Great Exhibition plan modified by a London builder, Matthew Allen*

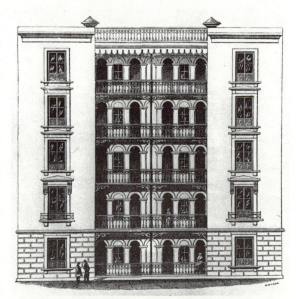

Derangement and breakages of sash-lines are thus avoided. The ventilation is perfect everywhere, and the honest solidity of the structure is an advantage that the humble occupants can boast over those unfortunate members of the middle class whose houses are generally called 'villas', and whose landlords are mostly speculative builders understanding but two qualities of domestic architecture – the showy and the cheap.[32]

There is, then, an interesting comparison during the course of the decade between the work of the Improved Industrial Dwellings Company and that of the Peabody Trust – one adopting the associated pattern, the other the self-contained – although the Company felt obliged to experiment with associated flats at one point in an attempt to make further economies. This was at Derby Buildings in Brittania Street, built during 1867–8, where two of the staircase units contained minimum flats which had communal sculleries and lavatories. The arrangement was not popular, it seems because the rooms were very much

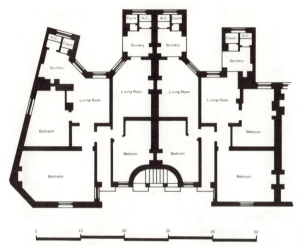

4.13 *Early plans developed from the Langbourne plan by the Improved Industrial Dwellings Company*

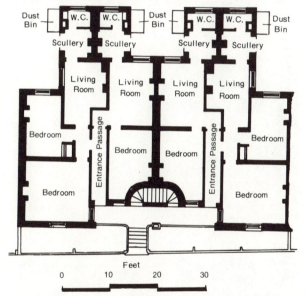

smaller than those provided by the Peabody Trustees, and it became necessary to convert these staircases into normal self-contained flats. The experiment was not repeated.[33]

The Company, like the Trust, was criticised because they did not provide dwellings suitable for the poorest class and, like the Trust, they admitted that this was not their objective:

We must take the class as of various degrees; the upper, middle and lower of the labouring classes; it would not have been right to build down to the lowest class, because you must have built a class of tenement which I hope none of them would be satisfied with at the end of 50 years; we have rather tried to build for the best class, and by lifting them up to leave more room for the second and third who are below them.[34]

It also seems to have been true that any hint of a management 'policy' alienated the very poor, because frequently they were not prepared to keep the rules of sobriety and the standards of cleanliness which

were demanded of them. Conversely, those who willingly accepted such standards were usually the same people who could afford the scale of rents charged by the Trust and the Company. The balance, nevertheless, was a delicate one, prospective tenants were poor and thrifty – as opposed to thriftless – but with care and a constant eye to possible economies it was possible to house them in the mid-sixties and still make a modest profit. In 1867 the Company declared a healthy five-per-cent dividend which was what Waterlow had promised the shareholders, and it continued to pay such a dividend for many years.[35] No organisation was as yet prepared to build what might be regarded as sub-standard accommodation in order either to make more profit or to reach down to a poorer class of tenant.

In one other respect, the work of the two organisations differed markedly. This was the actual nature of the estates themselves. Because of their vast resources and their philanthropic nature the Trust was able to buy large sites and redevelop them as separate estates: there was a clear Peabody 'concept'. Each estate was an open 'square', surrounded by building. The Company was more timid and less resourceful, it chose small sites, usually a row of cottages facing a street, which was replaced by a terrace, often of quite considerable height, but positioned exactly where the cottages had been because there was no spare land. Although they built on rather more sites during the decade than did the Trust, most of their individual developments were considerably smaller.

The Company's estates were also rather more visually attractive; the staircases were approached directly from the street and the cast iron balconies breaking up the façade added the architectural interest which was lacking in the ponderous blocks of the

4.14 *Gladstone Buildings, Willow Street, 1869–90; a fully developed linear block of the I.I.D.Co.*

Trust. Inside, too, the flats were less spartan and plaster was permitted from the outset. Nevertheless, they were curious, hybrid and complex buildings and often rather crudely designed.

Once established, however, the pattern of development changed very slowly; the reasons were concerned with building economics and were similar to those which tended to make the Trustees repeat a basic block once it had been proved effective and cheap. Waterlow, and his builder Matthew Allen, followed the lines of their Mark Street building for some time, modifying only the design of the sculleries and lavatories in 1866, at Palmerston Buildings, so that some of the unnecessary complexities of a separate 'off-shoot' for each W.C. were removed. The initial arrangement had been thought desirable on sanitary grounds although it must have increased building costs considerably, and in 1866 the number of projecting wings was halved and the lavatories made 'semi-detached'.

4.15a *I.I.D.Co., site plan of the Bethnal Green Estate; the Company's most ambitious venture, 1869–90*

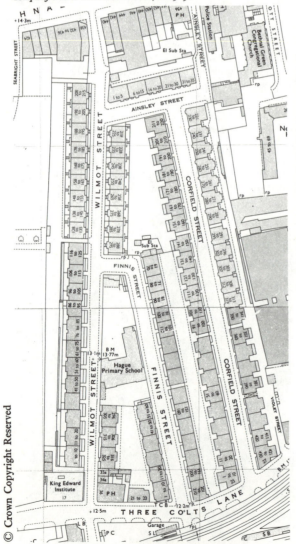

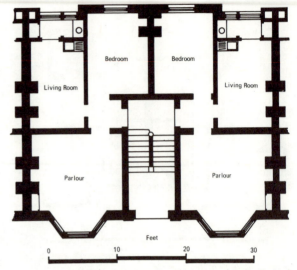

4.15b *New plans used during the development of the Bethnal Green Estate which show the adherence of the Company to the self-contained flat plan and the gradual decline in emphasis upon excessive ventilation of the W.C.*

4.15c *The Bethnal Green Estate*

That year a new Labouring Classes Dwelling Houses Act had been passed which made provision for companies such as Waterlow's to obtain government loans at low interest rates to assist them in their work. After the removal of certain technical difficulties, the Act proved beneficial, and in 1867 the Company had already borrowed £5,000.[36] By 1874, they had received loans amounting to £84,000.[37] Their relations with the Public Works Loan Commissioners were always good, and the additional revenue helped to keep the Company active during the difficult years after 1870. The Improved Industrial Dwellings Company, however, seems to have had little difficulty in obtaining capital in the normal way; the small but stable dividend seems to have attracted investment whenever the Company required it and, of course, the management remained free from scandal and accusations of mal-practices, which was not always true of 19th century organisations, philanthropic or commercial.[38]

In 1868, steps were taken to purchase land in Bethnal Green, a far-sighted decision which permitted work to proceed when land elsewhere became scarce and expensive.[39] During the early seventies Bethnal Green station was built, near to the estate; this greatly encouraged development and added to the popularity of the area. Work continued in stages until 1890 and various types of tenement blocks were used as the planning ideas of the Company were modified later in the century. But perhaps the most interesting aspect of the work at this estate was the concept of the layout itself, for here the Company had the opportunity to carry out a controlled development which would be comparable with the work of the Peabody Trust. Instead of taking consecutive plots of land and developing them with some kind of internal spatial organisation, they chose instead to adopt a linear approach, following to a great extent the existing street pattern, whilst increasing the height perhaps three-fold so that the effect is of great man-made canyons. The only relief is provided by a board school which, fortunately, the Company permitted to be built in the middle of the estate.

The Bethnal Green estate has all the qualities of grimness and harsh urbanism which brought the whole housing movement into such ill-repute later in the century. This cult of super-urbanism lies at the root of the subsequent violent reaction in favour of very low density, which became the objective of the working classes and inspired the founders of the first garden cities at the end of the century.

Land was also made available to the Company very cheaply by the Marquis of Westminster at the junction of Ebury Street and Pimlico Road where Coleshill Buildings were completed during 1870:

The neighbourhood being rather superior to the districts in which the company's tenements had been previously erected, and as the Marquis required the buildings to be made externally as attractive as possible, the directors had varied their general design of construction by the intro-duction of large shops with suitable accommodation for the shopkeepers on the ground floor, keeping all the upper storeys for small tenements, and had arranged high gable roofs in the fronts next to the main streets.[40]

Economies in construction to keep pace with the elaboration necessary to please the Marquis were probably achieved in part by the use of a novel 'patent stone' which they claimed reduced the total cost of building by about 20 per cent.[41] There were two large splayed blocks with 10 shops and 120 tenements, a large number having only one bedroom.

This was also the first scheme where Allen was not the builder, for apparently the Company felt obliged

4.16 *I.I.D.Co., Coleshill Buildings, 1870; built on land given by the Duke of Westminster and unusually lavish in detail*

to obtain competitive tenders in case their arrangement with him had been against the interests of the share-holders. In the event it was proved that his work in the past had been cheap, and the successful partnership was therefore hastily resumed.[42]

Further attempts to achieve economies can be the only explanation for the sudden change in design at the next estate, since it was once more the result of

4.17 *I.I.D.Co., Ebury Buildings, 1872; an experiment which was not repeated because it was not as economical as the standard block*

the partnership between Waterlow and Allen. The site in Flask Lane, Ebury Square, was again obtained at a price below its market value from the Marquis of Westminster. Work was carried out in two stages, the first completed in 1870, the second two years later; it consisted of two 'U' shaped buildings facing each other but without physical links, leaving an open court in the centre.[43] Access to the tenements was by external cast iron balconies on the courtyard side, and in order to maintain flat façades to the streets outside this necessitated bringing the sculleries and lavatories into the main block. There were 129 flats in the two sections of the building, all planned with a greater facility than at any of the earlier estates where the curved stair and numerous projecting wings had made for odd shaped rooms and had made adequate natural lighting extremely difficult to achieve.

The building had no precedent and it had no successor; it was a solitary experiment which doubtless failed to justify itself on financial grounds. Thereafter,

4.18 *I.I.D.Co., Leopold Buildings, Columbia Road, 1872; an ambitious middle-period linear block*

the Company reverted to the traditional model which was developed and modified for a whole sequence of estates completed during the early seventies on sites purchased in various parts of London, including one in the west end. An example of the Company's work at this period is Leopold Buildings, Crabtree Walk, Shoreditch, completed in 1872, a long terrace of blocks clearly still modelled on the Mark Street buildings.[44] The height of the terrace was varied along its length to relieve the cliff-like effect of continuous building and the accommodation included a greater proportion of larger tenements than was usual. Altogether, it is a rather grand set of buildings, yet it has little of the bleakness of Bethnal Green, mainly,

one suspects, because it is a single terrace and not a street lined on both sides with similar buildings

The Artizans', Labourers' and General Dwellings Company

The third important housing organisation to start work at this time, the Artizans', Labourers' and General Dwellings Company, adopted a rather different approach to the problem from those already discussed in this chapter, but its contribution to the total amount of organised housing was considerable, and it helped to make the sixties a veritable renaissance of private enterprise. The company was founded by a small-scale builder, William Austin, during 1867:

For the purpose of enabling workmen to erect dwellings combining fitness and economy with the latest sanitary improvements and to become themselves the owners of these dwellings in the course of a stated number of years by the payment of a small additional rent.[45]

There were various minor provincial ventures at first but the most important work was done in London where the houses were not in fact sold to the tenants but kept under the control of a central management.[46] The Company began, it could be argued, as a glorified building society, but it became much more than this, although it never achieved the respectability of Waterlow's Company. This was not because of its humble origins so much as the public scandal which surrounded certain unfortunate attempts to swindle the shareholders during 1877, long after Austin had been ousted from the board by a more commercially minded set of Directors.[47] Lord Shaftesbury and two of his sons were concerned with the Company over the

4.19 *Leopold Buildings, Columbia Road*

4.20   *I.I.D.Co. Torrens Buildings, City Road, 1884, an example of the last phase of the Company's work*

4.22a   *Shaftesbury Park, Battersea, the first estate of the Artizans' Company, begun 1872*

years, but even their good names could not entirely restore public confidence, and Artizans' remained outside the more respectable group of companies who took an active part in slum clearance work after 1875.

The important difference between Artizans' and all the earlier organisations was that they concentrated entirely on suburban low-rise housing until 1887.[48] They constructed three major estates during the seventies and eighties, the first, Shaftesbury Park, was situated between Lavender Hill and the South Western Railway near Clapham Junction, an outlying place for 'model' housing at that time.[49] Work started

in 1872, and although outwardly the estate might appear very like any other piece of suburbia, in fact the houses were better built and rather more spaciously laid out than was common before the advent of the model bye-laws in 1875. The idea of planting trees in the streets was a detail which greatly enhanced and humanised the whole appearance of the development: in addition all the houses possessed gardens. There were several different house-types all designed by a man who had apparently worked as a joiner for Austin at an earlier, more tentative, development consisting of houses built as normal speculation.

4.21   *Torrens Buildings, City Road*

4.22b   *Shaftesbury Park, Battersea*

A second estate was started during 1877 at Kilburn, known as Queen's Park. It was similar in appearance, although rather more tightly developed than Shaftesbury Park, and it was followed by a third scheme at Noel Park, in the next decade. At Queen's Park part of the accommodation took the form of cottage flats rather than some of the larger houses used previously and this was done to avoid sub-letting.[50] Noel Park, the third major estate, on the other hand, reverted to houses alone, although their size was kept down for the same reason. It was designed by Roland Plumbe and was a much more sophisticated piece of work than either of its predecessors, and deserves comparison with some of the early L.C.C. estates.[51]

The relative importance of the Company, in terms of a numerical solution to the housing problem, can perhaps be seen from the following figures, although the greater value to the poor and the magnitude of the attendant difficulties in building on more central sites, to some extent make the contribution of the other two organisations of far greater significance. By 1875, the Peabody Trust had built about 1,800 dwellings, the Improved Industrial Dwellings Company 1,500 and Artizans' 1,000. By 1895, the year in which the first council housing was occupied in London, the figures were 5,100, 5,350 and nearly 6,500.[52] In terms of well built, properly managed housing, then, the Company made an important contribution and it posed the opposite point of view from that offered by the endless tenements in barrack-like blocks, found in central London. That in itself was a useful thing to do, although the Company's more blatant commercialism made it less effective as a working class housing organisation because once again only the artizan could afford to live in the suburbs. By 1890, there was little to choose between speculative housing

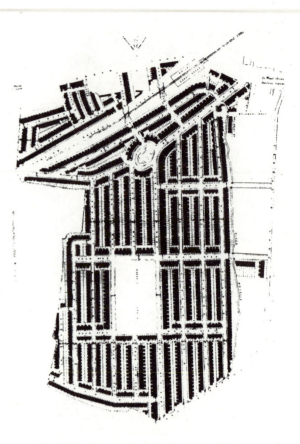

4.24 *Noel Park, Hornsea, built by the Artizans' Company after 1881*

and that built by the Company. The early estates can still be seen, however, as an interesting precedent for the garden suburbs of the first years of this century, so places like Shaftesbury Park occupy a unique place in housing history.

Another organisation which ran into similar troubles was the Suburban Village and General Dwellings Company,[53] founded in 1866:

To provide at the most rapid rate possible, healthy, pleasant and comfortable abodes, for the overcrowded population of the metropolis. The company will purchase estates in all the suburbs near to and having direct railway connection with London, and erect thereon complete villages. The houses erected will contain from four to eight rooms with every domestic convenience, each house to have a piece of garden ground. Educational establishments, etc., will be provided, as also a limited number of shops erected.[54]

Two hundred and fifty workmen subscribed, and the Manager, Edward Vigers, applied to the Ecclesiastical Commissioners for a site. However, the Secretary unscrupulously dissipated the funds and that was the end of the Company.[55] Fortunately, W. G. Habershon, of Habershon and Pite, a firm of architects practising in London, agreed to take over the site and develop it in accordance with the terms already agreed between Vigers and the Commissioners.

4.23 *Queen's Park, Kilburn, begun by the Artizans' Company, 1877*

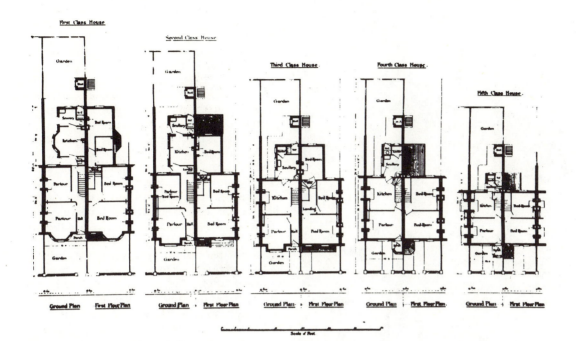

4.25 *Noel Park, Hornsea*
& 4.26

Early the next decade *The Builder* was able to write that it was:

A striking instance of the new suburban neighbourhoods rising up in succession in different places around the metropolis. About the present time last year (1871), the greatest portion of the land forming the estate was occupied as market gardens, but the entire area has now been laid out in wide and spacious streets, all drained and paved, and provided with ample footpaths, and upwards of two hundred private houses and shops have already been erected and occupied, whilst a larger number of new dwellings are at present in course of erection.[56]

The estate consisted of terraces, mostly of two but a few three storeys in height, all constructed in stock brick with red brick dressings and stone bay windows on the ground floor. The planning and the layout was quite orthodox.

New work in London

The effect of these three new organisations upon the housing movement was two-fold, they showed that there was scope for private enterprise and to some extent this stimulated fresh activity. At the same time their work appears to induce a feeling of satisfaction that something was being done, therefore the community as a whole might rest contented, despite the fact that in reality the scale of activity bore little

4.27 *Noel Park, Hornsea, today*

relation to the magnitude of the problem which still remained to be solved. The S.I.C.L.C. did not build at all in London during this period, and its housing development at Hull, completed in 1864, has already been mentioned.

The Metropolitan Association's estate at Beckenham in Kent, consisting of spaciously set out semi-detached cottages, makes an interesting comparison with the work of Artizans', but it was a solitary experiment. The first group were finished in 1866 and before the end of the decade there were 164.[57] It was a successful scheme; all the cottages had two or three bedrooms, and they were let to workmen from central London, despite the fact that concessionary fares were not at first obtained.[58] The estate paid a steady and handsome dividend of 7 per cent, but the Association seems to have thought that this kind of development was to some extent an easy way out, when the real problem was in the central area.[59] Here was the real difference between philanthropy and speculation.

The site at Beckenham had been obtained from the Duke of Westminster, and he also provided the land at very favourable terms for Gatliff Buildings in Chelsea.[60] This was a tenement block designed by a new architect to the housing scene, Frederick Chancellor, and the development was remarkable for its architectural quality, for the genuine attempt to create a humane housing environment and for the attempt to minimise the problems of scale and mass in tenement design.

Chancellor then converted the Artizan's Home in Spicer Street, long unpopular as a lodging house, into family dwellings, a difficult and expensive task which was completed in 1869. Then, in 1878, he extended the building, so popular had it now become, which shows how important the right kind of accommodation was to the success of any housing organisation.[61]

There were a certain number of new societies but none of course on the scale of those already described. One already briefly noted which reversed the normal trend by expanding from a provincial town, Hastings, into the metropolis, where it formed the London Labourers' Dwellings Society in 1862, and throughout the decade it successfully renovated cottage property.[62]

The conversion of existing property, and the erection of suburban dwellings, were the two solutions most frequently resorted to by a community which was finding it very difficult to grapple with the real problems of overcrowding; the increasing volume of written advice (and at the same time the decrease in building) in the early seventies was a symptom of the failure of society as yet to face up to the real problems of the later 19th century town.

Competitions for cottage plans were a favourite device used by organisations to stimulate interest and foster good design. They were rarely successful and were disliked by the architectural profession because competitors invariably falsified information, especially about cost, which usually made the designs quite useless. The effect of this was well illustrated by a Society of Arts cottage competition, held in 1864, which was won by John Birch. When the Great Eastern Railway Company decided to use his plan for some workmen's cottages the lowest tender they could obtain was twice the estimated cost of £203.[63]

Another organisation had a similar experience, this was the Central Cottage Improvement Company, which existed entirely for the dissemination of good design; it had established a network of provincial societies to make known its objectives, and by 1866 some fifty sets of plans had been sold to non-members.[64] The Company decided that year to hold a competition for a new design, and this attracted 112 entries; of these *The Builder* tartly remarked that 'whatever is good in them is old, and that whatever is new in them is not good'.[65] At the next annual meeting it was reported that the winning entry had proved much more expensive than was anticipated, and it was decided, therefore, that it might be more sensible for the Company to work out a solution based on its own solid practical experience.[66]

There was still a trickle of private schemes in London, pathetic not so much in their individual size as in their corporate effect. Those which attracted some attention included a group of houses erected by Sir S. Morton Peto at Notting Hill,[67] another group at Wimbledon were designed by Mr J. G. Smithers;[68] the Blakeney Ordnance Company at East Greenwich built houses for their workers and more centrally a block of tenements[69] and a club were built in Old Pye Street by Miss Adeline Cooper.[70] A group of gentlemen from Lincoln's Inn formed the Central London Dwellings Improvement Company, which renovated nearby property for the very poor, but we must count this as merely stop-gap work, useful at the time it was done, but of little lasting value in the search for a large scale solution to housing problems.[71]

One further scheme, this time in the City of London, is worthy of comment: it owed much to Waterlow and it was a rare example of 'council' housing. In 1864 the Court of Common Council were finally persuaded to use the Finsbury Estate Surplus Fund for the purpose of building tenements for the poor.[72] A site was found in Farringdon Road, and £37,043 was spent on blocks of two and three room flats for 160 families, built above a row of shops. The buildings were six storeys high, designed by the corporation architect Horace Jones, but very clearly modelled on Waterlow's Mark Street block.[73]

New work in the Provinces and Scotland

The picture of housing activity in London is now fairly clear; it centred around a group of companies and societies working steadily away during the sixties and on into the next decade. They made an important contribution, to which must be added a smaller number of private philanthropic schemes. It would be tempting to think that all this amounted to steady progress, the

easing of overcrowding and the improvement of living conditions for the population as a whole. For the few who were lucky enough to *obtain* a model dwelling and were able to afford the rent, it did very often mark a turning point in their lives,[74] but London continued to grow in size far faster than good cheap new housing could be built; the pressure for accommodation in the central area grew steadily worse and the slums consequently grew larger and denser throughout this period. Speculative building was still a dirty word, the sphere of the unscrupulous: there was still a gigantic task awaiting the sanitary and housing reformers. This account, outlining what was done in a few places, should not cloud the more usual scenes of abject misery that greeted the keen observer and which, alas, were typical of London as a whole. The metropolis was still an unattractive and an unhealthy place for the poor in the early seventies.

The typical provincial town, therefore, gives a much clearer picture of the failure of private enterprise, in all its forms, to cope with the problem of housing the poor. Lack of activity and lack of concern, these were the symptoms reported time and again from towns both large and small. Newcastle upon Tyne, for example, where cholera had raged more savagely than anywhere else during the great epidemics of the forties and fifties, had long since legislated

4.28 *Garth Heads, Newcastle upon Tyne, 1870, built by a local dwelling improvement company*

itself out of the public health code and, despite the grim housing conditions which were known to exist, there was no record of housing and sanitary reform. A private company, set up to build tenements or lodging houses, was first proposed in 1865 but it was so slow to start building that the city fathers were persuaded to take over their site and build a model lodging house. The proposal came to nothing and the site returned to the original company who managed to complete a five storey block of tenements in 1870.[75]

This pathetic account of sporadic inadequate activity could have been written of many other towns. Where there are records of more concerted effort, the reason for it can usually be found either in very special local conditions or in the work of a group of particularly public-spirited individuals.

Special local conditions had already provided the mainspring for work at Liverpool and Glasgow in the forties as we have already seen; twenty years later in both towns, civic action was still leading reform, in sharp contrast to neighbouring communities. At Liverpool, in 1864, the earlier private legislation of 1842 and 1846 was amended and the council was empowered to repair or demolish property which their Medical Officer considered unfit for habitation. As usual they took their responsibility seriously and as a result a considerable amount of insanitary property was demolished. This action was necessary, but it reduced the number of houses available for the poor and increased overcrowding elsewhere; it is not surprising, therefore, that the health committee were soon urging the council to: 'Instruct the finance committee to give every facility for the erection of model cottages on land belonging to the corporation.'[76]

A sub-committee investigated the problems involved and found that housing for the poor could only be built economically in the centre of the town if it was erected above shops on main streets. Alternatively, it would be possible to build in the suburbs although enquiries had shown that most outlying communities were unwilling to encourage working class housing development in case the poor became dependent upon the parish in lean times, thus adding to the rates.[77]

No action was taken, but the whole matter came before the council several times in 1866 – at one stage it was agreed that the Borough Engineer should prepare development plans for sites owned by the Corporation, and that they should then try and interest builders in carrying out the work on a leasehold basis.[78] No contractor, of course, was found who would take on the task, for the risk was considerable and the profit no doubt non-existent. When this was realised, the council evidently decided that they should build themselves, and negotiations began with the Public Works Loan Commissioners for a loan under the terms of the 1866 Labouring Classes Dwelling Houses Act.[79] They do not seem to have been very satisfied with the plans prepared by their engineer, however, and it was now decided to hold a competition for a site

in Ashfield Street, the winning scheme being the one which would house the maximum number of people without contravening the bye-laws issued the previous year in an attempt to curtail the worst practice of speculative builders. The competition caused all the usual problems associated with the system in the last century; but the final word went to the corporation, who calmly awarded the first prize to one scheme, while announcing that they would build another, which housed many more people only by breaking the bye-laws concerning the height and spacing of buildings.[80] Thus was St Martin's Cottages completed in 1869, the first municipal housing to be built in provincial England. The 'cottages' were four storey, self-contained tenements, except that the lavatories were placed on the half landing. The blocks were close together, rather bleak in appearance, and not really worthy of the city; well might *The Builder*, at the conclusion of its review of the buildings, recommend that those who built for the poor must 'Mix a little philanthropy with their per-centage calculations'.[81]

4.29   *St Martin's Cottages, Liverpool, 1869; a rare provincial civic development*

It was a step in the right direction, nevertheless, and it showed a laudable sense of civic responsibility in a sphere hereto exclusively that of private speculation. The experiment bore fruit in the much more carefully designed Victoria Buildings which the Corporation built in 1885.[82] A more immediate result of the St Martin's Cottages development was the renewal of public interest in housing problems, the formation of the Liverpool Labourers' Dwellings Company in 1871, and the construction by them, eighteen months later, of 132 tenements at the junction of Ashfield Road and Latimer Road.[83]

At Glasgow, where previously activity had been confined to the familiar pattern of lodging house associations, the most important event during the sixties was 'An Act for the Improvement of the City of

Glasgow and the Construction of New, and the Widening, Altering and Diverting of existing Streets in the said City; and for other purposes.'[84]

This private measure was obtained in 1866, and its importance was far reaching, not only in Glasgow itself but because it provided the model for a national Act some nine years later.

Anything more simple and straightforward in the shape of sanitary legislation than this it would be difficult to conceive. The simplicity of the measure, indeed, was never, as far as we are aware, called into question; it was its magnitude and the conflicting interests which were involved that excited the inveterate opposition which we are sorry to hear is now offered to the carrying out of the Act. It must be admitted indeed that this Glasgow Improvement Bill gave the corporation prodigious powers. They have power to take, in the first instance, enormous quantities of land, within the whole Parliamentary boundaries of Glasgow, and to construct no less than *thirty-nine* new streets; power to alter, widen, and divert at least twelve existing streets,... and power to stop up some thirty or forty back streets, wynds, lanes and closes, the very names of which we can understand are indicative of their antiquity or their infamy ...One section (the 22nd) gives power to pull down buildings and lay out the lands 'of new' and the section following provides that, 'the trustees may, on any land so acquired by them under this Act, erect and maintain such dwellings for mechanics, labourers, and other persons of the working and poorer classes as the trustees from time to time think expedient; and let the same when erected and fitted up to such mechanics, labourers, and other persons of the working and poorer classes, at *such weekly and other* rents, upon such terms and conditions as they might from time to time think fit; or the trustees may sell or dispose of the same'.[85]

These were the points that a contemporary reviewer singled out from this quite astonishing piece of private legislation which had been prepared by Dr Blackie, the Lord Provost, and a group of city officials including Carrick, the city architect. Glasgow's problems were no less considerable than twenty or thirty years earlier; in 1865 the density of the core of the old city was estimated at 583 people per acre, and the death rate 38.64 persons per thousand of the population. In certain pockets it was as high as 52.21 and it was to get worse before the end of the decade.[86]

Octavia Hill visited Glasgow at this time and described the conditions which existed:

But I saw there – what I have seldom or never seen in London – a perfect honeycomb or maze of buildings, where, to reach the "wynd" furthest from the street, one had to pass under narrow archway after archway, built under the houses, and leading from one squalid court to another. Some of these narrow tunnel-like passages appeared from the plans to have been many yards in length. The houses too were higher than is usual in London alleys, and the darkness and obscurity consequently greater.[87]

The administration of the Act was vested in Trustees appointed from amongst the councillors; they were empowered to raise £1,250,000 – the estimated cost of the scheme – either by means of a special rate or by obtaining a loan. The number of houses which might be demolished in any six monthly period was limited to 500, unless it could be proved to the Dean of Guild Court that adequate accommodation existed elsewhere; this was to prevent undue hardship to those displaced.

After a certain amount of local opposition the money was eventually raised by means of a special rate, spread out over 15 years. The Trustees set about acquiring the property as quietly as possible: 'A judicious person...was appointed to negotiate for the purchase of the property privately and as most of the buildings were old and dilapidated, and the owners willing to dispose of them, the committee succeeded in securing a considerable amount of property at very moderate rates'.[88]

They were in no hurry so they were also able to pass over owners unwilling to sell at a reasonable price and wait until such times as they were, consequently few properties were the subject of compulsory purchase orders. Re-development did not begin until all the property in the immediate vicinity was owned by the Corporation, so progress was slow, and by 1874 less than one quarter of the designated area had been re-developed.[89]

But the key to the success of the re-development scheme was that it did not involve the provision of housing on the cleared land. The Corporation wished to pursue a policy of dispersal, which was reasonable when it was still possible for workmen to reach their work from the suburbs with little hardship. At first the Corporation was afraid that private enterprise would not be equal to the housing demand, so they bought up two large sites in the suburbs, laid out the roads complete with sewers and then sold the plots to local builders rather surprisingly at a profit. But the perspicacious Scots builders soon saw the advantage of taking up the land themselves in the first place and there was always enough housing to satiate demand.[90] What is not clear, however, is how many people from the demolished slums actually moved into a new suburban house: one suspects few could afford the rent. The council never built housing, although the idea was frequently raised in council. The only buildings for which they were directly responsible were a number of lodging houses, and two experimental blocks of minimum tenements, built, as Baillie Morrison told the Royal Commission on Housing in 1885, 'by public clamour'.[91] They were apparently a failure and there were no more.

The cleared sites in the centre of the city were sold off during the seventies; very gradually, we are told, so that the market would not be flooded with land. The prices which the Corporation obtained exceeded all expectations, but this entirely ruled out any possibility of the private developers constructing even a small proportion of working class housing and Sir James Watson, at one time Lord Provost, freely admitted this in a lecture at the Royal Institute of British Architects:

It is proper to mention that ground in the centre of the city was found to be too high in price to allow the erection of workmen's houses. The buildings, therefore, which were erected thereon on the site of those pulled down, have consisted chiefly of shops and warehouses, along with other dwellings for the middle classes. Those built for the working class have been erected at some distance from the centre of the city, where the sites were less costly.[92]

The Act in practice possessed other, less obvious, defects, the most important was that no proper provision had been made for the very poor who were displaced from the demolished slums. In fact, they moved into the next ring of tenement houses turning them into new slums, while the rather better off artizans migrated to the new houses on the outskirts of the city. Furthermore, the policy of waiting until the purchase price suited the Corporation, slowed up re-development; and so did the piecemeal scale of cleared land. During the late seventies, the council found itself in the embarrassing position of owning considerable amounts of slum property, which had been temporarily improved in a rudimentary way, so that demolition could be delayed in case the market was flooded and the price of land brought down![93]

The problems which arose were obviously not anticipated in 1866, but they were not so great as those which beset the Metropolitan Board of Works, in London, under the terms of a similar Act, passed in 1875, which will be discussed later, and which was based on the experience gained from Glasgow's Act of 1866. The ratepayers of Glasgow never suffered, however, and the slums were demolished, As Octavia Hill expressed it during a visit in 1874: 'I felt as if some bright and purifying angel had laid a mighty finger on the squalid and neglected spot.'[94]

In the same years as the Improvement Act had been obtained, Glasgow obtained a Police Act which in Scotland, was the legal way in which building regulations could be made. They were administered through the Dean of Guild Court. Most of the speculative house-building which resulted from the Improvement Act was built under the terms of the bye-laws made by virtue of the Act, since these applied everywhere within the municipal boundary.[95]

New residential streets formed after 1866 were to be at least as wide as the buildings on either side were high; and no housing might be erected in an existing street unless there was a space in front of the windows equal in width to three-quarters the height of the wall in which the window was situated. There was no control over the height of non-residential buildings erected in streets formed before 1866.

Street widths in housing developments were well controlled, but the question of space at the rear of houses caused as much difficulty as in England. The Act required an open space at least 30 ft. wide behind each dwelling, which seems generous by typical English standards of the time until one remembers the traditional Scottish habit of building high. There was

apparently no means of preventing a builder who owned adjacent plots from making this distance serve for both houses, or indeed from erecting a solid square of housing with nothing more than a well 30 ft. wide in the middle, regardless of height.

Finally, the Act gave powers of inspection in order to abate overcrowding in certain kinds of dwellings, but the powers were circumscribed in a way which did not permit general inspection such as was possible later on in Chelsea and Hackney and Manchester.

On the other side of Scotland in the capital city, Edinburgh, the condition of the old town was probably little better than ancient Glasgow. The movement for reform which we traced in an earlier chapter blossomed after 1860 in a way which was, again, slightly different from the pattern either at Liverpool or Glasgow.

In 1860 there was published a *Report of A Committee of the Working Men of Edinburgh, on the present overcrowded and uncomfortable State of their Dwelling-houses* in which they set out their dissatisfaction with the current state of the town and the general lack of suitable dwellings. *The Builder* in a survey of cities published during 1861 noted that the visitor carried away with him from Edinburgh 'A sense of its extraordinary beauty and a horror of its unspeakable filth'.[96] And the same year, at the Annual Meeting of the Architectural Institute of Scotland, David Cousin suggested the revival of the co-operative building system which had apparently existed for a little while in the twenties.[97]

In fact, just such a company had been set up the previous year, known as the Edinburgh Co-operative Building Company, and their first work, Reid Terrace, Stockbridge, was a considerable success.[98] This was followed by a series of developments by similar bodies,

4.30 *Houses for Mechanics, Rose Bank, Edinburgh, 1866. Alexander Macgregor architect; privately financed cottage flats*

such as the Fountainbridge Church Building Society, the Cricket Park Building Association and the Edinburgh Workmen's House Improvement Company.[99] All these organisations built dwellings usually based on the traditional Scottish 'land', but occasionally experimenting with other housing patterns.

The corporation obtained an Improvement Act in 1867, very similar to that in operation at Glasgow, but rather less ambitious in its scope. The new housing was again provided by speculative builders, although,

4.31   *Co-operative Housing, off Glenogle Road, Edinburgh, begun in 1861 by the Edinburgh Co-operative Building Company*

as at Glasgow, an abortive attempt was made to build experimental dwellings. In Edinburgh they were sold off after they had stood empty for a while, because the poor could not afford the rents demanded.[100]

The various forms of co-operative buildings which were developing in Edinburgh were more popular in northern England where in many towns this was the only hope a working man might have of obtaining a sound house. Edward Akroyd, a local industrialist, and a few other mill owners were instrumental in founding building societies at Halifax; the movement flourished in other places without such substantial backing, and at that great Yorkshire boom town, Leeds, after Becket Denison had tried so hard to foster the co-operative spirit in the fifties and had eventually, almost in desperation, helped to set up lodging houses, after 1860 the housing movement began to develop very slowly as we have already seen.

It would be possible to find similar conditions and the same lack of activity in many industrial cities, and in fact the young Engels brought lasting ill-fame to Manchester by his book *The Condition of the Working Class in England in 1844*. He paints the usual grim picture, although with different motives from those with which we are concerned, and because he did not know so intimately the other northern cities he thought Manchester was exceptional, when in fact it was merely typical. The account given in an earlier chapter of Leeds, particularly, helps to redress this balance. Manchester obtained an Act in 1830 which contained a

clause fixing the minimum width of streets at 24 ft., and this rather meagre provision remained in force until the corporation prepared bye-laws in 1868 under the terms of the Manchester Improvement Act of 1867. These now regulated the provision of open space more carefully; the minimum street width was increased to 30 ft.; where the buildings were more than two storeys in height it was to be 36 ft. and more than three, 45 ft. Every new house was to have an open space at its rear of minimum area 70 sq. ft. A Medical Officer was appointed in 1867, but it was not until the early eighties that the apparently efficient controls just outlined were made effective and the work of slum clearance was begun. In 1891, the first corporation tenements were built. 'In appearance they were gaunt, gloomy, and barrack-like.'[101]

Manchester was a late developer in the housing movement and slow to make its sanitary powers effective: there seems to have been no individual, or group of individuals, able to galvanise the town into activity. And that was exactly what happened at Birmingham, a town which was typically lethargic between 1840 and 1870, although without the worst conditions which made Manchester and Leeds the subject of more frequent public attack. At Birmingham the situation changed during the seventies entirely because of the rise to civic power of Joseph Chamberlain, and between 1873 and 1875 the whole administration and its sense of responsibility was turned upside down. Chamberlain instigated the purchase of the Birmingham Gas, Light and Coke Company, the Birmingham and Staffordshire Gas Light Company and the Birmingham Water Works Company. A Health Committee was established, it was very active, and in 1875 a great Improvement Scheme was started, followed the next year by new bye-laws bringing Birmingham quickly into line with the model code produced the same year by the Local Government Board.[102] So, in a short space of time, years of sloth were replaced by efficient, responsible, local government, and here really was the start of a new movement, which had been hinted at at Liverpool and Glasgow. Here was the suggestion that private enterprise was not the most effective agency for reform either in public health or housing. A new era had been born.

4.32 *Dwellings at Holt Town, Manchester, 1883. Lawrence Booth architect ; built by the Manchester and Salford Workmen's Dwellings Company Ltd*

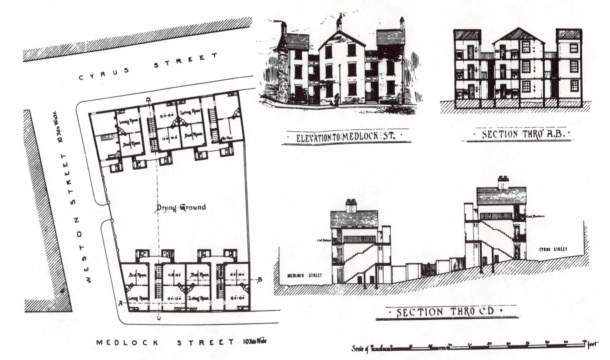

5

Towards a housing policy: the problems of permissive legislation in health and housing

The metropolis and the legal reforms after 1855

Some of the most important and decisive events in the whole history of housing took place between 1875 and 1890: they were in a sense the culmination of the work which has been discussed already. The account of this period revolves around new legislation and its effect upon metropolitan London, but at the centre of it all was the Metropolitan Board of Works, an organisation established in 1855 and creating for the first time a semblance of unity for that whole amorphous city. Before discussing the background to the events which lead up to the reforms of 1875 it is necessary, briefly, to outline the legal changes carried out during the previous twenty years. Once again these mainly refer to London and the problems of centralised administration.

The Public Health Act of 1848 had made elementary provision for the country as a whole, while excluding the metropolis, and many of the recommendations contained in the 1844–5 Royal Commission Report which referred to London were not implemented for another ten years. The year 1855 can be regarded, therefore, as the culmination of reforms started in 1848; what was now done was a necessary and an obvious corollary to the measures taken in the more famous parent Act. There were really a trio of Acts passed in 1855 which concern us here: they were the Metropolitan Management Act, the Nuisance Removal Act and the Metropolitan Building Act.[1] The first created a new framework for local government, replacing the innumerable petty vestries by twenty-three newly constituted and properly elected Vestries in the existing large parishes, and fourteen entirely new elected District Boards which grouped the remaining smaller vestries into more viable units. Over them, with responsibility for the sewerage system of the whole city, was the Metropolitan Board of Works replacing the moribund Commissioners of Sewers. The Board was also given powers to construct new streets and to control the alteration of existing streets as from time to time became necessary. It could not, significantly, appoint a Medical Officer of Health, or Nuisance Inspectors, to oversee the work of the Vestries and District Boards; nor was it able to coerce these bodies into carrying out its wishes. The local organisations were themselves given powers to appoint the officers denied to the Metropolitan Board and they were given the authority to organise paving, lighting, cleansing and refuse collection. In addition they were obliged to construct and flush local sewer networks leading to the main metropolitan system.

The Nuisance Removal Act was a national measure which this time applied equally to the metropolis. It extended the definition of nuisance, first made in the panic of 1848 to include: 'any premise in such a state as to be injurious to health, any pool, ditch, water-course, cesspool, drain or ashpit &c., so foul as to be a nuisance or injurious to health'.[2] At the same time the conditions under which the Act could be invoked were eased.

The third of these new measures, the Metropolitan Building Act, was to some extent a disappointment, since it was framed in much the same spirit as most earlier building legislation, paying particular attention to stability of structures and fire precautions, and little to space about buildings and general control of layout. The clause dealing with space at the rear of buildings was worded as follows:

Every building used or intended to be used as a dwelling house, unless all the rooms can be lighted and ventilated from a street or alley adjoining, shall have in the rear or on the side thereof, an open space exclusively belonging thereto of the extent at least of one hundred square feet.[3]

A provision which was inadequate and subject to abuse.

Many critics argued that the new organisation of local government was still too parochial, the councils represented the vested interest of property owners and this would continue to militate against the kind of activity which would cost their own class additional money.[4] On the whole, they were right: bad building continued and the legal provisions, such as they were, were not always enforced. Perhaps the most important result of the legislation of 1855 was the steady progress which was now made each year with the main sewerage network for London, but this was largely the result of centralised as distinct from local initiative.

Sir Benjamin Hall had intended that a major new Public Health Act should round off the legislation in 1855, but that was not possible and instead a stop-gap measure was passed, extending the life of the old General Board on an annual basis. This Act[5] made one innovation, however; it provided for a Medical Council and a Medical Officer of Health to be attached to the Board. Dr John Simon was appointed to the post and when, in 1858, a new Public Health Act[6] was finally passed, abolishing the General Board of Health, he was transferred to the Privy Council. At the same time a Local Government Act was passed transferring the few remaining powers of the Board to the Home Secretary. In 1861 a separate Medical Department of the Privy Council was formed. Simon's part in establishing the organisation for public health administration was one of the greatest contributions made by any one man to urban reform in the second half of the century.[7]

The 1858 Public Health Act was by no means an epoch making measure; the Derby government, which introduced it, was precariously situated and its provisions were only to last one year. The following year on his return to office Palmerston secured a permanent measure on similar lines, although he was obliged to force it through Parliament in the teeth of opposition.[8] Placed in perspective it was another step towards authoritative local government and the growth of centralised institutions, but to contemporary eyes, the whole public health situation was still open to much criticism.

One of the most interesting personalities who became involved with sanitary matters at this time was Henry Wyldbore Rumsey. In 1858 he published a pamphlet,

Sanitary Legislation and Administration in England, which pointed to the complexity and diversity of existing law, its all-pervading permissive character and its particularism. He showed how each new measure multiplied institutions, placing power in the hands of those most likely to be corrupted by it – the property-owning class. He believed, as did many others, that measures which did not reduce the density of towns failed to promote good health, and he called for new building laws which would be unified and all-embracing, controlling especially the speculative builders, working outside the legally defined boundaries of towns where at the moment there were no restrictions at all.

Perhaps most interesting of all was his restatement of a doctrine originating with John Stuart Mill: 'The removal of population from the overcrowded to the unoccupied parts of the earth's surface is one of those works of eminent social usefulness which most require, and which at the same time best repay, the intervention of Government.'[9]

He took this idea and made it specific, advocating state aid for the development of suburban villages which he suggested would consist of semi-detached cottages, not more than three storeys high, with a minimum of 80 sq. yds. of land per person.[10] This would fix the density at a maximum of eight houses or sixty people per acre, figures deliberately selected because he believed they would induce healthy living conditions. Rumsey believed that industry and a host of amenities would follow the people to the country; in this he was the fore-runner of William Morris and Ebenezer Howard, both of whom shared his philosophy and had a similar hatred of towns.[11] Finally, Rumsey made a strong plea for a vigorous, independent, public health organisation, staffed by well paid experts who did not rely for their security upon the favour of local councillors and here, of course, he touched upon the root cause why the existing legislation was not effective.

The law in action after 1860

The overall inadequacy of the law did not prevent certain real achievements during the next few years. Simon, largely through his own efforts, was slowly gathering together important and often significant information; his central organisation became the first efficient, independent, health department; its value to the housing movement was incalculable.[12] The Metropolitan Board by 1865 had nearly completed its task of reorganising the sewer system; there were 80 miles of new sewers disgorging into the Thames at a point much nearer to the sea than the outlets of any of the other networks.[13] In 1864 and again in 1865, Simon's department produced reports on the housing conditions of the poorer labourers in town and country, designed to show the results of the Nuisance Removal Acts. They made abundantly clear that the existing legislation was inadequate, and the reports of several Medical Officers reinforced this conclusion.

A house may be built anywhere, and almost anyhow, provided all the rooms can be lighted and ventilated from a street or alley adjoining. The object of the builder is to save as much ground, materials and expense as possible.[14]

and in another place, comment about the inadequacy of drainage:

Still there are large tracts of building land yet unprovided for, on much of which houses by the dozen are being squatted without any regard to this essential by the builders, save the horrid cesspool system.[15]

The Medical Officer for Whitechapel described how an area, 2 ft. wide and 50 ft. long, fulfilled the letter of the law while deliberately going against its spirit. And a complaint from a provincial town pointed out that their new legislation did not apply everywhere:

The Local Government Act, 1858 sec. 34, enacts that every Local Board may make Bye-Laws with respect (amongst other things) to 'the sufficiency of the space about buildings, to secure a free circulation of air, and with respect to the ventilation of buildings. With respect to the drainage of buildings to water closets, privies, ashpits and cesspools in connection with buildings, *and to the closing of buildings, or parts of buildings, unfit for human habitation, and to prohibit of their use for such habitation.*' But this power virtually becomes a dead letter, owing to the following proviso: 'Provided always that *no such Bye-law shall affect any building erected before the date* of the Constitution of the district.[16]

Building control, therefore, left a great deal to be desired nearly everywhere and in the provinces the only tangible improvements were very often the construction of sewers. Invariably this work brought about a reduction in the death rate and very often a considerable improvement in the expectancy of life.[17] Much attention, in fact, was given at this period to problems of public and personal cleanliness, and gradually cholera and typhoid epidemics became less severe.[18] But the position in most other ways was far from satisfactory; the law was patently inadequate but the real reason why it was ineffective was because the community as a whole would not at this stage accept what we would consider to be its responsibilities. It is doubtful in any case whether the existing local authorities would have made full use of any legal powers unless they were *forced* to do so.

In 1866 a Select Committee investigated Metropolitan Local Government and their deliberations were given added significance by the appearance of cholera first in the autumn of 1865 and then again in the following spring. The outbreak was sufficiently serious for the Privy Council to invoke the Disease Prevention Act and although the epidemic did not achieve the proportions of the frightening onslaughts in the forties – thanks to the work of sanitary reform – it was bad enough to ensure the safe passage of a new Sanitary Act,[19] despite a parliamentary crisis which brought the Earl of Derby back into office in June 1866 while the bill was still before Parliament. It did not remove all the faults and weaknesses which have just been outlined but Simon, writing later of the development of public health administration, saw it as an important step in the right direction.[20] Local authorities were now obliged to appoint inspectors and to suppress nuisances – overcrowding was for the first time specifically defined as a nuisance – and if they failed to do this, or to secure adequate drainage and water supplies, in certain circumstances they could now be coerced by the central authority. Furthermore, the Act made no distinction between the metropolis and the rest of the country; its provisions applied equally to both.

From our point of view the restraint of overcrowding was one of the most significant problems to receive attention. The Act stipulated that, 'Any house or part of a house so overcrowded as to be dangerous or prejudicial to the health of its inmates'[21] constituted a nuisance, so the provision which Lord Ashley had made for common lodging houses in 1851 was at last extended to all property:

It was the declaration of principles of the utmost importance. It was a declaration of the principle that the responsibility for the conditic of the 'house let in lodgings' should be on the shoulders of the 'owner' of the house. It was the declaration of the principle that the 'owner' should not be allowed to use his property to the detriment, to the injury of the public.[22]

The local authorities in Hackney and Chelsea made regulations to control overcrowding soon after the Act was passed, and they served their purpose well: overcrowding was reduced and the number of insanitary dwellings declined.[23] But there was no obligation to make regulations – although there was to suppress nuisances – and many parishes refused to make them, or sometimes when they did, to operate them impartially. It was often argued that the impartial operation of the Act would lead to undue hardship; there was probably some truth in this, if at the same time there was not a complementary rehousing policy, but it was usually a point of view voiced by those who would rather ignore overcrowding and rehousing, in the hope that the problem would solve itself. The problem was certainly worsening year by year; railway developments were a particular source of hardship as they invariably lead to the demolition of poor quality housing and in 1865, when the site for the new Law Courts was cleared in The Strand, a very large amount of slum housing was pulled down and considerable hardship resulted for the poor.[24] The solution to the problem did not lie in the removal of the nuisance by demolition and in endlessly permitting the poor to migrate into some other substandard and already overcrowded property, turning it into a potential danger to health. Little ultimate good would come from condoning this and turning a blind official eye to overcrowding; a progressive policy of house-building was urgently required, but who should carry it out? That problem remained so long as Medical Officers were able to complain, as did the Medical Officer for Fulham, that his authority was powerless in law to restrain unscrupulous speculative builders from constructing insanitary dwellings.[25] There was an urgent need for the expansion of the model housing movement, because they were the only organisations apparently capable of building sound, sanitary houses for at least one section of the working population.

For this reason, Sir Sidney Waterlow and many others agitated for government loans to support their work, and in 1866 the Public Works Loan Commissioners were given power to lend them money.[26] The first organisations to benefit were the Metropolitan Association, Waterlow's own Improved Industrial Dwellings Company, the Highgate Dwellings Company and Liverpool Corporation.[27]

Housing philosophy

These were the practical issues of the housing movement, then, but before it is possible to discuss the developments during the seventies it will be useful to try to distinguish the various strands in the discussions of housing philosophy. They were concerned not with practical implications of the law so much as with the rights and wrongs, the incipient dangers, of the various approaches put forward for the solution of the problems of the poor.

We have seen already the expression of the various ideas about housing standards, in terms of associated and self-contained tenements. The constant search for practical ways of reducing building costs occupied the minds of reformers during the forties and the fifties; and many people argued about which part of the working class should be rehoused by the model agencies and about the merits of allowing philanthropic ventures to pay a small return. These subjects were not just the concern of those actively engaged in building; they were the fundamental issues which provided the basis for the high Victorian housing 'philosophy' and they occupied the minds of learned societies as well as the press and Parliament. The sixties were probably the first years during which housing became a matter of broader and more fundamental concern to society, and a subject acceptable for philosophical discussion at the learned societies in particular. We have already seen that the Royal Institute of British Architects twice discussed the subject early in the decade under the guidance first of Henry Roberts and then Professor Robert Kerr, but the discussions were ultimately more widely based than the architectural profession itself.

The Society of Arts was probably the most important organisation to pay consistent attention to the problems of the poor; it made considerable efforts to appraise the situation and find some equitable solution. During 1864 it organised a conference on 'The Dwellings of the Labouring Classes', which set out to consider the extent of the problem, its causes and effect, and its ultimate solution.[28] Three questions were posed: first, what could be done by additional legislation; secondly, what improvements might come about without changes in the existing legislation; and last, what assistance, if any, could the Society make at either level? The conference came to the conclusion that the law as it then existed could be improved with advantage by providing a formula for housing societies to borrow money at lower rates of interest and with less stringent security requirements than was then possible. This point was to some extent met by the 1866 Housing Act. Secondly, they suggested that it could be a legal requirement for those demolishing housing for commercial purposes to provide an equal number of houses elsewhere. More stringent inspection of lodging houses was also recommended, and the simplification of the laws for property conveyancing.

As a result of the conference, a special committee of the Society was set up to consider further these recommendations. They suggested more specifically that there should be increased powers for corporations to sell land for the erection of dwellings and that loans should be made available for housing purposes from the Public Works Loan Commissioners at a maximum rate of interest of $3\frac{1}{2}$ per cent. They recommended that the appointment of sanitary inspectors should be obligatory; that there should be adequate powers for local authorities to force builders to construct adequate drainage systems for new houses; that there should be efficient inspection of overcrowded dwellings; and finally that Medical Officers should have security of tenure, their appointments terminable only with the permission of the Privy Council, an arrangement suggested because a lethargic council would sometimes dismiss an efficient medical officer if his efficiency proved embarrassing.[29]

These recommendations were contained in a report made to the annual meeting in June 1865;[30] it was approved and the committee was asked to remain in office during the following year to try to find the means of carrying into effect some of their own suggestions. In addition to these recommendations for reforms they had proposed that an analysis of the existing law should be published so that its provisions should be better known. This difficult task was undertaken for them by Martin Ware.[31] It was a necessary exercise because the legal provisions were frequently obscure and many local authorities often neglected their statutory obligations to such an extent that the public was completely ignorant of its rights at law. But by far the most ambitious part of the Committee's work was the preparation, in conjunction with the Social Science Association, of a new bill designed to remedy the existing legal defects. It was introduced in Parliament by Charles Buxton during 1866, and he described its function as being, 'To facilitate the removal of houses which are unfit for human habitation, and the erection of improved dwellings for artizans and labourers'.[32]

The timing of the new measure was ill-advised, for it coincided with the introduction of a bill by W. M.

Torrens, dealing with the same subject. *The Builder*[33] urged the Society to withdraw its bill in favour of Torrens' measure which, it claimed, contained better provisions, and eventually they were obliged to do this although not without some regret.[34] Torrens' bill did not become law until 1868, and then not in its original form. Many of the other recommendations of the Society were embodied in the Public Health Act of 1866 and the Working Classes Dwelling Houses Act of the same year: the pressure which the august institutions could exert, therefore, was growing in importance and it is clear that in the case of the Society of Arts their analysis of the housing problem was based on thorough knowledge, not just a superficial and passing interest, which would have been the case even five years earlier.

There was a marked increase, also, during the decade in the publication of books and pamphlets on housing and health. In 1864 George Godwin produced the third of his great pamphlets deliberately designed to shock and stimulate; this one was called *Another Blow for Life*:

Ten years ago, I pointed attention to the miserable condition of these districts, and said, 'From dirt comes death'. The warning, however, failed to produce any appreciable effect, or the country might have been spared the ghastly recitals which, day after day, have recently filled the public journals.[35]

He went on to describe, in his own inimitable way, the shocking conditions which he had recently seen, and then he suggested some remedies:

We want a class of house formed with especial reference to their inevitable occupation by more than one family; looking like ordinary residences, but with a separate entrance to each floor, and with separate conveniences...The increased value of land in towns forms necessarily a material item, and it seems to necessitate building *high* instead of building *wide*.[36]

However, he also criticised some of the recent high buildings which the societies and companies had built:

If we made them a little less like factories and barracks, it would go far to give an air of home to them – a quality those experimentally erected, can hardly be said to possess.[37]

He demanded the removal of cesspools, many of which still existed in the mid-sixties, and he described London as 'a bubbling expanse of putridity and filth, horrible to behold'.[38] He went on to plead for the improvement of building standards, for more light, air and ventilation, for the proper application of existing building legislation and adequate inspection to prevent overcrowded conditions.

Most writers dwell on these points, and it is important to remember just how little had been done during the previous twenty years to alleviate the evils of urban areas: *laissez-faire* was still a by-word in local administration.

Henry Darbishire, lecturing at the Architectural Association in 1863, was more specific:

I consider that a poor man's town dwelling should consist of a living room and bedroom, with provision for additional bedrooms when required; that it should possess a plentiful and accessible supply of water, both for ablutions and cooking; an E[arth] C[loset], sink and lavatory, distinct, but not far removed from his tenement; a wash-house, with the means of drying clothes in any weather without artificial heat; and lastly, when practicable, a play-ground for his children.[39]

One outcome of the close link between housing and public health was the inordinate attention given to curious constructional details. Witness the attention paid to fire-proof construction in a lecture by Henry M. Eyton, architect of the Hull model dwellings built by S.I.C.L.C.,[40] and in another lecture at the Society of Arts, John Taylor described the wide variety of patent devices available to cope with such problems as 'vitiated air'.[41]

The discussions continued apace: Edward Jenkins and Alexander Stewart, for example, discussed 'The Legal Aspects of Sanitary Reform' at the National Association for the Promotion of Social Science; they were particularly concerned with the evils of permissive legislation.[42] William Hardwicke wrote a pamphlet *On the Evils of Overcrowding in the Dwellings of the Poor, and the Means Suggested for their Removal*,[43] and the same year, 1865, an article in *Chambers's Journal*, called 'Where can Working Men Live?',[44] was concerned with the increasing amount of demolition for commercial purposes, and the lack of progress amongst the housing societies. The author placed his hope in the much discussed system of cheap loans from the Public Works Loan Commissioners. This was not a universal view, and Thomas Beggs, addressing the Society of Arts, believed that the poor could best help themselves through building societies and normal commercial channels rather than through government loans, of which he disapproved, or benevolent societies and companies which he considered to be a failure.[45]

There were many other views, some sensible, some quaint, but without doubt the most important publication and certainly the most exhaustive, was James Hole's *The Homes of the Working Classes with Suggestions for their Improvement* which was published in 1866. It was first written as an entry for a Society of Arts essay competition, and when Hole was awarded the prize he expanded it into a full-scale book. He was a Leeds man, with a specialised north-country knowledge of the housing problems of industrial communities, and he had played an active part in encouraging his home town to take an interest in housing matters.

When contemplating the ugly, ill-built town, where every little freeholder asserts his indefeasible right as a Briton to do what he likes with his own; to inflict his own selfishness, ignorance and obstinacy upon his neighbours, and upon posterity for generations to come; and where local *self*-government means merely *mis*-government – we are apt to wish for a little wholesome despotism to curb such vagaries.[46]

Hole was chiefly concerned with the absence of proper legal controls over space about building, over the width of streets and the prevention of back-to-back housing which was particularly popular in Leeds, and he showed how both Manchester and Bradford had provided themselves with bye-laws which successfully prevented back-to-back development.

All that is meant to be insisted upon here is that no real gain is achieved by permitting the continued multiplication of inferior dwellings under the plea of the low wages of the working classes.[47]

In common with many writers at this time, Hole did not favour high buildings, with their vastly increased densities, he argued that they had not been proved healthy, and one suspects he believed that eventually they would be proved actually unhealthy. His real enthusiasm was first for suburban development, which was fast becoming a reasonable proposition if cheap workmen's trains were exploited, and secondly, for new industrial settlements, and here he had in mind the successful experiments such as Saltaire, recently built by Titus Salt, in the Aire valley just outside Bradford. Hole believed that workmen could buy their own small house with the aid of what might best be called philanthropic building societies, of the sort then in existence at Leeds.

This might be a reasonable way to finance housing for the artizan, especially in provincial towns, but for the very poor, who formed the hard core of the urban housing problem, Hole recommended that there should be cheap government loans, effectively a subsidy and for this reason, that to provide a class of people now without hope with new homes would be to give them a new sense of purpose, a new incentive to live thrifty, decent lives.

Hole's book was perhaps the most comprehensive work produced during the decade, but increasingly after about 1870 the housing movement became a literary one, largely because of the frustrations which befell those who attempted to build. The issues remained the same, first and with increasing forcefulness the legal and economic problems, secondly those concerned with the construction and sanitation of the individual house. Many writers offered their own solution, like Banister Fletcher in *Model Houses for the Industrial Classes*, published in 1871, which contained a proposal for a complex tenement building which was designed specifically to look like a terrace of middle class houses. Fletcher and many others were highly critical of the model dwellings built by the societies and companies which we have already discussed. Many of their proposals, however, were little advance on the buildings already erected and *The Builder* rather harshly condemned Fletcher for what was in fact an honest attempt to find a new solution.[48]

One of the classic pieces of literature in the seventies was William Bardwell's *What a House should be, versus Death in the House*, published as a sequel to *Healthy Homes and How to Make Them*, which had appeared in 1853. It was directed not at the poor so much as at a nebulous class of house-owners and occupiers: 'Who are dwelling in habitations without knowing that DEATH IS IN THE HOUSE'[49] because they were blissfully ignorant that their drainage was inadequate. It still makes hair-raising reading, but it does show the degree of ignorance and apathy which was common at that time. A similar book, *Sanitary Arrangements for Dwellings*,[50] by William Eassie was less idiosyncratic and gave similar advice: it had begun as a series of articles in the *British Medical Journal*, and was a sequel to another volume which he described as: 'A handbook to the history, defects, and remedies of drainage, ventilation, warming and kindred subjects'.[51]

One of the last bodies to be set up during the period before 1875 was the Charity Organisation Society which was founded in 1869, not to raise fresh relief, but to attack the root causes of want and pauperism in a systematic manner. A small fund was raised for this purpose by a group of noblemen, but by 1873 it was exhausted and thereafter the Society was forced to rely upon public support. In that year they set up a Special Dwellings Committee which set about discussing the whole housing problem and the question of state aid.[52] They found it at first difficult to arrive at any clear-cut conclusion so it was decided to examine the work of provincial towns which had a reputation for municipal interest in housing problems; towns like Liverpool, Glasgow and Edinburgh which had obtained private development Acts. A deputation came from Glasgow to meet the Committee, but as the corporation had built nothing at that time, they could not be of help. The committee came to the conclusion that London needed a similar kind of improvement scheme to that at Glasgow and they favoured a new centralised system for local government in London. In the meantime they recommended that the Metropolitan Board and the City Council should be given compulsory powers to purchase land for housing purposes, and, furthermore, they advised an expansion of the loan facilities offered by the Public Works Loan Commissioners for housing purposes, by which they meant loans at lower interest rates. Finally, they suggested that all new railway extension Acts should contain a clause requiring the company to provide new housing in place of all that demolished by the proposed extension. During 1864–5 Lord Shaftesbury had estimated that 20,000 people had lost their homes in London as a result of railway extensions and street improvements,[53] and when the land was cleared for St Pancras station and its approaches the next year, a similar number were affected.[54] Railway companies chose to build over slum housing because it could be bought up cheaply and there had been little official objection to their policy until, in 1864, the Great Eastern Railway Metropolitan Station and Railways Act[55] became the first Act requiring a railway company to provide workmen's trains in return for what amoun-

ted to the virtual confiscation of their homes. Subsequent Acts usually contained similar clauses but it was another twenty years before cheap trains and workmen's fares became a useful and properly organised facility.[56]

Housing, in fact, had become a subject of public concern at a level never known previously. I have mentioned only some of the special organisations set up before 1875 and a few of the august bodies which heard papers and conducted lengthy discussions; these stretched from the Architectural Association to the annual conferences of the Social Science Association. Housing was even suitable material for ladies tea clubs. But it remained an open debate: no clear movement as yet existed supporting any novel approach and there was much distrust of what might be called a 'socialist' view of housing.

Octavia Hill and the problem of the poor

Hole's views were in some ways rather too advanced and they were not held universally; there were those who believed that the poor were beyond help because they were inherently thriftless, that they would only turn clean new homes into filthy new slums. The chief protagonist of this view was Miss Octavia Hill: her belief was that this class of persons must first learn to live decently within their natural environment before they were fitted for a new home – they must first regain their own self-respect, for the onus was upon them rather than upon society to take the initiative.

Octavia Hill's policy of 'self-help' was, on the surface, a hard one; it was based on social realism, perhaps even on a certain cynical attitude towards the lowest class of society. At the same time it was based on a belief that education was the means to all salvation; through it the poor might regain their self-respect, especially if the teaching was undertaken on a personal basis. She argued that if the poor felt that the community was genuinely interested in their welfare then they would be encouraged to help themselves. The idea of personal contact was fundamental to her work, and without doubt it was successful, for there were an increasing number of slum dwellings which had been purged through the activity of her band of lady workers.[57]

Octavia Hill was the grand-daughter of Dr Southwood Smith, one of the first social reformers; she began her work in 1864, partly with the financial help and always with the encouragement of John Ruskin.[58] That year she purchased a group of houses known as Paradise Place,[59] which were notorious both for their condition and for the class of people they housed. From the start her policy was built around ideas of personal management; she visited the tenants frequently, demanding that the rents should be paid on time, that the common stairs and landing should be kept clean, and in return she made such improvements as the rents allowed. But the greatest improvements were those that were made by the tenants themselves because they learnt that she would feel disappointed if they let her down.[60] Her work prospered and she became famous, in reality through the self-help she inspired in the people she was able to influence.

It is far better to prove that you can provide a tolerable tenement which will pay, than a perfect one which will not. The one plan will be adopted, and will lead to great results; the other will remain an isolated and unfruitful experiment, a warning to all who cannot or will not loose money. If you mean to provide for the family that has lived hitherto in one foul dark room, with rotten boards saturated with dirt, with vermin in the walls, damp plaster, smoky chimney, approached by a dark and dangerous staircase, in a house with no through ventilation or back-yard, with old brick drains, and broken down water-butt without a lid; be thankful if you can secure for the same rent even one room in a new, clean, pure house. Do not insist on a supply of water on every floor, or a separate wash-house for each family, with its greatly increased expense of water-pipes and drainage. Build a large laundry which shall be common to the whole house, and in other ways moderate your desires somewhat to suit the income of your tenant. Give him by all means as much as you can for his money, but do not house him by charity, or you will house few but him, and discourage instead of stimulating others to build for the poor.[61]

Socially there was much truth in what she wrote; there was a tremendous need for education for personal cleanliness and the revival of the self-respect which the poor very often had lost through years of degradation. The success of her work was proof of this, but the movement gained ground the more rapidly because it was seen as a satisfactory way to do something which would show results without much financial risk. While the economic difficulties which surrounded the erection of new buildings continued and prevented a radical attack on the housing problem, it was a convenient philosophy to support. But it only put off the evil day when the sub-standard property would have to be pulled down.

One other important aspect of her work deserves mention. This was the start of her interest in the problems of open space and recreation. In 1871 the first annual meeting of her People's Garden Company was held; already they had purchased fifty acres at Old Oak Common and soon it was opened as a public park.[62] The same year the Marquis of Westminster offered the garden in Ebury Square to St George's Vestry as a park for the local inhabitants.[63] From these very small beginnings there were to be significant developments.

The first slum clearance measure

The account of legal action and its effect between 1855 and the middle of the next decade is at once complex and clear cut; complex in that there were a variety of new Acts of Parliament dealing with widely differing aspects of housing and sanitary law, clear cut in that the outcome of each one was the same: whatever incidental improvements resulted or minor benefits accrued, the central problem of overcrowding, with its whole attendant train of sanitary and housing problems, grew steadily worse. If main drainage improved, building standards did not; the stultifying effects of permissive legislation were only too easy to find.

The first man to make any attempt to cope with the underlying issues of urban growth was William McCullagh Torrens who, in 1866, introduced a Bill dealing with slum clearance which was intended to deal with individual insanitary houses when the owner himself refused to undertake urgent repairs and remedial action to safeguard the health of the occupants. It provided for compulsory powers of demolition or repair, as the local authority thought necessary, and also for the erection of new and better dwellings, in place of those pulled down. This last clause met with fierce opposition and slowed down the progress of the Bill so that it did not pass that session. When re-introduced the following year the clause was at first retained, then dropped, and finally in 1868 when the Bill reached the statute book as the Artizans' and Labourers' Dwellings Act[64] it only provided for the local authority to secure improvement by repair or demolition; there was no mention of rebuilding. What it did do, however, was to establish that the owner was responsible for the condition of his property; if the community as represented by its Medical Officer and Council considered a property to be insanitary, they could require the owner to improve it in certain specified structural ways, to demolish it if it was beyond repair, or if he failed to co-operate they could do this work for him and require that he pay the cost involved. This made considerable inroads into the currently held ideas of the rights of property but, unfortunately, the Act made no provision for compensating the owner if the property was demolished, and as the initiation of proceedings under the Act was in the hands of the local vestries and district boards, property owning councillors were unlikely to act against their own class, so the whole measure was effectively nullified. Torrens believed wholeheartedly in the efficacy of local parochial administration, a faith that recent history might have taught him to abandon. He believed that the individual house and its owner was the level at which reform should be directed, but he failed to realise that the removal of single houses would make little impression on an area where wholesale demolition was required, not of one house but of whole streets and courts. Nevertheless, it is rarely possible to move public opinion at one revolutionary step and Torrens' Act, establishing as it did the principle of interference in an area of liberty which had previously been regarded as sacrosanct, was an important event in housing history.

The practical outcome of the new Housing Act, then, was negligible and the early seventies were marked by growing disquiet about the situation.

Water, air and light are nature's disinfectants and preventions of disease. They are abundantly provided, but more meagrely and inefficiently used, and indeed practically ignored by architects, builders, owners and occupiers.[65]

wrote a Medical Officer for Mile-End-Old-Town, and one of London's sanitary historians, Henry Jephson, later wrote of the years around 1870:

It is now almost incredible that the law should have been left in such a state as to enable builders, without any legal check, to put up the houses they did.[66]

The preparation for legal reform

If parliament needed advice on health or housing problems after about 1865 there was plenty available, it need look little further than the great wealth of literature appearing each year to see that there were innumerable opinions about all aspects of housing and public health. Much of the advice must have appeared contradictory and obviously it would be impossible to please all the pundits even part of the time. A joint committee representing the Medical Officers of Health and the Social Science Association was set up in May 1868, 'To promote a better administration of the laws relating to registration, medico-legal inquiries, and the improvement of public health'.[67]

They asked for a Royal Commission, a necessary prelude to legislation on health and housing and, after one false start, it was appointed by Gladstone in 1869 with a brief to investigate the sanitary administration of England and Wales and especially the function of a central authority, although administration within the metropolis itself was significantly excluded.[68] Its report was predictable, in the light of all the evidence which we have just examined from other sources, for there were salient faults in the existing provisions which few could ignore. It recommended the consolidation of existing laws and the streamlining of the administration within each sanitary area so that a uniform and universal building and public health code could easily be administered. It proposed the appointment of an independent Medical Officer in each district, responsible to a new central authority which would be under the direction of a minister of the crown. These were a fair, if not a radical series of conclusions, but the government was not prepared to carry many of them through Parliament at that stage and neither the Local Government Board Act of 1871 nor the Public Health Act of 1872 were epoch making measures.[69] The first abolished the central Poor Law Board, transferring its powers to a new department of central government, the Local Government Board and making various other minor 'tidying-up' measures which looked good on paper but in the context of a system of permissive legislation were still inept. The Public Health Act of the following year made provision for a national network of Medical Officers of Health who were intended to be men of experience, experts in their field, thus raising the standard of health administration. In practice it was

often an appointment held as an extension of the powers held by the Medical Officers of the local Poor Law Boards. Simon believed that there were still not enough properly trained men to fill the more onerous new posts if the job was to be done properly. *The Builder* thought the Act an imperfect measure which owed rather more to the recent attack of typhoid experienced by the Prince of Wales than to a proper consideration of the Royal Commissions proceedings![70] And there the matter rested until a Select Committee was appointed in 1874 to look into the working of the Metropolitan Building and Management Acts, which had not been revised since 1855. Their report did for Metropolitan London what the Royal Commission Report of 1869 had done for the rest of England and Wales; it completed the indictment of our sanitary institutions. An attempt was made that year to legislate for the various recommendations of the previous five years, but the Sanitary Law Amendment Act, as it was called, merely tampered with existing institutions, it was not the long awaited 'root and branch' reform that was necessary.

The Public Health Act 1875

The burning issues of sanitation and health were at last dealt with in the great Public Health Act of 1875, which, like its famous predecessor of 1848, became a landmark in the history of English sanitary institutions because of the way in which it cleared away the accumulated growth of contractory and often obscure legislation. It took account of the more successful experiments carried out under the terms of local Acts in the intervening years and for the first time it began to put teeth into the public health code.

The Act for Consolidating and Amending the Acts relating to Public Health in England,[71] as the 1875 Act was properly called, gave to the existing authorities, that is the town and borough councils, the Boards of Improvement Commissioners, the local Boards of Health formed under the 1848 Public Health Act, the Local Boards formed under the 1858 Local Government Act, and the Boards of Guardians, constituted by the 1872 Act as the Rural Sanitary authorities, a series of powers to control the conditions of their town or district:[72] but these powers were again only permissive, and the local authority could still proceed independently under a private Act if it possessed one, and this provided the traditional escape from activity. The authorities were also charged with the execution of the Bakehouse Regulation Act soon to be replaced by the Factory and Workshop Act of 1878; with the Artizans' and Labourers' Dwellings Act of 1875;[73] and also with the Baths and Wash-houses Acts and the Labouring Classes Lodging Houses Acts: if these were not in force, the authority might adopt them.

The sanitary provisions were numerous and all-embracing; sewers were to be vested in the local authority except in special cases, such as their ownership by sewer commissioners; the authority had power to purchase sewers, to make new ones, and keep them in good repair; to require house owners to connect their drains with the sewer, or if the distance was greater than 100 feet to discharge them into a cesspool. Each new house was to have proper privy accommodation, although there was a very lenient interpretation of what constituted a privy, but the local authority was given power to enforce this provision. It could also make arrangements for the scavenging and cleaning of streets, and should it not do so, in this particular instance, the Local Government Board was given coercive powers. There were also useful powers for the local authority to provide an adequate supply of water should there be no local company prepared to do so.

No new cellar dwellings were to be permitted and those already in use were only to continue as habitable dwellings if they fulfilled certain conditions. Stringent regulations were imposed upon common lodging houses, which were to be registered, regulated and inspected by the local authority in accordance with a series of bye-laws, and the Local Government Board could also empower the local authority to make similar bye-laws for ordinary houses let in lodgings. Very important duties were imposed upon the local authorities with regard to the suppression of nuisance, requiring inspection and giving additional powers of abatement. The definition of a 'nuisance' was again specifically made to include overcrowding.

Section 157 enacted the important provision for local authorities to make bye-laws for the layout of new streets, controlling their width and construction; for the construction of new buildings, the space regulations for them, and their sanitary requirements. It was under this section that most subsequent bye-laws were prepared, and for this purpose the Local Government Board, as the confirming authority, prepared its own Model Bye-laws. A new building was described as including

The re-erecting of a building pulled down to, or below, the ground floor, or of any frame building of which only the frame-work is left down to the ground floor, or the conversion into a dwelling house of any building not originally such, or the conversion of one dwelling house into more than one, of a building originally constructed as one dwelling-house only, are severally to be considered cases of 'The erection of a new building'.[74]

Finally, the local authority was obliged to appoint certain officials including a Medical Officer of Health, Surveyor, Inspector of Nuisances, Clerk and Treasurer, so that there might be adequate administrative machinery for the new and extended power granted to them. The provisions of the Act were in theory very adequate; but, alas, their implementation depended to a great extent upon the goodwill of the local authorities, like all the previous legislation which depended not upon force but upon the co-operation of people to whom the old dictum *Salus populi suprema lex est* at least in a sanitary sense could mean very little.

The final disappointment concerning the 1875

Public Health Act was the way it perpetuated the old tradition of excluding London from all its provisions, and the metropolis was obliged to wait a considerable number of years to reap the benefits which eventually accrued to the rest of the country as a result of the Act.[75] But the Act had established a new structure for local administration for the country as a whole and it had provided the important framework within which local government could set to work and make the necessary sanitary improvements and exercise the controls which were at that time so patently lacking. Although the Act was to a large extent permissive, it achieved greater effect than any previous Act because the climate of public opinion was changing and as the century drew to a close the sense of responsibility which was felt at a national level began to permeate through to a local level. When it did so, there was an adequate framework within which the responsible authority could work.

The origins of the Model Bye-laws

Spatially, one of the most important developments which resulted from the Act was the establishment by the Local Government Board of an acceptable standard for housing development, and the standard which they recommended became in time the basis for all bye-laws throughout the country.

Section 157 of the Public Health Act enacted that a local authority might make bye-laws:

1 With respect to the level, width, and construction of new streets and the provision for the sewerage thereof;
2 With respect to the structure of walls, foundations, roofs and chimneys of new buildings for securing stability and the prevention of fires, and for the purposes of health;
3 With respect to the sufficiency of space about buildings to secure a free circulation of air, and with respect to the ventilation of buildings;
4 With respect to drainage of buildings to water-closets, earthclosets, privies, ashpits, and cesspools in connection with buildings, and to the closing of buildings or parts of buildings unfit for human habitation and to prohibition of their use for such habitation.

In order that these bye-laws might be observed the local authority was also permitted to require developers to give notice of their intentions, and to deposit plans and sections showing the layout of proposed new streets. They could make arrangements for inspection; and they might acquire powers to remove, alter, or pull down any work which contravened their bye-laws. The chief weaknesses were first that the bye-laws did not apply to any building erected before this Act came into force; secondly, the local authority was under no obligation to make any bye-laws at all, since there was no power for a central authority to coerce the urban authority into adopting the Act if it did not so desire; and thirdly, there was apparently still certain ambiguity as to what constituted a new building.[76]

The local authority, if it wished to make bye-laws under Section 157 was obliged to seek the approval of the Local Government Board; and in order to give some kind of guidance about the standards which they thought were advisable, the Board decided to produce a series of Model Bye-laws. The proofs of these were examined by the Royal Institute of British Architects, who made such amendments as they thought desirable, and then in July 1877, the final version was circulated to all urban sanitary authorities.[77]

The Model Bye-laws were framed to include the four aspects of control mentioned in Section 157, but only those concerned with space about buildings will here be considered.

New streets were recommended to be 36 ft. wide except for those which were less than 100 ft. long, and these might be regarded as pedestrial roads and reduced to 24 ft. in width; all streets were to be open at one end throughout their full width and height.[78] There was no provision for the control of back streets in the Public Health Act, and a subsequent attempt to make a bye-law concerning them was found to be invalid in a court of law. Consequently, the Model Bye-laws suggest that any attempt to regulate the width of back streets might only hinder their provision. The minimum width for a carriageway was suggested as 24 feet, and the foot ways not less than one-sixth the total street width.

Turning 'to the sufficiency of the space about buildings to secure a free circulation of air, and with respect to the ventilation of building', the model clauses suggested were these:

Every person who shall erect a new domestic building shall provide in front of such building an open space, which shall be free from any erection thereon above the level of the ground, except any portico, porch, step or other like projection from such building, or any gate, fence or wall, not exceeding *seven feet* in height, and which measured to the boundary of any lands or premises immediately opposite, or to the opposite side of any street which such building may front, shall, throughout the whole line of frontage of such building, extend to a distance of *twenty-four feet* at the least; such distance being measured in every case at right angles to the external face of any wall of such building which shall front or abut on such open space. A person who shall make any alteration in, or addition, to such building shall not, by such alteration or addition, diminish the extent of open space provided in pursuance of this bye-law in connection with such building.[79]

This clause was aimed at the prevention of development on back land, making it necessary for any building to have in front of it at least the equivalent space of a street of minimum width; it was hoped thereby to prevent the building of narrow courts.

Space at the rear of buildings was also regulated:

Every person who shall erect a new domestic building shall provide in the rear of such building an open space exclusively belonging to such building, and of an aggregate extent of not less than *one hundred and fifty square* feet, and free from any erection thereon above the level of the ground, except a water-closet, earth closet, or privy, and an ashpit. He shall cause such open space to extend, laterally, throughout the entire width of such building, and he shall cause the distance across such open space from every part of such building to the boundary of any lands or premises immediately opposite, or adjoining the site of such building, to be not less in any case than *ten feet*.

If the height of such building be *fifteen feet* he shall cause such distance to be *fifteen feet* at least.

If the height of such building be *twenty-five feet* he shall cause distance to be *twenty feet* at least. If the height of such building be *thirty-five feet*, or exceed *thirty-five feet* he shall cause such distance to be *twenty-five feet* at least.[80]

There was the usual clause to the effect that future additions should not contravene the bye-law; but the most important point to note was the attempt made to prevent back-to-back development by requiring the open space for each house, regardless of its position, to be at the rear of the building; and not alternatively at the side, which in the past had provided a useful loophole for the unscrupulous.

A model clause was provided to govern the size of windows: they should have an area equal to one tenth that of the floor space inside the room; and at least half the window must open, and the opening part must extend to the full height of the window. Despite these carefully worded clauses dealing with light and ventilation there was a curious omission of any regulation concerning room heights.

The Model Bye-laws were received with mixed feelings. The discussion at the Royal Institute of British Architects showed that the architectural profession was not wholly convinced of their efficacy; one speaker feared that too great powers were already vested in local authorities by virtue of the Health Act; another that strict adherence to sanitary ideals would make working class housing too expensive; and a surveyor thought them 'as a whole, impractical, unworkable and inquisitorial...so stringent that local bodies would not dare to carry them out'.[81]

However, one eminent sanitarian, Dr Parkes, had more stringent views than those generally accepted. He thought that the minimum street width should be one and a half times the height of the buildings on either side.

It is not possible to state with any precision the number of persons who should be located on an acre. This will depend entirely on the construction of the individual houses, but it may be laid down as a general rule that whatever be the size of the houses the amount of ground not occupied by them in any given area should be considerably in excess of the amount actually taken up by houses.[82]

Alas, Dr Parkes was looking to a state of affairs which was not to receive commendation until the advent of the Garden City movement some twenty-five years later.

There was in existence, however, another method by which bye-laws might be made, and one which often seems to have been more successful, at least from the point of view of the local authority. During the 19th century, and particularly the early part of it, many corporate towns obtained private Acts of Parliament giving them special powers, usually for some specified purpose such as lighting or paving; but in addition under these Acts it was possible to obtain powers to make bye-laws. Many towns, therefore, already possessed bye-laws made in this way, without the obligation to submit them to any superior authority, such as the Local Government Board, and these towns continued to operate such regulations as they thought fit, despite the fact that they were often designed to be very lenient and convenient to the owners of property, thus thwarting the whole sanitary purpose of space control.

There was thus little immediate attempt in the country as a whole to follow the example provided by the Board, and a variety of anomalies gradually came to light.

In a report submitted by Dr Barry and Mr Gordon Smith to the Local Government Board in 1888 on the subject of back-to-back housing they were able to show that in a large number of Yorkshire towns the back-to-back house was legally permitted, and not merely permitted but also regulated and therefore condoned.[83] It was found that both occupiers and builders preferred the system, although there was said to be little real economy in their construction by comparison with any other kind of working class housing. The report examined a variety of housing topics such as the extent of recent back-to-back building; the space about building; housing standards and density figures; structural arrangements, methods of ventilation and provision for refuse disposal; the relative cost of different housing types, and the influence of these upon health and morality.

The results were quite astonishing; between 1876 and 1886, 61 per cent of the housing in Halifax had been built on the back-to-back principle; and in Morley, where bye-laws allowing this type of building were framed in 1883, 82 per cent of the houses were of this pattern. The bye-laws in Halifax, for example, regulated the building of back-to-back houses: there must not be more than four pairs, that is eight houses, in a block and between each block there must be an open space 15 ft. wide 'unless with the previous consent of the Corporation',[84] which, apparently, was freely given, so that the Report was able to cite blocks of 16, 28 and 30 houses built back-to-back.

Building standards were also abysmally low: 4½ ins. party walls were common; stopped off at ceiling level, so that the roof space was open throughout the block; but the report was unable to obtain sufficient statistics to show that the construction or the system was insanitary.

But this was only part of the picture; a few towns seemed more ready to accept the standards offered by the Local Government Board. Preston, for example, did so immediately the 1875 Act was passed, and on 23 October 1876 its bye-laws were confirmed after considerable correspondence between the town and the Board.[85] Preston's bye-laws required new streets to be not less than 36 ft., and back streets not less than 12 ft. in width; at the front of houses a minimum open space of 240 sq. ft. was necessary and at the rear 150 sq. ft. with a minimum depth of 10 ft. increasing to 25 ft. when the building exceeded 28 ft. in height.

It was not, then, that the small towns were behind the great cities necessarily, although this seems to have been more often the case. There was in all the towns, both large and small, a diversity of bye-law arrangements, but it was the model series which in time became the accepted standard, and in the years to come many followed the example of Birmingham which brought its own bye-laws into line with the model series in 1876.[86]

A new Housing Act

The Public Health Act proceeded on the assumption that there was an adequate supply of housing over which some form of control was necessary. It was also necessary to ensure that the supply existed in the right place, and in order to do this, parliament had already undertaken a different kind of legislative approach which was complementary to that adopted in the Health Act. The first attempt to control the provision of housing had already been made by the Torrens Act of 1868, a measure which had been much discussed and hotly contested:

'Strong objections are entertained', wrote the Earl of Caernarvon of artizans dwellings and Mr Torrens' Bill in particular in 1869, 'and not without reason, to state intervention in these matters; and it will doubtless be best if the desired end can be secured by the joint action of the private owners of property and of the local authorities; but, failing this, the evil is so great, and goes so deeply down into the roots of society, that larger and bolder measures may become necessary.'[87]

The Earl was very near to the truth when he wrote this, for the early history of the seventies showed the inadequacies of the legislation already in existence, and not least the failure of the housing provisions in Mr Torrens' Act, because nobody was prepared to exercise the permissive powers which it gave.

After 1870 it became increasingly evident that stronger, more direct powers were necessary to combat the growing need for housing in central areas, particularly of London. The *Report of the Special Dwellings Committee of the Charity Organisation Society*, published in 1873, and already discussed, urged that greater powers of redevelopment should be vested in the municipal authorities so that they might emulate the work done by Glasgow corporation.

The Committee were not the only body to call for such reforms; one of the more enlightened Medical Officers, John Liddle, of the Whitechapel Vestry suggested a very similar arrangement a year later;[88] and Captain Douglas Galton, another eminent sanitarian, saw the need for new legislation or the proper enforcement of the old.[89]

As a result, the Metropolitan Board instigated an abortive Bill, the Metropolitan Buildings and Management Bill, during 1874, which was universally criticised.[90] Parliament was, nevertheless, sympathetic to the whole problem, and *The Builder* commented upon the seriousness and earnestness with which the debate was conducted;[91] R. A. Cross, Disraeli's great Home Secretary, admitted that some measure was necessary and that the Government hoped to introduce a Bill, but he did not seem to know who might be entrusted with the administration of new legislation.[92]

Cross then proceeded to consult with the best authorities available, including men like Sir Sydney Waterlow and representatives of the Corporation of Glasgow, who, in their various ways, had great experience of solving different aspects of the housing problem. So far as London was concerned, Waterlow agreed with the Charity Organisation Society that there must be provision for the working population, as a whole, to live in the central areas. It was now impossible to obtain sites in just these places, the societies and companies had no means of obtaining slum property. He suggested that a public authority, and not the local vestries, should be given compulsory powers to purchase:

...the only question that I apprehend can be asked is, in what way can Parliament alleviate this evil without throwing too great a burden on the ratepayers, or dealing unfairly with the rights of private property?...In what way can Parliament assist in this work, which has hitherto been left so entirely to private philanthropy? What we ask is that this House, recognising the local authority which the Metropolitan Board of Works and the City of London exercise over the districts under their control, should impose upon these two public bodies,...the responsibility and the duty of submitting to Parliament, from time to time, schemes for public improvements involving the destruction of houses unfit for occupation, and the appropriation of the sites when cleared for the reconstruction of tenement-houses suitable for the labouring population, upon plans to be approved by the local authority, in the manner prescribed by the Metropolitan Improvement Act of 1872...[93]

The example of Glasgow was also very much in mind at this time; the Charity Organisation Society during its own investigations had already called a deputation to explain the provisions in Glasgow's private Acts.[94] It is clear, however, that public pressure was having its effect and Mr Kay Shuttleworth reminded the House when he introduced the subject, of the papers prepared by two bodies, of whom the Royal College of Physicians was one and the Charity Organisation Society the other.[95]

The long awaited Artizans' Dwellings Bill was introduced by R. A. Cross early in 1875. The vestries, of course, were against its provisions and voiced their disapproval from the outset; but it did not meet with strong Parliamentary opposition, and passed into law that summer as the Artizans' and Labourers' Dwellings Improvement Act, 1875.[96]

The provisions of the Bill, nevertheless, had raised a variety of very real problems; Shaftesbury, for example, was concerned with the problem of housing the people in the interim between demolition and rebuilding and with the problem of providing accommodation at a reasonable rent:

Well, what are we to do? Are we to construct a vast number of single rooms in order to meet the means of these poor people, or are we to build houses according to our new sanitary requirements? If we reconstruct single rooms, we shall maintain a most indecent and most immoral state of things; if, on the other hand, we do not, rents will be raised so high that it will be perfectly impossible for the people to bear the demands that will be made upon them. I am speaking now of labourers who have no regular work of any kind, and not of skilled artizans...Now I must repeat that, unless we reconstruct dwellings adapted to their means, great injury will be inflicted on the people who are displaced.
Yet there is one form of remedy well worthy of consideration. We can adapt, drain and ventilate old tenements, courts, alleys and *culs-de-sac* at a far less outlay than is required to construct anything new.[97]

He then went on to describe the work undertaken by S.I.C.L.C., and the alternative solution adopted by Octavia Hill, commending her scheme for consideration at least as a temporary and partial answer to the housing problem. Whichever solution was finally adopted he hoped that some kind of gradual clearance would be effected, rather than wholesale demolition.

Octavia Hill herself had had much to say about the principles contained in the bill, and especially about the possible provision of new dwellings in some non-remunerative way:

I enter more deeply, perhaps, than most of the objectors themselves into the full weight of this objection, and most heartily hope that whatever is done in building for the people may be done on a thoroughly sound commercial principle, I do not think it would help them the least in the long run to adopt any other principle; in fact, I believe it would be highly injurious to them.[98]

She allowed that the community had some responsibility for remedying the problem of the incoherent industrial town which it had permitted to develop over many years, and this was a considerable concession on her part, but her attitude to rehousing, and the fundamental importance of self-help through education, was typical of one particular school of thought then prevalent:

The people's homes are bad, partly because they are badly built and arranged; they are tenfold worse because their habits and lives are what they are. Transplant them tomorrow to healthy and commodious homes, and they would pollute and destroy them.[99]

The Act was of considerable importance, especially during the next decade, for under its provisions nearly all of the new working class housing developments in the central area of London were carried out. It is therefore necessary to examine the housing provisions which it contained in greater detail than has previously been found necessary. First, the purpose of the Act must be carefully distinguished from that of Torrens' Act of 1868, which dealt with single properties; the Cross Act – as it was popularly called – was designed to cope with larger areas; it was a comprehensive solution to the problem of a whole district.

Having made this distinction it is possible to turn to the machinery which the Act set up. The Metropolitan Board of Works and the City Commissioners of Sewers were the executant authorities for London, and in the provinces its powers were vested in the town corporation; and it could be set in motion through an official representation about the insanitary nature of the area by the local Medical Officer, either on his own initiative or that of two justices or twelve rate-payers. If the controlling authority agreed that the area was unhealthy it was obliged to prepare an improvement scheme, which might include additional land to that for which the representation was initially made, should it think it necessary for the completeness of the scheme. There was an important clause which required provision for rehousing at least as many people as were initially housed on the same site. After the scheme had been prepared it was then to be advertised during three consecutive weeks in September, October or November; and notices served on the various property owners requesting their approval or disapproval of the compulsory purchase order. The authority was then required to petition the Home Secretary, sending a copy of the scheme and a list of all the objectors. The Home Secretary then held an inquiry and issued a provisional order which might modify the scheme if he thought this desirable. He could not, however, increase the area to be purchased compulsorily. The provisional order then required confirmation by Act of Parliament and after this was obtained, the local authority was obliged to set about obtaining the properties included in the compulsory purchase order, arranging the amount of compensation to be paid to the mutual satisfaction of themselves and the owner; those claims which were not so agreed were sent to arbitration. When the land was all purchased and cleared, it was to be offered for sale with stringent rehousing obligations included in the sale agreement. The authority might only build itself with the express approval of the Home Secretary, but it was allowed to exercise control over the design of the buildings erected by the purchaser.[100]

The Artizans' and Labourers' Dwellings Act was applicable to provincial towns with a population of over 200,000, but the traditional bogy of permissive-ness made it inoperative in many places. Of about eighty towns in which the Act could be adopted, by 1879 sixty of them had taken no action whatsoever; eleven had begun discussions, and two or three had undertaken demolition, but none had erected the dwellings which were the *raison d'être* of the Act.[101] In Derby, for example, a scheme was proposed for an area of seven acres, but opposition arose as the work would have imposed too great a burden on the rates, it was said, and consequently the whole scheme was soon afterwards dropped.[102] Reports came from Liverpool, where sites were being cleared and although difficulties were experienced in disposing of them, dwellings eventually were built by the Council.[103] At Swansea the Council was undertaking demolition work, and in Manchester an association was formed for the improvement of dwellings.[104] But on the whole the response was poor, and no more satisfactory in its results than in London, although the reasons were entirely different. It was possible to argue, with much more conviction than in London, however, that the need for dwellings was not great in the centre of provincial towns since most artizans could depart to the nearby suburbs with little inconvenience and there find a wealth of speculative housing. This argument was put forward in both Glasgow and Birmingham as the reason for there being no rehousing provisions in the central area in schemes of a similar nature to those undertaken after 1875.[105]

Undoubtedly the most important work as a result of the 1875 Act was in London where the need for fresh action was absolutely urgent. It is, therefore, with the schemes undertaken by the Metropolitan Board of Works that any account of the problems and frustrations of the Act must be concerned, and it is to these that we must now return.

Slum clearance problems resulting from the new Act

On 27 July 1875, Dr John Liddle made the first official representation with regard to an area in Whitechapel, to which was later added another area in adjacent Limehouse.[106] The complicated proceedings just outlined took until 20 December 1877, when Sir H. A. Hunt made his final arbitration awards; and in the following February the Home Secretary gave permission for the first portion of the site to be cleared, but it was not until the following July that the Board satisfactorily settled all the outstanding legal claims. Clearance of the first area then began, and in December 1878, the Home Secretary, after a lengthy and protracted discussion, agreed to the condition of sale and the sites were advertised. No tenders were received, partly because the conditions of tender implied too great interference by the Board, so they were not acceptable to the majority of dwelling trusts and societies; and after the intervention of the Home Secretary the Board amended them. But it still proved impossible to attract bidders at the prices required by the Board; and finally, after much heart-searching, they agreed to sell a large part of the site to the Peabody Trustees at a price very considerably below that which they themselves had been obliged to pay in order to acquire the land. In January 1884, the remainder of the land on this clearance area was offered for sale, but the last plot was not sold until 1890!

The Act, then, could not really be called an immediate and outstanding success. The first scheme ran into difficulties which nobody apparently foresaw, and these were repeated in every later scheme: progress was inordinately slow because of the various separate stages outlined by the Act, which proved in practice to be exceptionally unwieldy. The Board was accused of causing unnecessary delay, and countered by complaining of their inability to obtain more than one third the value of the land when attempting to sell. Secondly, the arbitrator in all the schemes awarded compensation to the value of the property as if it had been in sound condition and on good ground, so no account was taken of its physical nature, only of its actual value by virtue of its position. Thirdly, the conditions of sale were unpopular; and last the Board was unable to obtain a price for the land which would cover the expense which had been entailed in acquiring it, since in practice all the sites were offered for sale as land for house-building, and only a minute proportion for commercial development. These practical objections prevented any new buildings arising on the now derelict sites during the first two years during which the Act was in operation, and *The Builder* could write:

It is discouraging to sanitary reformers to find, as they do year after year, their labours defeated by the procrastination of the authorities. The legislature passes Acts of Parliament that are intended to lead to *immediate* sanitary improvements, but the result is 'much cry and little wool'. The Artizans' Dwellings Act of 1875 is, so far as results, almost a dead letter...[107]

In all, some sixteen schemes were prepared and executed by the Metropolitan Board of Works before its demise in 1888 and a further six were started by the Board and completed by the London County Council.

There were, of course, many more representations than these twenty-two, especially during the first year after the passing of the Act; but the Board became increasingly unwilling to proceed with new schemes, either because it wished to see the outcome of the difficulties it was experiencing, or because it was unable to cope with the scale of the work involved. The first representation on which the Board deferred a decision was made as early as 12 August 1875;[108] but it did not begin consistently to delay activity until a representation made by the Medical Officer for St Giles on 6 November 1876, and this was done because of the quantity of work then in hand.[109]

It should be remembered that at this period the Metropolitan Board was also faced with considerable difficulties in connection with the rehousing obligations imposed by the Metropolitan Street Improvement Act of 1872 which were in many ways as onerous as those of 1875. Some of the worst problems seem to have centred around the Grays Inn Road Improvement scheme which dragged on for many years. The proposals made in 1876 by the Board were turned down by the Home Secretary:

The partial scheme appears to Mr Cross to be inadequate and also objectionable, from want of proper space, the street not being sufficiently widened in proportion to the height of the adjacent buildings. On the other hand, the entire scheme, as deposited, does not, as shown in Mr Nichol's report, provide accommodation for as many persons of the working class as would be displaced. The failure to comply with the statutory requirement would alone put it out of the power of the Secretary of State to confirm the scheme, even were it in other respects not open to objection...[110]

So far as the actual dwellings were concerned, the Board had proposed replacing many of the old courts with single room tenements, which led to a strong protest from Sir Sydney Waterlow.[111] Nevertheless, it was faced with a difficult problem: before it could demolish more than fifteen houses it must see that alternative accommodation was available on the site; and as usual, speculators were unwilling to take up the land which it offered them; so that eventually the Board was forced to sell at a loss. Questions were asked in the Commons about the delays, and Cross blamed the Board for mutilating the scheme prepared by its officers to such an extent that it was impossible for him to approve it. But in fact the problem was not quite so simple as that and the Board was faced with numerous very real difficulties: there were, no doubt, faults on the part of the Board, particularly with regard to its growing lethargy, but undoubtedly there were also faults in the legislature.[112]

By 1879, the Board had innumerable schemes under the 1875 Act still unfinished, and as there was little sign of any of them reaching completion in the near future it was becoming increasingly reluctant to undertake any more; the legal procedure was slow and tortuous; delays were legion, and the arbitrators had so far interpreted the Act in such a way that the owners of insanitary property received very lavish compensation.[113] It was in the summer of 1879 that the Board finally recognised its inability to fulfil the terms of the Act and at the same time to recoup its losses. For the schemes already undertaken, it agreed to accept the losses involved rather than prevent new housing being built and it agreed to the offer made by the Peabody Trustees despite the enormous burden which this would impose upon the rates.[114] At the same time the Board petitioned the Home Secretary for an amendment of the original Act of 1875 which would define the terms on which compensation should be made, so that the owner would only receive the value of the property in relation to its condition as hovels unfit for human habitation.[115] The existing compensation regulations, established in 1875, were described at this time as:

A premium to dishonest men. A man had simply to neglect his property...to extract as much money out of it as possible, and do nothing in return, and the result would be that his property would be presented as an insanitary property.[116]

The Board also asked for power to provide alternative sites elsewhere in London so that they might sell the cleared land at a more remunerative rate for commercial purposes and provide land for housing where it was cheaper to buy; and this idea for dispersal was one also favoured by *The Builder*.[117] Finally, the Board requested a simplification of the procedure, which was patently necessary since the so-called safeguards of 1875 proved a great hindrance to effective action in practice.

In addition to the machinery, there were problems connected with the rehousing policy set out in the Act of 1875. After a debate in the House of Lords on the housing situation, *The Builder* mentioned the fears which must have been in many minds concerning the densities which were achieved in the new buildings. Was it a good thing to replace the rookeries and slums with housing at an equal or even greater density? Socially, of course, perhaps it might well be argued that it was so, because the system provided the maximum accommodation; but no one could prove that high density interpreted as rookery or model tenements was really healthy: '... if the density remains the same, an element of anxiety still remains'.[118]

The Cross Act of 1879[119] was passed to give some effect to these complaints. The arbitrator was now specifically instructed to assess the compensation for property, which had previously been regarded as a nuisance, on its value after the cost of the removal of the nuisance had been deducted. The confirming

authority was also allowed to permit accommodation to be provided on alternative sites, and there were certain minor alterations in the procedure of the Act.

At the same time, the Torrens Act was amended,[120] for, like the Cross Act, it had proved unpopular in operation, especially as it did not make any provision for compensation. The authorities, too, found it difficult to take effective action in relation to such a small scale unit as a single house, and the Westminster District Board, for example, looking for a plausible excuse, claimed that the whole Act was too complex and for this reason they had not taken any action.[121] The amending Act made provision for compensation to the owner, and set up machinery for arbitration very similar to that provided under the 1875 Cross Act. In the case of Torrens' Act, of course, the executant authorities were the vestries and district boards, responsible to the Local Government Board in place of the Secretary of State. The Act also restored the powers to rebuild and maintain property acquired by the local authorities and it gave them powers to borrow money, and levy a rate for this purpose, thus restoring the second part of the original Bill proposed by Torrens in 1868.

These amendments concluded the legislation for the decade, and before considering subsequent developments it is necessary to trace the social and architectural implications of this series of Acts.

6.1   *Tenement housing at the Whitechapel Improvement Scheme*

6

The Indian summer of private enterprise

The events of 1875 were the first real steps towards a slum clearance policy and the establishment of a practical code for house builders. One should not expect rapid results from such innovations, particularly in an age which was so jealous of personal liberty and so suspicious of governmental interference, whether in the guise of the local authority or of the central administration itself. If we try to understand these fears and at the same time to realise the high, idealistic, motives of those involved in formulating the slum clearance and house building policies, then we can perhaps understand their reticence at over much interference and their sincere desire that slum clearance should not merely mean additional hardship for the poor. Their measures seem surprisingly obtuse to us because of these factors and since they were not radical enough, the outcome was a half-hearted slum clearance programme which continued to encourage the besetting sins of selfishness and inactivity, thus retarding the useful work suggested by the reformers and indeed by parliament.

As a result of the legislation reviewed in the last chapter there was, after 1875, a revival of interest in housing problems and several new organisations were founded, while at the same time some of the older ones seemed to take on a new lease of life. Some of the work was a direct result of the new measures, in other cases it was triggered off by the revival of interest presented by the endless discussions which surrounded each new scheme and the policy which the Metropolitan Board attempted to follow. Whatever the reasons, the years between 1875 and 1890 were the last during which private enterprise reigned supreme as the housing agency for the poor.

Architectural and spatial solutions under the 1875 Act

During the fourteen years that still remained of its life after 1875, the Metropolitan Board of Works completed sixteen schemes under the 1875 Act, displacing altogether 22,868 people.[1] The Board cleared over 42 acres of slum property, which meant that the original gross density had averaged about 540 people per acre, and the sites all consisted of a tangled mass of back streets and courts where there was little light and no ventilation, great overcrowding and even greater privation. The 1875 Act required, as we have seen, that the Board should buy entire areas, clear them of building and then sell this cleared land for the purposes of housing; it also imposed conditions upon the purchaser, who was required to provide accommodation for the same number of people as were displaced, in theory so that the poor did not suffer further privation because of increased overcrowding. Although this provision was later modified, on the whole the Board was able to ensure that the housing agencies provided more accommodation than had previously existed, and the societies and companies who actually built the housing were often able to improve still further on

these figures. They were legally bound by the Board to rehouse 23,188 people, and in the sixteen schemes on the same 42 acres they in fact rehoused 27,780 people, increasing the density from the previously existing 540 to about 660 people per acre. The Board had considerable difficulty in disposing of the sites and several years elapsed before they were all sold, and it only eventually succeeded at an enormous loss to itself, amounting to £1,323,415.[2]

Who, then, were the people who built the new dwellings, and what kind of buildings did they put up to replace the slums and rookeries? A large proportion of the land went to the Peabody Trustees who took the initative and made an offer for a group of sites at a time when the Metropolitan Board was unable to sell any of the land; in these circumstances the Trustees were able to name a price which was convenient to them, and the Board felt obliged to accept despite the financial losses involved.[3] The Trustees bought seven sites in their entirety and built all the required dwellings,[4] and they built on part of two others;[5] so that their contribution was the largest of any one organisation. The Improved Industrial Dwellings Company built on only three sites,[6] which at first sight might seem strange since they were so large an organisation; but it must be remembered that this land, even at the price for which it was eventually sold, did not allow any builder to make much profit out of the buildings he might erect. The Peabody Trustees were in a unique position as a large private trust, and were really the only organisation who could afford to buy at the price they paid; and they practised, therefore, a kind of subsidisation of the state; others were less able to do this since they were obliged to make a reasonable profit. The only other important organisations to take up land were both new, the East End Dwellings Company,[7] and the Rothschild family;[8] the remaining sites, usually in small portions, were bought by individuals, and their contribution was less important from the planner's point of view because they were rarely able to practise large scale spatial organisation.

The re-development of the land was planned partly by the Metropolitan Board, who undertook such street works as might be necessary before attempting to sell the land, and partly by the new owner of the site. The positioning of the dwellings was thus often predetermined by the Board before the land was sold, and the subsequent owner in any case was obliged to obtain the consent of the Board for any alternative layout. It is, therefore, incorrect to ascribe the housing policy in central areas, during the eighties particularly, entirely to the organisations who erected the buildings: the principle of high density was laid upon them as an obligation by virtue of the law. But, at the same time, they seemed to regard it as their moral duty to provide the maximum accommodation in an attempt to ease the acute problem of overcrowding, and there was therefore no real issue of force: the Trustees and the other Companies acceded willingly to the require-ments of the law. In view of the pressure on housing in central London it is difficult to see what alternative solution might have been adopted in principle, but in practice the rigid rehousing requirements of 1875 often required modification to suit special local circumstances, and this was realised in the amending Act of 1879 which released the Board from the strin-gencies of rehousing all those displaced upon the same site.

The best example of an actual housing layout which was beyond the control of the new owner was at Great Wild Street (now Wild Street; it is off Drury Lane) where the one-and-a-half acre site was originally almost completely built over and 1,903 people were displaced when it was cleared. The Board required 1,936 people to be accommodated in new buildings, despite the fact that the site was to be reduced in order to increase the width of two adjacent streets. In fact, the Peabody Trustees were only able to cram 1,620 people into their new blocks, despite increasing the height of the buildings to six storeys. It had become in this instance a physical impossibility to fulfil the requirements imposed by the Board, and indeed those of the law as it existed when the provisional order for the scheme was confirmed by Act of Parlia-ment.[9] The buildings proved unhealthy, unfortunately for the Trustees, and they were heavily criticised by the Royal Commission in 1885; but when such a redevelop-ment as this is criticised today the pressure which had been brought to bear upon the architect should not be forgotten.[10]

The Great Wild Street development, then, was an exceptional case, since the final density of the new buildings was about 1,080 persons per acre; and if one required a more typical example of an improve-ment scheme under the Cross Act it would be wiser to look at Old Pye Street – behind the new Victoria Street – where the density was slightly more than 600; or Bedfordbury, behind Charing Cross Hospital, where it was 720 people per acre.[11] Both schemes were built just after 1880, and they well illustrate how Darbishire, the Trustee's architect, set about developing such a site. The Old Pye Street site was the larger, but it was divided into two parts. The principle area he laid out with tall, six storey blocks, sited around a central open square of ample propor-tions. One of the sides was extended beyond the square because of the exigencies of the site, but other-wise it was a typical Peabody Estate. The buildings were high, almost the highest ever built by the Trustees, but there was not an unnecessary sense of overbearing enclosure, and the square was open at three of the angles so that there was always good ventilation. It should be noticed that the whole site was laid out with standard Peabody blocks, worked out over the years to provide the most economical accommodation; these were capable of slight ex-pansion or contraction to suit most sites, and there

was only one point at which a specially designed block proved necessary. The smaller site was not capable of this treatment because it was very much more constricted, but here again the development consisted basically of a single 'unit', this time linked together at the angles to save space, making a tight little three-sided court, to which was added a fourth block, smaller than the other three but nevertheless based upon another standard pattern. The site was completed with a diminutive version of the first type, incongruously squashed into the last remaining corner.

Darbishire began with a series of preconceived. designs for individual buildings which he knew could be built for a certain sum of money; these units were capable of modification, they could be linked to one another or arranged separately, depending upon the site; and they could be made four, five or even six storeys in height. It was thus only necessary to juggle ingeniously with a series of standard blocks until the required accommodation was obtained; and so long as it was unnecessary to build more than an occasional special block, it was merely a matter of simple arith-metic to equate the amount of accommodation neces-sary to produce the required return with the known cost of building; and it was by this means that the Trustees had first arrived at the price they could afford to pay for the cleared sites. So long as the site was rectangular and large, the principle worked well; but when they were small or irregular there were at once difficulties and problems which Darbishire seems to have been unwilling to solve. The sites used by the Peabody Trustees may not always have been chosen to suit the building, although the Trustees preferred large, regular, rectangular plots; but neither were the buildings really designed specifically for the sites.

On the whole, the Trustees seemed to strive for a spatial standard applicable to all their schemes: they were always unwilling to make complete en-closures, or to design long rows of continuous blocks separated by spaces little better than areas. Their concept of the tenement block based on staircase access did not lead to continuous extension, nor did it lend itself to complicated corner planning, and all these features tended to distinguish Peabody buildings from other contemporary work.

The second typical site, the Bedfordbury estate, was a mere acre in extent, and it is a good example of the Trust's treatment of a small site, on which it was not possible to plan according to their accepted principle. Most other housing agencies would have chosen to build a long single block running the length of the site; Darbishire, preferring as always the smaller detached unit, placed his blocks at right angles to the street, with a series of small courts open to it, and only at one point did he break away from his usual pattern and design a corner block.

The Peabody principle, then, on both large and small sites, was to arrange a series of individual blocks in the most economical pattern; neither Darbishire nor the Trustees seem to have conceived the problem as one essentially of the street façade, and in this particular sense they were not successful as comprehensive town planners. But their sites were usually open and free from hidden courts, and there were often a series of related spaces rather than one single court, which helped to break down the scale of the estate into more manageable proportions. If there was a central space it was usually very large and sometimes of sufficient size to permit the planting of trees.

These were the kind of buildings which replaced the rookeries on a large number of sites; they were, on the whole, typical of other Peabody developments outside the control of the Metropolitan Board, except for the occasional evidence of obligatory high density, so that it is true to say that the estates were considered completely satisfactory to the Trustees. On other cleared sites several companies worked together to provide the requisite accommodation. Two of these will suffice to show the alternative arrangements and approaches which were possible; the Whitechapel and Limehouse scheme, the first to be undertaken after the passing of the Act of 1875, and the Goulston Street and Flower and Dean Street scheme, near Commercial Street.

Two slum clearance schemes

The Whitechapel site was by no means easy to re-develop; the Great Eastern Railway divided it into two unequal portions with a continuously curving viaduct, and to the west lay the bulky buildings of the Royal Mint. The Board first reconstructed and extended Cartwright Street and also the portion of Glasshouse Street which was within the scheme; and then they proceeded to sell off the land, with what difficulty we have already seen. The whole portion to the east of the railway was bought by the Peabody Trustees and on it they built a series of nine blocks, very much after the manner already described. They were amongst the least rigidly laid out of the Trustees' estates and their appearance was dignified and not unpleasant. These buildings were completed in 1880, and four years later the Board sold two more sites on the western site of the railway, one to Mr Bond, the other to Mr Rothschild.[12] Bond purchased the long narrow site between the newly formed Cartwright Street and the Mint, for the recently formed East End Dwellings Company. The site offered no alternative but to build a long block facing the street, with an area between it and the back wall of the Royal Mint. Davis and Emmanuel were the architects, and later they designed several other similar buildings for the Company.[13] The Cartwright Street building had a plain five-storeyed brick façade facing the street, rising directly from the pavement, neat, simple and slightly more mellow than the work of other companies; the brick was warm red

6.2 *The Whitechapel Improvement Scheme: the site in 1875 before demolition*

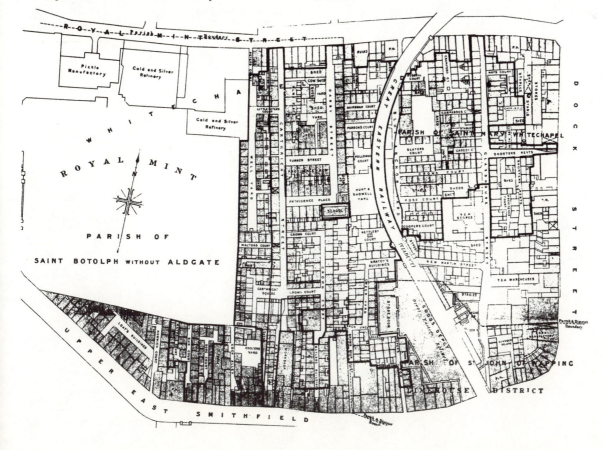

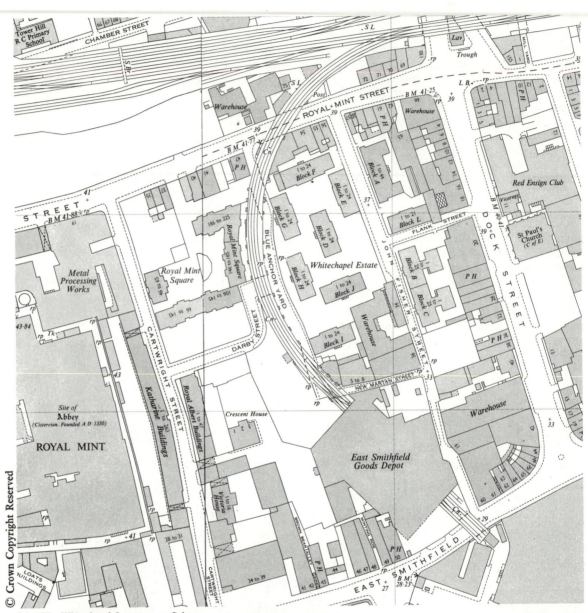

6.3 *The Whitechapel Improvement Scheme*

in colour and there were ornamental brick courses to take away the gaunt appearance of a plain wall. The entrances to the buildings were not from this street façade: a large archway led from the street to an area at the back, and from here stairs led up to cast iron external balconies, which ran the whole length of the building, creating an impressive and startling effect. There was little open space, but the architects wisely screened the small area from the street so that it formed a safe play space for children.

On the opposite side of Cartwright Street, Rothschild built a five storey block, based upon the staircase access system, but although the block again abutted the pavement, all the entrances were from the street. The block made extensive use of heavy terra cotta ornament and it was altogether much less pleasing in appearance than Katharine Buildings on the opposite side of the street. The housing work on the site was completed by another private development, Royal Mint Square, a simple three sided court with principal access from Royal Mint Street to the north. The scheme has curious architectural qualities, it was much ornamented with porches and bay windows; there is even an occasional coarsely detailed Ionic column! The building was a very poor example of private housing development.

The remaining portions of the site were sold for commercial development, one developer arranging with the Board to provide alternative accommodation elsewhere, and another portion of the site was found to have been a churchyard at one period, although subsequently built over, and the Board required that this should remain unbuilt on for ever.[14]

The site therefore represented an architectural pastiche, rather irregularly developed over a considerable period and with noticeable lack of relation and harmony between the several developments. The next scheme had fewer peculiarities about the existing site conditions, and development was therefore more regular. The Goulston Street area, which was separate from Flower and Dean Street, was small and need not detain us; on either side of the junction with Wentworth Street were five-storeyed blocks by the Wentworth Dwelling Company[15] and further down Goulston Street was another block at the junction of New Goulston Street, this time built privately. The Flower and Dean Street area gives a much better idea of a concerted and regular housing development when a redevelopment scheme involved complete clearance. The first site to be developed was in Wentworth Street, at the Commercial Street end, where E. J. Hoole designed College Buildings, in conjunction with Toynbee Hall, in 1885.[16] They were amongst the most original in appearance at this time, exhibiting Gothic tendencies, with plenty of detailing in terra cotta, and they were deliberately different in character in order to attract tenants. The next site was sold to the East End Dwellings Company, this was at the junction of the newly formed Lolesworth Street with

6.4 *The Flower and Dean Street Improvement Scheme; the site in 1875 before demolition and the redeveloped site*

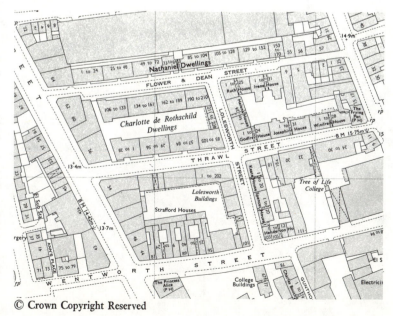

Thrawl Street. The Company built a trim 'L' shaped brick block, Lolesworth Buildings, designed by Davis and Emmanuel, again in a much less forbidding style than other contemporary work. In 1889 they obtained a further site in Wentworth Street, opposite College Buildings, and there they added Strafford House, similar in design, externally, to the earlier Lolesworth Buildings. The largest site, between Flower and Dean Street and Thrawl Street was taken by Rothschild for his 4% Industrial Dwellings Company, founded originally to provide homes for Jewish Artizans. This site presents the most intensive development in the area. N. S. Joseph, the architect for the scheme which was known as Charlotte de Rothschild Dwellings, built all round his site on the three available sides, the fourth being occupied by existing buildings facing onto Commercial Street which did not form part of the clearance area. The site was therefore almost totally enclosed, building being continuous on three sides around a central court which was below street level. The only break was where the buildings stopped off short of the older development facing Commercial Street, and at this point on either side of the court there were ornamental archways and gates allowing access from Thrawl Street and Flower and Dean Street, presumably to admit carts and vehicles, since it was possible for pedestrians to get into the court by any of the entrances to the public staircases. The two parallel blocks had staircase access in the normal way, but the connecting block facing Loles-

worth Street had balconies on the courtyard side. The buildings had simple regular façades facing the street,

6.5   *The Flower and Dean Street Improvement Scheme*

five storeys high above a semi-basement, and their character was reminiscent of the East End Dwellings Company scheme, although a little more mechanical and less human in appearance. From the courtyard the buildings rose to six storeys with a lower ground level than the surrounding streets, and the effect was of huge towering cliffs, divided by a long, narrow concrete yard. There was no sense of space or progression because of the continuous 'U' shaped building, and the general effect was of spatial finality, oppressive and overpowering, much more so than in the contemporary Peabody work with its sterner character, but less continuous building, and greater sense of spatial planning and of spaces continuing beyond the buildings.

In 1892 the 4% Industrial Dwellings Company bought further land, opposite Charlotte de Rothschild Dwellings in Flower and Dean Street; it was not part of the clearance area, but on it they built an additional block, Nathaniel Dwellings, which was similar in design but slightly more ornate in character. There was only the one very long and continuous building facing the street in this later scheme.

The redevelopment of the area was completed by the housing development on the east side of Lolesworth Street, between Flower and Dean Street and Thrawl Street. This was again not part of the improvement area, but it was an integral part of the spatial planning and as it completed a large area of housing development it is therefore right to include it here. The land was purchased by Abraham and Wolf Davis who themselves designed and built in 1897 a series of 'houses' based upon the staircase access principle. Following the example set by other adjacent developers, perhaps, they built continuously around the three available sides of the site; but their planning was very clumsy, with innumerable set-backs and re-entrant angles at the rear, which made a courtyard – already dark and cavernous – quite squalid.

Having described the way in which the area was redeveloped, it is now possible to judge it as a piece of town planning concerned entirely with housing since such a large number of adjacent properties were here entirely built to provide dwellings in a variety of tenement forms. If one stands in Wentworth Street looking north down Lolesworth Street, all the buildings in view except the first immediately to the right, consist of housing; tall cliffs of brick, rising vertically from the pavement, broken only by intersecting streets, devoid of open space or greenery. The architecture for the most part is simple and direct, free from eclectic detailing, and inoffensive if not pleasing. There is too much building, however; the streets are narrow and the effect is oppressive; there is no hint of the spaces which lie behind these great cliffs because the façades are unbroken; they greedily edge the street for the maximum possible distance, and as greedily they turn the corners. Those who care to penetrate behind the street façade find only bleak areas or badly proportioned alleys, certainly not useful or attractive open space. And this was the kind of development that commercial philanthropy was obliged to undertake, first because of the legal requirements of the Metropolitan Board, secondly because of the cost of land and building, and thirdly because of the urgent need to provide as many dwellings as possible in order to ease the acute overcrowding problem. It was as an alternative to this kind of environment that Ebenezer Howard a few years later presented his vision of the Garden City, but Howard chose to turn his back upon the existing city and built anew elsewhere: until it was possible to move industry outside the great towns, or to permit even the very poor to commute, this kind of high density central area development remained inevitable.

Liverpool and the 1875 Act

Outside London there was not a great deal of activity as a result of the new Act, probably because the structure of local government was still too liable to the pressures of reactionary forces. It is true that frequently there was not the same degree of urgency and the problems were never of the same magnitude as in the Metropolis, but slum clearance was none the less very necessary in many towns and the provisions of the Act might have attracted more interest had not the example of its practical implementation in London been so disastrous. Few towns sought to invoke its powers, fewer still actually brought schemes to fruition.

With typical Liverpudlian zeal the corporation decided very quickly after the passing of the Act to apply it to the Nash Grove district, and thus continue a policy of clearance begun under the 1864 Liverpool Sanitary Amendment Act which had so far had very limited success owing to the profiteering of the local speculative builders.[17] J. J. Clarke, the historian of housing law, points out that while there was a great demand for houses, there were few dispossessed people who could afford the rents of new ones and as a result some of those were actually unoccupied.[18]

In Liverpool, progress was equally as slow as in London. The Nash Grove site was cleared and offered for sale, but to no effect; no builder would accept the responsibility of rehousing the same numbers as had been displaced, in the tight terrace layout proposed by the Engineer. Consequently in 1879 the council decided to seek a modification of the rehousing figures whereby the only limitation imposed upon the developer would be those contained in the Liverpool Bye-laws and Building Act. It was estimated that this would allow accommodation for 920 people instead of 1,100.[19]

The Local Government Board asked the corporation to reconsider this modification but this they seemed unwilling to do. Terrace houses, they said, were very unpopular with the working classes, and the Health Committee wished to resort to the lower figure in order to give greater freedom. They also pointed out that speculative building had already provided nearly 10,000 houses since the first official representation on the Nash Grove scheme over four years ago – and indeed a correspondent of the *Liverpool Daily Post* had already called for some restraint on cottage building in the suburbs, because building had exceeded the demand.[20] The corporation went further in its demands; the land was objectionable for housing purposes and it was difficult to find buyers: it would be better if they were allowed to sell it on the open market, thus recovering the loss made on its purchase and provide land for housing elsewhere, as was by that time permitted in new schemes, by virtue of the amending statute of 1879.[21]

The Local Government Board must have remained adamant for the Health Committee later in 1880 recommended the council to apply for permission to have dwellings erected on the site together with a number of shops, and at the same time, to complicate matters, another committee was becoming interested in the site as one suitable for a new market![22]

Finally, in May 1883, the Council agreed, after a lengthy and by no means unanimous discussion, that they should seek permission to build and retain in their own ownership a high density scheme for the original site based on a design which had been prepared by the City Engineer.[23] The main objections to this proposal appear to have been concerned rather with the density of the development than with the ethics of corporation initiative. A councillor reminded the

members that at Birkenhead a high density scheme had been built many years ago and it was now a disgrace and an acknowledged failure; were they, with this knowledge, to repeat the same mistake? But in answer it was pointed out that the Birkenhead venture had been private speculation: the faults were mainly due to sanitary problems which could be controlled much more easily by a vigilant local authority. This point seemed to carry the day and the council agreed to seek the required permission.

The Local Government Board this time agreed to the council's proposals, except for their request to retain ownership of the dwellings beyond the ten year period. It was stipulated that the council should sell the buildings at such times as the Board should think fit, but that they should never be compelled to sell at a loss. The council agreed, and went out to tender, nearly eight years after initiating the clearance of the site.

In October, 1885, almost exactly ten years after the area had been designated, Sir Richard Cross officially opened the Victoria Buildings, Nash Grove.[24] The buildings had been designed by Clement Dunscombe, the City Engineer, and they provided accommodation for 271 families in tenements of from one to three rooms arranged in five storey blocks around a central court. The most remarkable feature about the scheme, especially by contrast with the corporation's previous attempt at housing, St. Martin's Cottages, was the

6.6a *Victoria Buildings, Liverpool, 1885. Clement Dunscombe architect; built by the corporation*

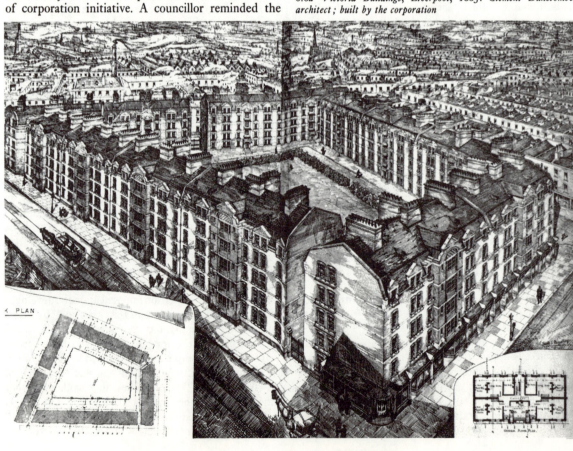

large and spacious central court, with its broad foot-walks, 15 feet wide carriageways and central playground surrounded by shrubs:

In judging the financial result of this scheme it has to be borne in mind that the object of the Corporation was not to cover this site to its full capacity with dwellings, but to erect buildings of the best class for their purpose and of the highest sanitary standard, thus affording an example to be followed in the future by private enterprise, while at the same time, providing a large unbuilt-upon space in this densely-populated district.[25]

The buildings were of Liverpool grey common bricks with pressed reds for window reveals and terra cotta detailing for the doorways and dormers. The effect was dignified, almost grand; Dunscombe had obviously striven hard to avoid the barrack-like quality which usually characterised tenement buildings by using every opportunity to achieve modelling and interesting detail in the lengthy façades. The actual height was masked somewhat by the use of an attic floor, set into a mansard roof, which was in many ways a considerable improvement upon the Peabody and Improved Industrial Dwellings standard designs. But it was obviously a 'designed' scheme in a sense that others rarely were; there was a care about detail which would have no place in standardised blocks repeated *ad nauseam* on each fresh site. The Victoria Buildings, therefore, stand between the Model Dwellings of S.I.C.L.C. or the Metropolitan Association, which were each consciously designed for their site, and the new tradition which was to come with the establish-

ment of the London County Council, largely inspired aesthetically by the school of design characterised by Norman Shaw and Philip Webb. Victoria Buildings, then, were in several ways a landmark, and it is well that they have been modernised and restored, for they have a place in the history both of housing architecture and the development of social responsibility.[26]

Birmingham and the rise of Joseph Chamberlain

Only one other town deserves mention at this point and that is Birmingham, where the efficacy of good local government was demonstrated for the first time in this country, largely due to the energy and drive of one man.

During the middle decades of the nineteenth century Birmingham was a typically lethargic provincial city; it took little action to improve the standards of drainage or the supply of water, and altogether the corporation evaded the kind of work which other northern cities, such as Liverpool or even Manchester, had undertaken. Birmingham was more typical of the large provincial town than either of these, however, for inactivity was more characteristic than a relish for reform; but Birmingham was in addition an important centre, rapidly developing the nature of a second metropolis, so its problems were more heavily underlined because they were larger.[27] There was one curiously wise provision in existence at the time of the 1844–5 Royal Commission on the Health of Towns which fixed the minimum width of streets at 42 feet. One witness reported that:

6.6b *Victoria Buildings, Liverpool*

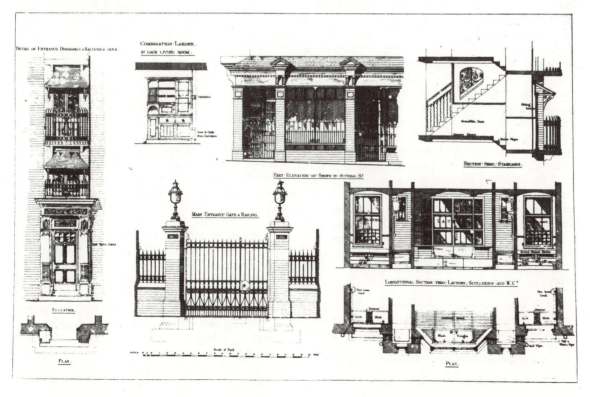

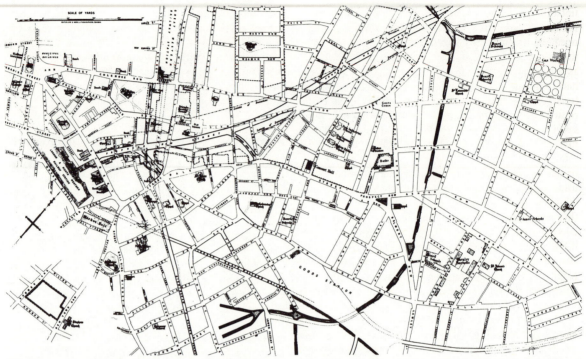

There are comparatively few narrow courts, back-houses being generally erected in square courts; some are well ventilated, others badly; most of them are approached by entries covered over, many of them are back to back; but there are not sufficient powers to enforce the cleansing of the courts...There are no cellar dwellings in the borough.[28]

Otherwise there was no mention of the kind of activity which took place elsewhere, and it was not until 1870 that the first lodging house was established.[29]

During that decade Joseph Chamberlain rose to power, and within the short time he was mayor, in the two and a half years after 1873, Birmingham made up for years of sloth in a rapid series of reforms which made the town, as well as Chamberlain, famous in progressive circles.[30] On his recommendation the council purchased the local gas company in 1874, and the following year they acquired the water company. New drainage schemes were started, and the bye-laws were strengthened in 1876 to bring them into conformity with the new model series, so that in a relatively short time the town had made up the leeway, and in some ways had overtaken the progress of other towns. Then, in July 1875, Chamberlain initiated the great Improvement Scheme which he proposed to carry through with the assistance of the new Artizans' and Labourers' Dwellings Act.[31] He subscribed to the school of thought which believed that the poor were the victims of circumstance:

Unless we go to the root of the evil, unless we deal with the dwellings themselves, unless we improve some of these dwellings off the face of creation, our arduous work will be useless. As for the labour of the minister of religion, the schoolmaster and the philanthropist, it will be thrown away.[32]

When the Local Government Board inquiry took

6.6c *The site of the new Corporation Street, Birmingham. One of the most successful late nineteenth-century town improvement schemes linked with slum clearance*

place, in the course of obtaining permission to make the required improvements, the case for the corporation was presented not by a retained lawyer but by the mayor himself, by Chamberlain; eventually he won approval for the scheme, and it was agreed by Parliament in August 1876. As a result Corporation Street was built, a wide and splendid thoroughfare, flanked on either side by fine shops and offices. Behind it, the slums were renovated and made more healthy by careful demolition and alteration. The scheme was unlike those in London either under the 1872 Street Improvements Act or the 1875 Act because it involved no rehousing. However, it did involve the construction of a new street of major importance, and this indeed was a sound idea, for it made the work financially successful because it encouraged prestige development which paid for the slum clearance. It was also an astute piece of planning, since it provided for the new street to run outwards from the centre of the city, thus ensuring its continued popularity for shops and business premises, increasing its desirability, and therefore its rateable value. All these things Chamberlain realised were essential to the ultimate success of the project but in addition he persuaded the Council that the sites should be leased on a 75 year basis so that eventually the Corporation would become the sole owners of the valuable property as well as of the land.

In certain respects, the scheme was similar to that started at Glasgow a few years previously, since the Corporation possessed the power of selection and was not obliged to purchase all the property included in the designated area. Furthermore, it was not obliged to provide any additional housing accommodation. Chamberlain maintained that there was no need to build housing in central areas since there was more than an adequate provision in the suburbs as a result of speculative developments and the same had been true at Glasgow.[33] Neither did the Corporation pursue a policy of complete clearance as was required in London but because the scheme was a special improvement as well as a slum clearance measure he was able to select badly placed houses for total demolition whilst permitting others to remain, provided they were altered. The Corporation never undertook any building work itself, and the only site which was set aside for dwellings was not sold for this purpose and eventually it was used for a school. Chamberlain believed that had the Corporation built, it would have upset private enterprise house building, and in consequence he disapproved of the action taken at Liverpool, although he supported Glasgow Corporation's limited building programme, restricted to lodging houses.[34]

Chamberlain's work at Birmingham showed very clearly that a provincial town, with its special problems involving central area redevelopment and slum clearance, could utilise the new Act to advantage, although Chamberlain did avoid most astutely the clauses about rehousing which upset the Metropolitan Board in London. Few towns possessed a citizen of the calibre of Chamberlain, however, so the Birmingham scheme remained a solitary example of vigorous civic activity. It is interesting to note that after the Corporation had taken the initiative the social conscience of the town seemed to reawaken, and public interest in housing and social problems began to increase. By this time, too, George Cadbury had moved his factory from central Birmingham into the country outside, where he began to create a new village for his workers which helped to revolutionise the traditional view of industrial and urban problems, because it showed that the pressures upon the centre of towns could sensibly be dissipated to the advantage of workers and management alike.

Each city possessed its own individuality so far as working class housing was concerned. Birmingham was exceptional in its concerted civic activity, and Liverpool equally for its long history of involvement. Elsewhere it was usually much more depressing. Manchester, for example, saw no activity until just before 1820 when a block of balcony access flats, known as Victoria Square, was built at Ancoats.[35]

The later companies: I

The Artizans Dwellings Act eventually provided scope for a considerable amount of new housing in the central part of London, because in reality it subsidised the housing companies by selling them land at an artificially low price. In fact it brought to life again a housing movement which had been declining quite

rapidly after 1870. Naturally, the Metropolitan Board became increasingly diffident about undertaking new schemes, first because of the great losses involved, but also because of the lengthy proceedings, lasting many years in most cases, which were necessary to complete a scheme once started. Its activities in this direction noticeably lessened during the eighties and there was consequently less land available at reduced prices for the various agencies to use. The effect of this was delayed because of the slow procedure under the Act; a scheme begun in 1876, for example, might still have building work in progress in 1890. It is clear, however, that during the penultimate decade of the century the rate of tenement building once again was waning. The Peabody Trustees appear at first sight to be more active than ever before between 1880 and 1885, but this activity was concerned exclusively with the sites obtained from the Metropolitan Board; after 1885 they did not build again in central London for nearly twenty years and after that long interval there was a marked change in their policy, for by that time they were no longer a major housing agency.[36] The Improved Industrial Dwellings Company remained modestly active, but its progress in later years was aided by gifts of land while developments begun on land purchased on the open market tended to be outside the central area.[37] It is true to say, then, that the two most vital forces in the housing movement between 1860 and 1885 had lost their real sense of purpose before about 1890. They were both criticised by the Royal Commission in 1885 because they housed a particular class which was not the poorest, and it was more than ever clear that the problems of this lowest class were outside the scope of this sort of commercial philanthropy.[38]

It is surprising, therefore, to find at this period a series of new dwelling companies; smaller, indeed, than the great organisations founded in the third quarter of the century, but nevertheless vital and prospering, making a useful contribution to the housing movement, as we have already seen in connection with the two clearance sites already discussed.

They fall into two distinguishable groups, the first consisting of those at work before 1880 and the second, those which were founded during the last twenty years of the century. The earliest of the new companies in the first group was the Victoria Dwellings Association; its first building, opened in 1877, was situated at Battersea Park and was designed by Charles Barry.[39] Barry planned the blocks around a court 84 ft. by 52 ft., and since the buildings were four storeys in height, he was criticised for his tight layout. Two classes of tenements were provided; the first, for artizans, were self-contained and mainly of three rooms; the second, for labourers, were either single or double rooms which were associated, three tenements sharing a lavatory. Barry planned the artizans' dwellings on the corridor principle and the labourers' with gallery access; his general internal arrangement of both types was approved by *The Builder*.[40] This reflected the growing body of opinion which supported a reduction in the standard of accommodation if this brought 'model dwellings' within the reach of poorer people. At the opening by Lord Beaconsfield, John Walter, M.P. – the editor of *The Times* – spoke about housing generally and his views were not without interest since they showed the general tendency at this time:

Instead of spreading London out, you must build upwards – you must raise it to the clouds. There is no other way of meeting the difficulty, for, in spite of all the poetry attached to suburban homes, of which you have an example at Penge, and in spite of cheap railway fares, it is an undeniable fact that the great mass of metropolitan poor, artisans and labourers, must live near their work; it may be a most disagreeable fact to contemplate, but that is the only way to provide for it.[41]

At first the buildings were not very popular since they were outside the immediate central area, and separated from it by the river; initially there was a toll to pay in order to cross the bridges, but after this was removed the buildings seem to have been more successful.[42] They were followed two years later by a more ambitious scheme, Beaconsfield Buildings in Stroud Vale, Islington, for which Barry was again the

architect. The first two blocks were finished by May 1879 and they were already accommodating 1,100 people, when R. A. Cross visited the site to lay the foundation of another block for a further 900 people.[43] There was also a third estate at Southwark, known as Stanhope Buildings.[44]

Another company building exclusively in one part of London, the South London Dwellings Company, completed a building at the junction of Kennington Road and Lambeth Road in 1879, which contained 200 tenements.[45] There were shops on the ground floor, four storeys of dwellings above them, and on the top were laundries and drying rooms; the tenements varied in size from two to four rooms, and in the angle between the two blocks was a coffee room. The buildings were designed by Elijah Hoole and he was also responsible for a subsequent addition consisting of two ranges of cottages built around a central quadrangle, formed between the earlier tenement blocks and the new buildings, which was laid out as a recreation ground.[46] Hoole built in red brick and seemed to favour gothic idioms rather than classical; some of his ideas no doubt sprung from his friendship with Octavia Hill, and indeed in later years he built several cottage schemes for her.[47] The first, and perhaps the most notable, was at Red Cross Street, Southwark,

6.7   *Beaconsfield Building, Islington*

BEACONSFIELD BUILDINGS, NEW MODEL DWELLINGS, STROUD-VALE, ISLINGTON.

6.8   *South Lambeth Dwellings, Lambeth Road, 1881. E. J. Hoole architect ; built by the South London Dwelling Company*

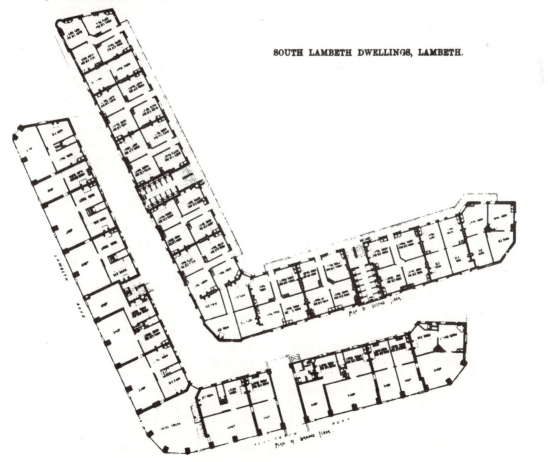

SOUTH LAMBETH DWELLINGS, LAMBETH.

6.9   *Cottages in Little Suffolk Street, Southwark, 1889. E. J. Hoole architect; one of the schemes managed by Octavia Hill*

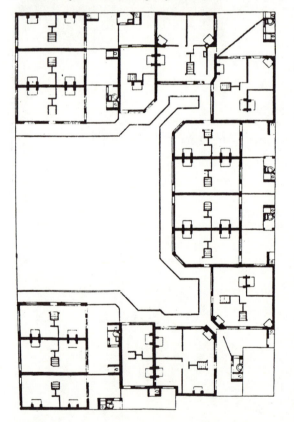

completed in 1888; it consisted of a group of cottages, again overlooking a garden, with a small community hall[48] attached to them. He designed another cottage scheme at Little Suffolk Street, in the Elizabethan style, which Octavia Hill managed, although she did not herself build it;[49] and for some dwellings he built rather earlier for the Chelsea Park Dwellings Company he had made an effort 'by adopting a rural style, to avoid the barrack-like appearance too common in industrial dwellings'.[50] This scheme, situated in King's Road, was again designed around a courtyard, with the existing trees preserved to form a garden. There were two four-storeyed blocks, the first had shops on the ground floor with flats attached to them on the floor above, and then two floors of tenements with one to four rooms; the second block which was parallel with the first had two and three roomed tenements on all floors. Between them was a two-storey link containing more tenements, so that altogether there was accommodation for sixty families arranged around three sides of the garden.

There were, of course, many other agencies active in the years following 1875 and it would be difficult to list all their works; it would also be of little assistance to this discussion since there were no other major societies or companies of significance. Of the minor ones, mention should be made of the National Dwellings Society who built Chichester Houses and Derby Buildings during 1877, both situated near Eastern Street between Shoreditch High Street and Old Street.[51] In the following decade, the City and Central Dwellings Company built a block of artizan tenements of 'warehouse' appearance at Seward Street, near Goswell Road in 1885.[52] The traditional character of the model dwellings seemed to die hard.

An unusual venture was that by the City Commissioners of Sewers, who purchased and cleared a site in Petticoat Square in 1884, and on it they built five blocks of dwellings each five storeys high.[53] Three of the blocks had shops on the ground floor with living accommodation attached; and the floors above, together with the whole of the two remaining blocks, contained tenements of up to three rooms, approached by a system of staircases. All the tenements were associated, with two lavatories and a communal scullery on each floor; the architect was Colonel Haywood, the Commissioners' engineer.

6.10 *Artizans' Dwellings, Petticoat Square, built by the Commissioners of Sewers for the City of London, 1885. Colonel Haywood, Chief Engineer*

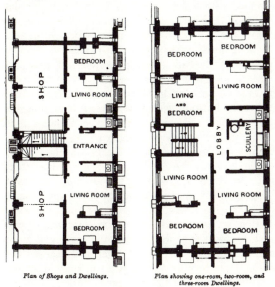

Plan of Shops and Dwellings.

Plan showing one-room, two-room, and three-room Dwellings.

renovations. It first turned its attention to the erection of new buildings in the sixties, when it built on part of Vauxhall Gardens;[57] then in 1879 came Murray Buildings, again at Vauxhall, containing 54 tenements, and at the same time it built a group of 20 cottages at 'the Ferry', Upper Clapton.[58] Model dwellings continued to be built by individuals, but the schemes were generally small and followed very much the pattern of

6.11a *Farringdon Buildings, Farringdon Road, 1874. Frederick Chancellor architect; built by the Metropolitan Association*

Of the older societies, the Metropolitan Association completed Farringdon Buildings in 1874,[54] and a block in Carrington Mews four years later, but these were its last ventures.[55] The Farringdon Road scheme was an important contribution to housing design, and it showed that the planning of model dwellings had not yet become stereotyped: Frederick Chancellor who designed it had evolved a new and more healthy version of the staircase access system, whereby the maximum ventilation was obtained, and it was a pity, therefore, that the association felt obliged to cram the buildings so close together that natural light was obscured to all the lower floors.[56] The other organisation which continued active work was the London Labourers' Dwellings Society, a branch of the Hastings Society, which had been set up ostensibly to conduct

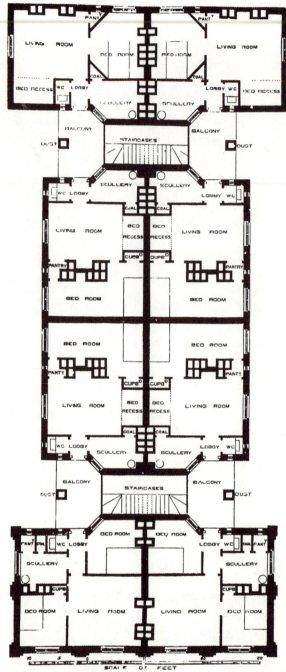

6.11b *Farringdon Buildings, plan*

previous decades.[59] In London, and some other large towns, the other interesting development was the growth of upper class interest in flatted dwellings and chambers after the French manner, largely because of high site values in central areas.[60] One of the best examples of this was the development around Victoria Street, that major new road running from Westminster Abbey to Victoria, cut through the slums between 1852 and 1871. Here there are several examples of tall rather ornate blocks of flats, such as Artillery Mansions built in 1885; Prince's Mansions, completed the following year, and in Caxton Street there are St Ermin's Mansions. Queen Anne's Mansions are now

demolished, they achieved enormous bulk, rising through twelve storeys to a total height of 100 ft.: 'the loftiest and ugliest of any similar structures in the metropolis'.[61] High density and grimness, therefore, were not the prerequisite of the poor by any means. Suburban development will shortly be mentioned in connection with the railways, its nature was invariably speculative, with the notable exceptions of the work of the Artizans' Company[62] and the Beckenham estate of the Metropolitan Association, but there were occasional organisations in this later period, too, which promoted house-building to a better standard than usual, such as The Real Property Investment Association which experimented with terrace house development in 1880–1 at Crownfield Road between Stratford and Leyton.[63] The chief advantage, of course, was that an architect was usually employed for organised developments of this nature. A slightly different association, the Bethnal Green House Property Association, which consisted of local tradespeople, was purchasing ruinous single storey property, of which there was a vast amount in that district, and replacing it with three-storeyed tenement buildings arranged with a more spacious layout wherever possible.[64] In the provinces, Manchester took a step which most other towns had taken many years before, and set up a dwellings company in 1882 as a result of reports which had brought to light existing bad conditions. The company started to build three-storeyed 'semi-detached cottages' at Holt Town, Ancoats;[65] but this kind of venture, as an innovation, seems to have been rare, and in other towns activity of this nature usually was the work of organisations set up in an earlier period of enthusiasm.

The implications of all this work were, I think, that the housing movement was not completely inactive even in the difficult years immediately following 1875. New ideas appeared in the work of existing societies, and a significant number of new small societies were formed, but the activity was now more diversified: particularly when it is realised that much of the new work took place in south and little in central London, which remained impregnable to the small societies, as indeed for the larger organisations until the Peabody Trustees broke down the Metropolitan Board. The societies and companies which continued building into the eighties showed signs of accepting some of the aesthetic changes which were taking place in the wider architectural field: there was greater emphasis upon the human qualities of design and a noticeable and novel attraction to the cottage and the rustic, ideas which were sometimes practicable in places where land could be obtained more cheaply, either through benevolent gifts, or because it was sufficiently far out of the central area to have little commercial value.

The later companies: II

After 1880 it was mainly to the Peabody Trustees that

STAIRCASE WINDOWS.   UPPER STAIRCASE WINDOWS AND CORNICE.

6.12   *A proposal in the 1850s for middle class flats*

the public looked for new housing developments, and in many ways they were not disappointed for the Trustees did an enormous amount of work between 1880 and 1885. But, in addition, a second group of important societies developed during the early years of the decade, this time once again concerned with central areas. At first glance this would seem entirely unexpected in the face of economic difficulties, but certainly not so in the light of the increasing evidence of the failure, on the part of authority and private enterprise alike, to deal with the problem of over-crowding, which both the Select Committee of 1881–2

and the subsequent Royal Commission found to be steadily worsening. There was, furthermore, a new generation of people eager to carry forward the social reforms first initiated by men of Lord Shaftesbury's age. There were, however, some quite important changes in attitude now, and the new housing agencies were seeking once again to put teeth into the movement.

On 1 November 1882, a meeting was held at St Jude's vicarage, Whitechapel, with the Rev S. H. Barnett in the chair, to consider the formation of a company to provide housing accommodation for the very poor in that part of London; and a little more than a year later, in February 1884, The East End Dwellings Company Limited was officially launched. Its first prospectus, issued the same month, made clear what its objectives were to be:

The main endeavour of the Company will be to provide for the poorest class of self-supporting labourers dwelling accommodation at the very cheapest rates compatible with realising a fair rate of interest upon the capital employed. Hitherto little or nothing of this kind has been done on a large scale, the buildings of the existing Companies and Associations being chiefly occupied by a class of industrial tenants more prosperous than those for whom this Company proposes to provide.

They are convinced, however, that, unless the enterprise can be made to pay a reasonable dividend to the shareholders, there is little chance of attracting into this kind of investment a sufficient amount of capital to enable this Company – or any other Companies which may follow in its wake – to extend their operations, and make any substantial contribution towards evolving the great problem of housing decently the poor of London.[66]

This, of course, was the problem which faced any organisation, other than one which was purely philanthropic, and it was an even greater problem to a company which set out to cater for a class with which all the existing companies had previously been unable to cope. The new company sought to do this by emulating the approach of Octavia Hill, although with one important difference: it chose from the outset to provide new buildings rather than to practice conversion. Its first venture was on the thin, difficult site bought from the Metropolitan Board at their Whitechapel clearance area. The company obviously tried very hard to achieve a satisfactory solution:

The plans were laid before the highest authorities, among those in personal touch with the poor. The prevailing ideas were that publicity should be courted, that the fittings should be of the simplest, in view of the destructive habits of the tenants, the buildings airy and wholesome, and the rents low.[67]

And this surely suggests that Octavia Hill had something to do with the final design for Katharine Build-

6.13 *Katharine Buildings, Cartwright Street, 1885, by the East End Dwellings Company. Davis and Emmanuel architects; their first venture on the Whitechapel Improvement site using a new minimum plan*

ings, which were built on the Whitechapel clearance site during 1885. The plan adopted was very reminiscent of that suggested by her during 1883, when she had recommended the adoption of flexible planning based upon single and double-roomed tenements, arranged so that a family might add or reduce its accommodation according to its needs. In order to achieve this she thought that it was unnecessary to carry plumbing into each dwelling, since her conception of a tenement building was of a communal 'core' surrounded by a series of rooms which might be related to one another in different ways according to circumstance.[68] And this, in fact, was the solution adopted by the Company. Katharine Buildings were designed as a long continuous block some 30 ft. deep and five storeys high with external balcony access at the back. Off these balconies were short corridors, around which were grouped 'nests' of rooms, as one writer aptly described them; each nest consisted of five rooms, four large and one small, and out of a total of 285 rooms more than 200 were intended to be let separately. There were three main staircases to the balconies and adjacent to each were situated the lavatories. Despite

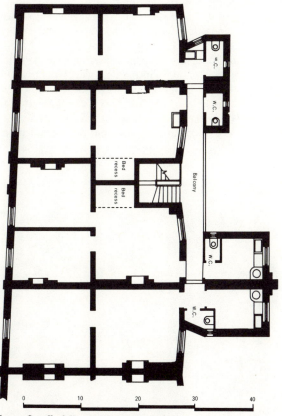

6.14   *Strafford House, Wentworth Street*

these economies the cost per room of these buildings was said to be greater than that of speculative housing in the suburbs; although it should not be forgotten that the standard of building was very much higher. The first part of the building was occupied in March 1885, but it does not seem that a large proportion of

the rooms was at first let singly, as originally intended; in April that year 167 rooms were occupied, and of these only 66 were let independently. It was also reported at the same time, that there was an enormous demand for the single rooms.[69] Henrietta Barnett, in her biography of her husband, Canon Barnett, comments on his great concern for the housing conditions in his parish and his own role in the foundation of the East End Dwellings Company. Katharine was named after Katharine Potter, the sister of Beatrix; she was then Mrs. Leonard Courtney and she it was who first undertook the important job of managing this block of dwellings.[70]

The Company's second venture, at Thrawl Street on the Flower and Dean Street clearance site, was very similar to the first scheme and was also designed by the same architects, Davis and Emmanuel. The only planning revision concerned the lavatories which were moved onto the balcony side of the building and placed at more frequent intervals, unrelated this time to the staircases. Lolesworth Buildings, as these were called, were opened on 1 April 1887.

Strafford Houses, which were built on an adjacent site in Wentworth Street three years later, showed a certain advancing standard, which was probably due to a decision on the part of the Company to build mixed dwellings, with a variety of types and standards of accommodation. This change in policy appears to have resulted from difficulties experienced in the management of blocks devoted exclusively to the very poor. The company had originally controlled their properties through a lady manager and a caretaker, with the assistance of other ladies, very much in the manner prescribed by Octavia Hill, but it was found necessary to have constant supervision in order to keep a new building in good order, despite its simplicity, and this might well have accounted for the decision to design composite blocks in which the very poor were mixed with a cleaner, more respectable class of tenant.[71]

On the ground floor of Strafford Houses were shops, with living accommodation arranged in the rear around small yards; and storage space provided in cellars beneath the shops. The block was of no great length and the architects provided only two staircases, each leading to a short open balcony on every floor; this time, however, the two balconies were not continuous. There were also no single room tenements; about two thirds were of two rooms, and the remainder of three. The major improvement upon previous practice was that each had its own separate scullery and lavatory in a small off-shoot on the opposite side of the balcony. The increased convenience was considerable, but it was achieved at the expense of good lighting to the main living rooms at the rear of the building.

Subsequent schemes showed a continued desire to experiment. At the Company's Cromer Street estate in St Pancras it was decided to compare the relative cost of buildings with staircase and balcony access; surprisingly it was found that the staircase principle was cheaper, and the balcony was therefore discarded.[72] A good example of the new staircase access plan was Meadows Dwellings in Mansford Street, Bethnal Green, consisting of two parallel four storeyed blocks. Here the balcony was dispensed with altogether as a means of access, and so were the rather unfortunate outbuildings of Strafford Houses. Each staircase gave access to five tenements on each floor; a single room facing the stair and four two-roomed tenements, one at the back and the other at the front, to the left and right of the stair, the second room leading out of the first along the length of the building as in many Peabody schemes. Lavatories, a sink and dust shoot were arranged on the landing for each group of rooms. To increase the number of single room dwellings one staircase was altered so that it led to a short passage off which it was possible to arrange four single rooms in place of the normal pairs. Another stair was redesigned to provide two three-roomed tenements at each floor, and these were the only tenements provided with their own scullery and lavatory.

These buildings were designed in 1894, and the following year came Cressy Houses in Hannibal Road, Stepney Green. This was a difficult site, with a sharp angle at the junction of Hannibal Road and Cressy Place, which involved some delicate planning to achieve continuous building on all three sides of the central yards. It allowed, however, certain larger tenements to be included, with as many as four rooms and a scullery. There were two basic plans used in this scheme: for the side wings the same solution as at Meadows Dwellings was adopted, but for the central block an entirely novel plan was evolved. Novel, that was, for Davis and Emmanuel the Company's architects, but it bore striking resemblance to the design which

Frederick Chancellor used exactly twenty years previously for the Metropolitan Association's building in Farringdon Road. The resemblance was so close that it could hardly have been a mere coincidence, and furthermore Chancellor's plan was published when the building was erected in 1874, and it must have been well known to housing architects.[73] Davis and Emmanuel perhaps borrowed the plan, as well they might, since it was in many ways an improvement on their own because it provided much better ventilation; but it was a plan only suited to a better class of dwelling: for the artizan, for whom it was no doubt intended by both the organisations which built it.

The next revision was again concerned with the old Cromer Street plan: the single room tenement on each floor of the standard staircase access block was now replaced by a wash-house serving the remaining four tenements. This plan was used in 1895 at Pollard Houses, Pentonville, and for the last work undertaken by the Company before the end of the century, Dunstan Houses, Stepney Green. This scheme included a number of two-roomed tenements, with large sculleries included as an integral part of the accommodation, and no doubt this movement towards self-contained dwellings was necessitated by the general rise in housing standards towards the end of the century. The East End Dwellings Company continued to build until 1911, which in the circumstances was a notable achievement, but most of its building work was financed through the Public Works Loan Commissioners, from whom it was able to borrow money at a low rate of interest.[74] Financially, it was successful, paying a five per cent dividend each year, but one should note

6.15 *Cromer Street Estate, East End Dwellings Company, 1892. Davis and Emmanuel architects*

6.16 *Dunstan Houses, Stepney Green, 1899, East End Dwellings Company. Davis and Emmanuel architects*

becoming increasingly out of step with official policy by the end of the century.[75] The London County Council prepared an improvement scheme in 1893 for Ann Street, Poplar, under Part Two of the 1890 Housing of the Working Classes Act, the successor to the previous Improvement Acts of 1875 and 1879. The East End Dwellings Company agreed to purchase the site in March 1896 and to erect dwellings for 180 people, provided their plans were acceptable to the council. These plans were submitted in July 1897 but the Council refused to accept them, so they were revised several times, and twice submitted to the Local Government Board, as an independent authority, for approval. The real objection to them seems to have been concerned with the single room dwellings, and the Board finally asked the Council to give an undertaking that the single rooms would be occupied only by child-less married couples, by two girls, or by two elderly people of the same sex. It was against the policy of the Company to accept conditions such as these, and it forthwith withdrew its offer to purchase the land, leaving the Council itself to build the new tenements, all of which were of not less than two rooms with a scullery and lavatory. The Company, then, was willing to accept a lower standard of accommodation than was accepted by local authorities, by the late nineties,

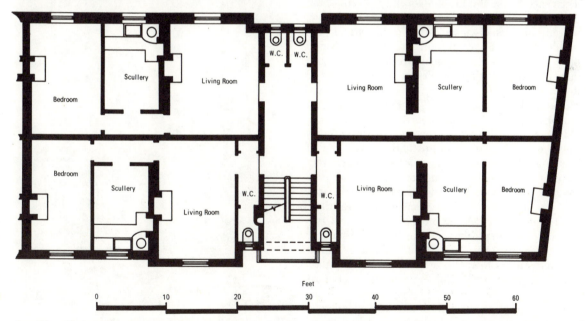

that like all the other societies, it eventually deviated from its original intention to house only the very poor. The Company continued to provide a number of single room tenements for those with the lowest incomes, which was one solution to their problem; but the proportion declined and for various reasons it was only able to provide even a limited number by combining them with more expensive accommodation, or with shops. It was one solution, but it was a solution which latterly began to shirk from the real issue.

There was also evidence that the Company was

and for this reason its part in the development of working class housing was played out soon after the new century began.

The second company to be founded during the eighties was the 4% Industrial Dwellings Company, founded in 1885 to provide the most accommodation, at the least rent, whilst yielding an interest of 4 per cent.[76] The Company owed its inception to Lord Rothschild, who intended that it should provide homes for Jewish artizans; but before the Company itself was started, Rothschild had bought a site from the

6.17 *4% Industriaʟ Dwellings Company, Cartwright Street, 1884,*
N. S. Joseph architect ; part of the Whitechapel Improvement Scheme

Metropolitan Board in 1884 on their Whitechapel
improvement area, and there he built a large block of
tenements. These and the subsequent properties built
in Spitalfields on the Flower and Dean Street site,
have already been discussed earlier in this chapter, but
in addition the Company built a large six storeyed
block in Brady Street, Bethnal Green during 1890,[77]
that is, between the completion of Charlotte de
Rothschild Buildings in 1887, and their extension,
Nathaniel Dwellings, opened in 1892. The largest
proportion of all these tenements were two roomed,
but there was a significant proportion of single rooms
and three-roomed flats, and in addition a very few of
four rooms. In the five subsequent schemes, built during
the next ten years, two tenements alone were of only
one room, and the three-roomed flats rapidly increased
until they dominated the developments, although there
still remained a reasonable proportion with only two
rooms. After 1905 the company ceased building
altogether until 1934. The architects for all the buildings were Messrs Joseph, and for the early group they
chose to build in brick, adopting a modified classical
style which became increasingly decorative, no doubt
in an attempt to get away from the rather ponderous
and oppressive quality of the first blocks, Charlotte de
Rothschild Dwellings; but this tendency must also
have echoed the rising quality of the accommodation.
Between 1887 and 1905 the company built a total of
about 3,800 rooms, so their contribution was quite
considerable, at least in terms of people housed.

The Guinness Trust, which was the next organisation
chronologically, was the first new philanthropic body
since the foundation of the Peabody Trust in 1862.
In November 1889, Sir E. C. Guinness gave £200,000
to found the housing trust which still bears his name:

6.18 *Charlotte de Rothschild Dwellings, 1886*

like the Peabody Trust the initial capital was intended
to provide dwellings for the lowest wage earners, while
at the same time paying a small rate of interest in
order to make the fund self-perpetuating. When the
gift was announced *The Builder* seized the opportunity
to castigate the Peabody Trustees for failing to do
either of these things: they were, it said, 'a conspicuous
failure';[78] and this no doubt was intended as a warning
for the new philanthropic body. At the same time
The Builder noted that a daily paper had exhorted

6.19 *4% Industrial Dwellings Company, Cartwright Street*

Guinness to take special care with the appearance of his buildings so that they might be more beautiful than those of other organisations; and this again, was probably an attack on the barrack-like Peabody Buildings which were still being completed at the end of the decade. *The Builder* was sanguinary, however; it did not consider that beauty and cheapness went hand in hand; and the former, it believed, must of necessity be sacrificed to the latter. The new Trust was further enlarged by a gift from the Goldsmith's Company in 1893 of £25,000.[79] Between 1891, when the first buildings were opened in Brandon Street, Southwark, and 1901, the Trust built in Finsbury, Chelsea,

Hammersmith, Bethnal Green, Southwark, Lambeth and Bermondsey. None of the tenements in these eight schemes were completely self-contained and like the two previous companies discussed in this chapter, they built a preponderance of two-roomed tenements; but the Guinness Trust contined to provide a large number of single rooms also, and this tendency was more marked than in the work of either of the other organisations. The other tendency common to most housing agencies at this time, of building a proportion of flats with three and later with four rooms, can also be traced, so that the Trust was following what we can recognise as a standard policy amongst this group of companies and trusts. The tendency to provide an increasing number of larger flats, with a multiplicity of rooms, took place slowly during these years, and at the same time the single room became less frequent, although at times it persisted rather unexpectedly; a reminder that while there was a gradual rise in the general standard of living, the problem of the very poor still remained unsolved in terms of commercial housing.

The architects for the Guinness Trust were Messrs. Joseph and Smithem, and their buildings show, on the whole, the effects of the changes in architectural taste which were reflected to some extent in the work of the other two companies, but even more so in the buildings of the Trust. It is possible to find the traditional tenement block planning arrangements at Guinness Trust estates; for example in Vauxhall Walk, Lambeth, where the blocks are still regimented in closely spaced parallel rows with barren concreted areas between them. But the architecture was less harsh and uncompromising, the choice of brick more mellow, and the effective height was minimised by treating the top floor as an attic; all of these were architectural devices, designed to reduce the scale and the effect of sheer physical bulk, qualities usually inherent in working

6.20 *Vauxhall Walk; Guinness Trust*

6.21 *Lever Street Estate, 1892, Guinness Trust. Joseph and Smithem architects*

class dwellings. The Lever Street Buildings were a good example of the real care which was taken in order to achieve pleasing modelling and decorative effect; and the result justified the effort, for buildings such as these showed that tenement blocks need not appear 'barrack-like'.

Another Trust was established in 1900 by the will of W. R. Sutton, the founder of Sutton and Co. Ltd., a firm of London Carriers; but for various legal reasons it was unable to build before 1909.[80] Only three schemes date from pre-war years, but unlike the other organisations the Trust was increasingly active again after 1918 and it continued to pursue a vigorous policy of building which, for the first time, was not confined to London. At the three early estates, the first at Sceptre Road, Bethnal Green; the second at City Road and Old Street; and the third at Cale Street and Elystan Street, Chelsea, the Trust built some single room dwellings; but by that time there was much greater emphasis upon the three-roomed flat, which nearly equalled in number those with only two rooms.

6.22 *Sutton Dwellings, Barrack Road, Newcastle, 1918*

Similarly, there were no associated dwellings in any of their schemes; each flat had its own lavatory and scullery.

After 1900, the importance of housing societies and trusts, in the sense that they were known during the 19th century, rapidly decreased; their work usually had been concerned with central area redevelopment and rising costs and values again made that proposition unattractive. Local authorities, such as the London County Council were now more convinced that the best way to implement their policies was to build on their own initiative, and this tendency, as we have seen, was often necessitated by the unwillingness of private bodies to build the kind of dwellings which the local authority wanted, on the land they wished to sell. Speculative housing development was at the same time moving outwards into the suburbs and even into the country, and the growing availability of cheap working class rail fares was encouraging this. The societies, with the one notable exception of the Artizans' Company, were not attracted to this kind of venture, indeed they never intended to cope with it, so new forms of working class housing were built by new organisations; for those who did not buy a speculatively built house, there were in addition to the local authorities such organisations as the co-partnership tenants. And so, although the housing movement was developed by private agencies working on into the 20th century, the last group who exercised real authority belong essentially to the penultimate decade of the 19th century. They were closely linked with the problems and anxieties which lead to the two great parliamentary enquiries of 1882 and 1885, while their solutions were the logical outcome of their predecessors' work in the same field. The years which witnessed this Indian summer of philanthropy and private social enterprise saw also the rise of the local authority and the great moral battle for state aided housing. New forces ultimately eclipsed the work of the private organisations; it is necessary, therefore, to return to the 19th century and trace their development.

7

The crises of confidence

We ought by this time to have seen the practical commencement, even the completion, of two or three rebuilding schemes under the Artisans' Dwelling Act; but they still hang fire, and the evils which the Act was intended to remedy are continuing unchecked, if not increasing.[1]

The pressure on housing accommodation, and the absence of organised house-building except for speculative work was, as we have already seen, an alarming fact throughout the whole country by 1880, when this comment was written, but it was particularly so in London, where the problem had reached a new level and a state of crisis existed. The housing movement was seen to be runnning down. Two series of Acts, those introduced by Mr Cross and Mr Torrens, both designed to provide the machinery for demolishing slum property and replacing it by new housing, had failed miserably and produced as yet no tangible results, despite the modification in the number of people to be rehoused made during 1879.

Public concern was growing both with regard to the worsening situation and to the nature of possible solutions. The Charity Organisation Society, for example, set up another special committee on housing which produced a very non-committal report during 1880.[2] The National Association for the Promotion of Social Science recommended a variety of sanitary reforms, pointing out the need to bring suburban districts within the control of the urban sanitary authorities, and in September 1881 they held a survey of all towns in which the Artizans' Dwellings Act was applicable, that is towns with more than 20,000 inhabitants.[3] The results were not encouraging; only fourteen towns had taken any action at all, and most of these had done very little. It noted the significant towns: Birmingham was the most obvious exception where the corporation had spent £1,000,000 on street improvements, clearance work and improvements to houses, but no new dwellings had as yet been built; in Liverpool a site had been cleared under the terms of the Act but no use had been made of the land and, under a local Act, Glasgow was undertaking similar improvements to those in Birmingham. Certain other towns had adopted the Act in the first flush of enthusiasm, but having found the arrangements for compensation unsatisfactory, and the sale of cleared land specifically for housing a very expensive business, they had abandoned it.

The situation throughout the country was very unsatisfactory, and finally in London a state of impasse was reached in 1881, when the Metropolitan Board informed the Holborn District Board that they could not proceed with any further schemes prepared under the Cross Act until the existing law was amended. And early in June the Home Secretary refused to permit the demolition of any further property by the Metropolitan Board, pending the setting up of a Select Committee.[4]

The Select Committee of 1881–2

Parliament set up the Select Committee on 9 June 1881, and shortly afterwards Sir Richard Cross was appointed chairman by the members. They were required to consider the various housing Acts from 1875 to 1879, to suggest how the expense and delay in carrying them out might be reduced, and to find out why the Acts had not been used to their full extent for the reconstruction of dwellings. Because it was appointed so late in the session, the Committee's deliberations were necessarily a little superficial, but it succeeded in making certain practical recommendations in its report published during August.[5] Amongst these were the suggestion that procedure should be simplified and speeded up, that the ground floor and basements of new dwellings might be used for shops, that convenient alternative accommodation or transport facilities should be taken into account when rehousing was arranged on alternative sites, as permitted in the amending Acts of 1879 which the Committee endorsed.

The Select Committee was reappointed the following session on 20 February 1882, and this time its deliberations were less hurried and, therefore, more thorough. The 1882 Report began with a review of existing legislation, and although the account is often quoted, its inclusion here is justified because it presents a clear analysis of the two distinct branches of the law then in existence.

The Acts of 1868–79 proceed upon the principle that the responsibility of maintaining his house in proper condition falls upon the owner, and that if he fails in his duty the law is justified in stepping in and compelling him to perform it. They further assume that houses unfit for human habitation ought not to be used as dwellings, but ought, in the interest of the public, to be closed and demolished, and to be subsequently rebuilt. The expropriation of the owner is thus a secondary step in the transaction, and only takes place after the failure of other means of rendering the houses habitable.

The Acts of 1875–79 proceed upon a different principle. They contemplate dealing with whole areas, where the houses are so structurally defective as to be incapable of repair, and so ill placed with reference to each other as to require, to bring them up to a proper sanitary standard, nothing short of demolition and reconstruction. Accordingly, in this case, the local authority, armed with compulsory powers, at once enters as a purchaser, and on the completion of the purchase, proceeds forthwith to a scheme of reconstruction. Though these two sets of Acts proceed upon different principles, they are each of them available for their own particular purposes, and are both, in the opinion of your Committee, alike necessary and useful.[6]

The great cost of executing the Cross Acts was the first point on which the Committee commented. The members thought that this was due to three factors: high compensation, expensive procedures and the obligation to sell land exclusively for housing. One of the arbitrators for the schemes prepared under the Act, Sir Henry Hunt, argued in his evidence that dwellings which were unfit for habitation should be valued only as land and materials, and this opinion was accepted.[7]

The obligation to sell land exclusively for housing had already been eased by the alternative site provision permitted under the 1879 Act, but this did not remedy the difficulties experienced for the large number of schemes initiated under the original Act of 1875. The rehousing obligation was also rather pointless in most schemes because the interval between demolition and rebuilding – which often amounted to several years – of necessity demanded that those displaced should meanwhile find alternative accommodation, and few were likely to return when new housing was built! Despite the pressure for homes in central London the Committee did not believe that more than half or two thirds of those displaced should be rehoused on cleared sites.[8]

The Committee endorsed the comments made in the 1881 Report about the simplification of procedure in order to gain speed; and in addition to the remedies then suggested they now recommended that there should be the minimum of control over street layout since this had proved particularly inhibiting in earlier improvement schemes. They also made a suggestion about the nature of the new accommodation which we have already seen was to become more popular during the decade: that 'in many cases it would be well to have a larger number of single rooms than have hitherto been provided, so as to suit the wants of the poorer class'.[9] An observation made, one feels, in desperation, and later reversed by the L.C.C.

With the conspicuous absence of a suitable authority in London who could carry out housing work they added:

Your Committee are of opinion that the Peabody Trustees, who may fairly be considered as a *quasi* public body, should specially undertake the duty of supplying the wants of the poorer class of persons displaced. Your Committee, therefore, hope that the Peabody Trustees may find it consistent with the provisions of their trust in any additional buildings which they may erect to make provisions suited to the means and to the wants and special callings of a poorer class than that for which they have hitherto provided.[10]

There was no hint, therefore, that responsibility as yet should lie anywhere but with private enterprise.

The problem of suburban development, and the role of speculative building in an expanding society, led the Committee to advise that all railway companies should be obliged to provide adequate workmen's trains; and that sanitary provision and regulations should be fully enforced, especially in the areas of rapid new growth. This resolution, then, recognised the importance of controlled suburban development as a complementary growth to central area redevelopment. And by attempting to secure better communications the Committee was seeking to remove the constant pressure on central London.

The report commented on the reason why the 1879 Act amending the original Torrens Act of 1868 failed to encourage any new activity. This was because of the 'prevalent misapprehension that an alternative method

was in *all* cases offered by Sir R. Cross' Act of 1875'.[11] It also sprung from the hope that the central authority would bear the financial responsibility for improvements under the terms of the Cross Acts, whereas the uses of the Torrens Acts were incumbent upon the local vestry or board.

Rehousing was also required in the provisions of the Metropolitan Street Improvements Acts of 1871 and 1877. The earlier Act had required the permanent dedication of certain areas to working class housing, and this provision had caused similar problems to those experienced under the Cross Acts. The second Act attempted to prevent the time lag between demolition and rebuilding by limiting the number of houses which could be demolished at one time, but its provisions were so strict that it was impossible for the Metropolitan Board to carry through any but the smallest schemes. The Report recommended that these stringent provisions whereby not more than fifteen houses could be demolished at any one time should be relaxed, and the equally stringent provision, requiring the provision of alternative accommodation within the area for the same number of people before the next fifteen houses could be demolished, should be modified so that the Metropolitan Board's proposals to use alternative sites, and to utilise street frontages for commercial purposes, might be legalised.

The 1882 Housing Act

As a result of this Report, placed before the House of Commons on 19 June 1882, the Artizans' Dwellings Act[12] was passed later that session, laying down new instructions about the purchase of insanitary property so that the owner did not receive excessive compensation. Secondly it permitted the Secretary of State to reduce the rehousing obligation to half those displaced; and thirdly, it allowed the Metropolitan Board to increase from 15 to 20 the number of houses which it might acquire without formally preparing a rehousing scheme.

The new Act legislated for some of the Committee's principal findings, but in truth neither the Committee nor the Act went to the root of the housing problem. One historian of London's health problems described it as 'mere tinkering with the subject removing some petty technical difficulties...something not far short of revolution was required if the housing of the people was to be reformed, and put on a proper sanitary basis'.[13]

There was one other practical result which followed the work of the Select Committee. This was the Cheap Trains Act,[14] passed in 1883, which gave the Board of Trade powers to require the railway companies to provide a proportion of accommodation at fares not exceeding 1d. per mile on certain suburban trains in return for some tax relief and to provide special workmen's trains at these fares between six o'clock in the evening and eight o'clock the next morning, the exact number being regulated by the Board of Trade. The

Act was not immediately effective because Chamberlain as President of the Board of Trade did not press the companies. Several of them did operate cheap fares, and it was one of the earliest attempts to ease the pressure on central areas: one destined ultimately to succeed.[15]

The immediate housing problem remained unsolved, and the succeeding years only served to emphasise its magnitude, and the consummate inability of Parliament to provide effective legislation which could actively encourage the building of new houses in places where they were most needed.

London, where the problems were always greatest, also suffered from the disadvantage of being specifically excluded from the provisions of the Public Health Act of 1875, so that the vestries and district boards established way back in 1855 were still in possession of considerable power over local administration. Furthermore they were still to a very great extent independent of the central authority. A typical example of this divided responsibility occurred in 1883 when the Home Office, as the supreme authority, was obliged to request the Newington vestry to make representation to the Metropolitan Board about an unhealthy area, so that it might be dealt with under the Artizans' Dwellings Act.[16] It appeared that the vestry was unwilling to act because of the cost involved and the unfairness of the law in rewarding the owner of insanitary property with compensation, at the expense of the other rate-payers. That was the kind of convoluted problem which still foiled the reformers.

The problem of controlling new development was as great as that of improving what already existed. In the metropolis there were inadequate powers and controls for those authorities willing to exercise them, and there were many more who were not interested in sanitary or building control at all. Two rather gruesome examples dating again from 1883 suffice to illustrate the predicament, and both come from Bethnal Green. The first concerned a disused cemetery known as Globe Fields, which was included in the land over which a railway company had been authorised by Parliament to construct a new line. Before the local Medical Officer could inspect the site the company had dug the foundations for a viaduct, exposing mortal remains and causing grave risk of epidemic. At even greater risk, it was then necessary to remove the bodies to other and more peaceful resting places while the progress of the railway went on unimpeded.[17]

The second example also concerns a burial ground, this time in Peel Grove. Eventually the site came into the possession of a speculative builder who excavated the foundations of a housing estate before submitting his plans to the Bethnal Green Vestry.

The Vestry of Bethnal Green are alive to the situation, and appear willing to do all in their power to avert the catastrophe. But the law on the subject is by no means clear...It is little short of scandalous that such doubts and difficulties should exist. It is repugnant to every feeling of decency and propriety to invite human beings to live in densely packed crowds over a charnel-house. Means already exist by which the local authority may legally acquire and manage such grounds as open spaces, but it is a necessary supplement to such wholesome legislation that building should be distinctly and absolutely forbidden.[18]

The lower middle class and the artizan were most affected by the malpractices of these speculative builders, and in London, where the 'model' bye-laws could not be adopted, the standards were now below those required by the Local Government Board for provincial towns. The need for centralised local government in London was by now recognised fairly widely, not least by the Medical Officers of Health who persistently agitated for unification.[19] London was still administered under laws dating back to 1855, patently inadequate by the standards of the eighties, their execution in the hands of bodies many of whom probably never had any real interest in the welfare of the community. Now they appeared exhausted and inept, the relics of a vastly different society which was rapidly passing away. The first attempt to change all this was the Local Government Bill of 1884 introduced by Sir William Harcourt; but the bill was strongly opposed by the powerful advocates of local administration and the voice of centralisation was silenced for a while. The time was not yet ripe.

The problem of administration and bye-law control seemed insoluble, and attention returned to the equally difficult and more pressing subject of overcrowding and housing. Information such as that produced by T. Marchant Williams in 1884 for the City, parts of Finsbury and Marylebone, showed that overcrowding was worsening, despite the spate of Parliamentary activity during the past decade.[20] At the same time the division of opinion about responsibility for the provision of new housing was becoming apparent; public attention was attracted to the struggle between the supporters of self-help as opposed to those of state aid, which was being fought out in the pages of contemporary journals, not by journalists or interested amateurs, but by experts, gentlemen and peers of the realm, the holders of high office and considerable reputation: by the men who in fact shaped the nation's destiny. It is clear then, that it was to issues of principle that public attention must now be turned, for the palliatives of recent years were patently inadequate because they interfered only with existing institutions, and it is the nature of this wordy battle that we must now try to understand.

The sequence of literary expositions really began in 1879, with the publication of an article by W. M. Torrens entitled 'What is to be done with the Slums'.[21] In it he gave an account of his own bill of 1868, the first piece of legislation to deal with the slums, and he described how it was his intention that it should give municipal authorities power:

1 To compel repair of unwholesome dwellings, under penalty of demolition;

2 To pull down, and sell the freehold of the site;

3 To compensate the owner for the fair value under the Land Clauses Act; and

4 To build workmen's dwellings with money borrowed at four per cent, charging the payment for thirty years upon the rates.[22]

This was Torrens' intention, and the Commons had agreed, but the House of Lords cut out the compensation and building clauses, so that despite his claims of activity, the Act was of little practical effect. The important point to note here was that the Act placed the onus upon the local authority, in whom Torrens seemed to place implicit faith, for certainly he was against centralised authority:

Yet we are told by empirics and quacks that it is no use trusting a reform of the slums to municipal bodies that have the greatest conceivable interest in their reformation; and that nothing will do but to give the whole matter as further prey into the maw of centralism to be crunched and gulped and ruminated at will by that unaccountable and unaccounting creature.[23]

But he goes so far as to agree that a central authority for London was necessary under the terms of the Cross Act of 1875:

But once more the misleading Will o' the Wisp of *laissez-faire* intervened, and lured the legislature from the high road to its purpose. The Act of 1875 stopped short at the point of rebuilding by the local authority where private enterprise failed to do so [and thus gave] no security whatever that the one thing needful would be done either promptly, economically or at all; but unbounded confidence was expressed in the efficacy of the wholesale temptations to individual builders and building companies, who it was said would do all that was required.[24]

His own faith, however, was not in the Cross Act with its wholesale demolitions and clearances; he still thought that piecemeal reconstruction was the soundest policy:

A region once left to run down socially and sanitarily may be redeemed court by court and street by street, and that is the best mode of doing it; but general reconstruction can only pay when planned and executed systematically and as a whole, and therefore, can only be effectual and remunerative when undertaken by a wealthy proprietor or by a public authority.[25]

So that on the one hand he was seeking more complete power for the local authority, while at the same time seeking to keep the framework of administration parochial in scale.

Despite the amendment of his own Act in 1879, which restored much of what had been omitted in 1868, it was still ineffectual; disproving yet again his sanguinary trust in the vestry and district board, the so-called responsible local authorities. Despite these further amendments of the Torrens Act the practical results remained few and the Act must be accounted unsuccessful. Torrens' polemical tract remains intrinsically a sound exposition of one point of view, and

one obviously not shared by Cross, whose own all-embracing approach showed greater scepticism of local initiative and paced its hope in centralisation. But in addition Cross was concerned with the larger problem of state interference in the housing movement, not necessarily in degree, but in principle, and it was Cross who publicly reopened the housing controversy in 1882, following the report of the Select Committee. 'How far is Parliament justified in interfering in the matter of the improvement of the dwellings of the poor?'[26] he asked, and he attempted thus to define his view of its limitations:

I take it as a starting-point that it is not the duty of the Government to provide any class of citizens with any of the necessaries of life, and among the necessaries of life we must of course include good and habitable dwellings. To provide such necessaries for any class is not the duty of the State, because, if it did so, it would inevitably tend to make that class depend, not on themselves, but upon what was done for them elsewhere, and it would not be possible to teach a worse lesson than this – 'If you do not take care of yourselves, the State will take care of you' – Nor is it wise to encourage large bodies to provide the working classes with habitations at greatly lower rents than the market value paid elsewhere.[27]

The state had a right to interfere, however, in sanitary matters; Cross argued that health was wealth, the government could ensure health through sanitary laws and controls, and it had sought to do so by two separate and independent series of measures, the first dealing with individual property, and the second with larger areas where a single land owner could not secure sanitary improvement of his own volition. Under the terms of his own legislation, dealing with the latter circumstances, the authority was responsible for the reorganisation of streets to ensure health and ventilation and also to secure the rehousing of a proportion of those displaced.[28] Cross did not hold the view that authority should itself be the rehousing agent, with what result after 1875 we have already seen. But having said this, it is clear that he remained aware of the existing problems concerned with the proportion of people that should be rehoused, of where they should be rehoused, of the role to be played by suburban housing and extended transport facilities, and last the effect of the buildings already erected upon the kind of people they housed. His attitude to social problems was closest to that of Miss Hill: the poor, he believed, needed education to fit them for new and better dwellings; and although the Peabody Trustees, who had built on most of the cleared sites, did not provide accommodation for the very poor, they at least alleviated the problem by adding to the amount of accommodation available generally, so that the effect was of levelling up: the artizan moved into the model dwelling and his old home became available to a poorer tenant; which was, of course, a popular defensive argument. Finally, he accepted that the financial losses on the cleared sites were the community's contribution to social and moral improvement, while at least a proportion of the site which could be sold for normal development would, in its turn, benefit the community financially by the greatly increased rateable value it would subsequently possess; this again was an argument frequently heard in these years, but one which was patently weak in view of the small areas usually available for commercial redevelopment.[29]

Further legislation followed during 1882 as we have seen, but with no more practical result than in time past, and the *Nineteenth Century* was publishing in 1883 a review of the housing movement by George Howell,[30] which spoke of the failure of legislative measures and practical works, and of the inability of either speculator or society to provide the necessary dwellings:

...there are cases where municipalities or local bodies alone can cope with the difficulties of the situation, and provide adequate remedies. In such cases it is their bounden duty to undertake the task, even at the risk of failing to realise a profitable return, calculated as a mere commercial investment.[31]

Then in October 1883, the Rev Andrew Mearns, a Congregationalist, published his tract *The Bitter Cry of Outcast London* which drew attention to the moral as well as the sanitary problems of overcrowding. Like the work of Chadwick and his team over forty years previously, Mearns was able to draw upon first hand information which, after the lapse of so much time, was all the more shocking to Victorian consciences.

Much more important, however, was an article written later in 1883 by the Marquis of Salisbury for the *National Review*,[32] since its repercussions were astonishingly widespread. It was hardly usual for a Tory of such eminence to set out to champion the poor in this way. He thought that 'increase of prosperity tends rather to aggravate the existing evil than to lighten it'[33] as far as the town was concerned, which had been the general conclusion of the 1882 Committee: overcrowding was increasing, the poor were worse off. Salisbury in his turn asked himself what else Parliament could be expected to do, and promptly returned the answer that it could make a public loan, which would be justifiable on humanitarian grounds and also for the improvement in health which it would bring about. But the real question was to whom the loan should be made and for what direct purpose, and about this there was no unanimity. Salisbury then proceeded to examine the situation as it appeared to him, finding that there were two alternatives: either of building high or building outwards, that is, of society or company built dwellings as opposed to speculative. His analysis led him to the perhaps somewhat desperate conclusion that the Peabody Trustees were the most suitable recipients of a public loan for they had 'already assumed an almost official position in their relation to the Metropolitan Board of Works'.[34] They were not interested in high returns, while at the same time their fund was self perpetuating; they were still building, when others had stopped, and they built well: they built to last, and although they built expensively and charged rents which could only be paid by the artizan who could also afford to live on a suburban estate if he chose to do so, they appeared to be the soundest body to whom such a loan as Salisbury proposed might be entrusted. He overcame the difficulty of rehousing the poor by the usual argument of alleviation and upgrading rather than direct rehousing. Salisbury's objections to municipal organisations were based upon his knowledge of the London School Board, whose activities had not been characterised by economy; and by his knowledge of local authorities, who were by their nature unsuited to positions of vigilance, and usually more interested in spending money where its effect would be most noticeable. So far as the very poor were concerned, Salisbury had little to suggest, apart from a series of minor palliatives, but he thought that Octavia Hill's methods might eventually prove the most satisfactory.

Coming as it did from the ranks of the nobility this view was a little surprising: on the one hand it was predictably reactionary – especially about the role of local authorities – while on the other it was clearly supporting a form of subsidisation. *The Builder*,[35] writing of a Communistic gospel in strange quarters, thought it superficial, choosing instead to lay the blame for the city's misery upon the lack of education, which in its turn was another favourite scapegoat.

Salisbury's article was published in the November, and the reply to it came from Joseph Chamberlain in the *Fortnightly Review*[36] during the following month. His review of existing problems differed but little from that of most other people, but he added 'In the Metropolis, where the evil is greater, the want of an efficient and thoroughly representative municipal government stands in the way of reform',[37] and this was the key to his first difference of opinion with Salisbury: Chamberlain was a firm believer in the latent efficiency of local government, and he could quote the example of his native Birmingham where Corporation Street had been successfully constructed through an improvement district by the city authorities. The cost was kept down because the corporation was not obliged to purchase the complete area designated for improvement, and in fact it purchased only half of it; leaving the remainder in the hands of the owner, where he made unreasonable claims, forcing him to improve the property himself. The intention to replace some of the slums with new housing was not obligatory and in fact did not prove to be necessary; Chamberlain tended to forget that this was a striking symptom of the difference between the problems of a provincial town and those of metropolitan London. Nevertheless, he made one point effectively: that municipalities were not necessarily ineffective organisations.

Chamberlain's second fundamental difference with

Salisbury was on the issue of the right of property as opposed to the right of the community, and he accused Salisbury of placing the burden of improvement upon the community, when it should rightly, he believed, be placed upon the land owners: 'The expense of making towns habitable for the toilers who dwell in them must be thrown on the land which their toil makes valuable, and without any effort on the part of its owners.'[38]

Chamberlain supported the idea of state loans – the expense involved at Birmingham seems to have convinced him of their value – but he did not support the granting of loans to organisations such as the Peabody Trustees, and he doubted whether they could make adequate return with the then existing high land values: Chamberlain's loans would be made to local authorities. Finally, he made a series of recommendations concerned with the practical interpretation of the measures necessary to control the right of property, so that the community would be protected from the unscrupulous property owner, and he concluded:

This is the age of municipal activity and enterprise, and there is not the slightest doubt that local authorities would under these conditions joyfully embrace the opportunity afforded to them, and that they would quickly put an end to the scandal and disgrace which has at last forced itself on public attention, and alarmed and shocked the public conscience.[39]

This article attracted as much attention as did that by Salisbury, but while the Marquis' article met with astonishment, Chamberlain's seems to have met with much more general approval by the daily press.[40] Approval, however, was not universal and the issues involved remained hotly debated.

The debate was now a matter of general concern, and a wide variety of views on all the facets of the subject were publicly discussed. Lord Brabazon, and the Rev S. A. Barnett wrote about the social implications of the housing movement: 'Until our working classes are decently housed, it is useless to look for any improvement in their moral, social or physical condition',[41] wrote Brabazon, and Barnett agreed: 'The first need is better dwellings. While the people live without adequate air, space or light, while the house arrangements are such that privacy is impossible, it is hopeless to look for them to enjoy the best things.'[42] And Earl Grey wrote to *The Times*[43] recommending the extension of the Common Lodging Houses Acts to the housing occupied by all working men.

At this point Octavia Hill joined the discussion, bringing to earth the excited politicians with her advice based upon much practical experience on the one hand, and what I think amounts to a rigidly inflexible social outlook on the other. She argued that housing must never be provided by the community, enabling 'the improvident to throw the burden of his support upon the provident'.[44] In her estimation this would amount to the restoration of the old Poor Law system, and it would attract more poor people

than ever into the towns. Neither, she observed, should the remedy of the housing problem be placed in municipal hands: 'Almost all public bodies do things expensively; neither do they seem fitted to supply the various wants of numbers of people in a perceptive and economical way.'[45]

Like many other people she was prepared to condone authoritative action in clearing the slum away, because this, she argued, was only the removal of an evil which the community itself had allowed to develop through generations of negligence. Another argument, which she used to overcome the moral problem of obtaining land under the clearance schemes at subsidised prices, was one used by Cross; namely that an improvement scheme, especially the portions devoted to commercial development, produced a considerably higher rateable value than the existing slums, and this money returned to the municipal coffers, and so indirectly benefited the community as a whole.[46] But housing itself must never be subsidised in any way: about that she was adamant.

Economic housing must of necessity, therefore, be based upon the single room tenement, with its communal scullery and lavatory; which was socially, she argued, also the most suitable solution for the very poor. It was necessary to realise:

That the problem before you is far more difficult than the financial one; that it is more complicated than that of building; that you will have, before you can raise these very poorest, to help them to become better in themselves.[47]

In the same symposium H. O. Arnold-Foster[48] reviewed the legislative provisions, pointing out the existing defects and drawing attention to the same anomalies which Chamberlain had noticed.[49] He concluded, like Cross, that the necessary legal powers existed but they had not been enforced because they relied too much upon the goodwill of the community rather than upon legal obligation. To these opinions, the ageing Shaftesbury added his view, writing about the 'Mischief of State Aid',[50] and his was indeed a voice from the past, despite the fact that he largely supported Miss Hill:

Hitherto we have done too little; there is now a fear that in some respects we may do too much...if the State is to be summoned not only to provide houses for the labouring classes, but also to supply such dwellings at nominal rents, it will, while doing something on behalf of their physical condition, utterly destroy their moral energies.[51]

Shaftesbury evidently still thought in terms of the kind of organisation which he himself had helped to set up, in the Society for Improving the Condition of the Labouring Classes, more than forty years previously; he was still recommending commercial ventures as the proper channel through which the housing needs of the community might be provided, and he wished to see further exertion to persuade new philanthropic action, despite the ample and clear evidence that these means were not able to supply either in quantity, or at the right price, the necessary dwellings. The only condition under which he could contemplate state aid showed how sincerely and earnestly he distrusted it as an aid to housing; and his point of view, although old fashioned and out of date in the penultimate decade of the century commands respect not only as the view of a previous generation, but of a considerable proportion of contemporary society, many of whom had done much to prepare the way for the step which they now could not in all conscience fully accept:

Should private bounty and private zeal be insufficient for the great issue now sought, it might be necessary for the Government to interpose and use the money of the State for the improvement of the domiciliary condition of some portions of the labouring classes by placing them in new homes at eleemosynary rents; but such interposition must not take place until every effort has been made, every expedient exhausted, and indisputable proof given that, if the State does not do the work, it will never be done at all.[52]

There were other voices raised against state aid in 1883, including that of Lord Claude Hamilton who believed that the improvement of the people, together with private enterprise housing, were the only solution to the problem of the poor. 'State aid should be entirely dismissed from the calculation and they depend upon their own exertions',[53] he said, and *The Builder*,[54] which should have known better, agreed. Nor was its editor prepared to condone further philanthropy, and now thoroughly imbued with the Hill doctrine he placed his hope in higher education, in the development of thrift and self respect, and confined his immediate recommendations to the enforcement of legal duties upon landlords.[55] Now that Godwin had gone, *The Builder* ceased to be an organ which was in the forefront of social thought and its importance to the housing movement rapidly declined.

The confusion which existed in the search for a solution to the housing problems – problems whose existence was not now frequently questioned, despite the disagreement about the method by which they might be solved – was further displayed in a series of articles in the *Contemporary Review* early in 1884, two at least of which posed diametrically opposing points of view. The first by Professor Alfred Marshall,[56] suggested that with the improvement in transport and communications it was no longer necessary to house so many workers and industries in the urban centres, since they could now be moved outside the towns with economic, as well as social and sanitary, advantage. He suggested, therefore, two ways of solving London's housing problem; first the regulation of people coming into the metropolis, and secondly a properly organised movement to take industry, and thus people, to new sites outside London.

The next article, by M. G. Mulhall,[57] saw the housing problem purely as one affecting the central areas of London; it was here that the people must be housed, and in order to do this he suggested four

solutions; first, that the state should itself build, using money at that time lying unclaimed in the Post Office Savings Bank, and also unclaimed dividends on the National Debt. Mulhall estimates these at four million pounds, and he suggested that the government build blocks of dwellings which the Post Office might manage. Secondly, he suggested that the municipalities might build, especially in London if a central local government organisation was created which could obtain large loans at cheap rates. His third idea was that Parliament should set up a trust committee with power to borrow large sums from the Post Office in order to build dwellings. The cost of the sites, when they exceeded a certain predetermined figure, would be subsidised by the Poor Law Board. Lastly he suggested that sites might be made available free of charge to various companies on condition that they let their tenements at fixed low rents.

Wildly impractical as the various solutions might be, they do show that a body of opinion existed which considered authority, either in the form of the state itself or the local municipality, as a possible agency in the solution of the housing problem.

The final major contribution, before the Royal Commission was appointed, came again from Cross;[58] he disagreed, of course, with Chamberlain about the function of the local authority in relation to the provision of houses and he still preferred to leave this in the hands of private enterprise. However, he seems to have been impressed by Salisbury's arguments, since he recommended the extension of loans to people like the Peabody Trustees; and he accepted that the trusts and societies could only afford to pay a certain price for their land, and that this price should be accepted as the fair value of the land for housing purposes. There were, however, other signs that his previous firm conviction was weakening; he mentioned the possibility of following the Glasgow experiment, which permitted the local authority to build for the very poor, as a temporary measure to relieve the immediate pressure upon accommodation; but he expressed this view in the most guarded terms. One cannot do better than to quote his own summary, for it explains better than any attempt at paraphrase the point of view which he represented:

First as to new buildings: we must take care that houses in future shall be properly built in the first instance, and strictly enforce the Metropolitan Building Acts: this is a matter of administration of existing laws. As a matter of legislation, strengthen these Acts if necessary, and, without delay, give like powers to local authorities in the suburbs.

Secondly as to maintenance, etc. Houses, though properly built, will soon become a nuisance if not properly maintained. Property has its undoubted rights. As a first principle of justice let these rights be properly protected. Property has also its undoubted duties; let us take equal care that these duties be properly performed...the Sanitary provisions of the law must also be duly enforced against occupiers as well as owners. This is a matter of administration only; fresh legislation is not needed.

Thirdly, as to old buildings. The old slums and insanitary houses must be got rid of – as economically as may be done, certainly – but they must go, the sooner the better, but only with convenient speed, or overcrowding will most certainly follow. The neglect of many years cannot be repaired in one. Mr Torrens' Acts for small places, my own Acts of 1875–82 for larger areas, give, as Mr Arnold-Foster has just stated in these pages, every requisite power …On this general head, therefore, my answer is, administration, not fresh legislation. Lastly, as to the question of rehousing. No legislation is here wanted. What is wanted is Patience, Perseverance, Determination, Firmness, so that these people may never be taught to forget that they must rely upon themselves. Encouragement in every legitimate way to those who are willing to invest money at a fair but moderate interest. Among local authorities themselves let us hope that there may be found willing and ready hearts, men alive to all the necessities of the case, and earnest in pressing forward measures of administration necessary for the work with energy, and never flagging exertion, though with prudence.[59]

The really significant point which emerged from this battle of principles was that certain people, who might be expected to support a strictly *laissez-faire* attitude, were prepared to say publicly, although patently without joy, that state aid in one form or another would be permissible as a last resort should their other recommendations fail for any reason. There were few people in 1885 with the singleness of purpose which Octavia Hill consistently displayed in her opposition to housing subsidisation; but then, there were also few people willing to accept her low standard of accommodation.

The Royal Commission 1884–5

It was inevitable that after all this discussion in the press, and the failure of the minor modifications made to the Housing Acts in 1882, following the Select Committee Reports, that there should be yet another Parliamentary enquiry, and this time it was at the highest level.

On 22 February 1884, the Marquis of Salisbury moved that a Royal Commission be appointed to investigate the housing of the working classes, a proposal which was accepted by the government. *The Builder* was very critical from the outset, probably because of the great delay which the procedure of the Commission would involve. Of Lord Salisbury it wrote: 'He is like a man who is annoyed at finding a flower bed overgrown with weeds, and proposes to clear it by cutting off the heads of all the weeds, leaving the roots in the ground.'[60]

This would have been a fairly apt description of all the activities which surrounded the housing problem since 1875, but there were signs, as we have just seen, that the roots were about to be examined, even if not immediately dug out.

The Royal Commission was duly appointed, with Sir Charles Dilke as President, and its members included the Prince of Wales, Cardinal Manning, Sir Richard Cross, Lord Salisbury, W. M. Torrens, George Godwin and many others familiar in these pages.

Its deliberations were along the now familiar pattern in housing enquiries, and during long sessions, it collected vast quantities of evidence, first from a series of specialist witnesses and then from the surveyors of a selected number of towns. In London the parishes of Clerkenwell, St Lukes and part of St Pancras, Bermondsey, Whitechapel, Southwark, Notting Hill, Marylebone, Hackney and Chelsea, were examined and in the provinces a series of towns representing three distinct groups: the large towns, including Newcastle upon Tyne, Birmingham, Merthyr Tydfil, Leeds, Liverpool and Gateshead; the medium size towns, such as Exeter and Doncaster; and the small towns, Camborne and Alnwick.

The Report was published the following year:

At the very outset of their inquiry Your Majesty's Commissioners had testimony to prove two important facts: first, that though there was a great improvement, described by Lord Shaftesbury as 'enormous', in the condition of the houses of the poor compared to that of 30 years ago, yet the evils of overcrowding, especially in London, were still a public scandal, and were becoming in certain localities more serious than they ever were; second, that there was much legislation designed to meet these evils, yet that the existing laws were not put into force, some of them having remained a dead letter from the date when they first found place in the statute book.[61]

The steady improvement in drainage and water supplies, which had resulted over the years in the decline of epidemics, was not paralleled by improvements in housing, and in nearly all the towns which were examined the problem of overcrowding was increasing. Middle class houses were frequently converted to tenements without any modification to their sanitary arrangements, and new housing for the working class was no better:

There can be no doubt but that houses are often built of the commonest materials, and with the worst workmanship, and are altogether unfit for the people to live in, especially if they are a little rough in their ways. The old houses are rotten from age and neglect. The new houses often commence where the old ones leave off, and are rotten from the first. It is quite certain that the working classes are largely housed in dwellings which would be unsuitable even if they were not overcrowded.[62]

There was little doubt, however, that low wages, uncertainty of employment and increasingly high rents were the root causes of overcrowding; and this was especially true of London, where cheap rail fares were not yet consistently operated and the necessity of living near to a source of employment usually overrode all other considerations in the eyes of the poor, making overcrowding a necessary evil. The three-fold reasons for demolition; to improve property, to widen existing streets and to make new ones, to create public amenities such as new schools and railways, were also continuously adding to the overcrowding problem, and thus by implication to the extension of the slum.[63] There were complaints, too, that demolition under the terms of the Torrens and the Cross Acts increased the pressure on existing accommodation for the very poor because the new tenement blocks, when built, were not for the kind of people who were displaced or needed rehousing.

Concluding their survey of existing conditions, the Commissioners went on to make their recommendations. Investigation of both Hackney and Chelsea had shown that local authorities willing to use the existing powers given to them, or which could be adopted from sanitary and building law, were able to reduce overcrowding to a minimum, and the first recommendation was, therefore, that all local authorities who had been lax and had either failed to make bye-laws or to carry them into effect should do so at once.[64] It was observed that there were too many local authorities and responsibility was often divided in futile ways; also that the prime need was for a greater public interest in local government, and here the Commissioners were underlining a fundamental weakness in the existing system.

The building act and bye-law provisions were considered to be inadequate, and it was recommended that space about buildings should be more carefully controlled. This did not mean the widening of streets alone, but in addition the control of backyards, where the Commissioners wished to see a minimum width throughout the whole length of the building, controlled by the height and not the frontage as was often the case at present.[65]

The Commissioners recognised the need for reform in the local government of London, and until this was possible they suggested that the responsibilities of the Metropolitan Board and the local authorities should be clarified with regard to the administration of the Torrens and Cross Acts, which in any case themselves required amending still further. As a practical step towards the provision of more housing land, it was suggested that the sites of several outdated prisons might be made available at nominal value for housing purposes, and that the government should make loans at low rates of interest to facilitate the erection of working class dwellings.[66]

Other practical suggestions included the revival of Lord Shaftesbury's Lodging Houses Acts, with their powers of inspection and the introduction of new buildings vested in the local authorities; and the extension of Waterlow's Chambers and Offices Act of 1881, which had brought into being a company to manage the common amenities of tenement blocks, so that individual tenements might be sold.[67] The principles of compensation outlined in 1882 were also reaffirmed, since there was still apparently a tendency to overcompensate the owners of slum property. The Commissioners thought that the provisions of the Cheap Trains Act of 1883, which required workmen's fares on certain suburban lines, should be enforced strictly, and that the railway companies should be obliged to rehouse all those displaced for new lines, and not permitted to evade the issue by a lump sum payment to bribe the tenant to leave his house before it was taken over by the company.[68]

The more vexed issues of the housing movement were treated with greater caution. The Commissioners were agreed that model dwellings did not reach down to the class most in need of help, and they noted the criticism levelled at the Peabody Trustees on this point, but on the subject of high density housing they failed to agree whether or not these were the fever nests of the future:

It would not be possible within the limits of this report to quote, to combat, or to support the views which were put forth on the general question of blocks of model buildings by witnesses whose opinions are worthy of the highest respect.[69]

The Commissioners also avoided the issue of subsidies and state aid, although the un-unanimous views of the members are mentioned in a series of memoranda at the conclusion of the main report. Here[70] Lord Salisbury reiterated his views that the housing problem was best solved by the law of supply and demand, except in London where he accepted the need to make available land, such as the disused prison sites, at a price below market value. He justified this as an 'eleemosynary' act, recompensing in some measure the land which had been used during the previous half century for road improvements.

Salisbury, as we have seen, was not alone in adhering to this point of view, but his basic philosophy represented the last outpost of the mid-19th century view of society. The breakdown of the whole structure of self-help was very near in 1885, and the vaccilating attitude which the report presented on one of the great issues of the time showed well the incongruity of the predicament in which the country found itself. Many thinking men were now prepared to accept some kind of subsidisation, but they were not prepared to recognise it as such, and in this they were only deceiving themselves.

There could not have been many, however, who supported the carping criticism of *The Builder*, which believed that the Commissioners were opening the way to special privileges for the working class.[71] The real evils, it said, had not been considered by the Commissioners: they consisted of idleness, ignorance and vice, and the solution to these problems lay in education.

Nevertheless, the Royal Commission Report outlined most of the reforms which were necessary to secure the proper provision of housing in the right places, and the proper control of housing everywhere. It gave added authority to the views expressed a few years earlier by the Select Committee, and in a sense it was the final summary of the 19th century view of the housing problem. But more than that it drew attention to the lines of progress along which future legislation must move if it were not to repeat the mistakes contained in the corpus of existing law. Perhaps the most important conclusions which it reached were concerned with the reorganisation of local government, and the acceptance of centralised authority. The most significant features were the failure to achieve unanimity about the nature of the housing solution, and the grudging acceptance of the role that the state must take in the future financial solution of the housing problem. But despite this, the tacit recognition of a changing pattern in society makes it fair to describe the 1885 Royal Commission as a truly epoch-making document. The next decade was not to see a repetition of the frustrations and failures of the years since 1875 and a new housing policy was soon to be evolved which was a product of an entirely different social outlook from that which has been described in the previous pages.

The 1885 Housing Act and the closing years of the decade

The 1885 Housing of the Working Classes Act[72] as it came to be called, was not the great Act that the Royal Commission had proposed: Parliament was too preoccupied with the Irish question at that time. But Salisbury's Act made provision for the extension of the conditions under which the Lodging Houses Acts of 1851–67 might be adopted, and substituted the Metropolitan Board for the local vestries as the authority under the Act; it extended the meaning of lodging house to include any labourers' dwelling containing one or more tenements; and it gave power for the sites of the Millbank, Coldbathfields and Pentonville prisons to be sold to the Metropolitan Board.[73]

Alterations were made to the Torrens Acts of 1868 to 1882 so that the local authority was no longer obliged to purchase a property which it required to be repaired or demolished. The Cross Acts were amended on certain points concerned with representation and arbitration, and the Secretary of State was given powers to decide, in doubtful cases, whether an area should be dealt with under the Torrens or Cross Acts.

The Torrens Acts were still especially defective, however; in 1882 the Artizans' Dwellings Act had directed that groups of houses numbering no more than ten were to be dealt with under these Acts, but there was no implied provision that they were to be treated as a group and the tendency was always to repair and patch up, never to remove and replace.[74]

Another weakness perpetuated in the Act of 1885 was its repetition of the directive to local authorities to use their permissive powers, a recommendation which Jephson thought to be 'futile, considering that the authorities in question had steadily ignored the same direction, made nineteen years previously, in the Act

of 1866'.[75] The legislation, therefore, toyed with the problem, but made little attempt to make any radical reforms, and it failed to reflect the spirit of the Royal Commission.

In some respects the position was quite desperate: in 1887, for example, the Medical Officer for Lambeth complained about the failure of the Building Acts to make adequate controls and he reported the gradual spread into the suburbs of the practice of building out to the maximum area on the site leaving only the mere 100 square feet demanded in law. The following year the Medical Officer for Camberwell was complaining that there was no machinery to ensure that drainage schemes were carried out according to the plans submitted to the local authority.[76] There was, therefore, during the eighties almost as much difficulty in controlling the quality of building and the standard of sanitation as in previous decades. The work of a Select Committee and a Royal Commission had merely shown what was wrong; they had not secured a radical solution to the problems.

The impact of these two great reports was delayed; it was, however, to be eventually forthcoming, and the first step towards righting some of the most flagrant abuses and solving the most outstanding problems was begun in 1888 with the passing of the Local Government Act,[77] which established a new system of local administration, the county council and the county borough; and perhaps most important of all the London County Council, making provision for it to take over the duties of the Metropolitan Board of Works which was to be abolished. The Board had come into great disrepute during 1888 when it was accused of various malpractices, most of which were substantiated by a special Royal Commission of inquiry set up as a result of the persistent rumours of corruption.[78] The life of the Metroplitan Board, therefore, ended in disgrace, but it was evident that the corruption which had been substantiated was the work of employees, of whom certain architects, alas, were amongst the most conspicuous offenders. The Board itself was equally as horrified as the Commission when these things were exposed. Nevertheless, as an institution it seemed to be an exhausted body, much buffeted by the government and the ratepayers alike, and at last without the real will to execute the law which was given into its hands. It caused unnecessary delays and appeared always unwilling to take action; and it is significant that its dissolution was decided upon before the accusations made against it had been verified, for they were only indicative of a continuing malignancy of long standing.

The first elections to the new Council took place on 17 January 1889 and the new body began work with a vigour and urgency which had long been absent from the metropolis. The Sanitary and Housing Committees at once began to examine the problems which confronted their work and to press for further legal reforms on the lines of the Royal Commission Report of 1885. In 1890 they obtained their objective with the passing of the Housing of the Working Classes Act[79] which set about organising the sanitary and housing legislation in a way which the Act of 1885 had completely failed to do.

The Local Government Act of 1888 had established a new system of administration throughout the country; but that was only one step in the reforms suggested by the 1885 Commission. It did not give the necessary powers to solve the housing problem, and in London, at least, it failed to make the new County Council a really authoritative central body since it did not interfere with the local authorities; so that the inevitable task of the newly established council, in order that it should not be balked by the problems which had made the old Board so ineffective, was to seek further legal powers to organise the metropolis in matters relating to public health and housing. The most pressing problem was the provision of working class dwellings, and a deputation from the Council saw the Secretary of State on 16 December 1889, less than a year after the first election to the Council.[80] It was as a result of pressures such as these that the Housing of the Working Classes Act was passed the following session, a great consolidating measure repealing and codifying no less than fourteen statutes. Before its provisions are discussed, there are certain other issues and events of the eighties which must be examined.

The open space question

Much of the discussion in this chapter has reflected the sense of desperation which existed throughout this decade. Many times we have noted the comment of observers or the evidence of witnesses with an intimate knowledge of housing, pointing to a worsening situation. The eighties were the crisis years of the housing movement, or so they appeared to those who lived through them. Yet if we attempt to place them in context they are the turning point in the development of a new housing movement. We have traced the growth of social awareness, the preparation for legal reforms and a new era of social responsibility which would bear fruit after 1890; there remains an account of some of the developments which were to be more important in later years and which passed with little notice before 1890. The first is the development of an anti-urban movement: not consciously to destroy the idea of the town, but to offer the recreational and visual qualities which the 19th century town so frequently lacked. In an age which believed that high density was in itself unhealthy, the breakdown of urbanism, in the sense of physical buildings and their inevitable over-occupancy, was regarded as a necessary step to healthy living.[81]

Open space, that is in this context public parks and gardens, was not an entirely novel subject in the last quarter of the century.[82] Particularly in London attention had been increasingly given to the problem as the metropolitan area extended, making the country less and less accessible to the common man. The same lack of amenity was evident, but to a much less extent because of a difference in scale, in the provincial towns, and for this reason London provided once again the necessary precedents. Before 1875 there was a certain amount of interest in the provision of public gardens particularly, and some of these have been noted in a previous chapter. They were, nevertheless, sporadic attempts either to salvage what was left, to reclaim what had been neglected, or to prevent the greedy speculator from building on every inch of the available land. There was a noticeable quickening of awareness and activity, however, about 1880: Professor Colvin, for example, spoke about the uncontrolled sprawl of the town into the country, a subject which caused increasing concern;[83] and there were two Metropolitan Open Spaces Acts: the first in 1877,[84] which permitted the owners of commonly held open space, such as a square, to make it over to a local authority as public open space, if all the owners were agreeable. The second Act, of 1881,[85] amended the first and required only two-thirds of the owners to agree to the conversion of ownership, thus preventing a selfish part-owner from obstructing the wish of the majority. It also permitted a variety of local bodies to 'drain, lay out, turf, plant, ornament, light, seat and improve' any churchyards of which they obtained the management; and it provided that these open spaces should never be built over in the future.[86] These Acts might well be described as a salvage operation, valuable in itself, but a mere palliative so long as the speculator was building his cheaper varieties of housing on virgin land without any relation to parks or public open space of any kind: 'why should houses be erected which their tenants can never possibly care to occupy when they have advanced even one step in the social scale?'[87] bewailed *The Builder*, and the effect of enlightenment in one quarter was rapidly counteracted by foolhardiness in another. There was a further Act in 1883,[88] which permitted the use of funds from London Charities for the purchase of open space, and in 1887[89] the provisions of the London Acts were extended to the rest of the country.

One of the chief figures in the growing movement for the preservation of open space was that doyenne of the housing movement, Octavia Hill; and it was natural enough that interest in the one should lead to concern for the other. In 1875 she joined the Commons Preservation Society, a body founded ten years previously to prevent the enclosure of the remaining commons around London, which were then rapidly becoming desirable building land.[90] The society had started work after a Select Committee had decided that the rights of common land were sufficient to prevent their enclosure if the issue was brought to a court of law, and they had considerable success in their subsequent legal battles. Complementary to this society, which dealt with land around London, Octavia Hill and her sister Miranda were instrumental in establishing the Kyrle Society in 1875; its Open Spaces Committee, formed four years later, dealt with the smaller areas inside the capital, and it was responsible for the laying out of burial grounds as well as a wide variety of other activities.[91] Miss Hill's greatest asset was her tenacity in badgering authority, for example in 1885 when she was largely responsible for stimulating public interest in the preservation of Parliament Hill.[92] Her own practical steps to create gardens in the hearts of the slums, often against tremendous opposition, also deserve mention, not least her first venture at Freshwater Place in 1866;[93] and another, rather later, at Redcross Hall, Southwark, on land given to her in 1887 by the Ecclesiastical Commissioners.[94] The Open Spaces Committee of the Kyrle Society, with Octavia Hill and her legal friend Sir Robert Hunter as the prime movers, were largely responsible for the Open Spaces Acts of 1881 and 1883.[95] Other triumphs of a similar nature were to follow, so that London owed her a considerable debt of gratitude for the open spaces which were preserved at the end of the century. The country as a whole owed her an equal debt, for out of this movement developed the National Trust, founded jointly in 1895 by Canon Rawnsley, Octavia Hill, Sir Robert Hunter and the Duke of Westminster who had done so much for housing and open space problems already.

Another important organisation was also inspired by a peer, this time Lord Brabazon; it was known as the Metropolitan Public Gardens Association and it came into existence in about 1884.[96] By 1885, when Brabazon was appealing for more funds,[97] the Association controlled some 14 acres, much of it in the form of old churchyards which it had laid out as gardens, very much in the manner which Octavia Hill had adopted in the work of the Open Spaces Committee of the Kyrle Society. Brabazon continued his activities, and his was one of the bodies mentioned in 1887 when *The Builder* commented upon the great activity in connection with the preservation of open space which was then so noticeable.[98] But it was activity on a small scale, and like the work in the housing field the intentions and ideals of the movement were of greater importance than the quantity of work completed. The public was made aware of a valuable asset which previously it had failed to cherish, and this alone was a promising advance. It provided the incentive, in addition, for the gift to London in 1889 of three parks; at Dulwich the governors of the College presented some 72 acres to form Dulwich Park; in Camberwell a builder gave 14 acres known as Myatt's Fields, and Sir Sydney Waterlow gave his Highgate estate to the newly formed L.C.C. for a public park, a generous gesture from one who had the welfare of the poor much at heart.[99]

In addition to the question of open space there was the broader issue of town growth as a whole: 'a subject of great interest, but which has not been hitherto much discussed' said Professor Hayter Lewis at the Bolton Congress of the Sanitary Institute in 1887:

extensions...have, almost invariably, been carried out by speculators without any general definite guiding plan, with little or no forethought for the future extension, and with slight provision for supplying the inevitable future wants of the inhabitants. Thus, in the course of time, spaces have to be cleared out for churches, schools, institutes, baths and such like edifices as are now required for a large population, and clearances have to be made to allow for its free breathing.[100]

He pleaded for some form of civic control over the layout of towns so that space was preserved for necessary community buildings as well as for open space and parks. The idea of open space inside the town for recreation, and around it as a means of controlling its growth and preserving a wider degree of amenity for the town-dweller was thus left to germinate; and so, too, was the idea of balanced development. They were fully envisaged by the early town planners of the twentieth century, but they were not realised until after the second world war, and by that time much of the damage done by uncontrolled growth was irreparable.[101]

Transport

The gradual realisation that open space was valuable as an amenity, then, was the first of these new trends discernible during the years following 1875. The second was the role of the railways, and there were two reasons for the critical attention which was now paid to them. Since the great booms of the thirties and forties the railway companies had been responsible for the demolition of large quantities of working class housing, because it was cheaper to construct their lines into the heart of the great cities through slum property. But the companies had taken a mean advantage of their privilege as a popular new public service, and their blatant misuse of the considerable powers they possessed by virtue of private parliamentary Acts had caused misery and mischief because they provided no alternative accommodation for the people whose homes they so freely demolished. In consequence, they eventually alienated public sympathy, and it was felt that they should be obliged to play some part in alleviating the distress which they had helped to create.[102] The second reason was concerned with the potential service that the railways could render to the community by increasing the area within which it was possible for the working classes to live. Despite the fact that all the housing authorities which have so far been discussed built high density tenement blocks, most of them to the exclusion of all other dwelling types, there was no great certainty that these buildings were inherently healthy; and with the ever increasing difficulties which were experienced in making even very high density housing an economic success in central areas where it was most needed, the railways were now seen as a splendid means of conveying large numbers of working people cheaply, and quickly, over considerable distances, to sites where land was cheap and housing could still be built economically.

Certain railway companies began charging special workmen's fares of their own accord during the sixties, such as the Metropolitan Railway Company in 1864 and the South Eastern Railway Company in 1868;[103] but as a rule they were introduced only because a railway extension Act made them obligatory, and parliament saw this as one form of compensation which could be required as retribution for the demolition of working class housing, which earlier as well as current railway expansion within urban areas always involved. Obligations of this kind were imposed upon the Metropolitan Railway Company and the Great Eastern Railway Company in 1864,[104] although this last does not seem to have introduced workmen's fares at once. Similar obligations were subsequently imposed on other companies, and several more voluntarily started to run special trains, especially in south London. The experience of the Great Eastern Railway Company was probably typical of most, and in 1882 William Birt, their General Manager was called to give evidence before the Select Committee on the Housing of the Working Classes. The company was running a considerable number of trains specially for workmen, the longest journey undertaken being from Liverpool Street to Edmonton, a distance of nearly 11 miles, for which the fare was twopence return. They were running, in fact, more trains than was statutorily required of them, and had been doing so for several years; but workmen's fares did not pay, and Birt said that had they foreseen the problems involved they would probably not have started to provide so many; but once started, it was impossible to withdraw such a service.[105] The service was not financially successful, but in addition there were certain less obvious difficulties; workmen wore dirty clothes and this meant that special coaches, which were idle throughout the rest of the day, were required; they also indulged in dirty habits, such as smoking and spitting on the platforms, which were deprecated by other travellers. Birt also thought that workmen's trains were injurious to suburban property since they encouraged the building of a poorer class of dwellings, incidentally, depriving the company of a potential middle class traveller; he mentioned especially Stamford Hill and Tottenham, where the number of houses for the working class had outstripped demand. The tendency to overbuild at that period was borne out by the complaints of the Northern and Eastern Suburban Industrial Dwellings Company, which had sprung up to satisfy the new suburban demand, and had succeeded in satiating it in particular places.[106]

Nevertheless, the Select Committee recommended an extension of the workmen's train movement,[107] and as a result the Cheap Trains Act was passed the following year. This established the principle of workmen's trains and placed them under the general control of the Board of Trade. As a concession and encouragement the companies were exempted from the passenger duty on fares costing less than 1d. per mile and they also received certain concessions on other fares, in addition. The Act made it obligatory for the companies to provide a proportion of accommodation at fares not exceeding 1d. per mile on all their trains, and to provide special workmen's trains at these fares between six o'clock in the evening and eight o'clock the next morning, the exact number being regulated by the Board of Trade.

The function of the railways was also discussed outside the confines of the Select Committee at this time; James Hole, for example, lectured on 'Suburban Dwellings and Cheap Railway Fares' at the International Health Exhibition Conference in 1884.[108] His ideas led him to think in terms of model villages in the surrounding country and it was only a short step further to Henry Solly's idea for completely independent village communities, intercepting the people before they reached the town.[109]

In 1885 the question was again discussed and the progress reviewed by the Royal Commission, which found that the Great Western, the London and North Western, and the Midland Companies had not, as yet, made any provision for workmen, although several other companies were providing more than their legal minimum. The Commissioners had evidence that the failure was probably not due to financial losses since these other companies provided in excess, and their general conclusion was that the Board of Trade should take the initiative and extract the full legal obligations from the companies rather than waiting first for representations to be made requesting the institution of workmen's trains, which had been its practice. The inference was that the Board had not chosen to exercise its powers; and this may have been true, possibly because Chamberlain, who was at that time President of the Board of Trade, did not see this as its function.[110]

The general feeling of the Commissioners was that the state had interfered in railway matters for the benefit of the community and it possessed the right to do this because the railways had a virtual monopoly. This rather strong directive was probably given because of the clear evidence of evasion, and lack of public spirit, on the part of the railway companies; evidence that the companies were paying tenants to leave their homes before they applied for compulsory purchase powers, thus avoiding the need to provide new housing in place of the old which they were to demolish; evidence, too, that the companies were sometimes building houses and quickly converting them for other more remunerative purposes. Undoubtedly, the railways were responsible for much totally unnecessary misery and overcrowding.

When the London County Council came into existence in 1889 it seized the initiative; and at a meeting between members of the Housing Committee and the railway companies, the Council suggested that the railways might encourage suburban housing by providing stations in suitable and desirable locations before the real need for them arose. But the companies were not prepared to take that risk, unlike London Transport in its Underground expansion before the second world war.

In preparation for further attempts to secure the assistance of the railways the Council conducted a survey of the existing facilities for workmen in the metropolis, and these reports provided the basis of discussion for an abortive Cheap Trains (London) Bill introduced by Sir Blundell Maple in 1893.[111] The introduction of the bill was quickly followed by another conference, organised at the request of the Council by the Board of Trade, between Council officials and representatives of all the railway companies, so that the Council could put forward a new series of proposals for the extension of workmen's fares; but the only proposals to which the companies were willing to accede were of minor importance; such as permitting the return journey on a workmen's ticket by any train after noon, and the issue of workmen's tickets daily.[112] Although agreement had not been achieved, the companies themselves undertook the extension of workmen's trains where they found it convenient to do so: and since the Council appeared to be unable to secure either general agreement through discussion or a general Bill in Parliament, it was obliged to pursue its objectives in other ways, namely by seeking to require special conditions in all the new railway acts. In order to do this it prepared a model clause to meet its requirements which was successfully inserted into several subsequent small scale extension Acts.[113] But a further report by the Council in 1897 showed that the provision of trains was still well below the estimated need. In 1896 an average of 99,919 workmen's tickets were issued each day, 28,000 less than the Council thought desirable, and there was a suggestion that the number of hours during which workmen's trains were run, especially in the morning should be extended up to 8 a.m. which, although required by the 1883 Act, had never been rigidly enforced by the Board of Trade.[114] Once again, therefore, the Council resolved to seek amendment of the 1883 Cheap Trains Act; this time so that it would be able to take the initiative in making inquiries and petitioning the Board of Trade to apply the Act, a right which the earlier Act only gave to the workmen themselves.[115] No new legislation resulted, but the Council managed to secure permission from both the Board of Trade and the Railway Commissioners, who heard appeals under the 1883 Act, to give evidence in all cases which came before them concerning London transport; and by this means, although it was only a private arrangement, the Council was able to use the great mass of statistical information, which had previously been collected, to secure from time to time a better provision of cheap trains.[116] This arrangement extended throughout the remaining years of the period, despite the fact that during 1903, 1904 and again in 1905 a Select Committee was appointed to

consider the working and administration of the 1883 Act with a view to its amendment.

The effect of workmen's trains in south London has been analysed by H. J. Dyos,[117] and he found that the railways encouraged a sporadic and uneven development because of the varying degrees of efficiency, regularity and cheapness of the facilities provided by the different companies. This unevenness was due, of course, to the lack of a generally enforced cheap fares policy. The development of working class housing was chiefly in a zone from six to ten miles out of central London; after about 1907 he found that an area up to fifteen miles out was being developed, but here traffic was mainly in ordinary third class fares, denoting the movement of a different social class.

In north London there is less documented evidence; but the effect is well illustrated by the growth of Edmonton, from which the Great Eastern Company consistently ran workmen's trains during the seventies and onwards.[118] In 1851, 1861 and 1871 the population was respectively 9,708, 10,930 and 13,860. At the next census, in 1881, workmen's trains had been running for a number of years, and the population had risen to 23,463; in the subsequent decennial intervals it increased with even greater rapidity, the highest figures being between 1891–1901 when the increase was 70 per cent of the 1891 population, and by 1911 the population had reached 98,409. Walthamstow, served by the same company, showed an even greater increase and successively doubled its population between the decennial censi of 1871–81–91 and 1901; so that before the first trains were started in 1871 its population was a mere 10,692 and in 1901 it had risen to 95,131. This was the effect directly attributable to the railway companies; the housing which was built in these areas was wholly speculative, of course, but the new travelling facilities were relieving the pressure on central areas. Over the whole of London the number of workmen's trains running each day increased from 257 in 1890 to 1,731 in 1911, and this was a measure of the new pattern of life available to the working man.[119]

The tram only became of importance towards the end of the century. There were statutory obligations to run workmen's tram services, very much in the manner of the railway provisions, and in south London there was an adequate service by 1895.[120] The L.C.C. became the tramway authority for the metropolis and it was able to pursue the kind of policy which it was unable to force the railway companies to follow; and consequently there was from the outset an adequate provision for workmen's fares and services.[121] The network was extensive and the fares cheap: in 1911, for example, it was possible for a workman to travel from Victoria Embankment to Norbury or Norwood, from Moorgate Street to Hampstead or Highgate for 1d. single, or 2d. return.[122] Buses did not make special provision for the working classes and thus were not really important, although no doubt they were an encouragement to the middle class. The contribution of the tram to the facility of movement into the metropolis can be shown by the increase of workmen's tickets on the Tooting route from 581,626 in 1902–3, to 8,426,140 in 1912–13.[123] This may not have represented traffic entirely in one direction, since Dyos found that in south London there was a considerable cross traffic,[124] and down traffic in addition to movement into the centre each morning and out from it to the suburbs each night. Nevertheless the tram was an important force in the development of the working class suburb.

Health and housing in 1890

Speculative building in London during this period was controlled by a series of Metropolitan Building Acts, administered with moderate efficiency by the local authorities, until the great amending Act of 1894 smoothed out some of the more glaring peculiarities and inefficiencies. In the provinces much of the housing built in the last two decades of the century followed the general standards set out in the Model Bye-laws, first published in 1877, which set out an acceptable minimum standard, hygienic and sanitary when followed in spirit, but in the hands of the average speculator capable of resulting in rigid, monotonous and desperate areas of packed housing.[125] As a result we speak derogatively of the 'bye-law street'. Much of the working class housing which has just been mentioned in connection with the developments attributed to the railways was built under the Metropolitan code rather than the model code which did not apply in London; and so, too, was much of the middle class housing, although usually with slightly better space standards.

One of the characteristic features of the eighties was the continued need to draw attention to household sanitation, not least amongst the middle and upper classes, where respectable people were prepared to live in older houses with totally inadequate sanitation: lavatories ventilated through bedrooms, or placed under the stairs so that they endangered the health of the whole household, were still a commonplace. The need in reality was for continued vigilance, and the dissemination of sanitary knowledge, rather than for innovation and reform of a fundamental nature, for there was a genuine improvement in sanitary knowledge and practice, as Douglas Galton pointed out in the year of the Queen's Jubilee.[126] The chief offender was still the cheaper speculative builder, and the quality of his work showed little improvement so long as control was inadequate or lax; reports made during the decade showed little real advance on previous years. The Society of Arts, for example, passed a resolution in 1880 to the effect:

That it is expedient that the Metropolitan Board of Works within the metropolis, and the County Board within each county should be empowered by the Legislature to make provision for the inspection and sanitary classification of dwellings, upon application being made by the owners thereof; and to grant certificates, of health worthiness in different categories, for terms of years, according to the perfection of sanitary equipment and fitness for habitation of such dwellings; and to determine the scale of fees to be paid for such inspection during construction and repair, and also upon delivery to the applicant of the certificate of classification awarded to such dwelling.[127]

Failure to construct adequate drains continued to be one of the chief speculative malpractices, and it was still possible very occasionally to find an example of an estate laid out without the provision of sewers. Such was the case with Newlands Estate, Camberwell, where the developer was summonsed and the drains built by the Council at his expense.[128] It is alarming, however, to find examples such as this because, while it shows the willingness now of local authorities to use their powers, it equally illustrates the weaknesses in the existing legislation that such a situation could even occur as late as the eighties. The legal controls were gradually tightening as local authorities took their duties more seriously but they were patently not yet adequate and the general standard of building at times still could be very bad. So bad, in fact, that in December 1883 the 'Mansion House Fund for Improving the Condition of the Dwellings of the London Poor' was established, and a special Committee was set up whose objects included the promotion of better dwellings and the supervision of their erection.[129] Its concern was chiefly with sanitary matters,[130] but it was instrumental in organising a useful conference, the following year, at the International Health Exhibition; an Exhibition which did much to publicise sanitary matters and which included two demonstration houses, one showing sound sanitary fittings, the other common malpractices and insanitary designs.[131] Another type of organisation which began to spring up during this decade, and one which was closely related to the interest of the Mansion House Committee, was the Sanitary Society: in London there was a body known as the London Sanitary Protection Association,[132] and there were many similar in other parts of the country. The active supporters consisted very often of clerics and ladies, who gave their time and advice gratuitously, and their chief function was to visit houses in their particular district and help the tenants or owners to rectify such insanitary features as they found.[133]

The continued need for the dissemination of sanitary knowledge amongst all classes was undoubtedly one of the most startling facets of the eighties; the second trend which became increasingly significant was the reduction in pressure on the central areas as the working population slowly began to move outwards. But there was a third important tendency at this time: the apparent failure of the housing organisations to achieve an acceptable standard of accommodation for the working classes. This has already been mentioned in connection with the work of certain societies who were building at this period, but it was not confined to those engaged in practical work. It was just as surprising to find a lecturer at the British Association meeting, held at Newcastle in 1889, recommending what was virtually a single room dwelling, or a 'state cabin' plan as he preferred to call it, reminiscent of the kind of solution used by Lumsden at Glasgow forty years earlier.[134] Economic conditions being what they were it was an idea which was increasingly palatable to capitalist and philanthropist alike.

1890 is one of the most clearly marked dividing lines in the history of 19th century housing and the events which followed belong more to the new century than to the old. The great parliamentary enquiries of the first half of the eighties came to fruition first with the Local Government Act of 1888 which, amongst other local government changes, established the London County Council; and then with the 1890 Housing Act. These were the novel innovations but at the same time the Metropolitan Board, which had played so important a part in shaping the housing policy of the previous twenty years, was abolished, disgraced; a body, nevertheless more sinned against than sinning. Another organisation which had frequently voiced its opinions in the past and served as a forum for the housing and sanitary movements was the Social Science Association, and in 1886 it was decided that it should meet no more, since there was a marked lack of interest in its objectives, perhaps because many of them had already been achieved.[135] And so, 'those bold, bad men who attend Social Science Congresses' as Matthew Arnold described them,[136] were left without a common meeting place, but perhaps they too had disappeared. Two of the most important figures in the history of housing and sanitation were also absent when the new decade began; for George Godwin, who had been editor of *The Builder* from 1844 to 1883, died in 1888; and two years later died also Edwin Chadwick, of whom it had but recently been said:

He may claim the distinction of having probably told more disagreeable truths than any Englishman of his generation; and he has had the satisfaction of living to see most, if not all of them, admitted and acted upon.[137]

And thus ended a great and eventful era.

8

The maturing of responsibility

The new decade was in nearly every way a contrast to the old; the sense of crisis which pervaded the eighties gave way to a growing optimism that the housing problem would be solved. This was in part due to the wave of fresh activity replacing the lethargy which seemed to surround the older generation and the existing institutions. But more than this there was, as far as the historian can judge, a distinct change in atmosphere: gone to a large extent was the age of selfish vested interest; gone too were the old microcosmic reactionary institutions, and rising to influence were the new civic authorities, more proudly representative of the people, new brooms anxious to sweep away the cobwebs of Victorian philanthropy. As usual, it was in London that the pace of reform was set and much of our discussion centres around the work done there, but the new decade began with the passing of a national measure, the Housing of the Working Classes Act, 1890,[1] the piece of legislation which at last carried through the spirit of the housing reforms outlined by the 1885 Royal Commission Report.

Root and branch reform in 1890

The Act was of national implication but its provisions were, as usual, most valuable in the metropolis, that vast city where it seemed all precedent was created. It was divided into seven parts, of which the first three were the most important so far as the practical issues of housing were concerned. Part I dealt with the revision of the Cross Acts and the new provisions for the redevelopment of large areas: in the provinces the urban sanitary authorities were the executant bodies, and their rights and obligations were similar to those of the London County Council, whose powers will now be described. The official representation setting the Act in motion could be made either by the Council's own Medical Officer, or by a local vestry or district medical officer. There was now an obligation upon the officer to represent, either when he saw just cause, or upon the complaint of two justices, or of twelve ratepayers. It was also possible for the ratepayers to complain directly to the Secretary of State if the medical officer failed to take proper action, and the Secretary could then require the Council to take action as if an official representation had been made.[2] The previous permissive loopholes were thus closed for the first time and the Act rendered more effective.

Provided that the area did not comprise fewer than ten houses, when it would be dealt with under a separate section of the Act, the Council would then prepare an improvement scheme which must provide for rehousing at least as many people as were displaced, but the Secretary could allow alternative accommodation, or reduce the numbers for whom accommodation was to be provided, so long as housing was provided somewhere for not less than half the people displaced.[3]

The scheme was then advertised during three weeks in September, October or November, and the Council was required to notify all those whose property would be affected. Following this, it was submitted to the Secretary of State, together with a list of objectors, and a Public Inquiry was held, presided over by a special Commissioner. Provided his approval was given, the scheme was then confirmed, either in whole or in part, by provisional order which in turn must be confirmed by Act of Parliament.[4]

The Council then set about acquiring the designated property, and it was required to complete all its purchasing within three years. It must first attempt to purchase by agreement; and failing this, provision was made for arbitration. Compensation for the compulsory purchase of good property required to complete a scheme was usually 10 per cent higher than its market value,[5] but for insanitary housing the Act laid down careful rules for determining the proper value.[6] This value was ascertained in three ways; on a basis of the rent obtained if the house had been used for its legal purposes, free from any overcrowding; secondly on the value of the house after the abatement of any nuisance and after it had been put into reasonable repair – less, of course, the cost of effecting the repairs; and thirdly, its value based upon the value of the land and the materials thereon.[7] These provisions were designed to prevent the owners of insanitary or overcrowded property from making a profit out of its clearance.

When the purchase of all the property was complete the Council could then proceed with the redevelopment scheme, preparing plans for streets and drainage – which must be approved by the Secretary of State – and then proceeding to execute them. It might prepare plans for working class dwellings, but it must first obtain special permission before undertaking their erection; and again, without special permission, it must sell any tenements which it had built after ten years.[8] There was also a provision similar to that in the 1875 Act, which allowed the Secretary of State to sell sites, which had remained unsold for more than five years, for housing purposes.[9]

Part II of the Act provided for the revision of the Torrens Acts; it was concerned, therefore, with areas too small to be considered under the First Part, and also with single houses. The executive authorities were the local vestries and district boards or, in special circumstances, the Council itself; and the confirming authority was the Local Government Board who, with the Secretary of State, also exercised certain supervisory powers. The Council could act by the default of the local authority, and there were provisions for the Council to give financial assistance to local authorities to facilitate the execution of schemes.[10] The most important new provisions were expressly designed to prevent inactivity on the part of the local authority, and they thus removed the factors which had previously made the series of Torrens Acts inoperative.

Part III of the Act was concerned with the consolidation and amendment of the Lodging Houses Acts of 1851 to 1867; it was necessary for a local authority to adopt this Part, whereas the first two Parts compelled action following representation. Provision was made for the purchase of land and lodging houses, for various corporations and trusts to borrow money in order to build, and also for the sale of lodging houses which for any reason became unnecessary or too expensive after a period of seven years.

This Act of 1890 was amended four years later by the Housing of the Working Classes Act 1894[11] which extended the borrowing powers, previously only allowed for the completion of purchase and compensation under Part II, to cover the expenses of preparing, sanctioning and approving schemes, for costs and fees involved in compensation, and the charges for new streets and sewers, all of which had previously been chargeable on the rates. The Act was amended for the second time by the Housing of the Working Classes Act 1900,[12] which permitted urban sanitary authorities to acquire land outside their own jurisdiction for housing purposes under Part III of the 1890 Act, and in London for the Metropolitan Boroughs to become the authorities under the same Part of the Act.

The 1890 Housing Act was the last major example of legislative interference for the country as a whole during the nineteenth century. It at last provided the necessary machinery for effective slum clearance, and with the gradual increase in the effectiveness of local administration, first by the reforms of 1888, and secondly those of 1894 when the Local Government Act[13] made elections to vestries direct, the country as a whole was equipped for most eventualities. The foundation of public health had already been laid in 1875; with the passage of time and this same growth of local responsibility the Public Health code and the Model Bye-laws with their wide ranging provisions bore fruit and the country was ready to move into the new century as a more responsible society: the battles for the control of building development, spatially and sanitarily, and for state interference in an effort to solve the housing problem were won, at least in theory, and it was only the method of effectively implementing the new policies which remained to be fully worked out after 1890.

Legally, then, the country as a whole was adequately equipped for the immediate future, but London anomalously was not: the provisions for slum clearance applied equally to the metropolis and the provinces, but the central authority was not yet fully established, and the petty local authorities under its wing were still in need of reorganisation. Nor did the L.C.C. possess an equivalent measure to the Public Health Act of 1875, for that great sanitary work, it will be remembered, excluded the metropolis. To complete this account of legal reforms, therefore, it is necessary to turn to the belated work of parliament to safeguard London in the same way as any other large town.

A Review of the metropolitan building controls

Before discussing the new stream of legislation for the metropolis, which was enacted after 1890, it is useful to outline briefly the history of building control in London so that the differences between metropolitan and provincial controls can be better appreciated. London was usually excluded from national legislation and proceeded under special Acts, as we have seen, while the provincial towns possessed permissive powers which gradually grew into mandatory directives as the climate for reform grew more stringent. In the years prior to 1875 they could also operate under private Acts. But gradually after 1875 most towns came to accept the standards established by the Local Government Board in its model code, which was published as a result of the 1875 Public Health Act. There was an increasing measure of unanimity in the country towards the end of the century and regulations were made of a more stringent nature than those still in force for London, which for the first time fell behind the national standard. It is true to say, too, that local government in the country as a whole gradually became more responsible.

The Building Act of 1774 was the last great codifying measure for the Metropolis before the middle of the nineteenth century;[14] it set out to control the construction of party walls by establishing four classes of property based upon value and area, and it was also intended to ensure that all houses were rendered as fire-resisting as possible. Aesthetically it led to a degree of standardisation of house building which the succeeding generation, the Victorians, found so distasteful and we, so attractive; but in other respects it did not set out to establish the kind of spatial controls which later became essential.

This Act was not replaced until the Metropolitan Building Act of 1844, although certain additional restraints were put upon projecting buildings by the Metropolitan Paving Act of 1817 and the Act for Consolidating the Metropolitan Turnpike Trust of 1828; but both of these were made inoperative by the lenient interpretations placed upon them by the magistrates.[15]

The Metropolitan Building Act of 1844[16] extended the metropolitan area to include the surrounding parishes such as Paddington, Hampstead, Tottenham, and Hackney to the north and Greenwich, Lambeth and Streatham to the south, and provision was made for the Act to become operative within a radius of 12 miles of Charing Cross if necessary. New streets were required to be not less than 40 ft. wide, or equal to the height of the buildings on either side, whichever was greater; and similarly, alleys and mews were not to be less than 20 ft. wide or equal to the height of the buildings. Each dwelling house was to have an open space at its rear not less than 100 square feet in area except in very special circumstances, but no minimum width was specified, nor was there any need to make the open space extend throughout the entire length of the property. Every new building was also required to have sufficient means of access to allow a scavengers' cart to reach it.

Nevertheless, the pressure on urban land was sufficient to make landowners determined to develop every available site; and without the adequate means of inspection and control to carry out the Act, the local authorities, even those willing to observe its clauses, were frequently quite helpless, and the unscrupulous developer found ways both legal and illegal to avoid its implied meaning.

The Metropolitan Building Act of 1844 was replaced eleven years later by another Act of the same name.[17] Most of the earlier provisions were re-enacted and in addition the height of all habitable rooms was not to be less than 7 ft. The authorities for enforcing the Acts were the newly created vestries and district boards, and the Metropolitan Board of Works which was created as a titular supervisory authority, was given special powers over street construction, but otherwise it was in reality quite powerless to enforce its wishes upon the local authorities, and thus the all pervading disinterest of vested property was allowed to continue.[18]

The real trouble lay in the relationship of the vestry to the ratepayers; the vestry was too closely dependent upon the goodwill of the ratepayers, and the temptation to curry favour was always paramount. Vestrymen were also usually men of property, or in some way dependent upon the evils of the existing property system, and it was unfortunately often true that the interests of property were best served by tacitly ignoring sanitary and building reforms:

...the exorbitant rentals obtained from certain classes of houses, create a powerful interest opposed to all sanitary reform, promote the maintenance of slums, and hinder the progress of public improvements...the Building Acts are flagrantly evaded in the newer districts, and in the older quarters whole tracts of land are depopulated and left unoccupied till house-farming capitalists build thereon.[19]

This was written as late as 1880, and the same had been true for the previous half century: the spirit of the legislation was continuously defied and its execution blocked by the great power of self interest.

The next legislative innovations were of a minor nature; and some of them did not affect housing. The Metropolitan Management Amendment Act of 1862,[20] however, stipulated that no building should be erected in a new street less than 50 ft. wide whose height exceeded the width of the street. A further amendment of the same Act in 1878[21] permitted the Metropolitan Board of Works to make regulations for the construction of foundations and site works and for controlling the kind of materials used in house construction; a measure very necessary to ensure that the worst kind of speculative building did not continue, and so discouraging the construction of insanitary dwellings.

A much more theoretically stringent Act was passed in 1882[22] controlling the open space at the rear of all new dwellings erected on sites not previously occupied by buildings. The area of open space at the side or rear, unless all rooms could be lighted and ventilated from an adjoining street or alley, was governed by the frontage dimension; at 15 ft. the area must not be less than 150 square feet; at 20 ft., not less than 200 square feet; at 30 ft., not less than 300 square feet; and when the frontage exceeded 30 ft. the minimum open space was 450 square feet.

Unfortunately the Act in practice was only applicable to suburban development, since sites previously not built upon were unobtainable in central areas.[23] As one observer tartly noted a few years later:

Now, as in London, there is hardly a spot which has not been previously occupied in whole or in part by a building, the exception is quite sufficient to warrant the assertion that the enactment might just as well have been omitted from the statute book.[24]

And, further, the Act had the most curious provision that the open space might be entirely covered at ground level, thus allowing unventilated basements. There was no provision for a minimum width to the open space regardless of length; its area was governed by frontage dimension, and with a long frontage it was possible to comply with the regulations by creating a mean and narrow strip of open space at the rear, so long as its area fulfilled the legal requirements. The witness who gave the Royal Commission this information told them that building in the metropolis was still in effect controlled by the legislation of 1855.[25] He suggested that there should always be a certain amount of open space at ground level so that all floors might have proper ventilation, and so that the lavatory could be placed outside the main building. The open space should have a certain minimum depth governed by the height of the building; and he thought it would be useful if the bye-laws secured adequate gaps at the angles of a block of buildings formed inside a square grid-plan of streets.

He also recommended that similar provisions for open space at the front of houses to those contained in the model bye-laws should be made applicable to the metropolis, and adequate windows should be required, overlooking either the open space at the front or the rear of the building.

The architect to the Local Government Board was not the only person who felt that open space should bear some relation to the height of building. C. L. Lewis, writing in *The Nineteenth Century*,[26] pointed out that the 1882 space regulations were very inadequate in the face of increasingly high building, which was rapidly becoming characteristic of central area development due to the high value of land. Lewis was concerned with the moral right of authority to interfere with private property, to control its development, and he argued: 'Liberty to do what you like with your own is the inalienable privilege of every Briton; but there is always the proviso *subauditium* that in doing what you like you shall not hurt others.'[27]

The difficulties and problems were again set forth most eloquently in 1889, at the time when the newly formed London County Council were considering a revision of the existing legislation:

One of the most crying evils of large cities is the close juxtaposition of the houses, and a regulation prescribing a minimum distance between the backs of all houses, large and small, is most urgently needed. The provision of the present Building Acts are practically a dead letter. Exception has been taken to the words of section 14 of the 1882 Amending Act (as to open spaces of dwellings), which only applies to buildings erected on a site not previously occupied, but I am bound to say – much as I regret it should be so – I see no help for this when dealing with such a city as London, or practically, rebuilding could not take place at all if the regulations were carried out in full. A building with 50 ft. frontage and 50 ft. height need only have an area at the rear 450 square feet, that is, nine feet deep! No restriction beyond this exists anywhere as to the distance of buildings from one another at the back...I should contend most confidently that the minimum depth of the open space that should be allowed at the backs of houses should depend on the height of the houses themselves, and that the frontage has nothing at all to do with the question, and I should say that this open space should equal the height of the building.[28]

Putting aside the moral issues, the practical use of existing building law was called into question from time to time, as for example in 1885 when a speculative builder laid out a continuous street some 509 ft. long and 24 ft. wide. It was a cul-de-sac, and the buildings were to be some 36 ft. high to their eaves. George Godwin wrote to *The Builder*[29] to complain about the advanced stage this work had reached: how it contravened the law by its length, by its breadth, by the height of the buildings and by the nature of its entrances. The local authorities concerned, the vestries of St Giles and St Lukes, were stirred into action and apparently agreed with Godwin's views, for they took the builder to court, on the ground that he had failed to give notice that he was constructing a street. In court, the builder countered that the street was to have gates at its open end, and was thus not a street within the meaning of the law, and, unfortunately, the magistrates agreed and dismissed the summons!

If the law was thus inefficient in that it did not make provision for such eventualities, it was also grudgingly applied, and it was ambiguous. The Act of 1855, and its amending Act of 1882, contained two clauses at variance with one another about the provision of space to the rear of a dwelling. *The Builder*[30] suggested that the latest clause should take precedence and that even when lighted from the side a dwelling must have open space at its rear. But what, it wondered, happened when a block of dwellings was situated between two streets? The correspondence which followed failed to produce a concise definition of the law. Banister Fletcher[31] argued that as the 1882 Act only amended the principle statute it did not necessarily supersede the original; and further correspondence showed that no one was clear on the real interpretation of the point.[32]

The law relating to cellar dwellings in the metropolis was also behind that for the rest of the country. A cellar occupied as a dwelling before 1855, and continuing to be so occupied, must have an area 3 ft. wide in front of the whole side, extending from 6 inches below floor level to street level. Of this area a portion at least 5 ft. in length and 2 ft. 6 ins. in width must be in front of the window with the top open, or covered only with a grill. In cellars not previously occupied before 1855 the minimum height was 7 ft., and the cellar must rise 1 ft. above street level; the external area was similar to that for a cellar first occupied after 1855.[33]

In the provinces the 1875 Act decreed that only cellars occupied before the passing of the Act might be used as dwellings, and then only if they were not less than 7 ft. high and reaching 3 ft. above street level. The requirements about the open area were slightly less severe: the area was required to be 2 ft. 6 ins. wide, extending the full length of the building, and vertically from 6 ins. below floor level to ground level, but unfortunately this rather stringent section of the Act was not always enforced.[34]

The legal reforms of the nineties in London: health and housing

When the L.C.C. was created, then, London was badly served by its legislation; clearly it lagged behind the rest of the country and there had been no dynamic lead from vestry, district board or Metropolitan Board. By 1889, for example, sanitary regulations had been made in 31 of the 43 sanitary districts of the metropolis, but in only 9 of these had any great use been made of them. Most local authorities had ingeniously rendered their bye-laws inoperative by such tricks as exempting houses above a certain value from overcrowding regulations, or failing to make the bye-laws of universal application in their district. Neither had the L.C.C. as yet been appointed the effective sanitary authority for London, and most local authorities could point to a carefully worded escape clause which protected them from the Council's interference.[35]

The important measure which began to rectify these faults, the Public Health (London) Act was passed in 1891,[36] amending more than thirty existing statutes and fulfilling many of the recommendations made on this particular subject by the 1885 Royal Commission. It required that a local authority should carry out regular inspections of the district under its jurisdiction and that it should secure the abatement of nuisances, which were so defined as to include premises dangerous to health; and a house, or part of a house, which was overcrowded might be considered such a nuisance.[37]

It was intended that the Act should be for the metropolis what the 1875 Public Health Act had been for the country as a whole. The existing local authorities were constituted the new sanitary authorities; these included the Commissioners of Sewers of the City of

London, and in greater London the local vestries and district boards. In addition the County Council were given certain powers to act in default of the local authorities except in the case of the City, where the County Council were powerless, thus preserving a time honoured distinction, which in the past at least had always permitted the City to manage its affairs a great deal more effectively than the Metropolitan area.

The Act greatly increased the powers of the local authorities in all matters of health and sanitation; but in addition it laid on them the obligation to look for nuisances and to secure their abatement; it laid upon them the duty to cleanse the streets and remove nuisances; it made it illegal for a house to be built which did not have one or more water closets, except where the sewers or water supply could be proved to be inadequate; and it provided for the London County Council to make bye-laws to this effect. The local authorities were in addition required to make bye-laws controlling houses let in lodgings (as opposed to common lodging houses) in order to prevent overcrowding, to provide for registration and inspection, to ensure adequate provisions of drainage, ventilation, cleansing and limewashing, and to ensure adequate provision of precautions in times of infectious diseases.

Strict regulations were set out for cellar dwellings, requiring a minimum height of 7 ft., 3 ft. of this above street level; the area in front of the cellar was to have a minimum width of 4 ft., quite the largest dimension required by any Act then in force. The area had to be paved and effectively drained, and to extend the whole width of the room. Other details, concerned with drainage and damp-proofing, were also included in the legal requirements, and these were entirely new provisions. The window area was required to be not less than one tenth of the floor area, and half of it must open to the full height. Furthermore, six months after the Act came into force all these provisions were to apply to every cellar let as a separate dwelling, and not merely to those brought into use after the Act became law, which made its provisions the more effective. A special escape clause, however, was included so that in cases where major structural alterations would be necessary the provisions of the Act might be modified.

The important provisions which allowed the L.C.C. to act in default of the local authority were contained in sections 100 and 101, and arrangements were made for the work involved to be financed out of the rates.

The local authorities were now obliged to appoint Medical Officers and Sanitary Inspectors, who were to be properly qualified, and the former was required to reside within one mile of his district. Medical Officers might be shared by more than one authority; but the important point to note was that a number of qualified and efficient officials were at last called into existence.

The effectiveness of the Act was greatly increased by a change which shortly took place in the organisation of local government by the Local Government (England and Wales) Act of 1894[38] which included London in its

provisions, and at last made elections to vestries direct, although Jephson did not think that in London this increased their sense of responsibility, at least so far as inspection was concerned.[39]

A year previously a Royal Commission had been set up 'to consider the proper conditions under which the amalgamation of the City and County of London can be effected, and to make specific and practical proposals for that purpose'.[40] Its report the following year recommended further centralisation and proper responsibility to the central authority by the local bodies. It was not, however, until 1899 that the administration of the metropolis was drastically reorganised by the London Government Act,[41] although even this failed to break down the impregnable bastions of the City. It removed the last outpost of Victorian self interest and *laissez-faire*: the system of vestries and district boards, which had thwarted the legislation throughout the whole period under discussion in a way which was at times criminal, and barely mitigated by their work in connection with drainage, refuse removal, lighting and the paving of streets, all of which had improved out of all recognition during the second half of the century. The Act created twenty-nine municipal boroughs in place of the forty-three vestries and district boards then in existence, and these became the new local authorities.

The legal reforms of the nineties in London: building controls

London was brought into line with the rest of the country so far as its sanitary and administrative arrangements were concerned by 1894, and it possessed through the national Housing Act of 1890 the means for continuing the slum clearance and rehousing programme begun under the Torrens and Cross Acts. It had not, as yet, adequate building controls; and this was the third and final step in the complete reorganisation of the metropolis. The picture of sanitary organisation before the 1891 Act, with its diversity of officials and authorities, its localised administration firmly pitted against central control, and its interest in thwarting the fullness of the law was paralleled by the appalling state of building control. As we have seen, of the 43 sanitary districts in London only 9 had made any real use of the building regulations which they were allowed to make under the various Sanitary Acts applicable to London. And the new legislation of the early 1890s did not give the London County Council absolute control over the local authorities, so that it was still possible for them to frame bye-laws, which were subject to Local Government Board approval and not that of the County Council, containing very useful escape clauses, thus successfully preventing the Council from intervening by making it virtually impossible to prove negligence.[42]

In 1894, therefore, the London Building Act[43] was passed, consolidating and amending the existing provisions and regularising the role of the L.C.C. as the central building authority for the metropolitan area. The spatial regulations were, from the point of view of this chapter, the most important, and this time they applied in the City of London as well. A carriage-way was defined as a street of minimum width 40 ft., and a pedestrian street 20 ft.; culs-de-sac were effectively prevented by the provision that no street longer than 60 ft., nor any street of less length in which the length was greater than the breadth, was to be formed without both ends open from the ground upwards.[44] The only exemptions were for the re-erection of buildings within the prescribed distances of the centre of the road – that is, within 20 ft. of the centre of a carriageway, or 10 ft. from the centre of a pedestrian way in the City of London – provided that it could be satisfactorily proved that during the preceding seven years a building had existed within the area which now infringed the prescribed distances.[45] No dwelling house built for, or converted to the use of the working classes might be included in this escape clause unless its height was less than the width of the street, except in the case of the re-erection of dwelling houses previously built by a local authority.

Building lines in each street were to be defined by general precedent, or they could be defined if necessary by the superintendent architect. No new building was to extend beyond this line within 50 ft. of the highway except under the special conditions just noted for rebuilding properties which had existed within the previous seven years.[46] The Council could give special consent for this rule to be broken, but it was made clear in the Act that a special case did not create a precedent.[47]

The provisions for the control of space at the rear of a building were very important; they began with regulations for the lighting and ventilation of basements. If a basement was habitable there must be an open space adjoining it at ground level of at least 100 sq. ft. but this need not extend to the boundary of the site. The other requirements were largely based around this provision.[48]

The Act dealt next with new domestic buildings[49] erected on streets laid out after 1894, and it required that each house be provided with an open space of 150 sq. ft. Where there was a cellar used as a habitable room and the 100 sq. ft. requirement was fulfilled, this open space could be provided above the level of the ground floor or above the 16 ft. level, irrespective of the use of the ground floor. The open space might also be provided at first floor level when there was no cellar and the ground floor was not used for purposes of habitation. In all other cases the open space must be at ground level, free from any obstruction except a lavatory or wall not exceeding 9 ft. in height.[50] In addition, the open space must extend the entire width of the building with a minimum depth of 10 ft. so that in certain cases 150 sq. ft. was not the minimum legal open space. For the first time there was a pro-vision for the regulation of height and open space in relation to one another: from the centre of the road an imaginary horizontal line was drawn, and it was intersected by another, at an angle of $63\frac{1}{2}$ degrees to it, at the boundary of the site in the rear, and no part of the building must project beyond this line.[51] In effect this meant either that the open space was increased in relation to the height, or the building was set back successively at each floor. This provision could be modified when the building was bounded by streets or open space to the rear as well as at the front, and a certain amount of building on the open space, to a maximum height of 30 ft., was permitted at junctions of streets. Similarly, a corner building might be returned along the secondary street to its full height for a distance of 40 ft., despite the $63\frac{1}{2}$ degree angle, so long as the other open space regulations were not fouled.[52]

The following sub-section dealt with new buildings in existing streets,[53] and the basic modification between this section and the one controlling new streets was that the $63\frac{1}{2}$ degree angle governing the relation between height and open space was to be constructed from a horizontal line drawn, not at ground level, but 16 ft. above the ground. The open space requirements concerning cellars, minimum widths and areas were nevertheless similar to those just described, but they too might be provided above this 16 ft. level also, except in the case of working class houses. This meant that back-to-back development was possible on the lower floor of certain buildings, which was not a very desirable state of affairs.[54] There were also certain provisions for exceeding the $63\frac{1}{2}$ degree angle if an equivalent cubic open space was provided to that required if the building had been erected in a new street.[55]

Working class dwellings were, therefore, specially regulated and the Act required in addition that when they were not erected in streets, plans were to be submitted to the County Council, and the open space requirements were to be equivalent to those for domestic buildings erected after the passing of the Act in existing streets.[56]

Complex regulations were also provided for courts which acted as wells within buildings, for the purpose of lighting and ventilating rooms which had no other means of communication with fresh air; these clauses were designed to prevent habitable rooms from having insufficient light and air[57]

The absolute height of buildings was also limited for the first time, perhaps because of the increasing tendency to build high at this period. With the exception of a church or chapel no new building or alteration to an existing building was to exceed 80 ft. in height to its eaves, without the special permission of the Council, although two additional floors might be placed in the roof. Existing buildings of a greater height might be rebuilt to the same height, and a person owning two adjacent buildings where one exceeded 80 ft. and the other did not, might rebuild the lower one to the same height as his other property.[58] Certain special regulations however were laid down for streets of less width than 50 ft. which were laid out after 7 August 1862; in these, old buildings were not to be raised above their existing height without the Council's consent. And similarly, no new building was to exceed in height the width of the street. At the junction of two streets the width of the wider was also to govern the height of building for the first 40 ft. in the narrower; but a building previously erected to what would now be a prohibited height might still be re-erected to the same height.[59] This provision also applied to working class dwellings which might be re-erected by a local authority to the same height and on the same site.[60] A further restriction was placed upon working class housing built or rebuilt within 20 ft. of the centre of a road laid out at any date, requiring that the height of these buildings must not exceed the width of the street.[61]

The Act increased the minimum height of rooms to 8 ft. 6 ins., except for attics which were required to have a minimum height of 8 ft. over not less than half the total room area. Every room must have a window with an area equal to not less than one tenth of the floor area, half of which must open at least to a height of 7 ft. above floor level. There were certain relaxations for rooms lit from the roof or by dormers or lanterns.[62]

Other related subjects with which the Act was concerned included the provision of powers to control or prevent house building on low lying ground;[63] the appointment of an official by the Council to be known as 'the superintending architect of metropolitan buildings',[64] and of district surveyors to control the erection of new buildings. Careful rules were laid down to ensure that properly qualified people were appointed to these offices and the R.I.B.A. was permitted to examine candidates for surveyorships.[65]

One of the significant innovations was concerned with building control; a builder was required to give notice to the surveyor two days before work first began on a building site, two days before work recommenced after having been stopped for more than three months; and when a new builder for any reason took over on a building site he was also required to give two days notice before starting work.[66] It was the duty of the surveyor by means of inspection to see that the provisions of the Act were enforced, and it was possible to take judicial proceedings against an offending builder or owner.[67] To regulate all these new legal provisions the Council could make bye-laws.[68]

Thus London was provided with a series of building controls the like of which it had not previously enjoyed, and which brought it more or less into line with the rest of the country. The Building Act was amended in 1898,[69] and the spatial requirements for working class housing were re-enacted. Further amendments were made in 1905[70] mainly concerned with fire precautions, and again in 1908 which,[71] so far as its references to the Building Acts were concerned, repealed the clauses dealing with warehouses, replacing them with more generous provisions. The London County Council (General) Powers Act 1909,[72] allowed the sanitary authority to require adequate storage for food in new tenement buildings, and provided regulations for framed structures in steel, iron or concrete.

The provisions made by the two Building Acts of 1894 and 1898 completed the legislation controlling house building before the war. It is worth noting, in conclusion, some of the variations between the controls which existed in London and those which applied in the rest of the country. The Model Bye-laws provide the accepted standard for the provinces, but it must be remembered that there was still room for considerable variation because they were not mandatory. The principal differences between the two standards were first, the distance which must separate buildings across a street which varied from the London minimum of 40 ft. to the Model Bye-law minimum of 24 ft.; secondly, in London there were a variety of controls over building height but elsewhere none. Similar slight discrepancies existed with regard to carriageways, the London minimum being 40 ft. and the Model 36 ft., although most authorities usually required more. The requirement that certain streets must communicate at both ends with other carriageways was also not paralleled in the provinces, since the Model series required only one entrance; and there were also minor differences about the height of rooms and the provision of damp-proof courses.[73] Undoubtedly the nature of London, its size and density, had provoked more stringent regulations than were elsewhere thought necessary at that time, so that before the end of the century the metropolis had again become the leader in matters of building control.

The public spirited way in which the L.C.C. pursued its role as the sanitary guardian and spatial arbiter of the metropolis made it clear that a new kind of local government organisation, more positive and willing to act for the public good, had sprung into existence. The preceding account of the Council's willingness to observe the sanitary and building law then in force, and its anxiety to obtain more efficient and stringent provisions marked the beginning of a new era of public responsibility.

In another and equally important way the Council made it clear that it was not merely an administrative authority, but one intent upon creating precedent by formulating its own housing policy and also carrying it into effect. The L.C.C. was the most important of the new housing agencies at the end of the century, in the first place because it set an example which was subsequently followed until local authority housing throughout the country became the most important source of all new working class housing; and secondly, because of the solutious, both spatial and architectural, which it adopted.

The Council succeeded the Metropolitan Board in 1889, and the most notable immediate change was one of attitude. The Board had become lethargic and had lost the will to take the initiative in the housing field, partly no doubt because its experiences had given it little incentive for activity: it had, for example, power to appoint a Medical Officer, but it had never done so; and it also had powers after 1879 to put into effect the series of Torrens Acts in cases where the local authority defaulted, but again it had not chosen to exercise them. The Council, on the other hand, saw itself as a new broom, and its activity was the more notable by comparison with the inactivity which characterised the Board's last years. It sought increasingly to take the initiative, especially after 1890 when its role in relation to working class housing was more clearly defined. The Board, as executive housing authority after 1885, was permitted to provide 'lodging houses', which included tenements and cottages as well as lodging houses, but it never sought to use these powers; and it was typical of the Council that the provision of dwelling accommodation was one important aspect of its policy from the outset, first by the provision of lodging houses, later by the purchasing of land.[74]

There was another important distinction to be made: the Board was faced with a single great task which to its credit during the early years of its life it had successfully completed, the reorganisation of metropolitan sewage, while the Council was faced more clearly with a housing and overcrowding problem, to which the Board towards the end of its life had found itself totally unequal.[75] It was perhaps a significant sign of the great new influence of transport that the Council's efforts were concerned less and less with slum clearance and the number of new clearance schemes dwindled after 1900. At the same time pressure on the central area of London for housing declined, and the emphasis moved on to the implications of outward expansion.

The number of additional rooms provided in central London after 1900, allowing for the replacement of demolished accommodation, showed a steady decline, this was more noticeable particularly after 1906, and in 1912 demolitions for the first time actually exceeded replacement. Building activity spread outwards, encouraged as we have seen by cheap transport, and the demand for housing was largely satiated during the early years of the new century, except for the cheaper working class accommodation, since the type of house built speculatively was often too large or too expensive for working class tenants, although at this point the L.C.C. was able to help with its cottage estates.

Looking back on this pre-war period from the beginning of the century, one can clearly see that, in the frenzy of building new houses – which spread constantly outwards, actuated by the traffic revolution – all sense of slum clearance was lost. The working-classes who could afford time and money were catered for; the middle-classes also tended to leave the town, leaving behind them fair-sized houses which were quickly invaded, divided and subdivided by the poorest classes since no provision, either by private enterprise or municipal action, had as yet been made for them.[76]

Local authorities, it must be remembered, were as yet a very minor housing agency, quantitatively, and there still remained an overcrowding problem which was gradually moving away from the centre into the inner suburbs. The problems we have discussed, therefore, still existed although to a lessening degree; but for the first time the physical centre of the overcrowding problem moved away from the geographical centre of the city and this created, perhaps, a false sense that the problem had apparently solved itself.

The Council took over from the Metropolitan Board of Works the administration of the whole of metropolitan London, and it inherited from the Board the remaining schemes, started under the 1875 Artizans' Dwellings Act, but never completed; as well as the urgent necessity in 1890 to start many more, which the Board in its laxity had failed to do. One of the first actions of the Housing of the Working Classes Committee was to review the existing legislation, and, in order to have their position clarified, they requested the government to revise the housing Acts, the result being the Housing of the Working Classes Act of 1890 which, as we have just seen, reorganised the existing series of Acts very much as had been suggested in the first place by the Royal Commission of 1885. The important point to note here is that the Act contained more definite provision for the local authority, in this case the London County Council, to build working class housing; and since the Council, like the Metropolitan Board, found great difficulty in disposing of the cleared sites, it became necessary for it to use this power, although it should be observed that its first intention was to sell the land in the same way as the Board had done. When it came to build, the Council proceeded on the following financial principle:

The rents to be charged for the dwellings erected in connection with any specified housing scheme or area shall not exceed those ruling in the neighbourhood, and shall be so fixed that after providing for all outgoings, interest, and sinking fund charges there shall be no charge on the county rate in respect of the dwellings on such area or scheme, and all such dwellings shall be so designed that the cost of erection may not exceed a sum which will enable the Council to carry out the foregoing condition. The interest and sinking fund charges shall be calculated upon the cost of erection, plus the value of the site, subject to the obligation to build dwellings for the working classes upon it.[77]

The design of the actual buildings remained subject to the approval of the Secretary of State, as it had done for schemes undertaken by the Board.[78] His requirements when the Council came into existence consisted of limiting the height of tenement blocks to four storeys, and fixing the minimum size of living rooms to 144 sq. ft. and bedrooms to 96 sq. ft.[79] The Council itself provided regulations to guide those building on cleared sites which incorporated these requirements; they also provided that staircases should not be totally enclosed, and established the general principle that the distance between buildings should be not less than one and a half times their height, and under no conditions whatsoever should this distance be less than the height of the building. The Council was obliged to modify these regulations when it tried to put them into practice in 1893, for reasons of cost, and it therefore increased the maximum number of floors to five, while reducing the width of staircases from 4 ft. to 3 ft. 6 ins., and the minimum height of rooms from 9 ft. to 8 ft. 6 ins.[80]

Subsequently the Council's housing standards were largely influenced by the views of the Secretary of State, and after 1894 these became more exacting. The Council, nevertheless, was anxious to set a standard of accommodation which 'would in all respects bear the closest investigation',[81] but at the same time it had itself established a financial policy by what came to be known as the '3 per cent resolution' of 1893. The early building policy was therefore, to provide an increasing number of self-contained dwellings while adhering to the minimum room sizes set out in 1889. Criticism, however, led to a gradual increase in areas until a new standard was reached in 1898 with a living room 160 sq. ft. and one bedroom 110 sq. ft., or two bedrooms, the first 100 sq. ft. and the second 120 sq. ft.[82]

The Council's policy was also influenced by other restrictions imposed by the Secretary of State; such as the limitation of the number of people using a common stair, the requirement that staircases should provide access to the yard, the disapproval of balcony access and the insistence upon a 45 degree angle of light. The Minister's opinion of the balcony access system must have undergone a considerable change since the Council later evolved a new and improved system which became standard practice. Similar conditions were imposed by the Local Government Board to whom the Council were responsible for schemes carried out under Part II of the 1890 Act, that part amending the Torrens Acts. In some of these schemes, however, the Council was obliged to revert to the space standards of 1889 for reasons of cost. It was faced, then, with increasing difficulties in fulfilling its financial obligations under the terms of its own three per cent resolution and the Treasury requirements during these years, and it was therefore only able to build with considerable difficulty.[83]

The L.C.C. as housing agent in central London

In March 1889, when the Council took office, there were a number of schemes which the Metropolitan Board had undertaken and never completed; the Council therefore became responsible for these, and its first efforts were largely a continuation of the

Board's policy: there were no immediate innovations.[84] Six schemes in all were outstanding,[85] and between 1889 and 1892 the Council made repeated attempts to sell the remaining sites, which had already been allocated for dwellings. Some of these were unfortunately arranged so that philanthropic societies refused to buy them, but nevertheless, they might not legally be used for any other purpose, and the Secretary of State refused to modify his ruling so that the Council was in a worse predicament than the Board.[86] In July 1889 the Council made its first attempt to secure the Secretary of State's permission to build, in connection with the Hughes Fields scheme at Deptford, but this was refused;[87] and it was not until April 1892 that the Council decided to seek permission to exercise the powers which it had then acquired under the 1890 Act, in order to build on the Brook Street site in Limehouse, and this time the permission was finally given.[88] The original scheme, which dated from 1876, had been modified so that only half those displaced were required to be rehoused, so long as the accommodation was provided in the form of houses. In fact, cottage property proved too expensive to build, and the bulk of the accommodation was provided in five storey tenements, known as Beachcroft Buildings, which were completed in September 1894 and only in 1900 were a small group of two-bedroomed cottages built in Brook Street.[89] Similar steps were taken with the other outstanding sites later in 1892,[90] and a variety of buildings were subsequently erected by the Council.

The tenements and cottages erected at Brook Street were designed in the Council's own architect's department; there had been an official architect appointed by the Council soon after it was created,[91] as well of course, as a Medical Officer and an Engineer; but it does not initially seem to have been regular policy to entrust all the housing work to the internal architects' department. In 1894 Rowland Plumbe was employed to design the housing for the Shelton Street scheme, and five blocks were completed in the autumn of 1896.[92] They consisted mainly of single room tenements, but unlike most work of this kind they were all self-contained whether of one room or larger. Plumbe was also engaged, when this scheme was being completed, to design cottages at Trafalgar Road, Greenwich; there were several delays and when tenders were received it was found that they could not be built so that the council's policy, contained in the three per cent resolution, could be followed, and the scheme was subsequently abandoned. In its place the Council's own architect provided an alternative design which also proved too expensive, but nevertheless it was built, and fifty-one cottages were completed in 1901.[93]

The completion of clearance and rehousing obligations inherited from the Board, fraught with difficulties as they were, established the kind of procedure which was to be followed to a large extent in the new schemes which were undertaken by the Council under the 1890

Act. The remaining sites were not so large as many of the more spectacular clearance schemes which had been completed by the Board before 1889, nor were they all central, so that demand for accommodation was not always great. In all 6,188 people were displaced on the six sites and 2,930 were rehoused;[94] the Secretary of State used his discretionary powers to reduce the total numbers, but it is noticeable that in other respects he was unwilling to comply with many of the council's requests, such as the substitution of alternative sites, or the complete abandonment of difficult sites; and he seems to have exercised his powers to the full with regard to the inspection of plans.

In 1890 the first representation was made to the Council under Part I of the new Act, and this came to be known as the 'Boundary Street, Bethnal Green, Improvement Scheme.' From most points of view it was an epoch making example of redevelopment, not least because it embraced a very large area, amounting to some 15 acres altogether.[95] The method of procedure, inquiry, provisional order and confirmation proceeded according to the modified system, based on that established in 1875 which was described earlier, and the approved scheme provided for the displacement of 5,719 people and the rehousing of 5,100.[96] Most of the existing streets were narrow, the widest only 28 ft., and provision was made for the widening of some which existed as well as the construction of several more, all of which were to be 40 ft. wide. The original intention was to divide the site into rectangular plots, which would be cleared in three stages, accommodation being found by the Council in adjacent districts for those displaced in the first stage. But before all the negotiations had been completed the Council decided to replan the area on a radial system. In addition to allowing a greater number of people to be housed than in the original rectangular plan, the second plan permitted a central open space from which the streets would radiate, and most of these were again increased in width: the main approach road to the site was made 60 ft. wide, the more important streets inside the site 50 ft., and only the secondary streets were 40 ft.[97] There was, in addition, provision for shops, workshops and costermongers' stores, and in this revised form the plan was approved late in 1893. Because of the new plan, the site was divided into five areas instead of three, as originally proposed; and the first was cleared in 1893, consisting of a detached site east of Mount Street. On it, two blocks designed by the architect's department, built by the Works Department and known as Streatley Buildings, were begun later that year and completed in 1895.[98] The next development was an independent communal laundry which was completed the following year; this was built partly because the Council seemed to have considered it to be more healthy than laundries incorporated in the blocks, and also because in that district it was difficult to obtain a good water supply at roof level, which was the traditional alternative position.

8.1   *Boundary Street Estate, L.C.C., begun in 1893 under the terms of the 1890 Housing Act; plan of the site before redevelopment and after*

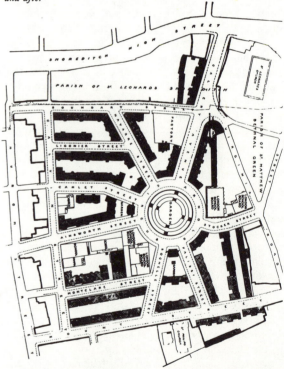

The next housing section, consisting of nine blocks, was begun in the autumn of 1894; they were designed in the architect's department and an estimate was prepared for their cost. The Works Department was then given the opportunity of building them for this figure, and if they refused – as they did in each case – they were to be put out for competitive tender. This group of buildings was completed during 1896 and 1897. It contained a variety of accommodation varying from single room to four room tenements, most of the multi-roomed tenements were self-contained, but some had shared sculleries and Culham Building which

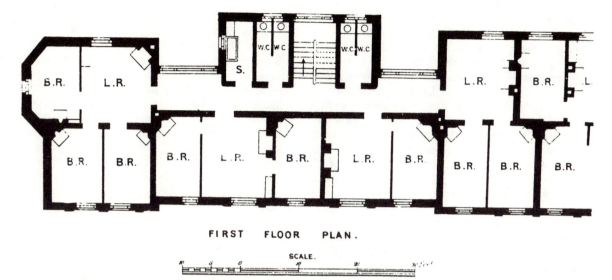

FIRST FLOOR PLAN.

SCALE.

8.2 *Boundary Street Estate, L.C.C.; typical flat plans*

contained mostly single rooms, had neither separate sculleries nor lavatories.[99]

The third section was made the subject of a limited competition. Six architects were selected and invited to submit designs in April 1894. This was done, it appears, to relieve the pressure of work on the council's own architects, and also to allow the building programme to proceed more rapidly. The winning

design was submitted by Rowland Plumbe, and additional premiums were paid to Davis and Emmanuel and Joseph and Smithem, all of whom were engaged in housing work elsewhere in London and have already been mentioned in connection with some of the private companies and trusts. This phase, which was known as Henley and Walton Buildings, consisted of two blocks, containing two and three roomed tenements,

8.3 *Boundary Street Estate, L.C.C.*

and they were built by the Works Department.[100]

Building work continued on the remainder of the site until 1900, all the new blocks were designed by the County Architect, some were accepted at the estimate and erected by the Works Department, others were put out to tender, although latterly it seems to have been impossible to obtain competitive tenders, and the Works department were able to build at their own estimate. The planning also continued to show a variety of arrangement and accommodation, but the later blocks showed an increase in the average area of the rooms reflecting the views of the Secretary of State, which were mentioned at the outset.[101]

It is necessary at this point to make some estimate of the contribution which this scheme made to the housing movement. The internal planning of the dwellings followed the precedents already established by other organisations, except that there was a definite attempt to increase the standard of accommodation within the individual tenement both in terms of the size of rooms, and in their number. One should not forget, however, that the Council was deliberately pursuing a policy similar to that of the Peabody Trustees in that it did not attempt to build for the very poor classes, and the reasons were similar to those contained in the evidence of Sir Curtis Lampson and Miss Hill to the 1885 Royal Commission. The problem of the poor was seen to be moral and educational, and so far as housing was concerned it required a kind of housing management which the council by its nature was totally unable to practise. Furthermore, the Council was aware that it must build for the future, as well as the present, if its housing policy was to have a lasting effect and it sought to provide dwellings which had a useful life as dwellings of at least 60 years, and as buildings of 100 years. Clearly this was not possible if the needs and the income of the very poor were to be considered. The Boundary Street estate, therefore, provided 51 per cent of its accommodation in tenements of two rooms, 37 per cent in tenements of three rooms and 10 per cent in four rooms; the remaining 2 per cent was composed of single room dwellings and a few larger tenements. Out of a total of 1,069 tenements, only 35 shared both lavatory and scullery; and a further 142, while having a private lavatory, shared a scullery.[102] This represented a reversal of the tendency which was noticeable in much contemporary work. The scheme was important, however, for other reasons than merely halting a downward tendency in housing standards. It was a very large development, and consequently it was possible to exercise proper spatial control, to pursue a planning policy, and this had not been possible since the days of the major Peabody schemes or the Bethnal Green Estate of the Improved Industrial Dwellings Company. It is only necessary to contrast the Boundary Estate with the Bethnal Green Estate, which was completed in 1890 just before the L.C.C. began its own development, in order to see the difference of outlook and of

character. The site planning, if it had any precedent, was a development of that practised by the Peabody Trustees which was probably the most consistent in the period before 1890; but the Council proceeded upon one important and different principle: the layout was based upon a road pattern, and nearly all the buildings were therefore conceived in a measure as street architecture. It was no longer a matter of simply juggling with a standard block on an unencumbered piece of land, the buildings were designed specially for the site, and they relate architecturally to each other as well as to the larger conception of the estate. Furthermore, there was provision for open space, both in the central raised garden and also between certain of the blocks, so that the usual pattern of buildings separated by paved wastes was abolished. The nature of the layout also relieved much of the scheme from the usual appearance of a regular internal area edged with parallel blocks, and now there was a variety of spatial experience and vista, so that the effect was no longer just one of respectability at the front with hidden languid courts behind, for the radial pattern exposed the back areas to the street and there was nothing to hide. The third quality which this scheme possessed was that of a new architectural sensitivity, new, that is, to the housing movement. At last the barrack-like block which had characterised working class housing for half a century was replaced by a more humane type of design, and in this perhaps lay the Council's greatest and most original contribution to the movement. Boundary Street was a new experience in housing architecture.

The Council undertook nine other schemes under Part I of the Act after 1895, but none of these involved an area so large as at Boundary Street.[103] The kind of site planning which was subsequently adopted was therefore severely limited because of this, and it fell very much into the pattern of previous work done by companies and societies, although, of course, the architectural treatment continued in the new tradition which the council's architects had introduced. Four schemes were also undertaken under Part II of the 1890 Act, since the Council were given power to assist local authorities, or to act in their default. These schemes represented areas dealt with previously by the Torrens Acts, and they were smaller in scale than those which came under Part I, the successor to the Cross Acts. At Mill Lane, Deptford, which was one of these, the Council built a small amount of cottage property, and at another, Falcon Court, Borough, it laid out a children's playground and provided housing elsewhere.[104]

Under the third part of the 1890 Act the Council, as well as the local authorities who eventually became the Metropolitan Boroughs, obtained considerably amplified powers to purchase, either by agreement or compulsorily, land and buildings both inside and outside the county; and power also to provide dwellings and lodging houses. It was under this portion of the

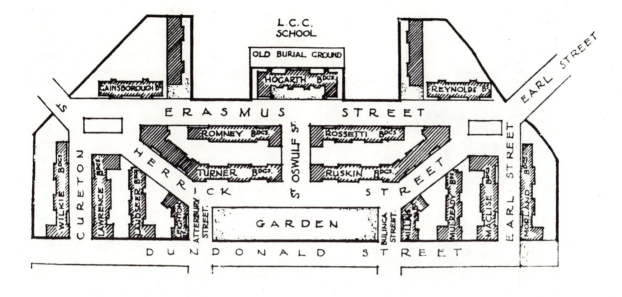

8.4   *Millbank Estate, L.C.C., begun in 1897*

Act that the Council undertook some of its most important work. The lodging houses do not occupy an important place in this discussion, but it is interesting to note there was still a need for such buildings.

Inside the county, the most important scheme undertaken was at Millbank. The Royal Commission had recommended that part of the Millbank prison site be sold to the Metropolitan Board at a very low price, as one practical means of providing more land for housing in central London at an uninflated price. The Council did not obtain the site, however, until 1896, and actual building only started late the following year.[105] The original intention was that the designs should be partly the work of the Council's architect and the remainder should be the subject of a limited competition. The Council advertised the competition and selected eighteen architects from those who replied, and the first premium was eventually awarded by W. D. Caroe, the assessor, to Spalding and Cross. But their designs proved too expensive and the whole site was developed by the Council's architect instead.[106] Like the Boundary Street estate, it is possible to judge Millbank as a fully worked out example of the council's planning and architectural policy. The site was smaller

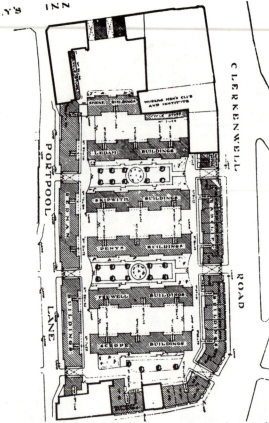

8.5 *Bourne Estate, L.C.C., begun in 1900; a very dense site like many earlier developments by the trusts and companies, the effect slightly modified by the new architectural approach*

and the layout necessarily more rectangular, but it showed the same tendency to avoid monotonous regularity; in the final solution it was broken down into small units, again arranged around a central garden, and there was the same insistence upon street architecture and the formation of an urban townscape which characterised Boundary Street. The detailing was less exciting, perhaps, but there was the same noticeable variety both in the massing of the individual blocks, which varied considerably in size although little in height, and also in the treatment of individual façades. The development of Millbank lasted from December 1897, when Hogarth Buildings were commenced, until August 1902 when Gainsborough Buildings were completed. The whole scheme accommodated 4,430 people.

There was one further scheme by the Council in central London which should be mentioned. The construction of Kingsway and Aldwych, which was begun in 1889 displaced a large number of people, like all major street works constructed through slum property. In order to provide sufficient alternative accommodation the Council acquired 2¾ acres of land between Clerkenwell Road and Portpool Lane, adjacent to a site which was developed independently as part of the Clare Market scheme.[107] The site came to be known as the Bourne Estate, and it showed the kind of solution which the Council's Architect adopted when faced with the same problems as those which had continually recurred in the work of the societies and companies. The site was not completely free from obstruction, so that it was impossible to develop the whole area; and there was the additional necessity to house as many people as possible. Consequently the layout was much less open than in the two previous schemes we have discussed, and it proved necessary to revert to the older principle of developing the internal area with a series of parallel blocks. The extremities of the site, facing Portpool Lane and Clerkenwell Road, were developed with continuous building, five storeys high, pierced at intervals with archways leading into a court which was filled with the six parallel blocks. The layout was not new and most of the dwelling companies could show similar planning solutions; but the treatment of the site and the appearance of the blocks was a great improvement. Between the blocks were gardens, and the planning of the buildings was arranged so that each tenement had at least one room which overlooked the garden, and although a balcony access system was adopted, the buildings were so designed that the living room and at least one bedroom in each tenement had unobstructed views and did not overlook a balcony.[108] The buildings, which accommodated 2,642 persons, 778 more than the Home Secretary had required, were all five storeys high and were built between 1902 and 1905. They were built in what might now legitimately be called the L.C.C. 'style', and it is perhaps most rewarding to contrast this set of buildings with the

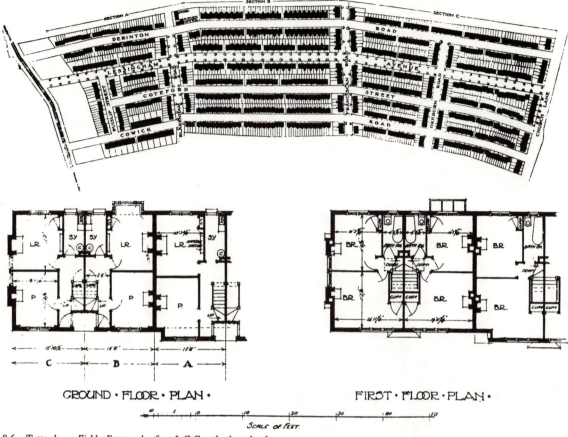

GROUND · FLOOR · PLAN ·   FIRST · FLOOR · PLAN ·

SCALE OF FEET

8.6 *Totterdown Fields Estate, the first L.C.C. suburban development 1903–11*

many similar schemes which had been erected in the past. Despite the high density, and the rather tight spatial standards, the buildings are surprisingly pleasant in appearance and lacking in the infamous barrack-like qualities of earlier decades. It is this, I think, which accentuates the importance of the architectural revolution carried through by the L.C.C. for it humanised the whole housing movement. The other points to notice are the care which was taken to secure a pleasing aspect for the main rooms, and the stress laid upon the provision of a garden even in a scheme of this nature.

The first L.C.C. suburban estates

It will be noticed that the Council exceeded the amount of housing accommodation which was required of them at the Bourne Estate, and this was a sign of a new development in their policy. In November 1898, largely because it was becoming increasingly evident that the supply of dwellings in London was still not equal to the demand, the Council decided that in all schemes under the 1890 Act, or any other Improvement Act, it should provide accommodation equal to that required for the people displaced, although not necessarily on the same site or even in the immediate neighbourhood. Secondly, it resolved itself to under-

take all the re-housing made necessary under the 1890 Act; and thirdly, and most important of all, it resolved to use to the full the powers granted under Part III of the Act; especially those for the purchase of land.[109] It was as a result of these decisions that the Council began to develop several large estates outside the central area.

The first of these was at Tooting, known as the Totterdown Fields Estate, which consisted of about 38½ acres. In 1899 the Council decided to purchase the land since it was suitable for working class housing, and situated conveniently at the terminus of one of their tramways.[110] The purchase was completed in January 1900 and the first houses were finished in June 1903.[111] The whole of the estate was laid out with cottage property and development proceeded from west to east, beginning behind Upper Tooting Road and finishing at Church Lane. Now this scheme, apart from the model villages, represents the first organised working class housing built on the cottage principle, and its importance as a housing experiment cannot, therefore, be overlooked; but at the same time it is necessary to distinguish between this type of estate which was an extension of an existing city, and the developments which belong more properly to the garden city movement. It was not intended that it should illustrate the garden city principles, for one thing the density was high even by normal housing standards; and the layout adopted made no pretence at romance. But in other respects the objectives were close to those of the early town planners; especially in the efforts to evolve a new cottages plan free from re-entrant angles.

The governing factors in planning are: (a) the economy of land and of road construction by limiting the frontage of plots where possible to narrow widths; (b) the avoidance of extensive back projections, as tending to cause insanitary pockets and to prevent a free current of air and proper ventilation at the backs of the cottages.[112]

The more important roads were 45 ft. wide, lined

8.7   *Totterdown Fields Estate*

with plane trees on either side, and the remainder were 40 ft.; the cottages, which were designed in terraces of up to twenty units, were set back from the street at distances varying from 5 ft. to 15 ft.

Development continued until 1911, but latterly the demand was for smaller houses at rents which the poorest class could afford, since private enterprise catered very adequately for the artizan who could afford a normal house with three bedrooms. In 1909 the Council therefore modified its layout to include a greater number of houses with only three or four rooms in addition to the scullery. All the houses, of course, had a small back garden in addition to the plot at the front, and there were open spaces between the individual terraced blocks, in some cases as great as 20 ft. wide.[113] The site plan consisted of a series of parallel streets, laid out with a slight curve because of the site, and intersected along their length by three transverse streets, so that the basic layout was a modified grid-iron: in other words it was an adaptation of the well known bye-law street. The architects were at great pains to minimise the effect which this kind of planning usually produced, first by breaking the multiple housing units into small and irregular lengths, instead of one continuous and monotonously even terrace; and secondly by achieving the maximum possible degree of modelling within the individual blocks, projecting either the central portion or those at either end to create a clearer sense of organisation and control. The houses were returned at the junction with each cross road, but no attempt was made to turn the corner with continuous building: that was a refinement which came later. Brick was used for the construction of all the buildings with selected blocks

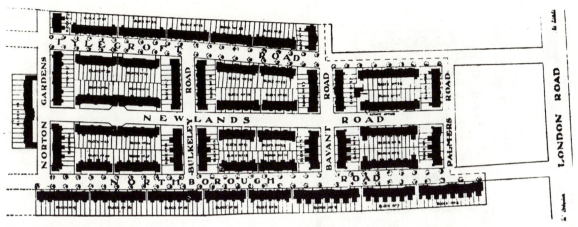

8.8 *Norbury Estate, Croydon, begun in 1902*

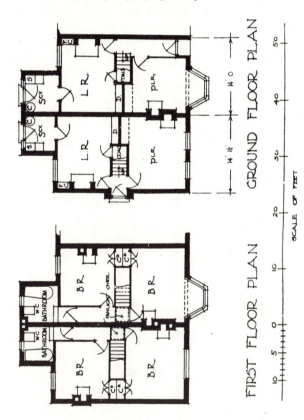

essentially rural in atmosphere. It was a piece of townscape in the best sense, for the buildings dominate and control although they never oppress, and once again the L.C.C. architects succeeded in creating out of material essentially quite mundane an environment which, for the working classes at least, was new and attractive.

When it was completed, the scheme had a density of 227 persons per acre, assuming an occupancy rate of two persons per room which was then acceptable. Today, with a lower figure of 1.1 persons per room, the density, theoretically, is still about 127 persons per acre, so that despite the absence of high buildings this was a high density housing scheme.[114]

The Council purchased an estate at Norbury, near Croydon, in 1901 and proceeded to develop it on similar lines to that at Tooting. The layout and the density figures were comparable, but the development continued over a much longer period and the estate was not completed until after the War. The whole site comprised 28½ acres, and by 1912 some 16½ of these had been used for building purposes. Again all the cottages were two storeyed, and some of the larger types, like those at Tooting, had bathrooms. The planning of the actual houses, on the whole, seems to have been less satisfactory than at the first estate;

8.9 *Norbury Estate, Croydon*

rendered above first floor level, but otherwise the architectural treatment was simple and logical so that it possessed an unaffected dignity and at the same time a personal scale which was lacking in nearly all the block dwellings. The design was slightly classical, with small-paned sliding sash windows; but it owed more to the influences of the vernacular revival, in the emphasis upon silhouette and the vigorous use of the gable, with the roof often carried down in great sweeping lines to within a few feet of the ground. The effect, therefore, was far removed from that of the bye-law street, despite the similarity in road pattern; nor was it reminiscent of the garden village, for that was

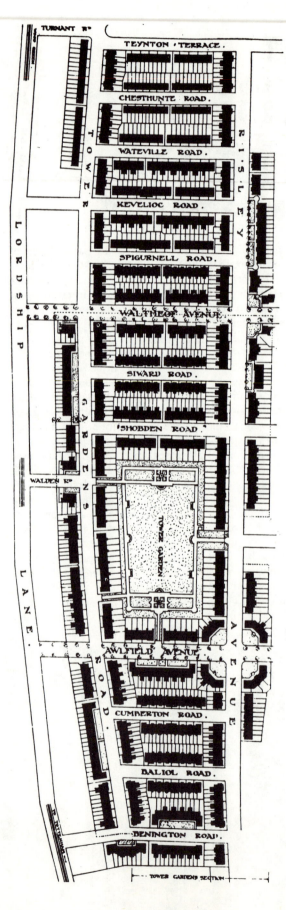

there was an unfortunate return to the small back offshoot in one plan, and there appears to have been some difficulty in finding a suitable position for the stair in the smaller units which would also give an economical solution. Another point which should be mentioned, because of its effect on layout arrangements and density figures, was that the locally prevailing bye-laws at Croydon required an average of 500 sq. ft. for each garden.[115]

The third scheme, known as the White Hart Lane Estate, at Tottenham, was in some respects a further development of the work carried out on the first two estates.[116] The section which was developed by the Council lay to the north of Lordship Lane and consisted of some $48\frac{3}{4}$ acres. Development did not start until 1912, and there was a special factor which influenced the planning: part of the estate was built with the assistance of a gift amounting to £10,000 from Lord Swaythling, which enabled the Council to lay out Tower Gardens and to increase the size of the individual house plots on part of the estate. On the western section the density was therefore slightly higher than that on the Tower section, which benefited from the gift, but nevertheless, the overall density was not a

8.10   *White Hart Lane Estate, Tottenham, L.C.C., begun in 1912*

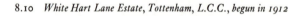

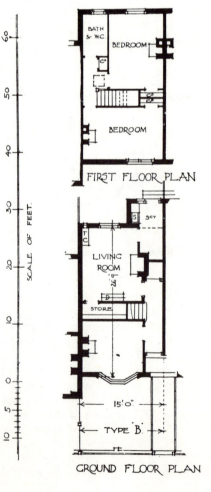

8.11a *White Hart Lane Estate, Tottenham, L.C.C.*

great deal less than at Norbury, and it is legitimate to include the estate as a high density cottage development. The streets were arranged so that they ran from north to south, giving the majority of the dwellings east–west orientation, and the garden was set in the centre of a group of houses. The cottage plans were again variants on the three, four and five roomed

house; and they differed only slightly from those built previously. There were still a number with back projections which must be regarded as an old fashioned planning device in an otherwise advanced design. The important innovation, however, was the attempt made for the first time, and only at one particular place, to design a corner unit which could be used at the junction of two streets; this was attended by considerable architectural success, and in addition it provided a useful place to incorporate additional and special accommodation.

8.11b *White Hart Lane Estate, Tottenham, L.C.C.*

It is but a short step from this innovation to the design for the Old Oak Estate at Acton, the last in this group, the land for which was purchased by the Council in 1905.[117] Its development goes on beyond 1914, but the portion which was built before the war, and much of the inspiration, belongs to the very end of our period, and it was perhaps the finest architectural experience of all the L.C.C. cottage estates. The idea that houses could be combined in a variety of groups around a small open space, that they could be used for visual effect to create an urban landscape, was here explored much more fully than before. The only comparable visual experience was at Port Sunlight, where similar architectural experiments were undertaken; but the comparison ends abruptly at this point for the model village was a private venture with totally different financial arrangements. At Port Sunlight the density was kept deliberately low, while at Acton it was high, although not quite so high as on the other three estates just described.

What, then, was the lesson which could, and indeed still can be learnt from these schemes? First, that quite high density could be achieved with two-storey development: it could be achieved by simple rows of cottages which give a variety of accommodation, from single room flats to five room houses; it could also be achieved with a spacious layout for the most part acceptable today. These questions of density are important today when architects and sociologists are revising their attitudes towards the relation of building height to density, to the flexibility of accommodation and the provision of open space, and on all these questions the early L.C.C. housing estates provide an object lesson. But they have more qualities than the mere ability to achieve a high density, and these qualities fundamentally are architectural. W. E. Riley and his team of architects at the County Council offices achieved a high standard of design, considering the amount of work which they undertook; and the most outstanding feature of it all was the absence of routine standardisa-tion. The buildings were usually specially designed for the peculiarities of the site, and each scheme was largely original: a special junction demanded detailing, and a new design was prepared which helped to achieve the individuality of each estate, and it was just this quality that made the speculative housing of the years which followed the war much less successful as architecture. The Council worked continually under the restraint of limited finance, which necessitated economical planning and detailing as well as relatively high densities, but these influences seem only to have enhanced the architectural and spatial qualities.

Riley also managed to evolve in the course of time a kind of vernacular character for these housing estates, and this was shown to best effect at Tottenham and Acton. The buildings were never monotonous, rarely dull; but there was little attempt, and there was no surplus money, to seek after effect and the solutions appeared direct and straightforward, surprisingly free from cliches. It is a long journey, aesthetically, from the work of the philanthropic trusts to that of the London County Council, but at the end of it one finds that sensitivity and delight are qualities which have again entered into the housing movement. It was unfortunate, therefore, that the developments after the war became less successful, less urban and more stereotyped because of a new and invigorating movement in support of very low densities. The bogy of this still haunts us, but its origins were sound and full of wisdom, and it is to the history of the Garden City Movement that we must turn in conclusion, for it was the last and the greatest influence upon housing in the first half of the century, and with its position in this history fully delineated our understanding of the historical forces which have created our problems today will be complete.

8.12 *Old Oak Estate, Acton, L.C.C.; the last estate to be started before 1914 and largely built after 1919; a sophisticated layout with a fine architectural approach to house design*

9

Housing, planning and the state

The development of the L.C.C. and its housing policies has carried us into the twentieth century. It is clear that the reforms of the nineties began to produce tangible results during the last years of the nineteenth and the early years of this century and the account of developments in London shows that the atmosphere was very different by 1900 from what it had been even around 1885. There was a new sense of purpose and renewed activity helped, it is true, by external factors such as the developments in public transport systems and the gradual rise in the standard of living which made a larger section of the working class more mobile and more independent.[1]

The work at the L.C.C. outlined the kind of policies which more large towns would sooner or later decide to embrace, it made clear once and for all that the community as represented by its elected council and their paid professional experts were the most effective as well as the most efficient organisation to lay down and carry out a housing policy. It is fair to conclude that this point had been made and probably accepted early in the new century. The financial implications of local authority housing were by no means so rapidly disentangled and this was one important issue of principle – to say nothing of its practical implications – which lingered on well into the twentieth century.

It would be easy to say also, at this point, that the housing problem was nearly solved because the pressure on central areas was removed. This was not true, however, the L.C.C.'s policy like that of the Peabody Trustees before it took no account of the hard core of the problem and the housing of the very poor remained, as it had done for two generations, a subject surrounded by ethical problems incapable of practical solution until the issues of subsidisation were solved, and those were debated until after the first world war.[2]

Housing and the state

The idea of state-owned and state-financed housing, whether at national level or that of the local authority was one not easily accepted in England. Some idea of the attitudes which existed in the first decade of this century will help to draw together one of the main philosophical arguments which has dominated this account of housing during the second half of the nineteenth century.

The London County Council first decided to build dwellings in March 1893 because it was unable to sell cleared land on the terms which it saw fit to impose. It was followed in 1896 by the borough of Shoreditch for whom Rowland Plumbe designed a scheme in Nile Street,[3] and thus began a long and honourable tradition of public housing.

The demand for Council housing, if we interpret that, as indeed we must, as housing initially for the artizan, was in reality not great in the early years: it was needed most urgently in London by the class of person who either must live centrally in order to be near his work, or by those who could not afford a suburban speculative-built house. Since this particular combination of circumstance existed in so few places the proportion of housing done by local authorities and the housing societies combined still only amounted to 5 per cent of all new housing built in the year before the first world war.[4] Perhaps for this reason the opposition to state-aided housing continued after its tacit theoretical acceptance in 1890. It was not yet clear that state interference was necessary to any large degree and, as we have already seen, private housing schemes continued to enjoy an Indian summer through the work of a new group of housing societies and trusts founded towards the end of the century, and working on into the new one.

In 1903 James Parsons investigated the 'Novel extension of public responsibility', largely to show the advantages of private enterprise: 'It seemed to many of those who had experience of the actual work of building and owning dwellings that the advocates of State intervention were deficient in knowledge and hasty in inference'.[5] This remark was based upon the statistical information about the relative amounts of housing built between 1891 and 1901. But what he seemed to fear most was that state interference would lead to the complete withdrawal of private enterprise from the housing movement, in the face of unequal competition, leaving the public with only the kind of housing authority cared to foist upon it; there would finally cease to be a choice:

Commercial enterprise, then, considered as an instrument for the supply of commodities, has well-marked traits. It acts through a free exchange of services, working with certainty and elasticity; it offers guarantees for the continuance of its good offices; it promotes efficiency and the personal qualities which conduce to efficiency.[6]

The state, on the other hand, acted from impulse, from party whim; it did not seek to make profit, and it was not under pressure to improve its design for aesthetic or economic reasons since it was only indirectly responsible to a client. Parsons argued that there were also other inefficiencies inherent in a local authority, such as the development of a vast system of officials and excutives, prone to extravagance, wire pulling, nest feathering, and to such vote catching tricks as irresponsible rent reduction.

Voluntary enterprise is conducting the business of house-building in London and the neighbourhood on a gigantic scale. Any drawback, therefore, which touches the business as an investment, and diminishes the flow of capital into it, will affect very large sums of money and prevent the building of very many houses.

The competition of the State is clearly such a drawback; it is formidable and looms still more formidable in the eyes of prudent and timid investors. It may, indeed, fairly be inferred that the more houses the State builds, the more houses will it prevent other people from building. The building work of the councils, however actively carried on, is likely to cause a loss and not a gain in the number of houses erected for wage-earners. Both in quantity and quality the State is likely to prove a less efficient instrument than voluntary enterprise of the improvement of the homes of the people.[7]

Parsons was arguing, in fact, that state-aided housing had all the inflexibility and extravagance of a large-scale organisation which did not depend for its existence upon the normal laws of supply and demand. With the huge financial resources of the municipality behind it, and an inherent desire to appear a cheap model landlord there was, he argued, the great danger that private enterprise would no longer feel able to compete with this gargantuan monster.

The opposite point of view, in support of local authority housing, was put a few years later by Kirkham Gray:

I maintain the thesis that: private philanthropy cannot provide a remedy for wide-spread want which results from broad and general social causes; that it ought not to be expected to do so; that the provision of such remedies is the proper responsibility of the State and should be accepted as such.[8]

and he went on the elaborate the role of civic authority in the twentieth century:

The due of the modern city is therefore freedom within the activity of State control. It becomes no longer a force *against* the State and *for* the citizens, but an instrument of the State for realising the highest life of individuals. The city appears as a member of the State. That is to say the city *is* the State because the State, by virtue of its philanthropic function, is *in* the city.[9]

This then, was the new view of society; it took the less jaundiced standpoint that the local authority was a responsible public body; philanthropic, because it has the greatest happiness for the greatest number at heart. In this context the social conscience is seen to have come full circle; instead of a reactionary local authority thwarting the right of the community

in order to preserve the 'vested interest' of a limited number of the community, Gray saw the municipality as the very epitome of the social conscience: through limited centralisation at a local level would come civic responsibility. And it was Gray's view which was to become acceptable to the basically socialist society of the twentieth century: 'For the city is an integral member of the great social purpose, whereas philanthropists can fulfil only their own personal sentiment of pity or justice. The philanthropists were unable to escape the disability of their arbitrary self-appointment.'[10] It is true that in his earnestness to present the state in a satisfactory light, Gray exhibited the same kind of faults, the same exaggeration, that Parsons in his turn had shown in his efforts to denigrate the state in the face of private enterprise; but these two works were, in effect, social tracts, written when these issues were of burning importance to their respective protagonists, and it so happens that in his conception of the state in modern society Gray was much nearer the truth, as we see it half a century later, than was Parsons. The role of the state has increased until it eclipses that of philanthropy and private enterprise, and Parsons' worst fears were never realised.

Model communities

If the problems of finance and ownership are one of the main strands in the early years of this century then the other is the far less tangible issue, the 'idea' of housing. The social and economic trends which marked the last years of the old century made possible the development of an idealism – which rapidly found effective protagonists – based on the idea of anti-urbanism.

During the course of the nineteenth century there had been several attempts to create paper dreams of

9.1 *New Lanark founded by David Dale in 1784 and developed by Robert Owen who took over from Dale in 1797*

9.2 *Bromborough on the Wirral, founded in 1854 by Price's Patent Candle Company*

ideal environments or to build model villages instigated by industrialists to encourage workers to move into outlandish spots where new mills or railway junctions were considered desirable. Nearly all of them had one thing in common: they were urban in character. In practical terms they began with Robert Owen's New Lanark outside Glasgow, more a social experiment than an architectural conception perhaps, which was built in the early years of the century and still survives. His views about society are contained in a remarkable book *A New View of Society* published in 1813 which inspired an ill-fated community at Orbiston and another at New Harmony in Indiana which was '...like a large prison or asylum on the outside with a sort of graveyard in the interior, and it is conspicuous for the absence of beauty in its architecture'.[11] There were those who poked fun at Owen and it is true that he spoilt his chances of success as a visionary because of his extreme views and particularly his own anti-religious outlook.[12] But he was not alone at that time in his search for a new

concept of an industrial society. There was, for example, Jeremy Bentham's *Building and Furniture for an Industry-House Establishment, for 2,000 persons, of all ages, on the Panopticon or Central Inspection Principle*.[13] In France Owen's work had a clear parallel in F.-C.-M. Fourier's *phalanstère* which was published in 1829[14] and as a semi-Owenite concept of living it was put into practice in 1859 by Jean Baptiste Godin at his iron foundry in Guise. His *Familistère* was in fact a series of block dwellings around courts, a system quite familiar to English working class housing architects who did not always need the social overtones to inspire their communities.[15]

Loudon included a scheme for the poor in his great compendium: *80 dwellings of the humblest class placed together, with a view of being heated by one common fire, and enjoying other benefits, on the co-operative system*[16] and elsewhere he published an *Outline for economical dwellings, fireproof, heated by steam, lighted by gas, and connected by an inclined plane*.[17]

Sydney Smirke, the architect, proposed model villages,[18] so did John Minter Morgan in *The Christian Commonwealth*,[19] and there were various other ideas along similar lines.

When it came to actually building such a community the designs were usually quite prosaic although there were perhaps more early model communities than one might imagine. For example, Samuel Oldknow built a small community around his factory at Mellor in 1790, Josiah Wedgewood some cottages at Etruria, the Ashworth family over 330 cottages at Hyde.

The Richardson family began a model village at Bessborough in Northern Ireland in 1846 and the Wilsons, who came from Lanark, started their interesting development at Bromborough Pool in Cheshire for Prices Patent Candle Company in 1853.[20] This was a surprisingly open village of short terraces and semi-detached cottages with large gardens and considerable public open space. There was evidence, too, of paternalism in the careful direction of the village during its early years, the construction of a school and church and the growth of social institutions which were watched over with interest and, often, with considerable financial help in addition.

Certainly the most famous of all the early model communities and the most ambitious was Saltaire, now on the outskirts of modern Bradford, but, when it was built, quite out in the country. Sir Titus Salt was a successful mill owner who discovered alpaca and out of it made his fortune.[21] His business success made it necessary to move in 1850 from the cramped site his family business occupied in central Bradford and he chose to build well up the Aire valley. The splendid new mill by the river was completed in 1853 and around it gradually grew up a complete community planned, like the mill, by his architects the famous local firm of Lockwood and Mawson. It took nearly ten years to complete a community of about 800 houses and to a modern eye the tightly planned regular streets with their equally narrow back lanes, the careful stratification of house types according to class and the dour architecture hardly suggest a model community. It was, of course, surrounded by open country originally and it is clear that nobody thought that any other plan form was necessary despite the high density which such a development must have achieved. The standard of building was beyond reproach – which was of course the argument used most frequently to defend the London model tenement blocks. But Saltaire does more than merely reflect the London pattern, it shows that, in a rural setting when all the economic pressures on land values were removed, the thoughtful mill owner and his architect still regarded the urban solution as the obvious answer to the housing problem. In other ways, however, Saltaire stands apart from the remaining model communities. Salt saw to it that the community was complete in a way which was not repeated until Lever endowed Port Sunlight. He built a sumptuous Congregationalist chapel; he provided a site for a church; he built the Sunday School, the institute, the alms-houses, the public baths and wash-houses and he provided a fine park across the river which was noticeably the only real open space designed in the community except for that in front of the almshouses and vestigial planting around the public buildings.[22]

9.3   *Saltaire, near Bradford, started in 1851 by Sir Titus Salt, Lockwood and Mawson architects*

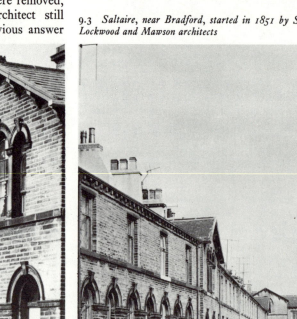

The other important group of model communities centre around Halifax, although by no stretch of the imagination do they measure up to concepts of Saltaire. The two great Halifax families, the Akroyds and the Crossleys, occupied a similar place in the development of housing in Halifax to that of Salt in Bradford, and just as there were links between the Wilsons at Bromborough and Owen at New Lanark, so too in Yorkshire, as Creese points out,[23] the Salts, Akroyds and Crossleys were friends and Sir Titus' son married a Crossley. Colonel Edward Akroyd began establishing mills at Copley outside Halifax in the 1830s and the housing development began in 1849.[24] Quite modest in scale it surprisingly was built on the back-to-back principle which was common in the north of England and much despised by the southerners. There is some architectural pretension but not a great deal at Copley and, as it is one of the earliest of the model communities, this reinforces the view that model housing was conceived on exactly the same lines as speculative housing. There was no concept of layout which was special to this kind of idealism.

Akroyd then undertook a more ambitious development in Halifax itself which came to be known as Akroydon. Work began in 1861, originally to the designs of Gilbert Scott, but it seems that working class housing was rather beyond that great master and he was soon replaced by a local man, W. H. Crossland.[25] There are quite clear signs of stylistic design of the gothic manner favoured by Scott and the attempts at some external character match those at Saltaire.

9.4 *Copley, near Halifax, 1849–53, started by Edward Akroyd, using back-to-back houses*

In some ways Akroydon was more ambitious in that the layout surrounds a central park although the earliest drawings show this filled with housing which was later abandoned very fortunately. It was never intended to be as large, however, but like Saltaire there were no private gardens, the houses fronting directly onto the street. The chief innovation of the development was in its financial arrangements. Akroyd intended that it should be a scheme for working men to buy their own homes through the fairly novel method of a building association, in this case backed by the Halifax Permanent Benefit Building Society of which Akroyd was a trustee. The venture was on the whole successful, although it looks a little forlorn today, which is the price one pays for home ownership rather than the preservation of the total environment.

It is also worth noting the other local development financed through the same building society and started by the Crossleys who, like the Akroyds, were amongst its trustees. It was begun soon after Akroydon was completed in 1863 and it was finished before the end of the decade. This was West Hill Park and it was composed of rather more expensive houses each with its own garden and like so much of the model housing as it moved towards the middle class it is nearly indistinguishable from the work of the speculative developer except for its higher standard of building and layout. Here, perhaps, was one way the building society movement was able to make a positive contribution to housing in its ability to control the quality of the development which it was financing.

The other important group of village communities were the three railway towns, Crewe, Wolverton and

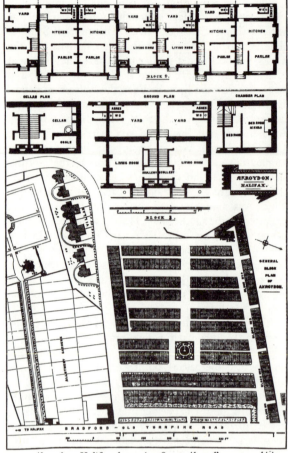

9.5   *Akroydon, Halifax, begun in 1855; Akroyd's most ambitious venture. G. G. Scott and W. H. Crossland architects*

Swindon, all of them started between 1840 and 1850.[26] Of Wolverton Sir F. B. Head, one of the earliest railway enthusiasts, had this to say:

...it would be impossible for our most popular auctioneer, if he wishes ever so much to puff off the appearance of Wolverton, to say more of it than that it is a little red-brick town composed of 242 little red-brick houses – all running either this way or that at right-angles – three or four tall red-brick engine-chimneys, a number of very large red-brick workshops, six red houses for officers – one red beer shop, two red public-houses, and, we are glad to add, a substantial red school-room and a neat stone church, the whole lately built by order of a Railway Board, at a railway

9.6 *Railway housing at Wolverton, built in the late 1840s by the London and Birmingham Railway Co.*

station, by a railway contractor, for railway men, railway women and railway children; in short, the round cast iron plate over every house, bearing the letters L.N.W.R., is the generic symbol of the town.[27]

To a large extent the work at all three towns echoed in a rather more prosaic way that of Salt. It showed the same physical qualities and the builders set their sights at firmness, commodity and certainly not at delight. It showed once again that the objectives at nearly every level in the housing movement were

9.7 *Railway housing at Crewe, built during the 1840s originally for the Grand Junction Line*

concerned with establishing a basically healthy community and there were few opinions at this point in mid-century concerned with the concepts of environment.

This idea of an urban non-romantic community extended as far as the most ambitious of the ideal visions, James Silk Buckingham's Victoria, appended to his *National Evils and Practical Remedies* which appeared in 1849. The book itself does not concern the housing or town planning movement, for it dealt with current social problems from a typically Owenite point of view, but the scheme for Victoria was quite novel and deserves mention because of the national way it was conceived. Its real importance to us was its vision of an urban community, whereas those which came later in the century were essentially rural, or semi-rural at best.

The objects chiefly kept in view have been to unite the greatest degree of order, symmetry, space and healthfulness, in the largest supply of air and light and in the most perfect system of drainage, with the comfort and convenience of all classes; the due proportion of accommodation to the probable numbers and circumstances of various ranks; ready accessibility to all parts of the town, under continuous shelter from sun and rain, when necessary: with the disposition of the public buildings in such localities as to make them easy of approach from all quarters, and surrounded with space for numerous avenues of entrance and exit. And, in addition to all these, a large intermixture of grass lawn, garden ground and flowers, and an abundant supply of water – the whole to be united with as much elegance and economy as may be found practicable.[28]

Victoria has the essence of the great ideal city, with its all pervading sense of perfection, and no hint of the means by which it might be achieved. Buckingham kept to the main principles of his development and did not concern himself too much with compromising practicalities. The town radiated out, in a series of concentric squares, from a central octagonal tower 300 ft. high crowned by a man-made sun, formed with an electric arc, so that the town need have no night. The outer hollow square, of which each face was a mile long, contained 250 dwellings on every side, each with a 20 ft. frontage and 60 ft. in depth. On one side was a garden, and on the other a 20 ft. wide colonnade which provided easy circulation in inclement weather, whilst its roof formed a balcony for fine weather promenading. This was the square in which the working classes lived. Between it and the next major square of housing was a street 100 ft. wide, then two parallel rows of workshops linked by a continuous arcade, and beyond them an open space 150 ft. wide, in which were set amidst lawns the dining rooms, schools, reading rooms and public baths. The second square of dwellings was then reached; it provided homes for shopkeepers, superintendents of labour and similar slightly superior people, and on each of the four sides were 140 houses this time each with a plot 28 ft. wide and 56 ft. deep and with a garden 14 ft. deep on the outer side, and on the other side another colonnade, this time detailed in the Doric style, the colonnade in front of the working class houses being reading rooms and restaurants, but in diminished numbers and increasingly elegant as the centre was approached and the residential character became more exclusive. The seventh square was then reached, with 30 dwellings on each side each 54 ft. wide, 100 ft. deep and with 100 ft. of garden. These were for superior professional people, and the ornament for their colonnade was Corinthian. The Grand Outer Square contained churches, museums and a concert hall; and the Grand Inner Square, which was the next complete hollow square, the houses of the most opulent citizens, 24 in number, 80 ft. wide, 150 ft. deep with an equal depth of garden, and the usual colonnade in front this time of the Composite order. The government offices form the inner square, with the residences of heads of departments, members of the Council of Ministers and the Governor himself above them, designed in the manner of Italian palaces. Finally, within this was the central Place 700 ft. square, the Greek agora or the Roman Forum of the city, in the midst of which was the great tower with its bell and electric sun.

Four avenues led into this square from the four angles of the outermost square, linking all the concentric streets together, and at the points where they entered the central space, and at their outer extremities, were great fountains. Outside the town were gardens and parks for recreation, and beyond them were the works and industries, the sewage farms and the gasworks.

The town itself occupied a square mile, and housed some 10,000 people, and the green belt around it, including the parks and local agriculture, would occupy a further 10,000 acres. Buckingham laid down that each single workman should have a room of his own and each married couple two rooms; when there were children there were to be not less than three rooms in the house and every house was to have its own lavatory. Various other regulations were laid down not strictly concerned with planning, notably that the town was to be organised on principles of co-operation without any form of private ownership. Intoxicating liquor was forbidden, which was a typical concern of Buckingham's, and the use of firearms and all weapons was prohibited. The Sabbath was to be strictly observed, but religious toleration was one of his main requirements, and so too was the regulation of working hours and the employment of children and women in industry, both of which were important contemporary issues. The advantages of Victoria which Buckingham extolled to his readers were its perfect ventilation, its covered colonnades and walks, the absence of culs-de-sac and wynds, of beer-shops, pawn-brokers, brothels and gambling houses, and the proximity of the working class to their places of employment and to the country, living as they did in the outermost square next to the parks and open spaces.

Like all ideal cities Victoria subordinated the individual to the pattern and modern critics have found it uncompromising and lacking in human warmth. Ebenezer Howard, comparing it with his own

9.8 *Railway housing at Swindon, built during the 1840s by the Great Western Railway Company*

Gothic. This hollow square faced another street 100 ft. wide, but instead of workshops there was an arcade of shops on the opposite side. The open space beyond the shops and before the next residential square contained further dining rooms and restaurants and in addition, a school for older children. The fifth square of buildings had 74 dwellings in each range, this time with plots 38 ft. wide and 76 ft. deep, with 84 ft. of garden and an Ionic colonnade: these were the residences of the professional classes. On the opposite side of the street was the public promenade, a covered gallery 100 ft. wide, and in the adjoining open space were the usual communal facilities, baths,

Garden City, saw that 'The members of Buckingham's city [are] held together by the bonds of a rigid cast-iron organisation, from which there could be no escape but by leaving the association or breaking it up into various sections',[29] and a modern biographer added, 'there is much in Buckingham's Utopia, which, from the twentieth-century point of view, is objectionable if not foolish and wrong, but his essential ideas compare favourably with those of his contemporaries, who, without having achieved anything like his synthesis, often appear quite as foolish and wrong'.[30]

The same critic, however, also saw that Buckingham for the first time provided an urban solution in place of the rural communities popular with earlier idealists and it was this that makes him so much more important to us; he attempted to achieve architectural quality and variety, increasing in scale and grandeur towards the centre. There were other qualities which are important, and chief amongst them was his use of open space, first within the town itself alternating gardens and parks with the housing and actually providing a setting for public buildings within the parks; secondly on the outskirts, where Buckingham limited the town by surrounding it with a green belt, and it is interesting that he placed the poorest class in closest proximity to the open spaces. His conception of a 'garden city' was in many ways a foreshadowing of Ebenezer Howard's great vision in *To-morrow*[31] some fifty years later, although it was considerably more urban in concept.

The housing standards which Buckingham required were also important; they reflect those established by Henry Roberts and the early housing societies which were contemporary with Victoria. Separate sleeping accommodation for parents and for children of each sex, a lavatory for each house; these things were ideal but they were not lavish, nor were they beyond the bounds of practicality in 1850, but they were beyond the grasp of a complete community. One wonders what plan form Buckingham envisaged for his houses since the minimum depth of a terrace block was 56 ft., and the largest was 150 ft.; neither would be easy to light in its interior! Finally, there was a suggestion of multi-level circulation, using the colonnade roofs and indeed the roofs of the buildings themselves as public promenades.

Buckingham was inhuman and naïve at times, but he never descended to the rigid social structure of Owen, and he possessed an architectural vision which is unique; if at times also a social crank, he was, nevertheless, acceptable to his contemporaries, and perhaps his great work was appraised to best effect in contemporary opinion:

We confess we opened his very interesting volume with some misgivings, that we might find in it much that would appear to be either impracticable or otherwise objectionable...from knowing how the subject has been so almost inextricably entangled and interlarded by others with impracticabilities quite inconsistent with the nature of man as he at present

exists; and more particularly as regards the evils of unmitigated *communism* contrasted with and apart from the benefits of individual *association*; but our mind was speedily re-assured on these points, and although we do not mean to bind ourselves down to the author's hopes and opinions, we do think his subject well handled and worthy of widespread perusal and careful consideration.[32]

A similar work to Buckingham's *National Evils*, *The Happy Colony*, by Robert Pemberton was published in 1854, but like Buckingham's Victoria it had no repercussions,[33] and the movement developed thereafter chiefly through practical ventures. One other rather small contribution, however, deserves mention, for it foreshadowed ideas which today are still occupying the minds of planners. It was for a model city, in which there was no building at ground level, all the buildings were carried instead on stilts so that the services such as drainage, water and gas could be raised above the ground and carried in easily accessible ducts beneath the buildings, at all times well ventilated. Transport throughout the city would be by rail, noiseless and cheap; and the roofs, freed from smoke, would become garden terraces.[34] Another scheme, this time of much later date and of French origin, suggested a series of 'Aerodomes', iron framed buildings not less than ten floors high with access by lifts, and each housing 1,000 people.[35] At the fifth floor was a terrace 10 ft. wide, linking each block to the next across wide avenues; so le Corbusier's scheme for Paris in the 1930s was not without precedent. *The Builder* thought it was an 'advanced idea', and was altogether sceptical.

The Romantic concept

All the housing which we have so far discussed, either speculative, model or idealistic had one quality in common; it belonged to the town tradition and it was essentially urban in that the houses were joined together in terraces, they were planned on a rectilinear layout or they were conceived as high city blocks. The difference between model and speculative housing was one of scale, or quality or quantity: the model dwellings in specially built groups were healthy and clean, well built and well drained, as opposed to the speculative housing which often possessed none of these qualities. In Buckingham's Victoria the scale and nature of the development was essentially urban, despite the fact that he tried to bring the amenities of the country within the town, alternating terraces of building with open spaces. This urban tradition in a sense was the legacy of the eighteenth century, although horribly debased and plagiarised; an aristocratic and essentially English tradition, humbled and interpreted for the myriad masses, continuing to be popular because the terrace was the cheapest way to build houses. The tradition died during the nineteenth century, slowly and imperceptibly; first the aristocracy lost faith in the town, were attracted to villa-dom and then the lure of suburbia percolated downwards until in the twentieth century the concept of the closely built town was replaced by a new and anti-urban attitude to housing, for every class. It took so long to replace this old tradition because it was necessary for the new kind of housing to reach down to the great mass of the people before its full impact was felt. Until this happened it was little more than the dilettante whim of the affluent.

Socially it is not difficult to see why this anti-urbanism developed, why it was received with such enthusiasm. The late nineteenth century conception of the great city correlated high density with disease and unhealthy conditions, and associated it with the grimness and uncompromising inhumanity of the model tenement blocks. The tall gaunt buildings retained the high density yet appeared to be healthy, although this was not proved in reality before the end of the century, and many people remained very sceptical of the lasting value of the new housing experiments. They asked whether the new buildings were not the slums of the future in which the unhealthy and insanitary drama would be re-enacted in a heightened form decades hence.

Alternatively, those who had found a house in a suburb, either because they prospered and were able to afford the additional expense of travelling, or whose horizons were extended by the railway and the cheap train, were but little better off because the standards of building could be notoriously, even dangerously, low. When the speculative house became sanitary, which was not until late in the century, at working class level, the legal obligations concerning space still remained meagre in the extreme so that the dangers of the central area and the suburb were to some extent similar. Nineteenth century suburbia did not mean semi-rural arcadia except for the wealthy; for the worker it meant urbanisation at its worst, because it was monotonously repetitive and extended on a scale hitherto unknown. There were few amenities to make the new suburbs into communities, and there was a dearth of open space; gardens were at a premium and parks were all too few, provided by haphazard munificence rather than accepted necessity. The reaction which set in, and which long had been the ideal and the hope of those who could have vision enough to look to the future, was one against the industrial town with its tremendous emphasis upon bricks and mortar and its negation of the country. The nineteenth century urban scene – one cannot call it a community – was architecturally, environmentally, and often socially barren, without the inspiration or the balanced planning of the eighteenth century town which we tend to eulogise today. The urbanity of Bloomsbury, Bath or Cheltenham bore no relation to industrial suburbia; and it was this fundamental change in the nature of towns which led to an almost pathological fear of spatial enclosure towards the end of the nineteenth century.

It is important to see the two architectural traditions in nineteenth century housing; first the projection of the classical and urbane town far into the industrial age until it degenerated into the bye-law street, secondly its antithesis the picturesque attraction of an accidental landscape imitative of rural scenes, what we can call 'anti-town'. The terrace became unfashionable in the nineteenth century, and there was a growing reaction against the monotony which many people thought it created. The identity of the individual had been lost in a Georgian terrace behind reticent, similar façades, designed to produce a harmonious street or square, rather than to glorify the separateness of each house. The rising class who possessed the money to own and build such houses were now no longer content with this reticence; they required that their social advancement should be more ostentatiously paraded by a showy individualistic house. The town, too, had become dirty, palled in smoke, the scene of heavy industry and vulgar commerce, unattractive as a setting for gracious living. So began the steady movement from the old town to a villa on its outskirts. The first sign was the professional office set up in the midst of a residential terrace and the upper floor let as a flat, or worse, in rooms. Now the street was seen to be sinking and more people moved out, while more offices and lodgers moved in. The final step to complete degradation would be the departure of respectability, in the person of the business man, and the arrival of more lodgers until the street was a veritable warren of tenemented houses: it was then a slum.

The second of these distinct architectural movements was, then, the emergence of the villa as the beau-ideal, the aspiration of the elite, of the middle class, and then finally of the working class, and with it in turn for each class the growing mark of respectability, of social arrival. The first of these more romantic and less formal town developments belonged to the Regency, to John Nash's great scheme for Regent's Park. In the original version of 1812[36] there were a large number of villas in the park itself, set amongst groves and gardens, but these were left out for economic reasons when the estate was finally developed. There remain, however, the two small developments known as Park Village East and Park Village West, except that part of the former was destroyed when the nearby railway was built. Nash added these to his larger scheme apparently as an afterthought, and the small detached and semi-detached houses were completed after his death by Pennethorne. The layout was essentially picturesque, with its curving streets and deliberate variety of houses, each with a different silhouette and roof line, set amongst trees and gardens. The villas contrasted sharply with the grandeur and rigidity of the terraces, and they were the precursor of much later work.

The Regency also marked the beginning of villa-dom in the suburbs and with it the first taste of the eclectic and the curious, which led to a startlingly wide variety of architectural idioms, all set off by miniature gardens. This was the kind of development which was to be practised by the rich throughout the century. In several towns there still exist areas of quite carefully arranged villas largely speculative in character, showing a positive approach to planning and in spirit not too far removed from the town planning schemes of this century. Two examples which are well known to me will suffice. The first at Sheffield where the Broom Hall estate was romantically laid out with villas and the park-like quality of the south facing slopes carefully preserved. This was in the 1830s. The other is The Park in Nottingham, a more formal layout but equally open and romantic with a wide variety of villas built over a rather longer period. Several other towns could provide similar examples. There were, however, sporadic examples of planned romantic development; notably that by Decimus Burton, who owed so much to Nash, at Tunbridge Wells,[37] which developed as a fashionable watering place during the last years of the eighteenth century and the early part of the nineteenth. Burton designed the Calverley Estate at Tunbridge Wells in 1828, with a series of villas overlooking a large park, and a crescent of shops with lodgings above them.

These were only early and rather tentative examples of what became a Victorian tradition; and a much more impressive development, because it continued throughout the century, was that of the complete town at Bournemouth.[38] In 1825 L. D. G. Tregonwell built himself a house, which still exists as part of a hotel, in the plain Italianate style which Nash had first popularised. This was followed late in the thirties by the development of the Tapp estate by Benjamin Ferry,

with the deliberate intention of making Bournemouth a fashionable watering place. The Westover Pleasure Grounds and Westover Villas belong to this period. Tapp decided that the whole of the development on his estate must be of detached villas in their own gardens, and this quality spread to subsequent developments, so that Bournemouth in the nineteenth century was a town of romantically laid out detached houses. The Tapp estate must have progressed well and the local guide thus described the town in 1850 '...a number of detached villas, each marked by distinct and peculiar architectural features, have sprung into existence, affording accommodation of varying extent, so as to be suited to the convenience of either large or small families, and adapted, some for extended, others for confined establishments'.[39] Tapp himself died in 1842 and the management of his estate passed to trustees, for whom Decimus Burton prepared several reports, recommending the preservation of the rustic appearance, and the deliberate avoidance of formality. The owners of other estates followed the example set by the Trustees and another local guide, written as late as 1875, described the current mode of building in a way which would not doubt have been approved of by Tapp:

When a villa is to be built, the trees and evergreens, the growth which has been carefully fostered all over the place, are not indiscriminately slaughtered; sufficient space only for planting the house is cleared and thus a picturesque appearance is given to the *ensemble*. Good roads intersect what were once plantations in every direction, and the natural sylvan beauty of the place has been aided by the

9.9   *Late nineteenth century villas, speculatively built*

addition of many ornamental and valuable native and foreign trees. In rambling about the town we come across Elizabethan and Gothic villas erected at every conceivable angle, almost hidden amongst the foliage of the trees, beneath which grow luxurient crops of ferns. The result is a *mélange* of architecture, timber, and foliage as unusual as it is agreeable.[40]

So when Richard Norman Shaw came to design Bedford Park for Mr Jonathan T. Carr in 1876 he was not creating a planning precedent, although by the simple brick Queen Anne style which he introduced, and by bringing organised and romantic garden and house design on a relatively small scale back to London, he made a contribution of another kind. Bedford Park,

Turnham Green, was an estate designed to provide small semi-detached or detached houses, with three or four bedrooms, arranged around a group of communal buildings which included a church, 'Not too near London, and yet not what might be called too far'.[41] There were two important characteristics which were quite novel at Bedford Park; first the deliberate idea of creating a new community of well designed small houses on the fringes of London; and secondly, the architectural quality which Shaw was able to infuse into the character of the estate in his own inimitable way. Sir Reginald Blomfield has described the effect

9.10 *Bedford Park, the new-look middle class garden suburb built by J. T. Carr to the design of Richard Norman Shaw in 1876*

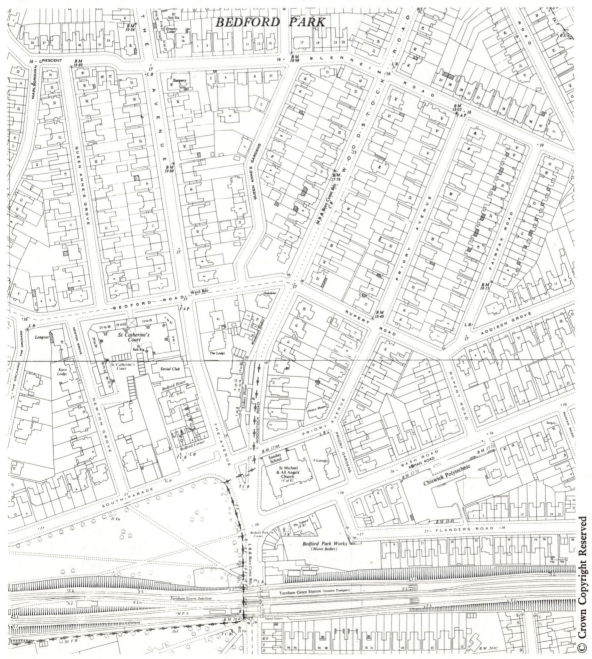

9.11   *Bedford Park*

Bedford Park had upon his generation, and this, I think, gives it the full measure of its importance:

I can recollect that we students used to visit Bedford Park much as students today visit the latest experiment in reinforced concrete and glass. Bedford Park meant a complete break with the small Victorian house with its bad ornament in stucco, its travesties of classical detail, the deplorable legacy of John Nash and the speculative builders of the thirties and forties of the nineteenth century.[42]

This was housing, but it was also architecture: that was a rare achievement in 1876 and this is the background to romantic design for the artizan too.[43]

Port Sunlight

The idea of a garden suburb in this sense first reached the working classes in the form of the model village. There were two important examples, both dating from the end of the century, but each was well under way when Howard published his book on Garden Cities. The first village was at Port Sunlight,[44] and it was very definitely a philanthropic, almost Utopian venture, the work of the first Viscount Leverhulme, who regarded it as a social duty to provide his workpeople with satisfactory homes regardless of cost, the rents paying only for the rates, and the upkeep and repair of the property.

The truest and highest form of enlightened self-interest requires that we pay the fullest regard to the interest and welfare of those around us, whose well-being we must bind up with our own, and with whom we must share our prosperity...If capital and management think of nothing but their own narrowest, selfish self-interest, without a thought for labour, care nothing for the comfort or welfare of labour, care nothing whether labour is well or ill-housed, whether labour is provided with opportunity for reasonable and proper recreation and relief from toil or not, then capital and management are blind to their own highest interest.[45]

Lever Brothers purchased some 52 acres of open land at Bromborough Pool in 1887 and the following year they started to build their soap factory and the first group of cottages. At the banquet given on 3 March, 1888, to commemorate the cutting of the first sod on the new site, William Hesketh Lever (as he then was) made clear his intentions to build houses for his workmen, and it is interesting to note the kind of housing he envisaged:

It is my hope and my brother's hope, some day, to build houses in which our work-people will be able to live and be comfortable – semi-detached houses, with gardens back and front, in which they will be able to know more about the science of life than they can in a back slum...[46]

The development of the village began four years later in 1892. Lever is said to have designed the layout himself, although two architects might well have had some influence;[47] nevertheless, he seems genuinely to have been the inspiration behind the scheme in more ways than merely financially; he thought that a density of twelve houses per acre was the maximum suitable for this kind of scheme, and Port Sunlight

was actually built at less than this, at about eight
houses per acre.[48] He argued that the speculative
builder by developing at a higher density was able to
pay large prices for the land on which he built; Lever
wanted the maximum number to be reduced by law to
twelve houses per acre which he believed was the
'maximum limit possible for the maintenance of healthy
life'.[49] By doing this the value of building land would
also fall, he believed. The layout was very loose, partly
owing to the nature of the land, which at first had
many ravines, subsequently filled in, and also because
of the open character which Lever desired. The site
was divided into a series of roughly rectangular blocks,
some left entirely open, others with public buildings
on them and the remainder devoted to housing. We are
told[50] that Lever deliberately made his roads wide;
the principal ones were 36 ft. wide with 12 ft. footpaths on either side, and his general rule throughout
the village was to make the footpaths the same width
in feet as the road in yards. The houses were arranged
around the perimeter of the plot with an open space

9.12   *Port Sunlight, on the Wirral, begun 1892 by Lord Leverhulme*

in the centre for allotments, but there were no back gardens as such. Various architects were employed so that the whole scheme did not have a tedious uniformity, although most of the designs were inspired by Tudor work, and there was plenty of half timbering, so that the effect of the houses was picturesque and cottage-like, rather than repetitive and urban.[51] Despite Lever's original intention to build houses only in pairs, most of the housing was finally erected in groups of up to seven, but no two blocks were identical in appearance. Two basic plans were used, the 'Parlour House' and the 'Kitchen House', the former with a parlour, kitchen, scullery and four bedrooms; the Kitchen House had no parlour and only three bedrooms, but both types had separate bathrooms. The front gardens were cultivated at first by the company in order to preserve uniformity, which seems to have been interpreted as meaning the absence of flowers and reliance upon evergreens, this was said to give a funeral appearance to the village so that in the twenties tenants were encouraged to take over the cultivation themselves should they so desire, the company offering reduced rents for the best kept gardens as an incentive and reward. Today, however, the original habit of cultivating the front gardens as an integral part of the village has returned much to the advantage of its homogeneity. But Port Sunlight was designedly a complete community, and Lever lavished upon it a series of public buildings which made it a much more elaborate and self-consciously architectural experience than any other village built by a less wealthy industrialist. Much of the detailing of

the cottages was also lavish far beyond ordinary contemporary standards, so that the importance of the village was more for its overall architectural and planning effect as a pleasant visual experience and environment than for its implications as a housing experiment which were, by its nature, small. But then, Lever's aims were different from Cadbury's at the later Bournville; he wished to make his own workmen well housed and contented, and he was not very interested to show that this particular kind of housing, with its extremely low density and wealth of open space, was capable of emulation by a utilitarian organisation such as a local authority. In a sense Lever did a disservice to housing, since by making Port Sunlight a merely philanthropic venture, he at once lifted it out of the realms of practical consideration, because he was admitting that it was not possible to achieve a low density garden village-type design and make it pay at the same time.

Bournville

The second, and equally famous, of these model industrial villages, was the work of George Cadbury outside Birmingham. Bournville was founded by the Cadbury family as a housing experiment with the purpose of: 'alleviating the evils which arise from the insanitary and insufficient housing accommodation supplied to large numbers of the working classes, and of securing to workers in factories some of the

9.13a *Bournville, outside Birmingham; George Cadbury's model village, first mooted in 1879, much of it built after 1895*

9.13b *Bournville*

advantages of outdoor village life, with the opportunities for the natural and healthful occupation of cultivating the soil'.52 It was never connected directly with the firm, nor was it ever intended primarily to house workpeople belonging to the Cadbury organisation, one of the principal intentions being to encourage a social intermixture of all classes, and that was the real difference between Bournville and Port Sunlight.53 The village was begun before Port Sunlight but the important developments came later. George and William Cadbury moved their cocoa factory from

Birmingham to Bournville, $4\frac{1}{2}$ miles away, in 1879, and they built the first group of cottages soon after this in order to house key workers; but the idea of a complete village came much later than this and really only dates from 1895. The 1879 houses were built in pairs, widely spaced, and set in large gardens. When the village was begun the intention was that it should be a financially sound concern, that after repairs and maintenance costs had been deducted there should still be a return of 4 per cent; and Cadbury's motive was that by doing so he would set local authorities an example, and encourage them to build similarly for the working classes generally. This in itself was an important step, since the financial arrangements at Port Sunlight only showed that heavy subsidisation was necessary to make such a venture possible, and it left the model garden village as an unattainable ideal. In 1900 George Cadbury founded the Bournville Village Trust to administer the village, which by that time consisted of about 330 acres, on which he had already built 313 houses.[54] The trust was independently endowed so that it would carry out research and other work connected with Town Planning, in which Cadbury became deeply interested, but the village itself remained a financially independent venture. Its layout was much less pretentious than that of Port Sunlight, and in character it was more typical of a suburban estate, except that the area of housing and private gardens was broken up by public open space, including a park, a recreation ground and a wood. There was no attempt to group the housing around them in a systematic way as at Port Sunlight, and no attempt to achieve organisation and coherence. Despite the purposeful way the estate was developed, the early stages do not suggest that there was a real grasp of planning and its implications. By contrast with Port Sunlight there were, of course, fewer public buildings, and in this the village was more typical of the garden city of the future than was Port Sunlight. Before the first world war, the Meeting House, School and Ruskin Hall provided the nucleus of the community centre, and there were of course some shops, but there was no lavish provision of public amenities.

The first housing the new village built after 1895 consisted of either semi-detached cottages, or short blocks of three or four houses; the planning was largely developed from the typical house patterns then common in Birmingham; but after the formation of the Trust it was decided not to build a greater number than four cottages in a block.[55] There were examples of the 'tunnel-back' arrangement and of the back off-shoot, both features associated with normal speculative development. The houses were closer together than those built in 1879, but there was still a gap of as much as 20 ft. between each pair or group, and each cottage had about 600 square yards of garden which was considered the amount that the average man could cultivate satisfactorily.[56] But this early work, although its planning was evolved from an urban pattern, did not bring with it the same urban quality which was characteristic of Saltaire; the planning at Bournville might lean heavily on local tradition, but the layout held tenaciously to the idea of a house in a garden. House plans which had been evolved to suit the terrace were incongruous in a setting where there was no longer any need to reach the back of the house through the actual building by means of a tunnel, since the units were short and not conceived as continuous

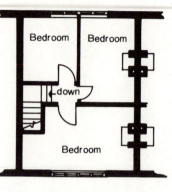

FIRST FLOOR

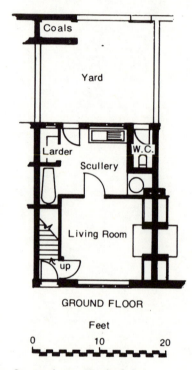

GROUND FLOOR

Feet

0   10   20

9.14 *Cottage plans at Port Sunlight*

terraces; and the outbuilding in the rear made the other back rooms unnecessarily dark. This inconsistency was soon realised and the first important change in design was to introduce a house inspired by the simple four-square country cottage, without any of the external back excrescences usual in town; and this resulted in a plan very similar to what later became the typical 20th century semi-detached house plan. The Bournville cottages had a living room, kitchen and sometimes a parlour, on the ground floor, and three bedrooms upstairs; there were no bathrooms in the cheaper cottages, since the rent was only 5s. a week, but there was often provision in the kitchen for a 'cabinet' bath, and the lavatory was arranged externally on the ground floor, although usually it was an integral part of the house structure. The density throughout the development remained low, at about seven houses to the acre, and the character was controlled by the

Trust, who themselves built most of the early housing to the design of their own architect. They pursued a policy of diversity, rather than uniformity, in order to achieve the greatest possible contrast with the bye-law street. In this sense the early developments at Bournville were a violent and purposeful aesthetic reaction against the normal working class conditions. It was not until 1907, we are told,[57] that the Trust architect, W. Alexander Harvey, began to study the relation of the houses to each other and to the street, so that it is legitimate to say that the first ten years saw the deliberate development of a rural character rather than an urban one.

In other respects, too, Bournville was important; Cadbury did not 'tie' any of the houses to his own works or organisation, and only about 40 per cent were at any particular time occupied by his employees; nor was the village a self-contained community, it rapidly became part of suburban Birmingham, and its own amenities were slow to develop, perhaps because of this. Its importance was in the way it sought to provide a different kind of housing, at economic rents which were commercially remunerative, in just the same way as S.I.C.L.C. had tried half a century earlier to be exemplary; and its significance was in the way it achieved this, denying the inherent nature of a community to be urban and close knit, and imposing a deliberate policy of low density and architectural diversity, considering the house as part of a picturesque landscape and not of a street. Cadbury proved that a low density layout could be a practical possibility even for the working classes, and unwittingly he opened the flood gates to a new kind of suburbia.

Harvey has left an account of the factors which should influence the layout and design of a model village, largely based upon the work done at Bournville under his supervision. The main streets should be planned with some degree of straightness for the convenience of getting to and from important places, there is no reason why regularity should be sought after for its own sake; at the same time an unnecessary irregularity should be as much avoided.[58] In residential areas the roads should not run east to west except where it was absolutely unavoidable, and then the houses on the northern side should be built on the front portion of the site. The building line in any case should be at least 30 ft. from the road, and there should be trees planted along the verges. The streets themselves should be 40–50 ft. wide with paths 8–12 ft. wide on either side. Variety in the appearance of the housing should be achieved by an irregular building line, by projecting the central cottage in a group of three, by the addition of a porch or a bay window; and in addition houses should not be arranged directly opposite to each other. For economical reasons Harvey admitted that a certain degree of standardisation both in planning and in detailing would be necessary, and in order to economise in road construction, children's playgrounds

might be sited at the back of the houses, beyond the gardens. These gardens would be about 600 square yards in extent which gave a density of eight to twelve cottages to the acre. In working class developments where it was necessary to plan the cottages in short terraces, Harvey recommended that the plan of the individual houses should be spread out laterally so that the gardens were not in narrow strips. Thus indeed was Bournville built, and many another less august suburb in its turn.

One other model village scheme deserves mention, that at Aintree, built by Sir William Hartley for the workers in his jam factory. Perhaps inspired by the more ambitious work at Port Sunlight across the estuary, which was then just starting, Hartley held a competition early in 1888 for the layout of a village to be built close to his factory. There were 85 entries and the winning design was by W. Sugden and Son of Leek; they planned the housing around a central green, giving a 'picturesque effect without eccentricity'.[59] Yet, in fact, the little development remains stubbornly Victorian in appearance, showing clearly the wide gap between the leading designers and their clients and those who tried to follow without fully comprehending. There were a variety of houses varying in size from five to seven rooms, and in all there were 71 cottages and five shops. The rents were from 2s. 6d. per week, a typical five-roomed cottage costing 3s. 6d., but some of the larger houses Hartley sold to his tenants over a period of twenty years, charging them $3\frac{3}{4}$ per cent interest on the purchase price. One of the features which he thought most important was the preservation of a wide passage to the rear, and at Aintree it was 12 ft. wide which Hartley thought was a minimum, and he had already struggled in the city council at Liverpool for the local regulations to be increased from 9 ft. to 12 ft.[60]

The ideal concept during the second half of the century: Howard

The development of Port Sunlight and of Bournville showed that low density 'garden suburb' planning was possible and could be visually attractive. Alone they might have made little impact but they were in fact part of a much wider movement which owed its real motivation to yet another idealist, but one who managed to turn his dream into reality. Ebenezer Howard was at one and the same time the prophet of the garden city movement and the man who codified a great mass of loose unrelated ideas.[61]

The continued growth of cities, and the related problems of overcrowding which became so noticeable during the eighties, were in part responsible for the idea that it might be possible to form new communities on the outskirts of existing towns which would perhaps attract industry and even working class commuters, as well as intercepting the influx of workers from the country. The idea became more realistic with the growth of the railways and the obligations placed upon the companies to run workmen's trains, and it received not a little consideration before Howard published *To-morrow*. In 1884, for example, the Social Science Association held a discussion 'for the purpose of considering the best means of promoting the formation of village communities, where manufactures and "Home industries" can combine with the cultivation of cottage or co-operative farms, as a remedy for overcrowding in great cities, and want of employment in agricultural districts'.[62] In the same year the Rev. Henry Solly wrote that the problems of London could best be solved by a similar solution: 'The remedy, unquestionably, seems to be to turn back the tide from town to country by finding these folks employment, profitable to themselves and the community, where they can be decently housed and fairly well remunerated'.[63] Perhaps under the influence of William Morris with his inspired vision, part romance, part socialist utopia, of London as a great garden,[64] these people were attempting to combine agricultural pursuits with a miniature industrial community, and with Howard this idea was fully expanded.

But even for those who did not see the solution in the form of new communities, there was great concern at the ever increasing size of the city, and it is worth quoting one view, at least, which was aware of this.

The main tendency of the future in consequence of the enlarged area of our towns must necessarily be not only an attempt to make the outskirts as accessible as possible to the centres, but also to prevent the further enlargement of towns and the consequent lengthening of distances. It is clear that towns will go on increasing in area without much check for a comparatively long period, but a time must arrive when the desire of the inhabitants is, if possible, not to go further but to utilise so much of the space as is already built over more than is done at present. The increase in areas must necessarily continue; but, on the other hand, a contrary influence strengthens and increases. At such time towns begin largely to increase in height, and it is in an increase in height of our town houses that the increase of the future is sure to be most marked.[65]

Ebenezer Howard published *To-morrow: A Peaceful Path to Real Reform* in 1898, and in 1902 it was re-issued, slightly revised, as *Garden Cities of To-morrow*. In it he brought together the two opposing concepts of a self-contained community and of economic housing which produced the famous Garden City concept. Howard was, if anything, an enigmatical figure, he earned his living as a parliamentary reporter, and moved in 'earnest circles of Noncomformist churchmen and less orthodox religious enthusiasts, circles overlapping with others of mild reformists, who in those days were largely concerned with the land question'.[66] He had been to America several times and his chief spare time activity seems to have been that of inventor. It was in America that he first read Bellamy's *Looking Backward*[67] with its communistic doctrine of equality, its belief in co-operation, and the social

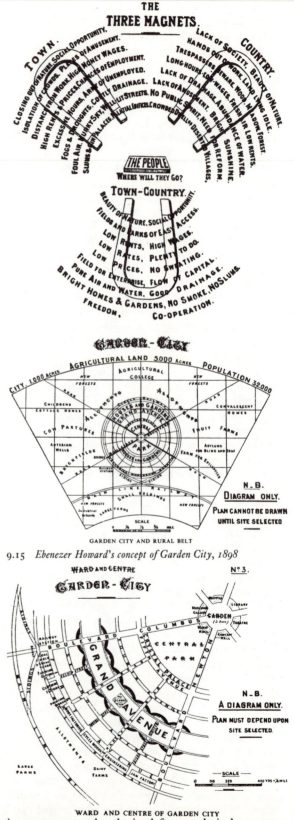

9.15 *Ebenezer Howard's concept of Garden City, 1898*

improvement to be obtained from technical progress; and this is thought to have been one of the chief influences upon him. But it would be wrong to think of Howard as a radical in thought or deed; his ideas, although novel, were mild by comparison with those of Buckingham or Owen, for example.

Howard looked afresh at the problem which had been vexing society since the onset of the industrial revolution, and more particularly since the middle of the nineteenth century: that of the persistent growth of cities and their fatal attraction for rural folk. He illustrated his conception of the existing condition and their solution with a diagram showing three magnets; the first representing the town, the second, of much less power, the country; and superimposed upon them Howard listed their several attractions with their corresponding drawbacks:

But neither the Town magnet nor the Country magnet represents the full plan and purpose of nature. Human society and the beauty of nature are meant to be enjoyed together. The two magnets must be made one...Town and country *must be married*, and out of this joyous union will spring a new hope, a new life, a new civilisation.[68]

And this was the third magnet, 'Town–country', the garden city ideal, in which the merits of both were combined, without their disadvantages, to produce an environment which would be better in all respects than either:

I will undertake, then, to show how in 'Town–country' equal, nay better, opportunities of social intercourse may be enjoyed than are enjoyed in any crowded city, while yet the beauties of nature may encompass and enfold each dweller therein; how higher wages are compatible with reduced rents and rates; how abundant opportunities for employment and bright prospects of advancement may be secured for all; how capital may be attracted and wealth created; how the most admirable sanitary conditions may be ensured; how beautiful homes and gardens may be seen on every hand; how the bounds of freedom may be widened, and yet all the best results of concert and co-operation gathered in by a happy people.[69]

The garden city was to be built on a 6,000 acre site, although the actual city would occupy only 1,000 acres in the centre of this. He suggested that the town might be circular in form, about 1½ miles in diameter: and from its centre would radiate six great boulevards, each 120 ft. wide, intersected by five concentric avenues. In the centre was a 5½ acre garden, the antithesis of the traditional city core, with the principal civic buildings, town hall, concert hall, theatre, library, museum and hospital set around it, each in their own grounds, and surrounded by another great ring of park land, comprising a further 145 acres. It is useful to contrast this arrangement with Buckingham's town which gradually built up to an urban centre with a great central square, an essentially civic space, whereas Howard placed the park at the heart of his scheme, deliberately bringing the country through and into the centre of his town concept.

Around the outer edge of Howard's central park was the 'Crystal Palace', a great covered arcade serving the purpose of shelter in wet weather, of winter garden,

and of shopping arcade; and this particular idea was probably culled from Buckingham who had incorporated a similar feature in Victoria.[70] Moving away from the centre there next came the fifth avenue, the innermost of the concentric ring roads; and bordering it, facing across to the Crystal Palace, were to be the first houses. Additional radial roads now began to run out to the circumference of the town, dividing the land into smaller plots, around which the houses were to be built in a manner reminiscent of Lever's arrangement at Port Sunlight. Howard made no attempt to keep his housing segregated from traffic, it bordered the principal boulevards, the circumventing avenues and the radial roads alike. The individual sites for houses were to average 20 ft. by 130 ft., and the minimum plot was 20 ft. by 100 ft.; there were to be about 5,500 separate sites, housing 30,000 people, while in the green belt outside the town there would be some 2,000 more people engaged in agricultural work. For the town itself this would give gross figures of 5.5 houses per acre and 30 people per acre, since Howard seems to have assumed a family of over five persons. He does not speak of densities, as such, however, but the implications of low density were nevertheless there.

The design of the houses was to be as varied as possible, and although the municipal authorities were to exercise control over the actual siting, Howard expressly stated that 'harmonious departure' from the general line was to be permitted so that 'the fullest measure of individual taste and preference is encouraged',[71] no doubt to avoid any semblance of the bye-law street. There was to be variety in other ways too: for example, some groups of houses should have co-operative kitchens, and others common gardens.

Mid-way between the Crystal Palace and the outskirts of the town, and dividing the residential area into two distinct concentric 'belts' was the Grand Avenue, a 420 ft. wide green area; an additional park, in fact, of 115 acres; and Howard pointed out that no house would be further than 240 yards from this park, in which were to be built the schools and churches. On either side of the Grand Avenue, Howard permitted a departure from the normal housing pattern, mainly for grand architectural effect, and here he suggested a series of crescents, but this was the only point at which he seems to have considered the visual appearance in terms of building.

On the outskirts of the town were the factories and works served by a circular railway, the outermost concentric ring of all, which connected to the main line. All the machinery was to be driven by electricity, so that the 'smoke fiend is kept well within bounds',[72] and beyond the industries was the green belt, with its allotments and farms, convalescent homes and asylum.

The greater part of *To-morrow* was taken up with the economic and financial problems involved in establishing a garden city of this type, and they do not concern us in this chapter; suffice it to say that Howard envisaged the common ownership of land,

and because the site would be obtained at its value as agricultural land, the increased population would be able to contribute through their reasonable rents to a fund which, in addition to paying back the capital initially necessary to buy the site, would provide for the further development and upkeep of the town.

Howard himself said that the inspiration for the Garden City came from three sources; first the idea of organised migratory movement of population by Edward Gibbon Wakefield and Alfred Marshall; secondly, the system of land tenure originated by Thomas Spence and developed by Herbert Spencer; and last, Buckingham's Victoria. Howard saw that his own Garden City differed from Victoria in the following way:

Now it will be seen that though in outward form Buckingham's scheme and my own present the same feature of a model town set in a large agricultural estate, so that industrial and farming pursuits might be carried on in a healthy, natural way, yet the inner life of the two communities would be entirely different – the inhabitants of Garden City enjoying the fullest rights of free association, and exhibiting the most varied forms of individual and co-operative work and endeavour, the members of Buckingham's city being held together by the bonds of a rigid cast-iron organisation, from which there could be no escape but by leaving the association, or breaking it up into various sections.[73]

Buckingham's two great evils, war and drunkenness, he sought to abolish by the prohibition of liquor and gunpowder; and he proposed a town in which the municipality possessed a complete monopoly in all things, a state of affairs which was anathema to Howard. Garden City was socially a much less radical scheme; the organisation was parochial rather than national, and there was scope for individual and private benefaction in the establishment of churches and asylums. Architecturally, too, Howard's city differed considerably from Victoria; there was no suggestion of an attempt to heighten the architectural experience by dividing the population into social classes, giving each a particular area in which to live, so that the structure of the town was characterised by successive squares of more imposing character. The only place where Howard deliberately sought after visual effect was on either side of the Grand Avenue, where he suggested a crescent treatment. Otherwise there was no sense of architectural urgency as the centre was approached, no sense of drama. The centre was a garden, and the city was dispersed.

Garden City differs from the extant garden villages in that it was a proposal for a complete community related to a group of industries, rather than to the factory of one man which would have been socially undesirable in a large scale venture. It was isolated by a surrounding green belt so that it was intended as a complete, independent and finite unit, connected with the outside world by railway, a means of communication on which Howard laid great stress, especially when he came to suggest the proper path by which a garden city should expand when it had reached its optimum size:

It will grow by establishing – under Parliamentary powers probably – another city some little distance beyond its own zone of 'country', so that the new town may have a zone of country of its own. I have said 'by establishing another city', and, for administrative purposes there would be two *cities*; but the inhabitants of the one could reach the other in a very few minutes; for rapid transit would be specially provided for, and thus the people of the two towns would in reality represent one community.[74]

Finally, Howard believed that if the garden city idea was successful and new cities sprung up all over the country, each owned by the local municipality who would establish the principle of low ground rents, the greatest magnet of all, London, would loose its power of attraction; its inhabitants would move out in number, and industry with them, because of the cheaper land in garden cities and the attractions of a wholesome life. London might then be redeveloped, the slums pulled down and replaced by parks, so that eventually the capital itself would become another garden city. The vision was splendid, but the complexities of realising a new community which could support itself were numerous, and it says much for Howard's tenacity that Garden City did not remain merely another dream city in the history of Utopias.

Letchworth

C. B. Purdom has recalled the universal appeal of Howard's idea: to the Socialist because of its 'semi-municipal character';[75] to the Conservative because it would give private enterprise scope to provide housing; to the Liberal because it involved land reform. Howard formed the Garden City Association in 1899, the year after the first publication of his book, and it quickly gained the support of influential people like Ralph Nevill and Thomas Adams.[76] In 1902 *To-morrow* was republished as *Garden Cities of To-morrow* and the same year The Garden City Pioneer Company Ltd. was founded. The initial capital of £20,000 was quickly subscribed, and the Company started to look for a suitable site:

To promote and further the distribution of the industrial population upon the lines suggested in Mr Ebenezer Howard's book entitled *Garden Cities of Tomorrow*....and to form a garden city, that is to say, a town or settlement for agricultural, industrial, commercial and residential purposes, or any of them, in accordance with Mr. Howard's scheme or any modification thereof.[77]

In 1903 a suitable site was found at Letchworth and the original company gave place to the First Garden City Co. Ltd whose avowed intentions were:

Firstly, the provision of hygienic conditions of life for a considerable working population. Secondly, the stimulation of agriculture by bringing a market to the farmer's door.

Thirdly, the relief of the tedium of agricultural life by accessibility to a large town. Fourthly, that the inhabitants will have the satisfaction of knowing that the increment of value of the land created by themselves will be devoted to their own benefit.[78]

Three firms of architects were invited by the company to prepare a town plan, and that submitted by Messrs Parker and Unwin was accepted, and in its broad outline followed when the town was built:

It would not be unfair shortly to describe that plan as a group of connected villages around a civic centre, with a factory district on the outskirts.[79]

At a glance, the plan showed little resemblance to Howard's ideal. The railway was already in existence, dividing the site into two almost equal parts; there were certain roads and natural features, but otherwise the site was fairly clear of existing development, and the architects were able to design freely around the company's requirement that provision should be made for a population of 30,000 to 35,000 in the midst of an agricultural belt, and with an area for factories and adequate sites for houses and cottages. The layout which was adopted radiated from a central square, but it was not in any real sense a symmetrical plan and it was modified by the position of the railway, the siting of the park and the factory site; and the use of minor centres elsewhere in the plan further modified Howard's diagrammatic approach. The winning architects became consultants, and Unwin helped to draft an initial pamphlet to prospective developers, which described the kind of control which was to be exercised over the town. The company itself prepared the street plan and laid out the building plots which were to be developed first, defining the general building line, the street width, and the depth of the gardens:

In certain cases it is not proposed to enforce a hard-and-fast building line, but some simple regulation as to building area will be made. Houses may be set back or forward within certain limits, and may be set at varying angles where this would be advantageous. A building line will be suggested in the first place by the company, and any alteration which the intending builder proposes to make will be carefully considered in each case.[80]

The pamphlet went on to draw attention to the importance of good aspect, and attempted to lead the developer away from the traditional housing types:

In Garden City ample frontage will be provided, and it is hoped that builders will not think of erecting those common, unsatisfactory rows of narrow houses, with unsightly 'backs' projecting behind to the exclusion of air and sunshine, for which the chief reason has been the high cost of frontage in existing towns. One suitable arrangement will be found to be that of having no out-buildings at all; the W.C. or E.C. being under the main roof and entered from the porch or from a lobby outside.[81]

In addition they attempted to exercise some form of aesthetic control, and they said that they would discourage 'useless ornamentation' and welcome 'simple building, well built and suitably designed and grouped together'.[82]

The early housing was the work either of speculative builders or private persons, often with their own architects, and Parker and Unwin at once ran into difficulties and arguments about the appearance of the housing. The result was very often unsatisfactory from their point of view, but without the company itself undertaking the complete development there was little hope of effecting a more rigorous control. But as Purdom pointed out, the variety of housing which has resulted makes a pleasant contrast to the monotony of the usual speculative estate development or the bye-law street, and with the spacious layout of trees and gardens the effect is still refreshing.[83]

9.16a *Letchworth, garden-city layout for small houses*

9.16b *Letchworth, founded 1903*

Industry came to Letchworth soon after its foundation and with it the need for workmen's cottages, but until the first world war the demand was met by private enterprise, and the cottages let at commercial rents. The Garden City Company built the first group of eight cottages for their own workmen, but these proved rather expensive, and the next work was influenced by the Cheap Cottages Exhibition of 1905 which produced designs illustrating a variety of structures and materials, the winning one being brick and tile. In the intervening years before the first world war a variety of societies were set up to build cheap cottages and the district council was also persuaded to build, since it could obtain loans on less onerous conditions than private organisations. Most of the cottages had a living room, scullery and three bedrooms, and a few larger types had a parlour in addition. The cottages were usually designed in short blocks with not more than four in each, often arranged around a cul-de-sac road. The early cottage building societies became expert at the problem of designing an economic yet attractive small house, and in this sense, Letchworth was developing the work started at Bournville and, of course, still going forward at this time. The working class housing had an architectural unity, at least within each individual group, which the better class housing had not; it also had the same advantage of open layout and a wealth of planting on its tree lined streets, which meant that the Garden City was not confined to any particular class; the whole town was a city in a garden, and in this Howard's idea of the marriage of town and country had achieved reality.

Development began along existing roads and in the old village centres, and this seems to have been at least in part deliberate; but it has meant that even today the central parts of the town have disconcerting gaps causing architectural hiatus; but the shopping centre, which developed from the start, now creates the atmosphere of a central area, and it is the real hub of the community, which unfortunately the Town Square still fails to be. But these are minor criticisms when the magnitude of the task which the First Garden City Company undertook with but meagre finance is fully appreciated. They achieved something which was entirely unique: they made out of a utopian concept a reality. The critic today, whatever he may think of the implications of Letchworth, cannot fail to appreciate its intrinsic merits; and comparing it with much speculative development between the two world wars he will perhaps be less harsh than one of its ardent supporters who criticised the general standard of domestic architecture. It is hard for us not to concur with his praise for the overall effect, however: 'Nature aiding, even encouraging, the efforts of man has brought beauty to the town, so that while hardly anywhere will you meet consistent architectural treatment of building, yet everywhere there is something at least to refresh the eye and give pleasure.'[84]

Letchworth itself was successful, but it grew slowly; partly because it did not attract industry very rapidly, and it is significant that when the first world war came, one factory withdrew its branch to the central works in London. Furthermore, it has so far failed to develop satellites of its own, and this is partly because it is set within the zone over which the metropolis now exerts an influence, so that the Second Garden City, even more than the first, acts at least in part as yet another dormitory suburb. The garden city therefore failed to provide a magnet whose attraction was greater than that of the town, and its lasting place in the history of urban development is likely to be small

9.16c *Letchworth, from the air*

because it failed to destroy irrevocably the existing concept of the town and replace it with another.

The idea of a garden city never exerted any influence on the rebuilding of a great modern capital. The most that resulted was the creation of new suburban settlements by co-operative societies and the introduction of better architectural schemes, but for the most part the idea degenerated into the building of conglomerations of small houses in small gardens.[85]

If this is indeed true, and it still remains a question for posterity to decide, the immediate effect was very considerable and the period before the first world war was characterised by the development of numerous garden suburbs, and a few garden villages, all inspired by the example of Letchworth and Howard's book. The original idea had been to establish independent communities, but most of the new developments which sought to emulate the garden city were no more than another kind of urban expansion, much more extravagant with land than the old bye-law street, but compensating for that in the new and popular housing patterns which were evolved.

New Earswick, Hampstead and the Garden City movement

Amongst the independent village schemes, the most important was the model community which Joseph Rowntree founded at New Earswick near York. It was started as a result of Howard's *Garden Cities*, and also

because of the example of Bournville, which George Cadbury was busily developing in the years after 1900 through the Bournville Village Trust. There was considerable similarity between the two villages, as there was between their founders, both of whom were Quakers; and both subsequently formed a trust to ensure the continuance of their work and to provide funds for research at the same time.

New Earswick was started before Letchworth in fact.[86] Rowntree purchased the site, adjacent to the firm's existing factory, in 1901; and he engaged Raymond Unwin to design a layout and the first cottages in the following year. The site consisted of some 150 acres, bounded on one side by the River Foss, and on another by the railway; through the centre passed the main road from York to Haxby, but otherwise the site was flat and featureless. Unwin's layout was designed around two of these existing features, the main road and the bend in the River Foss, and his network of streets dividing the area into smaller plots about five or six acres in extent. The plan provided a grid in effect, but it was an irregular one, without the suggestion of rigidity which would have been typical of a bye-law street planning system. There were no roads, on the other hand, which curved sensuously in all directions merely to be picturesque; the natural features, such as they were, moulded the design so that it seems eminently reasonable, logical and direct, and these were qualities which distin-

9.17a   *New Earswick, near York, begun by Joseph Rowntree in 1901*

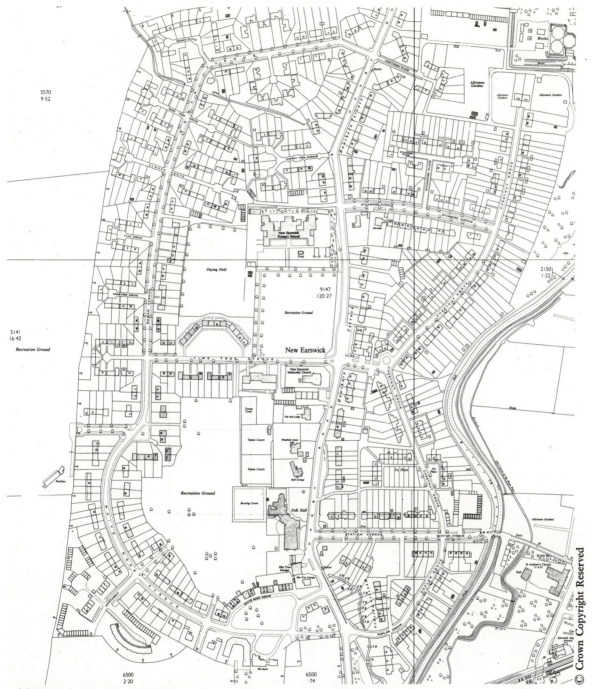

9.17b *New Earswick*

guished the best garden city planners from those who merely copied and came to seek effect for its own sake, regardless of reason or logicality.[87]

Unwin provided sites for church and chapel, school and library, shops and houses, together with a variety of open space in the form of village greens or park. The first houses which he designed were arranged in small groups, not always parallel to the road, but he planned them so that the living rooms had proper orientation, and each house had a large garden, not less than 350 sq. yards in area.[88]

Rowntree, however, was an old man by the time he was able to start his social experiments, and in 1904 he formed three separate trusts; the first two were concerned with social work, and the third was the Joseph Rowntree Village Trust. The actual trust deed was drawn up by the same lawyer who had prepared the deed for Bournville, and Rowntree had consulted Cadbury about the village before this date so that there was a real relationship between the two experiments. There were certain differences, however, between them. In York there was already in 1904 a surplus of housing, so the demand was not for more houses as at Bournville, situated on the outskirts of a large and growing industrial city, but for a demonstration that housing at an attractive rent, set in a proper environment and community, was a practical possibility and could be economically attractive. For this reason New Earswick was not necessarily intended to satiate an existing demand, thus developing over a continuous period into a large community, but rather to solve a social problem. Because Rowntree wished to provide a useful example he stipulated that the housing must pay an economic return, and it is therefore possible to trace the influence of rising cost upon the design and layout of the village.[89]

The most important contribution made by Earswick, as indeed by all the private organisations, came before the first world war, when it was still possible to produce original designs and build cheap cottages; after the war, with the advent of subsidisation, housing became more stereotyped, and financially it became impossible to build so cheaply at Earswick. The first group of houses were designed by Unwin before the Trust was formed in 1904, and he continued to design houses at Earswick until his appointment as architect to the Ministry of Health after the war, when his partner Barry Parker took over the whole of the practice. The first cottages were built in short terraces, not all of them with direct road access, since Unwin decided to use a pathway system in order to take the maximum advantage of aspect and correct orientation,

even to designing certain of the houses with their backs facing the main approach. Back access was achieved where necessary by means of the familiar short tunnel through the building, or alternatively around the end of a block, since most of them were of no great length. Unwin aimed to design a three bedroomed cottage without an excessively large ground floor, and to do this he incorporated a store and coal house within the dwelling itself. The lavatory, which was always at this period placed on the ground floor, was also incorporated into the main building; and if there were baths they were situated in the kitchen.[90] The character of the early cottages was very simple, Unwin made use of a traditional brick and tile construction, using a certain amount of colour-wash in the earlier examples, but otherwise he achieved his architectural effect by means of varied roof lines, prominent gables and ornamental bargeboards. By careful designing he was able to achieve a cheap cottage without great standardisation and he was able to retain some variety of treatment, all of which was denied to Barry Parker after the war, when economic considerations became so much more important in matters of planning and design. Despite economies, however, the Trustees found themselves unable to build as cheaply as the local authorities after 1918, and work was then halted until after the second world war. But Parker had contributed something new to the site planning of the village by the introduction of cul-de-sac planning in an effort to economise on road construction. Pathway access was now thought unsuitable because of growing traffic, and Parker adopted

9.18a *Hampstead Garden Suburb, the brain-child of Dame Henrietta Barnett, begun in 1907 to designs of Parker and Unwin in association with Lutyens*

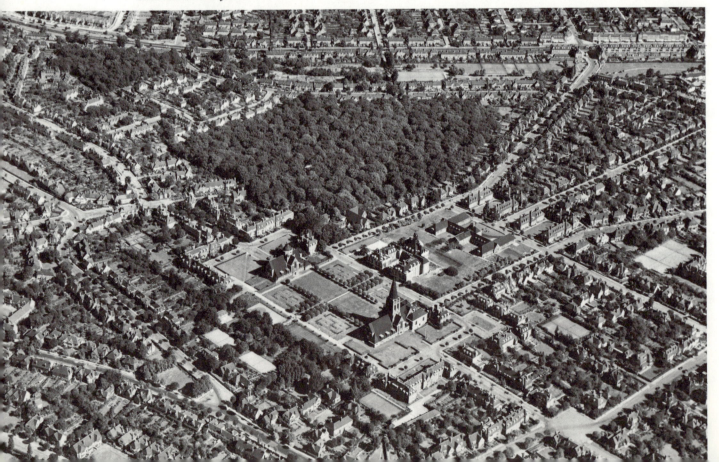

9.18b *Hampstead Garden Suburb*

the cul-de-sac because it allowed him to construct narrower and lighter roads for the access to small groups of houses. His final plan made economies of about 15 per cent on the road costs envisaged in the 1904 plan.[91]

The final example during this period which made any useful contribution to the development of the garden city idea, was the development of Hampstead Garden Suburb. In a way Hampstead was typical of the degeneration of the original intention of the garden city, because it was not conceived as a separate community, complete and inviolate, surrounded by an encircling green belt. It was always intended that Hampstead should provide a pleasing environment for the commuter, and when the site was purchased in 1906 by a specially formed company called the Hampstead Garden Suburb Trust, one of their avowed intentions was to provide cheap land on which cottages and houses with gardens might be built within a twopenny fare's distance of London. The other objectives included the intention to plan a suburb in a proper manner, with adequate open space and provision for public buildings, to preserve the natural beauty of the area and to promote a better understanding between the classes.[92]

The scheme originated with Dame Henrietta Barnett[93] who was a disciple of Octavia Hill, and the choice of site was largely made possible by the extension of the underground railway to Golders Green on the inner edge of the future suburb; for already Dame Henrietta had determined to preserve the Hampstead Heath Extension from speculative development.[94] In order to secure the kind of development that the Trust desired it became necessary to obtain a private Act of Parliament[95] which gave them greater freedom in the design of streets, permitting individual streets of up to 500 ft. in length and only 20 ft. in width so long as the houses themselves were 50 ft. apart. To compensate for these concessions the Trust agreed to restrict the density to eight houses per acre, and at this point the

Act was a precursor of the famous 1909 Town Planning Act.[96]

The layout for the suburb was the work again of Unwin and Parker, this time in consultation with Sir Edwin Lutyens, who was responsible for the more formal parts of the original plans and for the design of the central square with its two great churches and the Institute, which make the crowning hilltop such a magnificent architectural experience. The first phase of the development which was the most picturesquely laid out was completed during the years between 1907 and the first world war, but there were two later extensions which do not here concern us. It never proved possible to realise the founder's intention of housing a mixed community since there was no industry sufficiently near to attract the working classes, and they were not attracted to it as commuters; but in other senses a community developed which has proved satisfactory.[97]

The housing, which forms the largest proportion of the estate, was mainly of the detached or semi-detached variety, arranged in avenues or small squares; the trust exercised an aesthetic control over the development and it had power to refuse building permission for a design which they thought undesirable. This in turn gave some degree of unity to the development, and it also provided considerable scope for a series of architects with a mutually sympathetic outlook, including Baillie Scott and Voysey, to create an architectural environment of great quality and sensitivity. Three companies were involved in the development; Hampstead Tenants Ltd., Second Hampstead Tenants Ltd., and the Garden Suburb Development Company (Hampstead) Ltd.

The suburb was a spatial example of garden city development; it was patently not a working class

experiment in its final form, and today its chief characteristic is one of 'superiority'. It was not a fruitless experiment because of this, however, and it does exhibit many of the qualities which are necessary in a development for any class, and which became so depressingly absent in wealthy suburban development as well as council housing later in this century. Hampstead has organisation and a sense of purpose, despite the fact that some of the important facilities, for example the shops, are not situated near the central square, where logically they should be; it has unity and spatial cohesion which spring from the exercise of aesthetic control, and a proper sense of spatial drama in the initial planning; it has a wealth of planting, and where this has matured it compensates for any lack of urbanity, due to the enforced low density pattern, by providing a luxuriant landscape. The most singular, and perhaps the most important, of all the qualities it possesses is the real architectural achievement which no other garden suburb quite equalled.[98]

Some minor experiments

The garden suburb and the garden village had countless imitators during the next few years. Of the villages, only two were sufficiently important to deserve mention. The first was for the Brodsworth Main Colliery Company at a new pit some four miles from Doncaster, known as Woodlands and dating from 1908. The scheme was a private development but it was intended as an economic proposition, and the Company required that it should pay a 4 per cent dividend.[99] The architect was Percy B. Houfton, although in the first place the scheme had been won in competition by A. and J. Soutar, but it had subsequently become necessary to enlarge its scope. 'Woodlands' was the name of a

9.19a & b *Woodlands, a colliery village near Doncaster built by the Brodsworth Main Colliery Company, 1908. Percy B. Houfton architect*

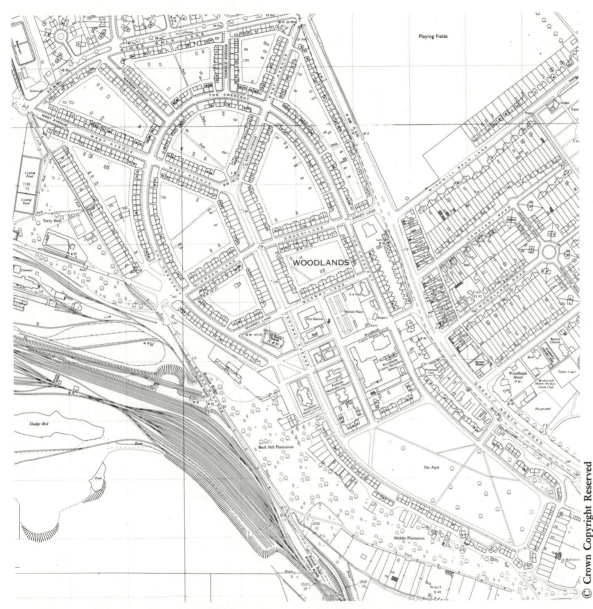

9.19c *Woodlands*

large house, set in its own grounds, which the company proposed to convert into a club, leaving the grounds as open space, even to the preservation of the fish pond. The site of the first stage of the village, consisting of 620 cottages, occupied about 127 acres, although this also included the grounds of Woodlands House. All the cottages were set back 25–30 ft. from the roads, and divided from each other with hedges of roses; the gardens were supplied with plants by the company and the gables of the houses were covered with creepers. The company was sufficiently keen about the effect of the landscaping to obtain advice from the resident forester at Letchworth about the planting in the village.[100] The initiation of the scheme filled Ebenezer Howard with joy; to see a private company develop a model village of its own initiative was indeed a mark of his own tremendous impact upon the country.[101] Howard was also well pleased with the solution adopted: 'It is

simply a wonderful advance – not a step forward, but a great leap.'[102]

The second village development was at Hull, where Sir James Reckitt was largely responsible in 1907 for the formation of a private company to build a model village which would house a large number of his own workmen; the site of some 130 acres was laid out by a local firm of architects, Runton and Barry.[103]

Garden suburbs became much more numerous than the villages, since they quickly became the most popular and novel way to develop a new estate on the outskirts of a town. The real advantage at the outset was that these estates, unlike nearly all previous suburban developments, were planned by one of the leading experts in the new field of town planning. Thomas Adams, for example, was responsible for the development of Sir Arthur Paget's estate, Fallings

9.20   Early garden city site planning showing the break up of the bye-law street concept

Park, at Wolverhampton in 1907.[104] The density was restricted to 12–14 houses per acre, and the housing was developed partly by private individuals building their own houses and partly by a co-partnership society. Adams also designed a small layout for a company formed at Bristol in 1909 to develop an estate at Shirehampton,[105] and another at Alkrington near Manchester, which was carried out by Pepler and Allen after Adams himself had moved to the Local Government Board.[106] Similarly at Knebworth the same firm was responsible for the execution of another design prepared by Adams in consultation with Lutyens.[107] Adams also prepared plans for the Newton Moor Estate near Stockport and for Glyn-Cory near Cardiff.[108]

Another firm who became very well known was that of A. and J. Soutar, who first made their name as town planning experts through several successes in competitions. They won the Woodlands competition but their scheme was subsequently revised, one for a Garden Suburb at Warrington, and another for the Ruislip Manor Estate which was one of the largest and most important developments of the period. The estate belonged to King's College Cambridge, who gave the development rights to the Ruislip Manor Company, which had been specially formed to carry out a scheme under the new Town Planning Act of 1909.[109] Inspired by this important gesture, the neighbouring Urban District Council for Ruislip and Northwood decided to develop adjacent land under the Town Planning Act, so that in all a considerable area was involved.[110] The scheme was of importance, partly because of its size, and also because of its density control, for in parts of the estate the density was only four houses per acre, and nowhere was it more than twenty. In the London region there were other ven-

tures, at Ilford for example[111] and Gidea Park[112] where a cottage exhibition was held which resulted in the publication of a book *The Hundred Best Houses*, illustrating the now fashionable extremes of picturesque effect in the architectural treatment of the small house.[113]

These examples are enough to show that the garden city ideal achieved a practical interpretation which amounted almost to a new cult in housing theory and practice. The result was not what Howard first envisaged, and the facets of his theories which were popularly adopted were mostly concerned with low density and anti-urbanism. Howard had therefore unwittingly unleashed a new and more rapid kind of town expansion which proved dangerous. But at the same time he had touched off the violent reaction to nineteenth century working class housing conditions which had long been smouldering just below the surface, and the proposition of a healthy home in a garden environment became the most sought after prerequisite of the early years of the twentieth century: it was considered so desirable because it was at last tangible, and within reach of the whole community, not merely the rich. Further, it was automatically assumed that because it was a low density concept of living, it would be healthy.

The contribution of Geddes

The garden city and the garden suburb had the most immediate effect upon housing and spatial problems, but they were at the same time both the cause and the expression of a movement whose implications were wider and more far reaching, and this was what came to be called 'Town Planning'. While Howard was developing his new communities another visionary, but of a different kind, was evolving the mental equipment which was necessary for a consideration of the wider implications of planning for the whole community, and this was the basis of Town Planning. The Garden City and the Town Planning movement were not synonymous, although for many years one was the only practical expression of the other, so that in a sense neither was a true expression of itself. In a sense, too, the whole history of housing discussed in these pages was a movement towards a town planning theory, but it was not the kind of all embracing doctrine which grew out of the Garden City movement.

The development of Town Planning during the early years of this century owed much to the work of Patrick Geddes; he was a supporter of the Garden City movement and of Howard, but he had an additional contribution to make which was both valuable in its own right and at the same time complementary to that of Howard.

Geddes was born in 1854 at Perth and his early training was that of a biologist, a subject which he taught first at Edinburgh then at Dundee, where he held a chair of botany from 1888 to 1919.[114] But this was in many ways a sinecure since it required his attendance only during the three months of the summer term. His home, therefore, was in Edinburgh and it was there that his interest in social problems was first aroused and fostered, after his marriage in 1887, by his wife who shared his interests and had contact with Octavia Hill, Josephine Butler and their associates in the movement for social and housing reform in London.[115] Geddes and his wife went to live in St James' Court, one of the slums of Edinburgh Old Town, partly to practise their own sociological ideas, partly to attract civic attention to the problems of the poor. During the next few years they were responsible for the purchase of a considerable amount of slum property, which they renovated and managed, some of it for the benefit of students in the University, the rest for the poor, and all of it was eventually turned over to the Town and Gown Association.[116] Geddes at this time was still predominantly a biologist, but perhaps more than most of his contemporaries he was conscious of the environment in which he had chosen to live, of its people and of their problems, and out of this grew his great vision for the improvement of cities.

In 1892 he bought the Outlook Tower in Edinburgh, where he began to collect his information about the nature of cities. The tower was in many ways a symbol, for even before Geddes purchased it there had been a camera obscura housed in the roof from which the visitor could see all Edinburgh laid out before him, and this he retained:

...alike for its own sake and as evidence of what is so often missed by scientific and philosophic minds, that the synthetic vision to which they aspire may be reached more simply from the aesthetic and the emotional side, and thus be visual and concrete. In short, here as elsewhere, children and artists may see more than the wise. For there can be no nature study, no geography worth the name apart from the love and the beauty of Nature, so it is with the study of the City.[117]

9.21 *A typical street scene in a suburb influenced by garden city ideals*

On the floor below the camera obscura Geddes gathered together in the course of time, illustrations of:

the analysis of the outlook in its various aspects – astronomic and topographical, geological and meteorological, botanical and zoological, anthropological and archaeological, historical and economic, and so on.[118]

The next floor down was devoted to the city, and in particular to Edinburgh whose history was outlined in a series of illustrations beginning with its origins and including the most recent photographs all gathered together and juxtaposed in what became a traditional, all-embracing, Geddes approach. Subsequent floors were devoted to Scotland, Great Britain, European civilisations and finally oriental civilisations.

But the general principle – the primacy of the civic and social outlook, intensified into local details with all the scientific outlooks of a complete survey; yet in contacts with the larger world, and these successively in enlarging social zones, from that of the prospect outwards – will now be sufficiently clear; and of course be seen as applicable to any city.[119]

Geddes did not achieve this synthesis at once, it was evolved over many years, and these accounts were written in 1915 when his whole philosophy had matured; but he was from the outset searching after a great truth which was to form the genesis of town planning as an art and an applied science. His idea was that cities and indeed great regions, such as his own centres which he called for convenience Greater London, Lancaston, West Riding, South Riding, Midlandton, Southwaleston, Tyne–Wear–Tees and Clyde–Forth, should look afresh at themselves, should gather statistical information and organise illustrative exhibitions to stimulate interest in themselves from within, in order that they might rejuvenate their own town or city, or even the whole region, and thereby control its growth so that the surrounding countryside was preserved. From the Outlook Tower, Geddes himself conducted a survey of open space in the slums of the Royal Mile, and he found some 76 separate areas, in all about ten acres of wasteland, many of which he was able to reclaim, and through the activities of voluntary agencies to turn them into gardens. It was practical work such as this, on a small and intimate scale, which proved the value of the Outlook Tower technique.

Geddes became a well known figure in sociological and planning circles in the years following 1900, and more especially after the publication in 1904 of his town planning report for Dunfermline entitled *City Development: A Study of Parks, Gardens and Cultural Institutes.* Unfortunately, his solution would have cost more than twice the amount offered to the city by its philanthropic son Andrew Carnegie, for the town's renovation, and consequently it was never implemented; but it established Geddes' reputation as something more than a gifted amateur. The same year the Sociological Society was formed in London by Victor

Branford, a friend of Geddes, and in it he took great interest. One of the best known actions which they undertook was the rebuilding of Crosby Hall in 1909.[120]

It was during these years at the beginning of the century that Geddes moved in the circles of planners such as Raymond Unwin, Patrick Abercrombie and H. V. Lanchester, and together they were largely responsible for the introduction of the first Town Planning Act of 1909. Geddes' own views on the architectural implications of planning were very much those of contemporary enlightened opinion, that is of the garden city group, and the evidence for this comes from his own writings. For example, after discussing German town planning and the work of Camillo Sitte he wrote:

It is still from Letchworth and Hampstead, from Woodlands and Earswick, and the like, as of course from the old-world villages they continue to renew, that we may best learn to house our people in moderate numbers to the acre, and with that most essential of conditions of health for children, wife and man alike – that is, of cottage and garden.[121]

He was critical, too, of the Scottish adherence to continental building practice:

The evil Continental tradition of walled cities and crowded population, and consequent persistence of high site values, still weighs heavy upon our long war-worn land, so that even at new industrial villages – say Duddington, a mile out of Edinburgh – the brewery workers' tenements are already towering up as high as the malt barns.[122]

At the same time he was conscious of the need to limit the city, but he seems to have accepted the natural method of linear growth, following the line of main roads:

For all the main thoroughfares out from the city...and around every suburban railway station, the town planner is arranging his garden village, with its individuality and charm; but we, with our converse perspective, coming in from country towards town, have to see that these growing suburbs no longer grow together, as past ones have too much done. Towns must now cease to spread like expanding ink-stains and grease-spots; once in true development, they will repeat the star-like opening of the flower, with green leaves set in alternation with its golden rays.[123]

The culmination of Geddes' work for town planning was two exhibitions, in one of which he took part, and the other which he completely organised. In 1910 the London Town Planning Conference was held following the passing of the great Act the previous year, and accompanying it was an exhibition at the Royal Academy, organised jointly by the Royal Institute of British Architects and the Royal Academy.[124] For it Geddes brought sufficient material from Edinburgh to fill a complete gallery, over which he presided almost daily. He himself described the scene:

From the 'Survey of Edinburgh', for many years in progress at the Outlook Tower, a selection had been made and developmentally arranged; so that here, more than elsewhere before, the essential conditions and phases of a city's historic past were shown as determining its qualities and defects in the present. Past and present were also shown as presenting the problems of the city's opening future, and as conditioning their treatment also.[125]

Geddes felt that this exhibition was only the beginning of his exposition, and consequently the following year he produced his own enlarged version at Crosby Hall, the 'Cities and Town Planning Exhibition':

The principle of this new exhibition was no longer simply that of seeking and accepting examples of good contemporary work as it comes, important though this always must be. It involved an ordered design; that of presenting a type-selection of housing and town-planning schemes of suggestive character towards city development; and further of working towards the comparative presentment and study of the evolution of cities – historic, actual and possible.[126]

The exhibition was in three parts, the first dealing with the Classical Cities and Great Capitals, from Athens, Rome, Babylon and Jerusalem to Vienna and Washington; the second with Race, Population and Child Welfare; and the third with the Geographical and Historical origins of cities in which were the sections on Garden Suburbs, Villages and Towns, Surveys of Towns and Cities, and Civic Study. In fact, a complete exposition of Geddes' philosophy, culminating at the end in a model for an Outlook Tower, 'as incipient Civic Observatory and Laboratory together' with its watchword 'Civic Survey for Civic Service'.[127] That indeed was the essence of Geddes. From Chelsea the exhibition went successively to Edinburgh, Dublin and Belfast, and after further material had been added it appeared at Ghent as the 'Exposition des Villes' of the Ghent International Exhibition in 1913. When war broke out it was on its way to India, whence Geddes had gone to advise on various town planning schemes, but the ship in which it was travelling was sunk by the Germans, and the whole exhibition was lost. Following this disaster a second exhibition was gathered together by his friends in England, men such as Lanchester, Unwin and Pepler, and this was shown in India in 1915. After much adventure it is apparently still in existence at the Town Planning Department of London University, a great monument of faith and love.[128]

In 1910 Geddes wrote his first version of *Cities in Evolution*, which described the philosophy which I have attempted to illustrate, but his publisher did not find it suitable for the popular series it was intended to join, and the work did not reach the public until 1915, when it appeared in a much extended form, although the original material apparently remained largely as it had been written five years previously.

Finally, then, what is the implication of Geddes' work in terms of the housing movement? So far as his views on density, and thus his sense of a spatial concept, were concerned, he represented the typical garden city standpoint, equating low density with health; and in this he added strength to an existing body of opinion, rather than contributing something new. His real addition to current thought lay in the vision he had of the whole structure of communities; cities were for him living organisms composed of people, who required amenities in order to live happily. Cities required to be set into a regional pattern, to be related to one another, and to be controlled in their growth so that the country was not swamped by ever extending urban expansion. To achieve this, and to rectify the faults of the existing city he developed a new science for looking at communities: the survey, at once technical and humane. It was Geddes' great virtue that he was not an idealist in the sense of the grand unified vision of Buckingham, or even Howard; he was an empiricist, building upon information already collected and adding fresh evidence to it so that the image of the city grew from the small to the great, from the individual to the community, and was never imposed from without. The best known of his theories, the relationship of Place and Work and Folk, provides the key to his qualities and his virtue, and the greatest of these qualities was surely his emphasis upon 'Folk'. Geddes enlarged the whole scope of planning, and he provided new tools for its study in order that cities might become congenial places in which to live; and to us who are concerned with the city, his contribution must seem more constructive and positive than does that of Howard who in his heart saw no hope for the city as we conceive it.[129]

The growth of town planning

The Garden City and the almost synonymous Town Planning movements did not merely produce a great series of village and suburb developments characterised by low density, they sought to do more than that; they attempted to create a completely new approach to town development and the nature of housing in particular. The Garden City Association, or the Garden City and Town Planning Association as it subsequently came to be called, was set up in 1899[130] as a direct result of Howard's book, and it was followed by the National Housing and Town Planning Council, which was a propaganda body, and it was the Bureau set up by them which organised the cottage exhibitions at Sheffield and Newcastle.[131] The first exhibition of this nature, however, was held at Letchworth in 1905 in order to experiment with plan forms and methods of construction.[132] Twenty-one different types of cottage were built, either singly or in pairs, and most of them were criticised in the *Architectural Review* for their immature planning and poor design.[133] The exhibition showed that there was at this time no standard against which it was possible to measure cottage planning, no accepted minimum space requirements; and if nothing else the exhibitions helped to publicise the need for research, while at the same time showing new ideas of planning and construction to the public, and thus providing from the best of the new ideas a foundation on which to work. But as we have already seen much of the real research was done by Unwin himself at Letchworth and Earswick, and by the Bournville Village Trust at Birmingham. The Letchworth competition was privately organised for the *Country Gentleman*,[134] and it was intended to assist in the design of rural housing, although its implications about cost and space standards were of universal application. The first exhibition held by the Housing and Town Planning Bureau was at High Wincobank, between Rotherham and Sheffield, in 1907;[135] and the second at Walker, down river from Newcastle upon Tyne, during 1908.[136] The exhibition sites were both developed as a result of competitions and were laid out on garden city principles with picturesque curving streets and low densities. The houses were of the cottage variety with short terraces of three or four houses, but some were semi-detached and a few detached. Both the schemes were municipal ventures, but Abercrombie thought that, like most exhibitions, they should be pulled down since they were unsatisfactory as town planning, displaying too much variety and ingenuity; and this, alas, was to be true of many similar developments in the future.

Another type of organisation which had grown up with the garden suburb movement were the co-partnership tenants organisations, which were intended to enable a group of working class families to build and own a group of houses. The co-operative movement grew out of the mid 19th century desire amongst working men to protect their own welfare as well as their jobs. It started in Rochdale in 1844 and grew first as a shop and distributive organisation. Then in 1884 they established their own building society and building ventures soon followed. Tenant Co-operators Ltd built several housing estates but it was not until 1901 when Henry Vivian, at that time Secretary of the Labour Association, founded Ealing Tenants Ltd that a true co-partnership organisation came into existence. Their chief contribution was to link co-partnership building policies with town planning concepts and for their first major venture Raymond Unwin and his partner Barry Parker were called in to design the layout. This was Brentham Garden Estate.[137]

Similar ventures followed at Leicester (1902), Sevenoaks (1903), then a group associated with the garden city developments at Letchworth, Bournville and Hampstead. Other provincial towns soon followed and there were examples in such unlikely places as Keswick. A typical example from the provinces is Fallings Park Tenants Ltd (1907).[138] In 1906 a central organisation of the Co-partnership Tenants Council was formed.[139]

The official organ of the movement, *The Garden City*, was first published in October 1904; the various numbers were published sporadically over the years, sometimes monthly at other times quarterly, recounting the developments at Letchworth and elsewhere. In August 1909 it changed its name to *Garden Cities and Town Planning*, a change necessitated by the growing scope of the movement, and in February 1911 the magazine was re-established on a monthly basis, for Town Planning had by now achieved an important place in society. By that time the magazine had been joined by the *Town Planning Review*, which appeared in April 1910 and was thereafter published steadily as a quarterly, quickly establishing itself as the important vehicle for planning thought under the able guidance of Patrick Abercrombie. The *Town Planning Review* had been made possible largely by the endowment of a department of Town Planning and Civic Design at Liverpool University by Lord Leverhulme in 1909; he had shown considerable interest in planning since the inception of Port Sunlight but in reality it was deeper than this because of the movement's wider implications in the much larger field of national housing. His gift, which included various other works at Liverpool University, was made possible out of damages amounting to some £91,000 which he obtained from the press, and particularly from Lord Northcliffe's organisation, as a result of a libel action.[140] The following year, Cadbury endowed a lectureship at Birmingham, which was held first by Raymond Unwin, and London University also quickly established a School of Town Planning.[141] The Town Planning Institute followed, inevitably, in 1914, and the new profession was then fully fledged.

The first Town Planning Act: The suburb salubrious

The development of the Garden City principle in housing layout and the simultaneous growth of planning as an applied science, the first inspired by Ebenezer Howard and the second by Patrick Geddes, were the outward manifestations of a new spirit within the housing movement itself. The logical outcome of the various practical experiments in low density planning was a growing volume of opinion in favour of legislative reform, and during the early years of the century this began to crystallise first through the medium of the Garden City Association, and then through the Workmen's National Housing Council.[142] It was at a joint meeting of the last two organisations, held at Leeds in 1904 during the Trades Union Congress, that the first public resolution in favour of 'town planning' was passed. The resolution had been proposed by T. G. Horsfall,[143] one of the leading figures in the early stages of the movement, and the same year he published a work which showed his wide knowledge of town planning; it appeared under the title of *The Example of Germany* and it was published as a supplement to a report on the housing situation in Manchester.[144]

At Birmingham, which had already gained a great reputation for enlightened activity because of the work of Joseph Chamberlain and George Cadbury, a third figure appeared who was to play an important part in housing reform, and who secured one of the earliest low density housing developments for the city.[145] This was John Nettlefold who was a firm supporter of the low density approach adopted by Cadbury and Lever in their model villages.[146] Nettlefold belonged to that school of thought which believed that private enterprise was the right agent to provide the actual housing, and consequently he did not support the full ramifications of the German attitude, which was at this time attracting considerable attention because it usually necessitated the civic authorities undertaking the erection of the housing in addition to their planning duties.

I prefer to see wages rise to meet the higher rents, as they have done in England, rather than houses provided by the State at lower rents in order to meet the lower wages...To my mind the rock on which municipal house builders have split is the desire to regulate rent...Local Authorities will increase rather than diminish the difficulties of the subject by attempting to interfere in a matter which they cannot control; but they can do enormous good by insisting upon sanitary houses and taking those steps which lie in their power to keep down as low as possible the cost of erecting these houses.[147]

The steps which Horsfall regarded as the municipal prerogative, however, included the objectives for which the town planners sought legal approval; the right to plan the street pattern, to control the nature of the development, and to create or preserve open space.

The third important figure in the growth of the planning movement was William Thompson, the chairman of the National Housing and Town Planning Council, and he it was who led the deputation in 1906 which finally requested the Prime Minister, Sir Henry Campbell Bannerman, and the President of the Local Government Board, John Burns, that the housing laws should be amended to create the legal powers necessary to carry through the new kind of planning proposals inspired by the garden city ideal.[148] Two years later John Burns introduced his Housing and Town Planning Bill, which legislated for the deputation's proposals; it is one of the most important measures in the history of the whole housing movement.

The object of the Bill is to provide a domestic condition for the people in which their physical health, their morals, their character and their whole social condition can be improved by what we hope to secure in this Bill. The Bill aims in broad outline at, and hopes to secure, the home healthy, the house beautiful, the town pleasant, the city dignified, and the suburb salubrious. It seeks, and hopes to secure, more and better homes, better houses, prettier streets, so that the character of a great people, in towns and cities and villages, can be still further improved and strengthened by the conditions under which they live...On its housing side, the Bill seeks to abolish, reconstruct and prevent the slum. It asks – at least I do for it – the House of Commons to do something to efface the ghettos of meanness and the Alsatias of squalor that can be found in many parts of the United Kingdom. It hopes to take effective steps to put down many of the unpleasant features of our purely industrial towns. It hopes to render model dwellings similar to those that are so prevalent in Germany less frequent in the future than now...The Bill seeks to diminish what have been called by-law streets with little law and much monotony. It hopes to get rid of the regulation roads that are so regular that they lack that line of beauty which Hogarth said was in a curve. It seeks to improve the health of the people by raising the character of the house and the home and by extended inspection, supervision, direction and guidance of central control to help local authorities to do more than they now do.[149]

The Bill was sympathetically received and earnestly debated, which delayed its progress so much that it was necessary to withdraw it that session and re-introduce it in 1909 when it was duly passed as the Housing and Town Planning Act.[150] It is perhaps of interest that the important provision which permitted the limitation of density in town planning schemes was one of the provisions not originally included in the 1908 Bill; it was inserted during the committee stage, which was an example of the new attitude in the Commons, now so desirous of serving best the needs of the community, by contrast with the obstructive attitude so characteristic of the nineteenth century House.[151]

The Act was divided into four parts, of which the first two were the most important. Part One was concerned with housing, and its intention was to make the statute of 1890 more effective; but it did not seek to make fundamental or radical changes in the structure of housing law. It first enacted that Part Three of the 1890 Statute, which amended the Lodging Houses Acts and made the important provisions for local authorities to erect dwellings, should be effective in every urban and rural district, whether or not it had been formally adopted. The Act gave the local authority additional power to purchase land compulsorily in order to carry out these provisions, and it eased the repayment of loans, directing the Public Works Loan Commissioners to grant loans at the minimum current interest rates, with extended periods for repayment.[152] The Act in fact stressed the role of the Local Authority in the provision of housing for the working classes. In addition, the Local Government Board, as the central authority, was given wider powers to act in default of the local authority and to force it to exercise its powers under all parts of the 1890 Act.[153] A further restriction was placed upon cellar dwellings, requiring the local authority to close a cellar which had a floor level more than 3 ft. below ground level if it was used as a sleeping place – in other words as a separate dwelling – because it constituted a dangerous dwelling. The only exception to this rule was in certain cases where the average height was not less than 7 ft. and where the cellar complied with the local authority's regulations concerning ventilation, lighting and dampness.[154] The authority was to make these regulations if it had not already done so, and it was permitted to demolish dangerous dwellings if the owner refused to remedy the defects after a closing order had been made.[155]

Part Two of the 1909 Act was concerned with Town Planning, and this was the most important as well as the most novel portion of the whole measure.[156] It was adoptive, and it only applied to the development of a new area, so that it was concerned with town expansion rather than town redevelopment, and it is important to make this distinction at the outset. Part Two made provision for a local authority, with the approval of the Local Government Board, to make a 'Town Planning Scheme' for a particular area, and within the boundary of this land it was able to exercise unique powers. First, it could establish a maximum density over the whole area, which in one step established the character of the development, and this was undoubtedly of great importance since in practice it meant a limitation to the figures acceptable to the garden city point of view. Within the scheme the local authority could regulate the construction and width of roads, departing from those established by the bye-law system either to create new and wider arterial highways necessitated by increasing vehicular traffic, or alternatively, it could reduce the width of minor streets in purely housing areas and extend their length beyond those previously allowed. It will be remembered that at Hampstead a special Act had been necessary to construct roads of this nature in order to achieve the character which the developers required, at a reasonable expense and without breaking the law. The local authority was also able to control the relation of the elements within the scheme, to decide where the areas of housing, shopping and industry should be sited in relation to one another and to the whole development. It could control the positioning of the individual buildings upon their sites, governing their height and character, and the proportion of the site covered by building in relation to that left exposed. It could regulate the use and condition of private open space, and purchase open space for the benefit of the community as a whole.

These powers gave the local authority a unique opportunity to develop new districts in a balanced and organised manner; they gave them the means of control which had never before existed in this country, so that it was possible, at last, to create for the first time the 'suburb salubrious', as Burns described it. And the effect, in a period tempered by the new vision of working class, as well as middle class arcadia, and freed from the shackles of intense central area development by the transport revolution of the previous twenty years, was that the garden suburb had received the official imprint of authority, and this was now the acceptable form of development for all classes. The garden suburb was Town Planning, and in 1909 the converse was true: Town Planning was the garden suburb. Just before the Act was passed Raymond Unwin, the greatest of the early planners, published his *Town Planning in Practice* which defined very clearly exactly what the movement had been fighting for, and in fact what it won that same year. The nineteenth century conception of housing was, to him,

monotonous in the extreme; typified by the bye-law street which permitted a high density development with no more control over space than that contained in the code of 1875. Aesthetically it was ugly, and he believed it was also unhealthy, which provided him with two firm arguments in favour of low density. This caused him to argue in favour of the relaxation of the bye-laws not, this time, to allow inhuman speculative high density development but to permit a new kind of development where the relation of building to open space was radically altered, where the frontages of houses could be increased; in fact, where the principles of the garden city could be practised freely and unhindered. Unwin believed that in a low density development there lay the possibility of a better environment, more healthy and more beautiful; he believed that the changes which John Burns made in 1909 were necessary in order that people might be healthy and happy, that architects might now design an adequate aesthetic environment, for previously they were constricted and limited by existing legal controls. Unwin, too, knew how to handle the vocabulary of the garden city, he was an able and a sensitive designer, and his intention was not to destroy spatial qualities just because the buildings were now spread out in a less dense way; on the contrary he sought to achieve a new kind of spatial control, and his concern was for the detailed progression of one enclosure to another, for the design of street junctions so that the ugly gaps typical of the denser nineteenth century urban developments were abolished.

The early planners possessed a confidence in their medium and also an ability to handle it which commands our respect; for them the garden city concept was right, and they made a contribution to planning and housing which must never be denied. They gave to an aesthetically impoverished working class the hope, and often the chance, of a new and better environment, within the town yet not of the town; and this was in a sense the objective for which the whole housing movement had worked since the days of Chadwick and the early Public Health reforms.

There were wider implications which were evidently not fully realised in 1909 in the full flush of achievement, the implications of low density upon town expansion in the future, for example; and there was the later debasement of the garden city ideal into the extreme case of semi-detached ribbon development in mock Tudor disguise after the war. These things have turned the intentions of the first Town Planning Act sour and bitter in the mouths of those who still feel the same concern for people and towns which Burns and Unwin felt so urgently in the first decade of the century. This chapter ends, then, with the reversal of eighteenth and nineteenth century housing thought completed; we look back upon the struggle for decency, for the separate rights and responsibilities of the state, the community as well as the individual. All these problems apparently were solved in theory, if not always satisfactorily in practice, before the outbreak of war in 1914, and some working class folk now lived in an environment which was the realm of the visionary in 1840. So there was a solid sense of achievement, of purposeful progress, and the future seemed bright and full of hope, as indeed it remained, at first, after the war. The town which had mastered the people and enslaved them was negated, and William Morris' symbolic dream of the palace of Westminster reduced to a rural dung-hill was a little nearer reality. This was a massive reversal of the eighteenth century attitude delighting in urbanism for its own sake, but then that was separated from the twentieth century by the weary industrial wastelands of the nineteenth. The garden city movement had the full vigour and force of violent reaction, the causes of which have been my concern in the previous pages. If now we understand a little better the reasons why it was so successful we may be more willing to condone the acclamation which it received, for in 1909 the garden city movement seemed to proffer for the first time the health and happiness which had been denied the Victorian working man as the high price of progress.

Endnotes

Introduction

1 There is now a great deal of literature dealing with industrial archaeology which helps to reinforce this point. The rational position economically was very clearly put many years ago in: P. Mantoux, *The Industrial Revolution* (1928); see bibliographical references to other works.

2 See J. L. and L. B. Hammond, *The Town Labourer, 1760–1832* (1917); *The Skilled Labourer, 1760–1832* (1919); *The Age of the Chartists* (1930); E. P. Thompson, *The Making of the English Working Class* (1963) and Asa Briggs, (ed.) *Chartist Studies* (1959).

3 The classic example is Lord Shaftesbury and his work in connection with factories, mines and many other aspects of human exploitation; see G. F. A. Best, *Shaftesbury* (1964), which is a recent and manageable biography. For the earlier and fuller study see E. Hodder, *Life and Works of the Seventh Earl of Shaftesbury* (1886).

4 See A. W. Pugin, *Apology for the Revival of Pointed or Christian Architecture* (1943); see also M. Trappes-Lomax, *Pugin* (1932); P. Stanton, *Pugin* (1971) and Sir Kenneth Clark, *The Gothic Revival* (1928), for general comment about architectural problems in the industrial age.

5 The relevant novels are listed in the bibliography.

Chapter 1

1 The two standard works are S. E. Finer, *The Life and Times of Sir Edwin Chadwick* (1952), and R. A. Lewis, *Edwin Chadwick and the Public Health Movement 1832–1854* (1952).

2 *Poor Law Board Report*, 1842, 40.

3 *Ibid.*, 233.

4 *Ibid.*, 273.

5 By A. Briggs, *The Age of Improvement* (1959), 295.

6 Royal Commission, *Second Report*, 1845, 60.

7 *Ibid.* There were, of course, many other documents on housing, the most famous single book is still F. Engels, *The Condition of the Working-Class in England in 1844* (1845), often reprinted; latest edition 1968.

8 'Proceedings of the Health of Towns Association, 11 December 1844', quoted by Finer, *Chadwick, op. cit.*, 237.

9 Finer, 341.

10 George Godwin, F.R.S., F.S.A., Vice-President R.I.B.A., R.I.B.A. Royal Gold Medalist 1881; was born 1815 and died 1888, he edited *The Builder* 1841–1883 and practiced in a small way usually with his brother Henry. His work was mainly ecclesiastical and his most important job was the restoration of St Mary Redcliffe, Bristol. At one time he was also District Surveyor for Islington.

11 This problem of permissive legislation makes a study of building control peculiarly difficult. As a broad generalisation the evidence suggests that towns which were active in obtaining legal powers were likely in the end to avail themselves of their powers before those towns which were more lethargic.

12 See A. Errazurez, 'Some types of housing in Liverpool', *Town Planning Review* XIX (Spring 1946), 57; also J. N. Tarn, 'Housing in Liverpool and Glasgow', *Town Planning Review* XXXIX (Jan. 1969), 319.

13 *Labourer's Friend*, Oct. 1844, 81.

14 *Ibid.*, April 1846, 62.

15 *Ibid.*, March 1845, 182.

16 *Ibid.*, Oct. 1846, 182; Nov. 1846, 195; March 1848, 35; Oct. 1848, 162 and in other pages of this journal during these years.

17 A fact pointed out in *Labourer's Friend*, Oct. 1847, 182.

18 *Builder* III (1845), 220.

19 H. Roberts, *The Dwellings of the Labouring Classes* (first pub. 1851) 1853 ed., 13.

20 'The land we live in' – *Labourer's Friend*, Oct. 1847, 182.

21 *Builder* III (1845), 220.

22 *Labourer's Friend*, Sept. 1847, 165 and *Builder* V, (1847), 341.

23 *Builder* VI (1848), 524; see also Roberts, *op. cit.*, 16 and J. Wylson, *Remarks on Workmen's Houses in Town Districts* (1849?), 6–7.

24 I have written more fully about this in *Town Planning Review* XXXIX (Jan. 1969), 319.

25 *Labourer's Friend*, 1850, 194.

26 For a more detailed treatment of Edinburgh see J. N. Tarn, *Working Class Housing in Nineteenth Century Britain* (1970), ch. 7.

27 The pages of *The Builder*, the *Poor Law Board Report* (1842), and the Royal Commission 1844–5, all are full of references to speculative building methods.

28 Select Committee, 1840, 13.

29 H. Jephson, *The Sanitary Evolution of London* (1907), 13 *et seq.*

30 Royal Commission 1845, app. 20.

31 Royal Commission 1844, app. 186.

32 Royal Commission 1845, 79.

33 A useful contemporary annotated edition of the Act is D. Gibbon, *The Metropolitan Building Act, 1844* (1844?).

34 *Metropolitan Building Act, 1844*, Schedule 1; a square was equal to 100 sq. ft.

35 Jephson, *op. cit.*, 24–5.

36 On the complicated subject of health legislation see Jephson, *op. cit.*, and more particularly Sir J. Simon, *English Sanitary Institutions* (1890).

37 Morpeth's speech introducing the Bill, *Hansard* XCVI (third series, 10 Feb. 1848), 391.

38 *The Economist* VI (13 May 1848), 536.

39 See R. Lambert, *Sir John Simon, 1816–1904, and English Social Administration* (1963).

40 Jephson, *op. cit.*, 44.

41 The full story of the General Board is outside the scope of this chapter, it will be found fully documented in the biographies of Chadwick by Finer and Lewis.

42 Finer, *op. cit.*, 384.

43 *Report of the General Board of Health on the Administration of the Public Health Act and the Nuisance Removal and Disease Prevention Act, from 1848–54* (1854).

44 'The Condition of our Chief Cities, Newcastle upon Tyne', *Builder* XIX (1861), 241.

45 Simon, *op. cit.*, 233.

46 *Hansard*, CXV (new series, April 1851), 1260–1.

47 *Hansard, Ibid.*, 1267.

48 *Ibid.*, 1273.

49 *The Times*, 4 Jan. 1853; see W. Hay, *Report on the Common Lodging Houses Act, presented to the House*

of Lords, December 28th, 1852, and reprinted in full in Labourer's Friend, Feb. 1853.
50 Ibid., 15 Jan. 1853.
51 Ibid., 16 May 1853.
52 See Labourer's Friend, Aug. 1853, 123.
53 Ibid., Dec. 1855, 195.

Chapter 2

1 Labourer's Friend, June 1844, 1.
2 W. Bardwell, 'The Labourer's Friend Society', Healthy Homes (1853), 10 et seq.
3 Loudon, Encyclopaedia (1833), 237.
4 Bardwell, op. cit.
5 Willis's Rooms, King Street, St James's were the fashionable Assembly Rooms of the first half of the 19th century although they began to decline after about 1835 (information supplied by the City of Westminster Librarian), see also the Survey of London, XXIX (1960).
6 Labourer's Friend, June 1844, 1–2.
7 Ibid., 28.
8 Chadwick to Southwood Smith, 1 July 1844, quoted by Lewis, Chadwick, 117.
9 Labourer's Friend, July 1844, 33.
10 See Labourer's Friend, Sept. 1844, 66 and Dec. 1844, 129, also Builder II (1844), 63.
11 See H. Roberts, Dwellings, op. cit., 6.
12 Builder III (1845), 1.
13 Labourer's Friend, April 1846, 50 and May 1846, 73.
14 Treated more fully later in this chapter.
15 Labourer's Friend, July 1846, 116.
16 Builder V (1847), 287; see also Quarterly Review CLXIII (Dec. 1847), 142.
17 Roberts, Dwellings, op. cit., 8.
18 The design was published in Builder VII (1849), 325; see also Labourer's Friend, Jan. 1848, 2; Feb. 1848, 18; June 1848, 81 and Aug. 1849, 113.
19 Roberts, Dwellings, op. cit. 10.
20 Labourer's Friend, July 1850, 97.
21 Ibid., June 1850, 83; taken from the Morning Chronicle.
22 Ibid., July 1850, 97 and July 1851, 97; see also Builder VIII (1850), 297.
23 The material for this book was first gathered together for a lecture at the R.I.B.A. in 1850. See also for other favourable comment on the concept of the Exhibition Cottages Builder IX (1851), 174 and The Times, May 26, 1851.
24 Each flat had a living room 14 ft. 2 in. × 10 ft. 4 in., a small scullery and separate lavatory; bedroom 1 was 11 ft. 6 in. × 9 ft. and bedrooms 2 and 3 were both 9 ft. × 5 ft. 9 in. They were subsequently re-erected in Kennington Park; see L.C.C. Survey of London XXVI, 1956, 34.
25 See the monthly notes in Labourer's Friend after 1851.
26 Labourer's Friend, July 1853, 97, from the 9th Annual Report of the Society.
27 See, for example, Labourer's Friend, March 1853, 34; June 1853, 89; July 1856, 105 and Builder X (1852), 705; XII (1854), 153; XIV (1856), 525 and 556.
28 A Society such as this which operated with a tight profit margin was particularly susceptible to economic stringencies. For general comment on building costs at this time see J. R. T. Hughes, 'Problems of Industrial

Change 1859'; Entering an Age of Crisis, ed. Appleman, Madden and Wolff; also S. G. Checkland, The Rise of Industrial Society in England 1815–1885, ch. iv, sect. 9 and vii, sect. 6.
29 Labourer's Friend, Dec. 1854, 187; the editor noted with evident delight that the scheme had been well written up in the daily press. Builder XII (1854), 589 carried a typical account, 'Wild Court, Drury Lane, and What is Intended'.
30 Dickens, C., Household Words X (16 Dec. 1854), 409.
31 Ibid., XII (25 Aug. 1855), 85.
32 Labourer's Friend, Nov. 1848, 186 and July 1850, 97.
33 Builder XXI (1862), 890, and Labourer's Friend, Jan. 1863, 182.
34 C. Gatliff, On Improved Dwellings and their Beneficial Effect on Health and Morals, and Suggestions for their Extension (1875).
35 Builder V (1847), 16.
36 This was W. B. Moffatt, one-time partner of Gilbert Scott, see Builder V (1847), 37.
37 Builder XXV (1867), 473.
38 Roberts, Dwellings, op. cit., 16. The Birkenhead buildings are those built by the Dock Company and mentioned in Chapter 1.
39 Builder VI (1848), 376 and 386.
40 Ibid., VII (1849), 589. The lodging house – known as 'The Artizans Home' – was officially opened on Wednesday 12 Dec. 1849.
41 Roberts, Dwellings, op. cit. 15; the charges in 1849 at George St. were 2s 4d per week and at 'The Artizans Home', 3s 0d.
42 Builder X (1852), 413. See also the version of the 10th Annual Report, published by James Bowie as part of his compendium Healthy Homes (1854).
43 See Builder XI (1853), 337 and 360.
44 Gatliff, op. cit.
45 See 10th Annual Report.
46 'Report of a Meeting to Consider the best method of extending the operation of the Metropolitan Association for Improving the Dwellings of the Industrious Classes, held at the London Tavern on Saturday, 18th February, 1854. Thomas Baring in the Chair', published by James Bowie in Healthy Homes (1854).
47 Builder XII (1854), 101. The figure rose to £18,475 – see 10th Annual Report.
48 Southwood Smith, 'Results of Sanitary Improvement, 1854', published as an appendix to James Bowie's Healthy Homes.
49 See 10th Annual Report and C. Gatliff, Tabular Statement (1867).
50 C. Gatliff, Practical Suggestions (1854), 31.
51 Ibid.
52 See M.A.I.D.I.C., General List of Members and Officers (1854).
53 See Builder XIII (1855), 311; see also for this and other provincial schemes J. Bowie, Healthy Homes (1854).
54 Builder XIV (1856), 290.
55 Ibid., XIII (1855), 59.
56 Gatliff, Tabular Statement, 1867; see also L.C.C. Survey of London XXVII (1957), 273.
57 Builder XXIV (1866), 494 and Labourer's Friend, Oct. 1869, 79. See also Gatliff's Evidence to Select Committee (1881), 141, the Tabular Statement appended, 287; the Tabular Statement of 1867 and his On Improved Dwellings (1875).

Chapter 3

1 The Viscount Ingestre, *Meliora* (1852), 172.
2 *Builder* X (1852), 506 and XI (1853), 251; Lee worked subsequently for the *Metropolitan Association*. He was another of the minor architects who were involved in housing.
3 The Viscount Ingestre, *Meliora II* (1853), app. 6.
4 See Chapter 2.
5 *Builder* VII (1849), 537 and XV (1857), 662; see also A. Ashpitel, and J. Whichcord, *Town Dwellings* (1855), 33.
6 *Labourer's Friend*, June 1855, 96; Aug. 1855, 121; July 1856, 97 and May 1857, 75.
7 Roberts, *The Improvement of the Dwellings* (1859), 28 and *Builder* XV (1857), 500.
8 *Labourer's Friend*, Nov. 1850, 179.
9 *Builder* X (1852), 78 and 469; see also Roberts, *Dwellings*, 59.
10 *Builder* XII (1854), 97.
11 *Labourer's Friend*, June 1855, 85.
12 *Builder* XXX (1872), 634.
13 *Labourer's Friend*, June 1850, 86 and Roberts, *The Improvement of the Dwellings*, 33.
14 *Builder* XIV (1856), 179 and 196.
15 *Illustrated London News* XXIV (1854), 258. See also *Builder* IX (1851), 209, which seems to be the first suggestion of such a venture and is taken from *The United Services Gazette*.
16 *Builder* XV (1857), 225 and 615.
17 *Illustrated London News* XL (1862), 256. I have dealt more fully with Columbia Square and Market in *Working Class Housing in Nineteenth Century Britain*, ch. 3.
18 *Illustrated London News* LVI (1869), 445.
19 *Labourer's Friend*, Apr. 1855, 54 and Oct. 1855, 157.
20 M.A.I.D.I.C. *10th Annual Report*; *Builder* XIII (1855), 498; XIV (1856), 291 and 576; XV (1857), 68.
21 *Builder* XVI (1858), 361.
22 Nottingham, *Builder* X (1852), 646; Wolverhampton, *Ibid.*, XI (1853), 237 and XIII (1855), 24; Worcester, *Labourer's Friend*, Sept. 1854, 149; Saffron Walden, *Builder* XII (1854), 384; Norwich, *Ibid.*, XIV (1856), 35; Hertford, *Ibid.*, XVII (1859), 448; Halifax, *Labourer's Friend*, Jan. 1852, 11; Cambridge, *Builder* XIII (1855), 84. Liverpool and Glasgow were of course already involved in the movement as the towns receiving the brunt of the Irish problem: see J. N. Tarn, 'Housing in Liverpool and Glasgow', *Town Planning Review* XXXIX (Jan. 1969), 319.
23 *Builder* XIII (1855), 84.
24 For the context of this legislation see Ll. W. Woodward, *The Age of Reform* (2nd ed. 1962), 605.
25 This is a separate subject in itself, a rather more amplified account will be found in the early chapters of W. L. Creese, *The Search for Environment* (1966).
26 *Builder* XIX (1861), 289.
27 Royal Commission 1845, quoted in *Labourer's Friend*, Apr. 1852, 53.
28 *Labourer's Friend*, June 1851, 94, quoting from the *Leeds Intelligencer*. See also Denison's own account 'Notice of the Leeds Model Lodging House' published as an appendix to Henry Roberts' *The Improvement of the Dwellings* (1853).
29 *Labourer's Friend*, Oct. 1853, 155.
30 *Ibid.*, March 1853, 42.

31 *Ibid.*, Feb. 1852, 19; Denison's letter and statistics, *The Times*, 21 Jan. 1854 and a leading article 23 Jan. 1854.
32 Denison's account, *op. cit.*
33 *Builder* XVIII (1860), 809.
34 *Ibid.*
35 *Ibid.* The population in 1861 was, in fact, 207,165.
36 *Builder* XIX (1861), 21.
37 *Ibid.*, XIX (1861), 289.
38 J. Hole, *The Homes of the Working Classes* (1866), 88.
39 Hole, *op. cit.*, and *Builder* XX (1862), 647; XXI (1863), 285; XXIII (1865), 287; XXIV (1866), 239.
40 Hole, *op. cit.*, 125.
41 *Ibid.*, 129.
42 *Ibid.*, 142–3.
43 *Builder* X (1852), 123 – in a public lecture at Doncaster.
44 *Ibid.*, XXV (1867), 173.
45 *Ibid.*, XXXI (1873), 739; on Leeds particularly see also W. L. Creese, *The Search for Environment* (1966), 61 *et seq.*
46 *Builder* XXXII (1874), 844.
47 *Builder* XXXVI (1878), 683.
48 'The Pestilence at Newcastle and Gateshead', *Builder* XI (1853), 652.
49 *Builder* XI (1853), 601 – Sept. 24.
50 *Ibid.*, XI (1853), 625 – Oct. 8.
51 Smith, Dr Southwood, 'Results of Sanitary Improvement', published as an appendix to J. Bowie, *Healthy Homes* (1854).
52 See *Builder* XI (1853), 673.
53 'The Life and Death Question – The Condition of Disease – an appeal for Preventative Measures', *Builder* XII (1854), 433. This was an editorial, warning of the folly of abandoning precautionary measures during the previous winter when the epidemic had abated. It was imminent again now. For report of its outbreak in London see 473. See also 486 and 531.
54 *Builder* XV (1857), 55.
55 Pub. Edinburgh 1857 under same title.
56 *Journal of the Society of Arts* V (1857), 317; see also *Builder* XV (1857), 220 and 232.
57 *Ibid.*
58 See Ingestre, *Meliora II*, 153. Chambers (pub.) *Papers for the People*, XI (1851), 87, adds a comment about the way investors forced up the dividends in Building Societies by more or less auctioning their money to the highest bidder: this in turn encouraged a poor standard of building and skimping to raise profits.
59 *Builder* XIV (1856), 98.
60 G. Godwin, *Town Swamps and Social Bridges* (1859), 60 and *Builder* XVII (1859), 581.
61 H. Mayhew, *Home is Home, be it never so homely*, see Ingestre, *Meliora* (1852), 276.
62 See *Builder* XVIII (1860), 809; XIX (1861), 1, 241, 293, 349 and 421; XX (1862), 69, 813, 833 and 849.
63 *Ibid.*, XIX (1861), 893.
64 *Town Swamps*, 8.
65 *Ibid.*, 11.
66 *Ibid.*, 102.
67 *The Times*, 27 Oct. 1853.
68 *The Times*, 29 Oct. 1853.
69 See for example W. Hoskin, *Builder* IX (1851), 429.
70 This particular section was also published separately: Dr Southwood Smith, *Results of Sanitary Improvement* (1854).

71 A. Ashpitel and J. Whichcord, *Town Dwellings* (1855), 25.

72 *Builder* XV (1857), 77.

73 *Ibid.*

74 *Ibid.*, XVIII (1860), 409, in *The Builder*'s Survey of society properties.

75 The *Hertford Society* already mentioned. Roberts makes this claim in *The Progress and Present Aspect* (1861). I have found no further societies either.

76 Ref. to Mulhouse. Roberts, *The Improvement of the Dwellings* (1859), 24; see also Leonard Benevolo, *The Origins of Modern Town Planning*, 127–8.

77 *Ibid.*, 13; Roberts, *Ibid.*, 13.

78 See *Labourer's Friend*, April 1857, 57.

79 A point made by G. M. Trevelyan, *Illustrated English Social History* IV, 65.

80 Quoted *Labourer's Friend*, Feb. 1853, 26.

81 *Ibid.* This, I suspect, is the start of a new 'hardline' which becomes more common during the next decade. The only earlier reference to this need to improve the people first is: 'Fitting the Poor for their Dwellings', *Builder* XI (1851), 646.

82 *Builder* XVIII (1859), 572.

83 H. W. Rumsey, *On Sanitary Legislation and Administration in England* (1858), 27, quoting from J. S. Mill, *Political Economy* II, 542.

84 Rumsey, *op. cit.*, 27–32.

85 *Ibid.*, XIX (1861), 63.

86 *Ibid.*, XVIII (1860), 829.

Chapter 4

1 See J. N. Tarn, 'The Housing Problem a Century Ago', *Urban Studies* V 8 (Nov. 1968), 290.

2 *Transactions, R.I.B.A.*, 1861–2, 95, later published separately as *The Essentials of a Healthy Home* (1862).

3 *Transactions, R.I.B.A.*, 1866–7, 37.

4 *Builder* XXIV (1866), 890, 900, 915, 935, 945 and 960.

5 *Ibid.*

6 *Ibid.*, 915.

7 *Labourer's Friend*, April 1867, 34.

8 *Builder* XXIV (1866), 960.

9 *Ibid.*

10 *Transactions, R.I.B.A.*, 1866–7, 80.

11 *The Times*, 26 Mar. 1862.

12 On Peabody himself, see F. Parker, *George Peabody 1795–1869, Founder of Modern Philanthropy* (1955). For details of the early deliberations of the Trustees see: *Peabody Donation Fund, Reprint of the First Report of the Trustees, issued on December 1865, together with a Summary of operations up to the Year ending 31st December 1906.*

13 Letter dated 12 March 1862 from Peabody to the Trustees.

14 *First Report, op. cit.* It was quoted: *The Times*, 11 Jan. 1866.

15 To the original sum of £150,000 was added, in 1866, £100,000; in 1868 a further £100,000; and in 1873 a legacy of £150,000 making in all £500,000. By 1906 the accumulated Fund stood at £1,531,919.

16 *The Times*, 17 Feb. 1863 and *Builder* XXI (1863), 547.

17 *Builder* XXII (1864), 67 and Peabody archives.

18 See *Ibid.*, XLVI (1884 i), 192.

19 Islington, opened 1865, *Illustrated London News*, 10 March 1866, 232. Shadwell, opened 1867, *Ibid.*, 23

Feb. 1867, 193. Westminster, opened 1868, *Ibid.*, 27 Mar. 1869, 317. Chelsea, opened 1870, *The Times*, 28 Feb. 1870.

20 *The Times*, 11 Jan. 1866, a description of the Shadwell estate.

21 *Builder* XX (1862), 228.

22 *The Times*, 11 Dec. 1869.

23 *Builder* XXIX (1871), 601.

24 *The Times*, 11 July 1871. See also *Illustrated London News*, 23 March 1872; the estate was opened 1 Aug. 1871.

25 *Builder* XXX (1872), 102; XXXI (1873), 171; XXXII (1874), 707.

26 G. Smalley, *The Life and Times of Sir Sydney H. Waterlow* (1908).

27 *Builder* XXI (1863), 198.

28 *The Times*, 14 Apr. 1863.

29 *Builder* XXI (1863), 429.

30 *The Times*, 15 March 1865.

31 *Ibid.*, 23 July 1866.

32 J. Hole, *Homes of the Working Classes*, 57–8, quoting the *Daily Telegraph*.

33 *The Times*, 9 Feb. 1867; *Builder* XXIX (1871), 654: see also Waterlow's Evidence, Royal Commission 1885, 426; the earlier evidence of the Company Secretary James More is also relevent: Select Committee 1881, 176.

34 Royal Commission 1885, 425.

35 *Builder* XV (1867), 137, and subsequent half-yearly reports.

36 *The Times*, 7 Aug. 1867.

37 *Ibid.*, 31 July 1874.

38 There was actually one period when they appeared to turn away investors; see *The Times* 11 Aug. 1869.

39 The site came into their possession on Lady Day, 25 March 1868; see *The Times*, 27 Aug. 1868.

40 *Ibid.*, 11 Aug. 1869.

41 *Builder* XXVIII (1870), 963.

42 *Ibid.*, XXVII (1869), 675; *The Times*, 11 Aug. 1869.

43 *The Times*, 2 Feb. 1870 and *Builder* XXX (1872), 110.

44 *Builder* XXXI (1873), 112.

45 Quoted in *Labourer's Friend*, Oct. 1872, 71.

46 *Builder* XXX (1872), 273. The properties were sold off 1882; see *The Times*, 9 March 1882; also *Charity Organisation Society Report 1881*, 68–9.

47 *Builder* XXXV (1877), 247, 432, 502, 593, 599, 745, 816, 1116; the major attack on early policy came in an unsigned article entitled 'Scientific Philanthropy (Limited)', 599.

48 *Builder* LIII (1887 ii), 901.

49 *Labourer's Friend*, Oct. 1872, 71; Jan. 1874, 2 and Oct. 1874, 69. See also 'The Workman's City', *The Standard*, 20 July 1874.

50 *The Times*, 9 March 1882, and *Builder* XXXVII (1879), 1405.

51 *Builder* XLI (1881 ii), 591; XLV (1883 i), 880 and LIII (1887 ii), 901.

52 Figure drawn from the annual reports of the three organisations.

53 *Builder* XXIV (1866), 144.

54 *Ibid.*, XXV (1867), 231.

55 See L.C.C. Survey of London, XXIV (1952), 138.

56 *Builder* XXX (1872), 536.

57 C. Gatliff, see Select Committee, 1881, app. 287.

58 *Ibid.*, 141. See also C. Gatliff, *On Improved Dwellings* (1875).
59 C. Gatliff, Select Committee, 1881, 149.
60 *Builder* XXV (1867), 473. See also Gatliff, Tabular Statement, 1867.
61 See Gatliff, Select Committee 1881, 287 and *Builder* XXXV (1877), 647.
62 *Ibid.*, XX (1862), 415; XXIII (1865), 198; XXV (1867), 215; XXVI (1868), 683 and XXVII (1869), 743.
63 *Ibid.*, XXII (1864), 952, and XXIII (1865), 295.
64 *Ibid.*, XXIV (1866), 291.
65 *Ibid.*, 462.
66 *Ibid.*, 291.
67 *Labourer's Friend*, April 1866, 29.
68 *Builder* XXIV (1866), 685.
69 C. B. P. Bosanquet, *London: Some Account of its Growth, Charitable Agencies and Wants* (1868), 273.
70 *Labourer's Friend*, April 1866, 40 and Jan. 1867, 5.
71 *Builder* XXIV (1866), 493.
72 *Ibid.*, XXI (1863), 850.
73 *Ibid.*, XXII (1864), 317 and XXIII (1865), 484.
74 There is evidence in the Peabody Trust records that tenants frequently prospered once they came to live in the stable environment of the model estates.
75 *Builder* XXIII (1865), 842; XXV (1867), 506 and XXVI (1868), 272. See also J. Price, *Homes for the Poor* (1875), 27; the evidence of the journals and pampleteers is uneven for the provinces, but I think that Newcastle was fairly typical of this period. Activity was slight and usually privately inspired. One of the most august patrons was the Dean and Chapter of Christ Church, Oxford, who built some family dwellings in 1868 to the design of Henry Roberts: *Builder* XXIV (1866), 785 and XXVI (1868), 477; also *Labourer's Friend*, Oct. 1868, 60.
76 *Builder* XXII (1864), 907.
77 *Ibid.*, XXIII (1865), 635.
78 *Ibid.*, XXV (1867), 175.
79 A loan of £13,000 was subsequently granted – *Labourer's Friend*, Oct. 1868, 72.
80 The saga of the competition can be found: *Builder* XXV (1867), 883, 906, 921; XXVI (1868), 49 and 57; XXVII (1869), 98.
81 *Ibid.*, XXVII (1869), 99.
82 *Ibid.*, XLIX (1855 ii), 563. See also J. N. Tarn, 'Housing in Liverpool and Glasgow', *Town Planning Review* XXXIX (Jan. 1969), 326.
83 *Ibid.*, XXIX (1871), 453 and XXX (1872), 972; see also *Journal of the Society of Arts* XIX (1871), 602 for Lord Derby's speech at the inaugural public meeting.
84 29 and 30 Vict. C. lxxxv.
85 *Builder* XXV (1867), 383–4.
86 J. Morrison, 'Glasgow and its Improvements', *Transactions, N.A.P.S.S.* (1874), 594, reported in *Builder* XXXII (1874), 839. See also Sir J. Watson, 'Improvements to Glasgow and the City Improvement Acts: Origin of the Artizans Dwellings Act', *Transactions, R.I.B.A.*, 1878/9, 153, reported in *Builder* XXXVII (1879), 448.
87 *Macmillan's Magazine*, June 1874, 135.
88 Watson, *op. cit.* See also Morrison's Evidence in the Glasgow section of Royal Commission, 1885 (Scotland), 44 *et seq.* Three witnesses appeared for Glasgow: Sir William Collins, Dr J. B. Russell and Baillie J. Morrison.

89 *Builder* XXXII (1874), 861, Report of the Trustees.
90 *Builder* XXXVII (1879), 449, and 496.
91 Royal Commission 1885 (Scotland), 55.
92 Watson, *op. cit.*
93 Royal Commission 1885 (Scotland), 45, Evidence of Sir William Collins.
94 *Macmillan's Magazine*, June 1874, 135.
95 Royal Commission 1885 (Scotland), 4 and 50–1 make comment on the legal position, so too does Watson in *Builder* XXXVII (1879), 449–50, *Glasgow Police Act*, 29 & 30 Vict. C. cclxxiii.
96 *Builder* XIX (1861), 422.
97 *Ibid.*, 899.
98 *Transactions, N.A.P.S.S.* (1863), 627. See also Sir Hugh Gilzean-Reid, *Housing the People, an example of co-operation*, 1894(?).
99 *Builder* XXI (1863), 900.
100 Royal Commission 1885 (Scotland) 22 *et seq.* Evidence of J. K. Cranford, Solicitor and Clerk to the Improvement Trustees, J. Gowan, Lord Dean of Guild and J. Colville, Manager of the Edinburgh Co-operative Building Co. for further comment on the situation.
101 E. D. Simon and J. Inman, *The Rebuilding of Manchester* (1935), 10–11.
102 See A. Briggs, *Victorian Cities*, 1963, chapter V, 'Birmingham: The Making of a Civic Gospel'.

Chapter 5

1 Respectively 18 & 19 Vict. C. 120, C. 121, C. 122; Jephson, *London*, and Simon, *Sanitary Institutions* are invaluable in the interpretation of this legislation.
2 Jephson cites this, 83.
3 18 & 19 Vict. C. 122, Section 29; there is a useful annotated edition by E. W. Lowes, 1855.
4 Jephson, *op. cit.*, 88–9.
5 18 & 19 Vict. C. 115.
6 21 & 22 Vict. C. 97.
7 Lambert, R., *Sir John Simon* (1963).
8 22 & 23 Vict. C. 3.
9 H. W. Rumsey, *On Sanitary Legislation* (1858), 27.
10 His scheme depended initially upon the co-operation of the railway companies and the provision of cheap workmen's fares. The first example of such a step came in 1864 when the *Great Eastern Railway Co.* agreed to provide workmen's trains in return for development rights contained in the *Great Eastern Railway Metropolitan Station and Railway Act, 1864* – see *Builder* XXII (1864), 634. H. J. Dyos, 'Workmen's Fares in South London 1860–1914', *Journal of Transport History* I (May 1953), 3, comments that one or two companies at this time operated workmen's fares of their own accord.
11 W. Morris, *News from Nowhere* (1890).
12 Simon, *Sanitary Institutions*, 279 *et seq.*
13 Jephson, *op. cit.*, 158–9.
14 *Ibid.*, 162.
15 *Ibid.*, 159.
16 Letter from the Town Clerk of Wolverhampton to Sir George Grey Home Secretary – see J. Hole, *Homes of the Working Classes*, 190.
17 Take for example Leek where the local Burial Society reported in 1867 that a new drainage scheme had reduced the death rate and increased the expectancy of life by 8½ years – *Builder* XXV (1867), 81.

18 See for example H. Roberts, 'On Healthy Dwellings and Prevailing Defects in the Homes of the Working Classes' – a lecture to the *Ladies Sanitary Association* reported *Builder* XVIII (1860), 474 and 'On the Sanitary Instruction of the Labouring Classes, and their Training in those Domiciliary Habits which Conduce to Physical and Moral Well-Being', *Transactions, N.A.P.S.S.* (1862), 751. Godwin, G. 'What is the Influence on Health of the Overcrowding of Dwelling Houses and Workshops? And by What Means Could Such Overcrowding be Prevented?', *Transactions, N.A.P.S.S.* (1864), 512.

19 29 & 30 Vict. C. 90.

20 Simon, *op. cit.*, 299.

21 29 & 30 Vict. C. 90.

22 Jephson, *op. cit.*, 195.

23 Royal Commission 1885, 28–9.

24 *Builder* XXIV (1866), 497.

25 Cited by Jephson, *op. cit.*, 204.

26 29 & 30 Vict. C. 28; Waterlow's correspondence on this subject will be found in J. Hole, *Homes of the Working Classes*, 187, amended with regard to rate of interest which was reduced by 30 and 31 Vict. C. 28.

27 *Builder* XXVI (1868), xi. M.A.I.D.I.C. received £18,000; Highgate D.I.C. £2,500; I.I.D.C., £48,000; Liverpool £13,000.

28 *Journal, Soc. of Arts* XII (1864), 263, 472 and 489.

29 *Op. cit.* XIII (1865), 145, 427.

30 *Ibid.*, 532.

31 Ware, M., *A Handy Book of Sanitary Law*, 1865; see also *Journal of the Soc. of Arts* XIV (15 Dec. 1865), 79.

32 *Journal, Soc. of Arts* XIV (1866), 443; see also 543.

33 *Builder* XXV (1867), 99.

34 T. Hawksley, 'Suggestions for a Mode of Supplying Cheap and Healthy Dwellings for the Working Classes, with Security and Profit to the Investor', *Journal, Soc. of Arts* XIV (1867), 308.

35 *Another Blow for Life*, viii.

36 *Ibid.*, 31 and 41.

37 *Ibid.*, 62.

38 *Ibid.*, 85.

39 *On the Construction of Dwellings for the Poor*; reported in *Builder* XXI (1863), 821 and 823. This quotation taken from a report in *Labourer's Friend*, Jan. 1864, 4.

40 Eyton, H. M., 'On the Fireproof Construction of Dwellings', *Journal, Soc. of Arts* XII (1864), 91.

41 J. Taylor, Jnr., 'On the Construction of Labourers' Cottages, and Sanitary Building Appliances', *Journal, Soc. of Arts* XI (12 Dec. 1862), 68.

42 *Transactions, N.A.P.S.S.* (1866), 478.

43 Reviewed in *Builder* XXIII (1865), 603 which also in the leading article for that issue notes the revival of interest because of the current fears of a cholera epidemic.

44 'Where can Working Men Live?', *Chambers's Journal*, 16 Sept. 1865, 584.

45 Beggs, T., 'Dwellings for the People – How to Multiply them and How to Improve them', *Journal, Soc. of Arts* XIV (1866), 177.

46 *The Homes of the Working Classes*, 26.

47 *Ibid.*, 42.

48 *Builder* XXIX (1871), 860.

49 W. Bardwell, *What a House Should Be, versus Health in the House* (1873).

50 Published in 1874.

51 W. Eassie, *Healthy Houses* (1872).

52 *Builder* XXXI (1873), 318, 361, 381–2, 430, 461, 480, 560, all contain reference to the committee's debates and its report is summarised, 893. It was published as the *Report of the special Committee of the Charity Organisation Society on the Dwellings of the Poor* (1873). There is a good summary in a subsequent and more readily accessible document, *Report of the Dwellings Committee of the Charity Organisation Society* (1881).

53 *Builder* XXIII (1865), 243.

54 *Journal, Soc. of Arts* XIV (1865), 31.

55 27 & 28 Vict. C. 313.

56 See Chapter 7. The 1883 *Cheap Trains Act* was the most important measure in the evolution of workmen's fares on the railways.

57 O. Hill, 'Experiences of Management', *Builder* XXIV (1866), 770. 'An Account of a Few Houses Let to the London Poor', *Transactions N.A.P.S.S.* (1866), 625; see also *Fortnightly Review*, Nov. 1866.

58 W. T. Hill, *Octavia Hill* (1956) 56 *et. seq.*

59 Paradise Place is now Moxon Street, Marylebone. The buildings no longer exist.

60 Octavia Hill's evidence, Select Committee, 1882, 158 is an important summary of her views; see also 'Common Sense and the Dwellings of the Poor and Improvements now Practicable', *Nineteenth Century* IV (1883), 925.

61 O. Hill, *Homes of the London Poor* (1875), 193.

62 See *Builder* XXIX (1871), 233 and 424; XXX (1872), 433.

63 *Builder* XXX (1872), 583. The growing interest in public gardens was reflected in the formation of a society in 1874 to buy up some of the more desolate London squares – see *Ibid.*, XXXII (1874), 211.

64 31 & 32 Vict. C. 130; for views against the earlier drafts, see: *Transactions, N.A.P.S.S.* (1866), 619 and *Builder* XXV (1867), 615.

65 Quoted by Jephson, *London*, 227.

66 *Ibid.*, 226–7.

67 See Simon, *Sanitary Institutions*, 322–4.

68 The Royal Sanitary Commission, appointed 24 November 1868; it reported early in 1871.

69 Respectively 34 & 35 Vict. C. 70 and 35 & 36 Vict. C. 79.

70 *Builder* XXXII (1874), 3.

71 38 & 39 Vict. C. 55.

72 See G. F. Chambers, *A popular Summary of Public Health and Local Government Law* (1875).

73 See below.

74 Section 157.

75 In fact until the various reforms of the nineties dealt with in Chapter 8.

76 See note in W. G. Lumley, *The Public Health Act, 1875, Annotated* (1875), 135.

77 *Transactions, R.I.B.A.*, 1877–8, 277.

78 The most useful source of information about the model code is *Knight's Annotated Model Bye-Laws, 1883*.

79 Knight, *op. cit.*, 86.

80 *Ibid.*, 87–8.

81 *Transactions R.I.B.A.* (1877–8), 287.

82 Parkes, E. A., *Public Health*, 1876, 17.

83 See *Builder* LV (1888 ii), 223.

84 *Ibid.*

85 Information supplied by the Town Clerk. Preston was unusual so far as I can gather, but a great deal more work in the problem of bye-laws and particularly the spirit in which they were implemented is necessary before it will be possible to analyse the full effect of the Model Code.

86 An examination of Birmingham's case shows that it was specifically Chamberlain's influence that brought this step about following years of neglect. This strengthens the argument for specific cases rather than generalisation.

87 See *Labourer's Friend*, Jan. 1869, 7.

88 *Builder* XXXII (1874) 273 see also J. Liddle, 'Defects in the Sanitary Provisions of the Metropolitan Building Act', *N.A.P.S.S.* VI, 1872–1873, 129, reported *Builder* XXXI (1873), 63.

89 *Builder* XXXI (1873), 802.

90 *Builder* XXXII (1874), 347, 403 and 430.

91 *Ibid.*, 441.

92 *Hansard, ibid.*, 1983.

93 *Hansard, ibid.*, 1967.

94 *Builder* XXXI (1873). It continued to be so right through to the Select Committee 1881–2 and the Royal Commission 1884–5. Sir James Watson lectured to the British Association 'How to Meet the Requirements of Population displaced by the Artizans Dwellings Act', in 1878 – see *Builder* XXXVI (1878), 891 and in 1879 he was at the R.I.B.A. – see *Builder* XXXVII (1879), 448.

95 *Hansard, op. cit.*, 1943.

96 38 & 39 Vict. C. 36.

97 See *Labourer's Friend*, Oct. 1875, 70.

98 O. Hill, *Homes of the London Poor* (1875), 2.

99 *Ibid.*, 7. I think this shows that both Octavia Hill and Shaftesbury were adopting entrenched positions which became increasingly at variance with the growing body of socially liberal thinking.

100 See L.C.C., *The Housing Question in London*, 5–7.

101 *Builder* XXXVI (1879), 1249.

102 *Ibid.*, 326 and 551.

103 Victoria Buildings already referred to.

104 *Builder* XXXVII (1879), 1139 and 1299.

105 It was not a very convincing argument because the really poor who were the hard core of the slum problem everywhere could not afford to live in suburban houses even if they could reach them.

106 L.C.C., *The Housing Question in London*, 112 *et seq.*

107 *Builder* XXXVI (1878), 723.

108 L.C.C., *The Housing Question in London*, 146.

109 *Ibid.*, 151.

110 *Builder* XXXIV (1876), 647.

111 *Ibid.*

112 *Builder* XXXV (1877), 796 and 842; XXXVI (1878), 549.

113 *Ibid.*, XXXVII (1879), 724 and 1359.

114 *Ibid.*, 785.

115 *Ibid.*, 813.

116 *Ibid.*, 896.

117 *Ibid.*, 846.

118 *Ibid.*, 905; the L.C.C. work, Simon and Jephson are all valuable on the problems after 1875. I have used *The Builder* here because it was able to make week-by-week comments on the progress of negotiations.

119 42 & 43 Vict. C. 63.

120 42 & 43 Vict. C. 64.

121 *Builder* XXXIV (1876), 196.

Chapter 6

1 L.C.C. Housing Question in London, 294–5, Appendix C.

2 *Ibid.*, 296–7 and figures derived from Appendix C.

3 The plight of the Board is unemotionally set out in L.C.C., *The Housing Question in London*, 36; see also the evidence of Robert Vigers, Surveyor to the Peabody Trustees and G. B. Richardson, a member of the Metropolitan Board, to Select Committee 1881 and that of F. W. Goddard, Surveyor to the Metropolitan Board, to Select Committee, 1882.

4 There were Bedfordbury, Great Wild Street, Pear Tree Court, Whitecross Street, Old Pye Street, Little Coram Street and Great Peter Street.

5 Whitechapel and Essex Road.

6 St. George-the-Martyr, Southwark: High Street, Islington and Bowmans Buildings, Marylebone.

7 Part of Goulston Street.

8 Part of the Goulston Street and Whitechapel sites.

9 See L.C.C. Housing Question in London, 130 *et seq.*

10 Royal Commission 1885, 414. A rather biased case is made out against the Peabody Trust in: H. Quigley and I. Goldie, *Housing and Slum Clearance in London* (1934), 41 *et seq.*

11 The initial populations did tend to decrease – see A. Newsholme, 'The Vital Statistics of the Peabody Buildings and other Artizans' and Labourers' Block Dwellings', *Journal of the Royal Statistical Society* LIV (March 1891), 88, Table XVIII.

12 L.C.C. Housing Question in London, 113.

13 See below.

14 L.C.C. *op. cit.*, 114.

15 A small company of no special importance.

16 *Builder* LI (1886 ii) 713.

17 See J. N. Tarn, 'Housing in Liverpool and Glasgow', *Town Planning Review* XXXIX (Jan. 1969), 321.

18 J. S. Clarke, *The Housing Problem*, 372–3.

19 *Builder* XXXVII (1879), 1088.

20 Noted *ibid.*, 1188 and XXXVII (1880), 427.

21 *Builder* XXXVIII (1880 i), 427.

22 *Ibid.*, XXXIX (1880 ii), 322.

23 *Ibid.*, XLIV (188 i), 693.

24 *Ibid.*, XLIX (1885 ii), 563.

25 *Ibid.*, L (1886 i), 881.

26 *Architects Journal*, 18 March 1954, 336.

27 For accounts of local conditions see *Labourer's Friend*, June 1845, 234; *Builder* XV (1857), 55 and XIX (1861), 1.

28 Royal Commission 1845, app. 24.

29 *Builder* XXVIII (1870), 750 and *Labourer's Friend*, Jan. 1871, 27.

30 J. L. Garvin, *Chamberlain*, 186.

31 *Builder* XXXIII (1875), 1072. The construction of Corporation Street itself was carried through by means of a local Act.

32 From a speech by Chamberlain, quoted by Garvin, *op. cit.*, 195.

33 Royal Commission 1885, 447, Chamberlain's Evidence.

34 *Ibid.*

35 Designed by Spalding and Cross; see N. Pevsner, South Lancashire (Buildings of England series), 270.

36 J. N. Tarn, 'The Peabody Donation Fund: the Role of a Housing Society in the Nineteenth Century', *Victorian Studies* X (1966/67), 7.

37 The Duke of Westminster helped in the seventies with

a site in Pimlico and during the eighties with land in Grosvenor Square, the Marquis of Northampton the previous decade with a plot in Goswell Road. Otherwise the Company was buying land in less expensive areas. By 1890 its role was largely played out. See J. N. Tarn, 'The Improved Industrial Dwellings Company', *Transactions of the London and Middlesex Archaeological Society* XXII (1968), 43.

38　The evidence and the cross-examination of representatives of both organisations testify to this. Attention is drawn to this point in Quigley & Goldie, *Housing and Slum Clearance*, 32 and 34.

39　*Builder* XXXV (1877), 669.

40　*Ibid.*

41　*Ibid.*

42　*Illustrated London News*, 31 May 1879, 519.

43　*Ibid.*

44　Bowmaker, *Housing of the Working Classes*, 96.

45　*Builder* XXXVII (1879), 1158 and Bowmaker, *op. cit.*, 96.

46　*Ibid.*, XL (1881 ii), 572.

47　W. T. Hill, *Octavia Hill*, 169.

48　*Builder* LIV (1881 i), 352 and LVII (1889 ii), 333; see also Hill, *op. cit.*, 121–2 and Bowmaker, *op. cit.*, 73.

49　*Ibid.*, LVII (1889 ii), 333.

50　*Ibid.*, XLIX (1885 ii), 151.

51　Bowmaker, *op. cit.*, 130.

52　*Builder* XLIX (1885 ii), 137.

53　*Ibid.*, XLVII (1884 ii), 645 and XLIX (1885 ii), 424.

54　*Ibid.*, XXXII (1874), 987 and 1003.

55　Select Committee, 1881, 287.

56　*Builder* XXXII (1874), 1057, contains a contemporary criticism.

57　Bosanquet, *London*, 274.

58　*Builder* XXXVII (1879), 291.

59　See, for example, Burdett Buildings, junction of Burdett Road and Westminster Bridge Road, designed by a Mr Sinclair for a Mr Hobbs in 1882: *Builder* XLIV (1883 i), 223. A scheme for Messrs Chubb in Glengall Road designed by Elijah Hoole, so arranged that the rooms could be let off in any combination from 1–4: *Builder* XLVIII (1885 i), 600. St James' Dwellings in Silver Place and Ingestre Place off Regent Street, designed by H. H. Collins for St James, Westminster Vestry who paid for them out of a trust fund – they were for widows and their children, minimum dwellings of 1 or 2 rooms each. *Builder* L (1886 i), 471 and LI (1886 ii), 123.

60　For example, St James's Residential Chambers at the junction of King Street and Jermyn Street – *Builder* LXIII (1882 ii), 320; Oxford and Cambridge Mansions, Marylebone Road and Lisson Street – *Builder* XLIV (1883 i), 140 and XLV (1883 ii), 144; Hyde Park Mansions, *Builder* XLVI (1884 i), 351 and 380; Newman Mansions, Oxford Street, *Builder* LIV (1888 i), 340.

61　*Builder* LIV (1888 i), 128.

62　See Chapter 4.

63　*Builder* LX (1881 i), 165, the architect was William Crisp of Chancery Lane.

64　*Labourer's Friend*, April 1881, 57.

65　*Builder* XLV (1883 ii), 747.

66　From the 1884 Prospectus.

67　J. Parsons, *Housing by Voluntary Enterprise*, 38.

68　O. Hill, 'Common Sense and the Dwellings of the Poor, Improvements Now Practicable', *Nineteenth Century* XIV (Dec. 1883), 925.

69　*Builder* XLVIII (1885 i), 446 and 603.

70　H. Barnett, *Canon Barnett, his Life, Work and Friends*, I, 138.

71　Parsons, *op. cit.*, 40.

72　*Ibid.*

73　See *Builder* XXXII (1874), 1057.

74　Much of the information about the Company was provided by C. W. Baker of Charlwood Properties Ltd.

75　L.C.C., *Housing Question in London*, 242–3.

76　*Builder* XLIX (1885 ii), 140.

77　Information supplied by the Company.

78　*Builder* LVII (1889 ii), 361; other details from the Trust records.

79　See Bowmaker, *The Housing of the Working Classes*, 125.

80　Information supplied by the Trust.

Chapter 7

1　*Builder* XXXVIII (1880 i), 2.

2　*Dwellings of the Poor. Report of the Dwellings Committee of the Charity Organisation Society, Presented to the Council 2 August, 1880.* Criticised in *Builder* XXXIX (1880 ii), 215.

3　C. H. Cameron, 'Results of the Town Labourers Dwellings Acts', *Transactions, N.A.P.S.S.* (1881), 687 *et seq.* See also in same volume, p. 596: E. Spencer, 'Artisans' and Labourers' Dwellings Improvements Act, 1875, and Local Acts'.

4　See *Builder* XL (1881 i), 666 and 747.

5　*Report of the Select Committee on Artizans' and Labourers' Dwellings, 1881.*

6　*Report of the Select Committee on Artizans' and Labourers' Dwellings, 1882, iv–v.*

7　Select Committee, 1882, 11, Evidence of Sir H. A. Hunt.

8　*Ibid.*, x; it was suggested that the City of London might be allowed to rehouse on alternative sites and then to rehouse no more than half those displaced.

9　*Ibid.*

10　*Ibid.*

11　*Ibid.*

12　45 & 46 Vict. C. 54.

13　Jephson, *London*, 297.

14　46 & 47 Vict. C. 34.

15　William Birt, General Manager of the Great Eastern Railway Company which had the obligation of providing workmen's fares imposed upon it as early as 1864 gave evidence before the Select Committee 1882, 87. The 1885 Royal Commission found that the Act had not been widely effective in the first two years.

16　*Builder* XLV (1883 ii), 232.

17　Cited by Jephson, *London*, 309.

18　'A curious site for Industrial Dwellings', *The Times*, 18 Dec. 1883.

19　*Builder* XLV (1883 ii), 583.

20　*The Times*, 22 Feb. 1884. 'The School Board for London and the Over-pressure of Poverty and Drink'; Williams was a London School Board Inspector.

21　*Macmillan's Magazine* XXXIX (April 1879), 535.

22　*Ibid.*, 536.

23　*Ibid.*, 538, see also W. M. Torrens, 'The Government of London', *Nineteenth Century* VIII (Nov. 1880), 761.

24　*Macmillan's Magazine, op. cit.*, 540.

25 *Ibid.*, 543.
26 *Nineteenth Century* XII (Aug. 1882), 231.
27 *Ibid.*, 235.
28 Cross had first insisted upon rehousing all those displaced, but had subsequently found it necessary to modify his view.
29 *Nineteenth Century, op. cit.*, 238 *et seq.*
30 *Nineteenth Century* XIII (June 1883), 992.
31 *Ibid.*, 1007.
32 'Labourers' and Artisans' Dwellings', *National Review* II (Nov. 1883), 301.
33 *Ibid.*, 304.
34 *Ibid.*, 313.
35 *Builder* XLV (1883 ii), 577.
36 'Labourers' and Artisans' Dwellings', *Fortnightly Review*, 1 Dec. 1883, 761.
37 *Ibid.*, 766.
38 *Ibid.*, 775.
39 *Ibid.*, 776.
40 See 'Mr Chamberlain on the Housing of the Poor' *Pall Mall Gazette*, 26 Nov. 1883, 11. *The Times* and the *Daily Telegraph* were favourable; the *Standard* and *Morning Advertiser* hostile.
41 Lord Brabazon, 'Great Cities and Social Reform', I, *Nineteenth Century* XIV (Nov. 1883), 802.
42 S. A. Barnett, 'Great Cities and Social Reform', II, *Nineteenth Century* XIV (Nov. 1883), 813.
43 *The Times*, 24 November 1883, The level of interest and discussion can be seen elsewhere in columns of this newspaper; see a letter from J. Llewelyn Davies, 16 November, and in the same issues reports of speeches by Messrs Fawcett and Shaw-Lefevre at a Liberal party occasion at Reading. *The Times* also printed a leader that day touching upon the Reading meeting and generally arguing caution in housing reform particularly with regard to financial implication on the part of the community. Another long and anonymous letter in support of lodging houses was published on 30 Nov.
44 O. Hill, 'Improvements Now Practicable', part of a Symposium 'Common Sense and the Dwellings of the Poor', *Nineteenth Century* XIV (Dec. 1883), 925.
45 *Ibid.*, 926.
46 A similar argument is put forward in *Quarterly Review* CLVII (Jan. 1883), 144. See *Builder* XLVI 19 Jan. 1884.
47 Hill, *op. cit.*, 933.
48 He was the son of William Arnold, brother of Matthew; as an orphan he was adopted by Matthew's sister and her husband W. E. Foster.
49 'Existing Law', *Nineteenth Century* XIV (Dec. 1883), 940.
50 *Nineteenth Century, op. cit.*, 934.
51 *Ibid.*, 935.
52 *Ibid.*, 938.
53 *Builder* XLV (1883 ii), 803.
54 *Ibid.*
55 *Ibid.*, 773.
56 A. Marshall, 'The Housing of the London Poor, I: Where to House them', *Contemporary Review* XLV (Feb. 1884), 224.
57 M. G. Mulhall, 'The Housing of the London Poor, II: Ways and Means', *Contemporary Review, op. cit.*, 231.
58 R. A. Cross, 'Homes of the Poor', *Nineteenth Century* XV (Jan. 1884), 150.
59 *Ibid.*, see also a further article by Cross under the same title, *Nineteenth Century* XVII (June 1885), 926.
60 *Builder* XLVI (1884 i), 291.
61 Royal Commission 1885, 4.
62 *Ibid.*, 12.
63 *Ibid.*, 16 *et seq.*
64 *Ibid.*, 28–9.
65 *Ibid.*, 34.
66 *Ibid.*, 34 *et seq.*
67 *Ibid.*, 40 *et seq.*
68 *Ibid.*, 51–3.
69 *Ibid.*, 55.
70 *Ibid.*, 60.
71 *Builder* XLVIII (1885 i), 715.
72 48 & 49 Vict. C. 72.
73 Millbank alone was used for dwellings; Coldbath fields was used for a Post Office & Pentonville continued in use as a prison.
74 See L.C.C., *Housing Question in London*, 17–18.
75 Jephson, *op. cit.*, 326.
76 *Ibid.*, 329.
77 51 & 52 Vict. C. 41.
78 See *Builder* LIV (1886 i), 434, 446, 466, and LV (1886 ii), 8 etc.
79 53 & 54 Vict. C. 70.
80 L.C.C. *Housing Question, op. cit.*, 19.
81 By far the best expression of this point of view is William Morris' *News from Nowhere*, 1890.
82 The subject is treated more broadly in G. F. Chadwick, *The Park and the Town, Public Landscape in the 19th and 20th Centuries* (1966).
83 See *Builder* XXXVI (1878), 1092.
84 *Open Spaces (Metropolis) Act, 1877*, 40 & 41 Vict., C. 35.
85 *Metropolitan Open Spaces Act (1877) Amendment Act, 1881*, 44 & 45 Vict. C. 34.
86 Attention to this provision was drawn in *Builder* XLII (1882 i), 38.
87 'The Practical Utility of Public Gardens', *Builder* XLV (1883 ii), 314.
88 *City of London Parochial Charities Act, 1883*, 46 & 47 Vict. C. 36.
89 *Metropolitan Open Spaces Acts Extension Act, 1887*, 50 & 51 Vict. C. 32.
90 W. T. Hill, *Octavia Hill*, 104.
91 For an account of the Kyrle Society, see O. Hill, 'Colour Space and Music for the People', *Nineteenth Century* XV (May 1884), 741.
92 *Builder* XLIX (1885 ii), 595.
93 W. T. Hill, *op. cit.*, 70–2.
94 *Builder* LIV (1888 i), 352.
95 For Hunter's views see 'Commons, Parks and Open Spaces', *Contemporary Review*, Sept. 1886, 387.
96 *Builder* XLIX (1885 ii), 177.
97 *Ibid.*, 492.
98 *Builder* LII (1887 i), 73, 277 and 560.
99 *Ibid.*, LVI (1889 i), 275 and LVII (1889 ii), 345.
100 T. H. Lewis, 'On the Laying Out of Town Areas', *Builder* LIII (1887 ii), 424.
101 See for example Pepler, G. L., 'A Belt of Green Round London', *Garden City* I (March 1911), 41.
102 See *Builder* XLI (1881 ii), 596.
103 For a study of one specific area see H. J. Dyos, 'Workmen's Fares in South London, 1860–1914', *Journal of Transport History* I (May 1953), 3.

104 *Ibid.*, and also Select Committee 1882, 87 *et seq.*, evidence of William Birt of the Great Eastern Railway Co.
105 Birt, *op. cit.*
106 *Builder* XLII (1882 ii), 172 and XLV (1883 ii), 233. Not a company which falls within the true meaning of 'Industrial dwellings' as they have been defined in early pages – this in itself a sign of changing times.
107 Select Committee, 1882, x.
108 Reported in *Builder* XLVI (1884 i), 871.
109 Rev. H. Solly, *Rehousing of the Industrious Classes*.
110 Royal Commission 1885, 50.
111 L.C.C., *The Housing Question in London*, 98.
112 *Ibid.*, 100.
113 *Ibid.*, 101 where the clause is printed in full.
114 *Ibid.*, 107–8.
115 *Ibid.*
116 *Ibid.*, 109–11.
117 *Journal of Transport History, op. cit.*
118 L.C.C., *Housing after the War*, 31.
119 L.C.C., *Housing of the Working Classes*, 108.
120 Dyos, *op. cit.*, 17.
121 L.C.C., *Housing of the Working Classes*, 109. Obviously the L.C.C. would wish its readers to believe this and it was largely true: the municipal broom was efficient.
122 *Ibid.*, 110.
123 L.C.C., *Housing after the War*, 31.
124 Dyos, *op. cit.*, 17.
125 The divergence of official opinion, however, can be well illustrated by the paper read at the York Congress of the *Association of Municipal and Sanitary Engineers and Surveyors* in 1882 by the Borough Surveyor of Halifax in which he recommended back to back housing as the best and cheapest form of working class housing. It should be added however, that his colleagues unanimously condemned this north country practice; see *Builder* XLII (1882 ii), 265.
126 'A Sanitary Review', *Builder* LI (1886 ii), 752; see also a report of Professor Corfield talking on 'Household Sanitation' at the Architectural Association: *Builder* LII (1887 i), 199.
127 *Ibid.*, XXXIX (1880 ii), 88.
128 *Ibid.*, XLV (1883 ii), 199.
129 *Ibid.*, XLIV (1888 i), 41.
130 See J. Hammer, 'Improvement of the dwellings of the 'Poor', *Transactions, N.A.P.S.S.* (1884), 459.
131 *Builder* XLVI (1884 i), 735, 819, 853, 871, 881; XLVII (1884 ii), 107, 118 and 221. A typical pamphlet of the period was John Allan, *Healthy Homes* (1885) – progress was patently very slow.
132 *Builder* LII (1887 i), 372 and LIV (1881 i), 165.
133 *Ibid.*, LII (1887 i), 561.
134 D. G. Hoey, 'Dwellings for the Poor' reported *Builder* LVII (1889 ii), 204 and 275.
135 *Builder* L (1886 i), 633.
136 *Ibid.*
137 *Ibid.*, LIII (1887 ii), 386, in a review of B. W. Richardson (ed.) *The Health of Nations*, which was a collection of Chadwick's writings.

Chapter 8

1 53 & 54 Vict. C. 70.
2 Sections 16–19.
3 Sections 6, 11 & 12.
4 Section 8.
5 L.C.C., *Housing Question in London*, 22.
6 1890 Act, Second Schedule.
7 Section 21.
8 Section 12.
9 Section 13.
10 See L.C.C., *Housing Question in London*, 26 *et seq.*
11 57 & 58 C. 55.
12 63 & 64 Vict. C. 59.
13 56 & 57 Vict. C. 73.
14 There are several summaries of the early building legislation for London: see J. Summerson, *Georgian London*, and W. R. Davidge, 'The Development of London, and the London Building Acts', *Journal, R.I.B.A.*, XXI (2 Mar. 1914), 359.
15 Jephson, *op. cit.*, 24.
16 7 & 8 Vict. C. 84.
17 18 & 19 Vict. C. 122.
18 Jephson, *op. cit.*, 83–4.
19 *Builder* XXXIX (1880 ii), 187.
20 25 & 26 Vict. C. 102.
21 41 & 42 Vict. C. 32.
22 45 & 46 Vict. C. 14.
23 Royal Commission 1885, 712, Evidence of P. G. Smith, who was architect to the Local Government Board.
24 W. Woodward, 'London As It Is And As It Might Be', *Transactions, R.I.B.A.*, 1885–6, 13.
25 P. G. Smith, Royal Commission 1885 *op. cit.*
26 'How to ensure breathing spaces' XXI (May 1887), 677.
27 *Ibid.*, 679.
28 J. Slater, 'Building Legislation', *Transactions, R.I.B.A.* (1889–90), 128–9.
29 *Builder* XLIX (1885 ii), 478, 562, 625 and 745.
30 *Ibid.*, XLVIII (1885 i), 469.
31 *Ibid.*, 530.
32 *Ibid.*, 567.
33 Royal Commission, 1885, 12.
34 *Ibid.*
35 Jephson, *op. cit.*, 375 *et seq.*
36 53 & 54 Vict. C. 76.
37 See *The Public Health* (London), *Act, 1891*, edition of A. MacMorran (1891).
38 56 & 57 Vict. C. 73.
39 Jephson, *op. cit.*, 382 *et seq.*
40 From the Commissioners Brief, see Royal Commission on the Amalgamation of City and County of London, 1894.
41 62 & 63 Vict. C. 14.
42 Jephson, *op. cit.*, 376.
43 57 & 58 Vict. C. ccxiii.
44 Section 9.
45 Section 13.
46 Section 22.
47 Sections 26–7.
48 Section 40 i.
49 The term dwelling house referred to 'a building used, or constructed, or adapted to be used wholly or principally for human habitation'.
50 Sections 40 i and ii.
51 Section 41 iii.
52 Section 41 iv and v.
53 Section 41. 2.
54 See J. F. J. Sykes, Public Health and Housing, 92–3.
55 Section 41. 2.

56 Section 42 i and ii.
57 Section 46.
58 Section 47.
59 Section 48.
60 Section 51.
61 Section 13.
62 Section 70.
63 Section 122.
64 Section 136.
65 Sections 138 *et seq.*
66 Section 145.
67 Section 153 and 166 *et seq.*
68 Section 164.
69 The *London Building Act 1894 (Amendment) Act, 1898*, 61 & 62 Vict. C. cxxxvii.
70 The *London Building Acts (Amendment) Act, 1905*, 5 Edw. 7 C. ccix.
71 The *London County Council (General Powers) Act, 1908*, 8. Edw. 7 C. cvii.
72 The *London County Council (General Powers) Act, 1909*, 9 Edw. 7 C. cxxx.
73 L.C.C., *Housing of the Working Classes 1855–1912*, 117.
74 *Ibid.*, 25.
75 Quigley and Goldie, *Housing and Slum Clearance*, 52.
76 *Ibid.*, 65–6.
77 Known as the 3 per cent resolution, quoted L.C.C., *The Housing Question*, 47.
78 After 1905 the Local Government Board became the responsible authority.
79 L.C.C., *The Housing Question*, 48.
80 *Ibid.*
81 *Ibid.*, 43.
82 *Ibid.*, 49.
83 *Ibid.*, 49 *et seq.*
84 L.C.C., *Housing of the Working Classes, 1855–1912*, 26.
85 These were (1) Tench Street, St Georges in the East; (2) Brook Street, Limehouse; (3) Trafalgar Road, Greenwich; (4) Hughes Fields, Deptford; (5) Cable Street, Shadwell; (6) Shelton Street, St Giles.
86 L.C.C., *Housing of the Working Classes 1855–1912*, 26.
87 *Ibid.*, 177.
88 L.C.C., *The Housing Question in London*, 170.
89 *Ibid.*, 170–1.
90 Except for The Tench Street site which was used as an open space after the Council had obtained a special Act for this purpose in 1889; L.C.C., *The Housing Question in London*, 167.
91 Thomas Blashill, 1830–1905; appointed architect to the Metropolitan Board of Works, 1887, transferred to L.C.C. and retired in 1898, previously he had been a district surveyor in London and in private practice.
92 Known as Aldwych, Cotterell, Lindsay, Powys and Wimbledon Buildings, see L.C.C., *The Housing Question in London*, 188–9.
93 *Ibid.*, L.C.C., *The Housing of the Working Classes*, 32.
94 L.C.C., *The Housing Question*, Table IV, 300–1.
95 *Ibid.*, 190.
96 *Ibid.*, 192, subsequently reduced to 4,700; see 194.
97 *Ibid.*, 194.
98 *Ibid.*, 200.
99 *Ibid.*, 201.
100 *Ibid.*, 203.

101 *Ibid.*, 208–9.
102 These figures are taken from or derived from *Ibid.*, 209.
103 *Ibid.*, all the estates are here treated in some detail. Details of the L.C.C. schemes are contained in the Council's own publications *The Housing Question in London 1855–1900* (1900), and *Housing of the Working Classes 1855–1912* (1912).
104 *Ibid.*, 236–45.
105 *Ibid.*, 268.
106 L.C.C., *The Housing of the Working Classes*, 66 *et seq.* See also D. G. Jones, 'Some Early Works of the L.C.C. Architect's Department', *A.A. Journal* (Nov. 1954), 91.
107 L.C.C., *The Housing of the Working Classes*, 42.
108 *Ibid.*, 88.
109 L.C.C., *The Housing Question*, 63–4.
110 *Ibid.*, 275.
111 L.C.C., *The Housing of the Working Classes*, 70.
112 *Ibid.*, 72.
113 *Ibid.*
114 *Ibid.*, and deduced from statistics.
115 *Ibid.*, 76–8.
116 *Ibid.*, 72–3.
117 L.C.C., *Housing of the Working Classes 1855–1912*, 82.

Chapter 9

1 The changing housing situation is a symptom of a gradual shift in the economic position of the working man. By the last years of the century the artizan was relatively better off than he had been at any other time and this made the task of housing him less of a problem – see Sir Robert Ensor, *England 1870–1914*, 274.
2 The L.C.C. decision in 1898 to provide accommodation somewhere equal to that demolished, in quantity, demonstrates the continuing gravity of the situation.
3 J. N. Tarn, *Working-class Housing in 19th-century Britain* (1971), 49.
4 Quigley and Goldie, *Housing and Slum Clearance*, 47.
5 J. Parsons, *Housing by Voluntary Enterprise*, 9.
6 *Ibid.*, 59.
7 *Ibid.*, 66–7.
8 B. Kirkham Gray, *Philanthropy and the State*, x.
9 *Ibid.*, 68.
10 *Ibid.*
11 *Garden City* IV (Aug. 1909), 231; this of course reflects the early planners' antipathy towards this unromantic concept. See also G. D. H. Cole, *The Life of Robert Owen*, 239 for further details.
12 Thomas Love Peacock, Crotchet Castle, 1831, has this to say '...Mr Toogood, the co-operationist, who will have neither fighting nor praying; but wants to parcel out the world into squares like a chess-board, with a community on each, raising everything for one another, with a great steam-engine to serve them in common for tailor and hosier, kitchen and cook.' 61 (Folio Society Ed. 1964) and a little later he has Mr Toogood saying 'Build a grand co-operative parallelogram, with a steam-engine in the middle for a maid-of-all-work', 75 (*ibid.*).
13 See H. Rosenau, *The Ideal City*, 132–3.
14 *Ibid.*, 134–5.

15 See L. Benevolo, *The Origins of Modern Town Planning*, 65.

16 J. C. Loudon, *Encyclopaedia*, 244.

17 *Mechanics Magazine* XVI (1831–2), 231.

18 S. Smirke, *Suggestions for the Architectural Improvement of the Western Part of London*, 60.

19 Published c. 1845; see W. Ashworth, *The Genesis of Modern British Town Planning*, 123–4.

20 See Ashworth, *op. cit.*, 121–4; Select Committee 1840, 110; and J. N. Tarn, 'The Model Village at Bromborough Pool', *Town Planning Review* XXXV (Jan. 1965), 329 and A. Watson, 'The Price's Bromborough Village', *Progress: The Unilever Quarterly*, 3 (1964), 138.

21 J. Burnley, *Sir Titus Salt*, gives all the details of Salt's career.

22 For Saltaire see C. Stewart, *A Prospect of Cities*, 148 *et seq.*; J. M. Richards, 'Sir Titus Salt', *Architectural Review* LXXX (Nov. 1936), 216.

23 W. L. Creese, *The Search for Environment*, ch. 2, 'The Bradford-Halifax School of Model Village Builders'.

24 On Copley see *Builder* XXI (1863), 109; J. Hole, *The Homes of the Working Classes*, 70–2; for Akroydon see *Builder* XXI (1863), 116–7; Hole, *op. cit.*, 75; E. Akroyd, *Transactions, N.A.P.S.S.* (1862), 806; and R. Bretton, 'Colonel Edward Akroyd', *Transactions, Halifax Antiquarian Society, 1948*, 61.

25 See also Creese, *op. cit.*

26 See W. H. Chaloner, *The Social and Economic Development of Crewe 1780–1923*; also H. B. Wells, 'Swindon in the 19th and 20th Centuries' and J. Betjeman, 'Architecture' both from: L. V. Grinsell, H. B. Wells, H. S. Tallamy and John Betjeman, *Studies in the History of Swindon* (1950).

27 F. B. Head, Stokers and Pokers, 82.

28 Buckingham, 183.

29 E. Howard, *Garden Cities of To-morrow*, 127.

30 R. E. Turner, *James Silk Buckingham*, 440. See also: P. Abercrombie, 'The Ideal City, Victoria', *Town Planning Review* IX (March 1921), 15 and C. Stewart, *A Prospect of Cities*, 169.

31 Howard first published the account as *To-morrow, A Peaceful Path to Real Reform* in 1898 but in its revised form of 1902 it was given what has become its most well known title: *Garden Cities of Tomorrow*.

32 *Builder* VII (1849), 401.

33 S. Lang, 'The Ideal City from Plato to Howard', *Architects Review* CXII (Aug. 1952), 91.

34 From the Spectator, quoted in *Builder* XIV (1956), 476.

35 'Piling up the People; M. Jules Barie's "Aerodomes"' *Builder* XXVI (1868), 255.

36 See T. Davis, *John Nash, The Prince Regent's Architect* (1966), 63 *et seq.*; see also T. Davis, *The Architecture of John Nash* (1960), 99 *et seq.*

37 R. Turnor, *The Regency Style 1800–1830*, 90.

38 The account of Bournemouth is taken from W. Ashworth, *The Genesis of Modern British Town Planning*, 42.

39 *The Visitors Guide to Bournemouth and its Neighbourhood* (3rd ed. 1850), 11 quoted by Ashworth, *op. cit.*, 42.

40 *A Descriptive Guide to Bournemouth*, 1875, 3.

41 'Ballad of Bedford Park', *St James's Gazette*, 17 Dec. 1881, quoted by R. Blomfield, *Richard Norman Shaw*; interesting light is cast on the estate in M. Glazebrook, (ed.) *Artists and Architecture of Bedford Park 1875–1900* (1967), which was the catalogue for An Exhibition held at St Michael's Vicarage during Bedford Park Festival Week 10–18 June 1967.

42 Blomfield, *op. cit.*, 37.

43 See R. Turner, *The Smaller English House, 1500–1939*, 174.

44 M. E. Macartney, 'Mr. Lever and Port Sunlight', *Architectural Review* XXVIII (July 1910), 43 and P. Abercrombie, 'Port Sunlight', *Town Planning Review* I (April 1910), 33.

45 T. Raffles Davison, *Port Sunlight*, 6; quoting from a paper by Leverhulme of Nov. 1900.

46 The Viscount Leverhulme, *Viscount Leverhulme by his Son*, 49.

47 These were William Owen, who designed the factory and Jonathan Simpson who was a personal friend, see *Viscount Leverhulme by his Son*, 86–7.

48 J. Reynolds, 'The Model Village of Port Sunlight', *Architect's Journal*, 27 May 1948, 495.

49 From a paper read at the A.A., 21 March 1902, quoted *Viscount Leverhulme by his Son*, 89. See also, The Viscount Leverhulme, *The Six Hour Day*, 146. He deals very fully with the issues of density limitation and the provision by the municipality of free land for housing, in a lecture 'Land for Houses' given to the *North End Liberal Club*, Birkenhead, 4 Oct. 1898; see *The Six Hour Day*, 155.

50 *Viscount Leverhulme by his Son*, 87.

51 William Owen designed the first group then various firms assisted until in 1910 J. L. Simpson was appointed architect to the firm and thereafter designed much of the housing. His speciality seems to have been half-timbered work.

52 W. A. Harvey, *The Model Village and its Cottages: Bournville* (1906), 9.

53 J. J. Clarke, *Town Planning Review* VIII (April 1920), 118.

54 They have published their own history: Bournville Village Trust *The Bournville Village Trust 1900–1955* (Birmingham, 1956).

55 Harvey, *op. cit.*, 17.

56 *Ibid.*, 10: see also on subsequent garden experiments, Bournville Village Trust, *Landscape and Housing Development*.

57 Harvey, *op. cit.*, 12.

58 *Ibid.*, 64.

59 *Builder* LV (1888 ii), 16 and 141.

60 *Ibid.* See also A. S. Peake, *Sir William Hartley*.

61 The 1946 edition of *Garden Cities of To-morrow* with its perceptive Preface by F. J. Osborne. Howard lived 1850–1928, for biographical details see Dugald MacFadyen, *Sir Ebenezer Howard and the Town Planning Movement*.

62 *Builder* XLVII (1884 ii), 79.

63 *Rehousing of the Industrial Classes, or Village Communities and Town Rookeries*.

64 In *News from Nowhere*, 1890.

65 *Builder* XLII (1882 i), 730.

66 See F. J. Osborne, in his preface to the 1946 edition of *Garden Cities of To-morrow*, 20.

67 Edward Bellamy, *Looking Backward* (1887), frequently reprinted.

68 *Garden Cities of Tomorrow* (1945 ed), 48.

69 *Ibid.*, 48–9.
70 The account of Garden City is taken from chapter I; Osborne notes the derivation of the Crystal Palace on 32.
71 *Ibid.*, 52.
72 *Ibid.*, 55.
73 *Ibid.*, 126–7.
74 *Ibid.*, 142.
75 *The Building of Satellite Towns*, 55.
76 Nevill a well known K.C. who subsequently became Mr Justice Nevill, and Adams one of the important early town planners who later worked at the Local Government Board.
77 Purdom, *op. cit.*, 57–8.
78 Prospectus of the First Garden City Co., quoted Purdom, *op. cit.*, 60.
79 Purdom, *op. cit.*, 83.
80 *General Suggestions and Instructions Regarding Buildings other than Factories in the Garden City Estate*; quoted by Purdom *op. cit.*, 97.
81 *Ibid.*
82 *Ibid.*
83 *Ibid.*, 97.
84 *Ibid.*
85 S. Giedion, *Space, Time and Architecture*, 510.
86 *One Man's Vision, The Story of Joseph Rowntree Village Trust*, 3.
87 *Ibid.*, 15–17.
88 P. Abercrombie, 'Earswick', *Town Planning Review* I (April 1910), 37, is a good account of the early development.
89 *One Man's Vision*, 5–8.
90 *Ibid.*, 23–4.
91 Parker worked out his views more carefully in an article 'Site Planning as Exemplified at New Earswick', *Town Planning Review* XVII (Feb. 1937), 79. His argument, briefly, was that on land costing less than £300 per acre a system of peripheral development was cheaper than that involving a series of intersecting roads. Increased density involved increased road costs which consequently increased the cost of the housing over that of a low density layout based upon the cul-de-sac principle.
92 P. Abercrombie, 'Hampstead Garden Suburb', *Town Planning Review* I (April 1910), 30.
93 Wife of Canon Barnett the Founder of the East End Dwellings Company.
94 P. Johnson-Marshall, 'Hampstead Garden Suburb', *Architect's Journal*, 11 July, 1957, 83.
95 *Hampstead Garden Suburb Act, 1906*, 6 Edw. 7, C. 192.
96 Abercrombie, *op. cit.*
97 Johnson-Marshall, *op. cit.*
98 The other useful account of Hampstead is W. A. Eden, 'Hampstead Garden Suburb, 1907', *Journal R.I.B.A.*, Oct. 1957, 489.
99 'A Model Mining Village; Woodlands', *Garden City* III (Sept. 1908), 125.
100 *Ibid.*, and *Town Planning Review*, I (July 1910), 111.
101 *Garden City, op. cit.*, 125.
102 *Ibid.*
103 *Architectural Review* XXII (March 1910), 179.
104 *Garden City* II (June 1907), 348; (July 1907), 371; (Jan. 1908), 496 and IV (May 1909), 206.
105 P. Abercrombie, 'A Comparative Review of "Garden City" Schemes in England, Part II', *Town Planning Review* I (July 1910), 111.
106 *Ibid.*, and *Garden City* I, new series (May 1911), 98.
107 Abercrombie, *op. cit.*, and *Garden City, op. cit.*, 97.
108 Abercrombie, *op. cit.*
109 *Garden City*, I new series (March 1911), 36.
110 *Town Planning Review* IV (April 1913), 133. For plans of the Ruislip Common, Clack Lane, Eastcote and Northwood Schemes, see *Town Planning Review* VIII (Dec. 1920).
111 *Town Planning Review*, I (Jan 1911), 339.
112 *Town Planning Review* II (July 1911), 124.
113 *The Hundred Best Houses* was published as a history and advertisement for Romford Garden Suburb in 1911, it included contributions from Arnold Bennett, Thomas Hardy, H. G. Wells, Sir Fredrick Treves, Sir Hiram Maxim, Sir Arthur Pinero.
114 P. Mairet, *Pioneers of Sociology, The Life and Work of Patrick Geddes*, 3.
115 *Ibid.*, 47.
116 *Ibid.*, 76.
117 P. Geddes, *Cities in Evolution* (Ed. 1949), 114.
118 *Ibid.*, 115.
119 *Ibid.*, 116.
120 *Architectural Review* XXVIII (July 1910), 14.
121 Geddes, *op. cit.*, 68.
122 *Ibid.*
123 *Ibid.*, 53.
124 See Abercrombie's account quoted by J. Tyrwhitt in her new introduction to the 1949 ed. of *Cities in Evolution*, xii.
125 Geddes, *op. cit.*, 81.
126 *Ibid.*, 82.
127 *Ibid.*, 96.
128 According to Tyrwhitt, ix.
129 For other estimates of Geddes see T. F. Lyon, 'After Geddes', *Planning Outlook* I (July 1948), 7 and G. Peper, 'Geddes' Contribution to Town Planning', *Town Planning Review* XXVI (April 1955), 19.
130 See Osborne's Preface to 1946 ed. of *Garden Cities*, 12.
131 See W. Ashworth, *The Genesis of Modern British Town Planning*, 178. See also *National Housing and Town Planning Council 1900–1910, A Record of Ten Years' Work for Housing and Town Planning Reform*.
132 Purdom, *The Building of Satellite Towns*, 66.
133 'Cheap Cottages and the Exhibition at Letchworth', *Architectural Review* XVIII (Oct. 1905), 154.
134 'Cheap Cottages and the Exhibition at Letchworth', *Architectural Review* XVIII (Sept. 1905), 108.
135 *Town Planning Review*, I (April 1910), 23.
136 *Ibid.*
137 See M. Tims, *Ealing Tenants Limited, Ealing Local History Society, Members Papers, No. 8* (1966). Miss Tims deals with the development of the movement in some detail.
138 *Town Planning Review* I (April 1910), 23 and (July 1910), 111.
139 *Ibid.*
140 *Lord Leverhulme, by his Son*, 139.
141 Geddes, *Cities in Evolution*, particularly chapter 5 'Ways to the Neotechnic City'.
142 Ashworth, *op. cit.*, 180.
143 See his book *The Improvement of the Dwellings and Surroundings of the People – the Example of Germany*, 1904. He was a layman deeply interested in planning,

at the time Chairman of the Manchester Citizens' Association and an influential figure in the pressure group which prepared the way for the 1909 Act. He died in 1931.

144 T. R. Marr, *The Housing Condition of Manchester and Salford* (1904), Manchester and Salford Citizens Committee on the Housing Conditions of Manchester and Salford.

145 At Harbourne.

146 See his book: J. S. Nettlefold, *A Housing Policy* (1905), and for his views on Birmingham and its problems. *Town Planning Review* II (1922–12), 99 and *Garden City* I (1911), 44.

147 *Ibid.*, 35–6.

148 H. R. Aldridge, *The Case for Town Planning* (1915) Manchester and Salford Citizens Committee on the Housing Conditions of Manchester and Salford, contains the statement presented to the Government, the speeches and the replies, 161 *et seq.*

149 *Hansard*, 1908, quoted in L.C.C. *The Housing of the Working Classes*, 1912, 14.

150 9 Edw. 7 C. 44.

151 Aldridge, *op. cit.*, 155.

152 Sections 1–4.

153 Section 10 *et seq.*

154 Section 17.

155 Section 18.

156 The Town Planning provisions attracted wide attention and they are printed in full in Aldridge *op. cit.*, and *Garden City* IV (Feb. 1910), 276 *et seq.* See also *Town Planning Review* I (1910–11), 39, 44, 129, 132, 164, 323 and II (1911–12), 26.

Bibliography

The works listed below are intended to provide a concise list of the sources used in the preparation of the book. It is not suggested that they explore thoroughly all the related fields covered in the previous pages. Periodicals used only rarely are referred to only in the footnotes.

PAPERS AND PERIODICALS

Architectural Review, from 1896.
Architects' Journal, The, since 1919 (formerly *Builders' Journal and Architectural Record* and the *Architects' and Builders' Journal*).
Builder, The from 1842.
Contemporary Review, The, from 1866.
Chamber's Edinburgh Journal, 1832–53, then *Chambers's Journal*.
Economist, The, from 1843.
Fortnightly Review, The, 1865–1934.
Garden City, The, 1904–8; later Garden Cities and Town Planning and now Town and Country Planning.
Halifax Antiquarian Society papers, reports &c. c. 1910–28, now *Transactions* 1928–.
Illustrated London News, The, from 1842.
Labourers' Friend, The, 1834–84.
Macmillan's Magazine, 1859–1907.
Mechanics' Magazine, The, 1923–73.
New Monthly Magazine, The, 1821–81.
Nineteenth Century Review, The, 1877–1950. Subsequently *The Twentieth Century*
National Association for the Promotion of Social Science, Transactions of, 1857–84.
National Review, The, 1883–1950, then the *National and English Review*
Pall Mall Magazine, The, 1893–1914.
Quarterly Review, The, from 1809.
Royal Institute of British Architects, Transactions of, 1835–41, subsequently, *Papers read at the Institute, Sessional Papers, Transactions, Proceedings* and now *The Journal of the R.I.B.A.*
Society for the encouragement of arts, manufacturers and commerce, Journal of the, from 1852.
Times, The.
Town Planning Institute, Papers and discussions, 1914–23, then *Journal of the*, from 1924.
Town Planning Review, The, from 1910.
Transport History, The Journal of, since 1953.
Victorian Studies, since 1957.

PARLIAMENTARY PAPERS

Report of the Select Committee on the Health of Towns, 1840.
Poor Law Commission Reports:
  On the Sanitary Condition of the Labouring Population and on the Means of its Improvement, 1842.
  Local Reports for England, 1842.
  Report on Scotland, 1842.
  Supplementary Report on the Practice of Interment in Towns, 1843.
Royal Commission for Inquiring into the State of Large Towns and Populous Districts;
  First Report, 1844.
  Second Report, 1845.
Royal Sanitary Commission;
  First Report, 1868–9.
  Second Report, 1871.

Select Committee on Artizans' and Labourers' Dwellings Improvement;
  First Report, 1881.
  Second Report, 1882.
Royal Commission on the Housing of the Working Classes, Report 1884–5.

BOOKS AND PAMPHLETS

Abercrombie, P. *The County of London Plan*, 1943 (with J. Forshaw).
  The Greater London Plan, 1944.
Adshead, S. D. *Liverpool Town Planning and Housing Exhibition*, Liverpool 1914 (with P. Abercrombie).
  Town Planning and Town Development, 1923.
Aldridge, H. R. *The Case for Town Planning*, 1915.
Allen, J. *Healthy Houses*, 1885.
Armytage, W. H. G. *Heavens Below: Utopian Experiments in England, 1560–1960*, 1961.
Ashpitel, A. *Town Dwellings: An Essay on the Erection of Fireproof Houses in Flats: A Modification of the Scottish and Continental Systems*, 1855 (with J. Wichcord).
Ashworth, J. *The Genesis of Modern British Town Planning*, 1954.
Austin, H. *An Instance of Faulty Arrangement of Dwellings and a Plan for its Improvement*, 1855.
Baines, T. *Liverpool in 1859*, 1859.
Balgarnie, R. *Sir Titus Salt, Baronet: His Life and its Lessons*, 1877.
Bannington, B. G. *English Public Health Administration*, 1915.
Bardwell, W. *Healthy Homes and How to Make Them*, 1853.
  What a House should be versus Death in the House, 1873.
Barnes, H. *The Slum: its Story and Solution*, 1931.
Barnett, H. *The Story of the Growth of Hampstead Garden Suburb, 1907–1928* [not published, ?1928].
Barton, M. *Tunbridge Wells*, 1937.
Beames, T. *The Rookeries of London: Past, Present and Prospective*, 1850.
Bellman, H. *The Building Society Movement*, 1927.
Berlepsch-Valendàs, *Die Gartenstadtbewegung in England, ihre Entwickelung und ihr jetziger Stand*, Munich, 1911.
Besant, W. *London in the Nineteenth Century*, 1909.
Best, G. F. A. *Shaftesbury*, 1964.
Blomfield, Sir R. T. *Richard Norman Shaw, R. A., Architect, 1831–1912*, 1940.
Boardman, P. *Patrick Geddes: Maker of the Future*, 1944.
Bosanquet, C. B. P. *London: Some Account of its Growth, Charitable Agencies and Wants*, 1868.
  The History and Mode of Operation of the Charity Organisation Society, 1874.
Bosanquet, H. *Social Work in London 1869–1912: A History of the Charity Organisation Society*, 1914.
Bournemouth, The Visitors Guide, 1850 (3rd ed.).
Bournemouth, A Descriptive Guide, 1875.
Bournville Village Trust, *Bournville Housing*, Bournville, 1922.
Bournville Village Trust, *When We Build Again*, 1941.
  Sixty Years of Planning, Bournville, 1943.
  Landscape and Housing Development, 1949.
  Bournville Village Trust, 1900–55, Bournville, 1955.
Bowie, J. (ed.) *Healthy Homes*, 1854.
Bowle, J. *Politics and Opinion in the Nineteenth Century*, 1954.
Bowley, M. *Housing and the State, 1919–1944*, 1945.

Bowmaker, E. *The Housing of the Working Classes*, 1895.

Briggs, A. *The Age of Improvement*, 1959.
History of Birmingham, 2 vols. 1952 (with C. Gill).
Victorian Cities, 1963.

Buckingham, J. S. *National Evils and Practical Remedies with a plan of a Model Town*, 1849.

Burnley, J. *Sir Titus Salt and George Moor*, 1885.

Burn, W. L. *The Age of Equipoise*, 1964.

Chadwick, E. *Commentaries on the Report of the Royal Commission on Metropolitan Sewage Discharge, and on the Combined and Separate Systems of Town Drainage*, 1885.
The Health of Nations, 1887 (ed. B. W. Richardson).

Chaloner, W. H. *The Social and Economic Development of Crewe, 1780–1923*, Manchester, 1950.

Chambers, G. F. *A Popular Summary of Public Health and Local Government Law*, 1875.
The Law Relating to Public Health and Local Government, 8th ed. 1888.

Chambers, W. *The Sanitary Movement*, 1850.
Industrial Investment and Associations, 1851.
Improved Dwellings for the Humbler and other Classes, based on the Scottish Dwelling House System, 1855.

Chapman, J. M. & B. *The Life and Times of Baron Haussmann*, 1957.

Chapman, S. D. (ed.) *The History of Working-class Housing*, Newton Abbot, 1971.

Charity Organisation Society, The *Report of the Special Dwellings Committee*, (1) 1873; (2) 1881.

Checkland, S. G. *The Rise of Industrial Society in England, 1815–1885*, 1964.

Cleary, E. J. *The Building Society Movement*, 1965.

Clark, G. K. *The Making of Victorian England*, 1962.

Clarke, J. J. *The Housing Problem, Its History, Growth, Legislation and Procedure*, 1920.

Cole, G. D. H. *The Life of Robert Owen*, 1930.
The Common People 1746–1946 (with R. Postgate), 4th ed. 1949.

Cullingworth, J. E. *Restraining Urban Growth : The Problem of Overspill*, 1960.

Culpin, E. G. *The Garden City Movement up to Date*, 1914.

Davison, T. R. *Port Sunlight, A Record of Artistic and Pictorial Aspect*, 1916.

Dewsnup, E. R. *The Housing Problem in England: its Statistics, Legislation and Policy*, Manchester, 1907.

Dickens, C. Many of his novels contain authentic descriptions of working class homes and life, see particularly *Oliver Twist*, 1838–9, *Dombey and Son*, 1846–8, *Hard Times*, 1854.

Disraeli, B. His social and political novels are relevant:
Sybil, or The Two Nations, 1845,
Tancred, or The New Crusade, 1847.

Dove, P. E. *Account of David Yarranton*, Edinburgh, 1854.

Dutton, R. *The Victorian Home*, London 1954.

Dyos, H. J. *Victorian Suburb, A Study of the Growth of Camberwell*, Leicester, 1961.

Eassie, W. *Healthy Houses. A handbook to the history, defects, and remedies of drainage, etc.* 1872.
Sanitary Arrangements for Dwellings, 1874.

Engels, F. *The Condition of the Working Class in England in 1844*, Leipzig, 1845 (modern edition of W. O. Henderson and W. H. Chaloner, 1958).

Farr, W. *Vital Statistics*, 1885 (ed. N. A. Humphreys).

Finer, S. E. *The Life and Times of Sir Edwin Chadwick*, 1952.

Fletcher, B. *Model Houses for the Industrial Classes*, 1871.
The London Building Acts, 5th ed. 1914.

Fraser, P. A. *On some of the Causes which at present retard the Moral and Intellectual Progress of the Working Classes*, 1857.

Gale, S. *Modern Housing Estates*, 1949.

Galton, D. *Observations on the Construction of Healthy Dwellings*, 1880.

Garvin, J. L. *Life of Joseph Chamberlain*, 1933.

Gaskell, E. C. *Mary Barton*, 1848.
North and South, 1855.

Gatliff, C. *Practical Suggestions on Improved Dwellings for the Industrious Classes*, 1854.
On Improved Dwellings and their Beneficial Effect on Health and Morals, and Suggestions for their Extension, 1875.

Gavin, H. *Sanitary Ramblings*, 1848.
The Habitations of the Working Classes, 1851.
City Development, A Study of Parks, Gardens and Cultural Institutes, Edinburgh, 1900.

Geddes, P. *Cities in Evolution, An Introduction to the town planning movement and to the study of civics*, 1915 (new edition of A. Geddes and J. Tyrwhitt 1949).

George, W. L. *Labour and Housing at Port Sunlight*, 1909.

Gibberd, F. *Town Design*, 1953.

Gibbons, D. *The Metropolitan Building Act 1844*, 1844.
The Metropolitan Building Act 1855, 1855 (with R. Hesketh).

Giedion, S. *Space, Time and Architecture*, 1943.

Gill, C. *History of Birmingham*, 2 vols., 1952 (with A. Briggs).

Girdlestone, C. *Letters on the Unhealthy Condition of the Lower Class of Dwellings*, 1845.

Glen, A. *Glen's Law of Public Health and Local Government*, 1858, and numerous subsequent editions.

Goldie, I. *Housing and Slum Clearance in London*, 1934 (with H. Quigley).

Godwin, G. *London Shadows*, 1854.
Town Swamps and Social Bridges, 1859.
Another Blow for Life, 1864.

Gomme, G. L. *London in the reign of Victoria 1837–1897*, 1898.

Goodwin, M. *Nineteenth Century Opinion*, 1951.

Granville, A. B. *The Spas of England*, 2 vols, 1841.

Gray, B. K. *Philanthropy and the State*, 1908.

Grinsell, L. V. (and others) *Studies in the History of Swindon*, Swindon, 1950.

Halevy, E. *A History of the English People in the Nineteenth Century*, 4 vols., 2nd ed., 1950.

Hammond, J. L. & B. *The Age of the Chartists*, 1930.
The Bleak Age, 1947.
The Town Labourer, 1917, ed. of 1966.

Hares, T. *Thoughts on the Dwellings of the People, Charitable Estates, Improvements and Local Government of the Metropolis*, 1862.

Harling, R. *Home : A Victorian Vignette*, 1938.

Harris, G. M. *The Garden City Movement*, Hitchin, 1905.

Harrison, J. F. C. *Social Reform in Victorian Leeds, The Work of James Hole, 1820–1895*, The Thoresby Society, Leeds, 1954.

Hart, E. *A Manual of Public Health for the use of Local Authorities, Medical Officers of Health and Others*, 1874.
London Old and New, A Sanitary Contrast, 1885.

Harvey, W. A. *The Model Village and its Cottages: Bournville*, 1906.

Hashick, P. H. *Cheap Dwellings*, 1906.

Head, F. B. *Stokers and Pokers*, 1849.

Hill, M. D. *Charge to the Grand Jury of Birmingham*, 1854.

Hill, O. *Homes of the London Poor*, 1875.
Letters to my Fellow-Workers, 1904.
Letters on Housing (ed. E. Ourvy), 1933.

Hill, W. T. *Octavia Hill*, 1956.

Hiorns, F. R. *Town Building in History*, 1956.

Hitchcock, H. R. *Early Victorian Architecture in Britain*, 2 vols., 1954.
Architecture, Nineteenth and Twentieth Centuries, 1958.

Hobson, O. *A Hundred Years of the Halifax. The History of the Halifax Building Society, 1853–1953*, 1953.

Hodder, E. *The Life and Works of the Seventh Earl of Shaftesbury*, 1888.

Hole, J. *The Homes of the Working Classes with Suggestions for their Improvement*, 1866.

Hole, W. V. *The Housing of the Working Classes in Britain, 1850–1914: A study of the Development of Standards and Methods of Provision* [unpublished University of London Ph.D. Thesis, 1965].

Holroyd, A. *Saltaire and its Founder, Sir Titus Salt, Bart.*, 1871.

Horsfall, T. C. 'The Improvement of the Dwellings and Surroundings of the People: The Example of Germany', Manchester 1904 (appendix to T. R. Marr, *Housing Conditions of Manchester*).

Hoskin, W. *A Guide to the Proper Regulation of Buildings in Towns, as a means of promoting and securing the Health, Comfort and Safety of the Inhabitants*, 1848.

Howard, E. *To-morrow: a Peaceful Path to Real Reform*, 1898 (republished as *Garden Cities of To-morrow*, 1902; modern ed. 1945).

Hughes, J. R. T. 'Problems of Industrial Change' (see Appleman, P., Madden, W. A. and Wolff, M., eds., *1859: Entering an Age of Crisis*, Bloomington [Indiana] 1959).

Hundred New Towns Association, *A Hundred New Towns for Britain*, 1933.

Illustrated Carpenter and Builder, *Modern Cottages and Villas*, n.d. [1908].

Ingestre, the Viscount, *Meliora, or Better Times to Come*, 1852.
Meliora II, 1853.
Social Evils, their Causes and their Cures, 1853.

Inman, J. *The Rebuilding of Manchester*, 1935 (with E. D. Simon).

Jennings, H. *Brynmawr, A Study of a Distressed Area*, 1934.

Jephson, H. *The Sanitary Evolution of London*, 1907.

Judge, M. *Sanitary Arrangements of Dwelling Houses*, 1884.

Kellett, J. R. *The Impact of Railways on Victorian Cities*, 1969.

Kingsley, C. *Yeast*, 1848.
Alton Locke, 1850.

Knight's Annotated Model Byelaws, 1883, and various other editions.

Korn, A. *History Builds a Town*, 1953.

Kropotkin, P. *Fields, Factories and Workshops*, 1907.

Laing, S. *National Distress: Its Causes and Remedies*, 1844.

Lambert, R. *Sir John Simon, 1816–1904 and English Social Administration*, 1963.

Lavedon, P. *Histoire de l'Urbanisme – Renaissance et de temps modernes*, Paris 1959.

Leverhulme, The Viscount, *The Six Hour Day and Other Industrial Questions*, 1918.

Leverhulme, the second Viscount, *Lord Leverhulme by his Son*, 1927.

Lewis, C. L. *Dr Southwood Smith*, 1898.

Lewis, R. A. *Edwin Chadwick and the Public Health Movement, 1832–1854*, 1952.

Little, B. *The Building of Bath*, 1947.
Cheltenham, 1952.

Lloyd, N. *A History of the English House*, 1931.

Lock, M. *The Hartlepools, A Survey and Plan*, 1948.
A Plan for Middlesborough, 1945.

London County Council, *The Housing Question in London 1855–1900*, 1900 (ed. C. J. Stewart).
Housing of the Working Classes in London, 1855–1912, 1913.
Housing, 1927.
Housing, 1928–30.

London County Council, *Survey of London*, see particularly:
vol. XXI, 1949, *Tottenham Court Road, and neighbourhood*.
vol. XXVI, 1956, *The Parish of St Mary, Lambeth. Pt. 2. Southern area*.
vol. XXVII, 1957, *Spitalfields and Mile End New Town: the parishes of Christ Church and All Saints, and the liberties of Norton Folgate and the Old Artillery Ground*.

Loudon, J. C. *Encyclopaedia of Cottage, Farm and Villa Architecture*, 1833.

Lower, E. W. *The Metropolitan Buildings Act 1855*, 1855.

Macfadyen, D. *Sir Ebenezer Howard and the Town Planning Movement*, Manchester 1933.

Macmorran, A. *The Public Health (London) Act 1891*, 1891.

Mairet, P. *Pioneers of Sociology – The Life and Letters of Patrick Geddes*, 1957.

Marr, T. R. *Housing Conditions in Manchester and Salford*, Manchester 1904.

Mayhew, H. *London Labour and the London Poor*, 1851 (abridged ed., P. Quennell, *Mayhew's London*).

Meakin, B. *Model Factories and Villages: Ideal Conditions of Labour and Housing*, 1905.

Mearns, W. C. *The Bitter Cry of Outcast London: An Inquiry into the Condition of the Abject Poor*, 1883 (see ed. of A. S. Wohl, Leicester 1970).

Metropolitan Association, *Report of a Public Meeting to Raise Funds, etc.*, 1854.

Middlebrook, S. *Newcastle upon Tyne, Its Growth and Achievement*, Newcastle, 1950.

Millington, F. H. *The Housing of the Poor*, 1891.

Morgan, J. M. *The Christian Commonwealth*, 1850.

Morris, W. *News from Nowhere*, 1890.
Architecture, Industry and Wealth, 1902.

Mumford, L. *The Story of Utopias*, 1923.
Technics and Civilisation, 1934.
The Culture of Cities, 1938.
City Development, 1946.

Nettlefold, J. S. *A Housing Policy*, 1905.
Practical Housing, Letchworth, 1908.
Practical Town Planning, 1914.

Newsholme, A. *Fifty Years in Public Health*, 1935.

Olsen, D. J. *Town Planning in London, The Eighteenth and Nineteenth Centuries*, New Haven, 1964.

Osborne, F. J. *New Towns after the War*, 1918 and 1942.
Greenbelt Cities: The British Contribution, 1946.

Owen, D. *English Philanthropy, 1660–1960*, 1965.

Owen, R. A. *A Statement Regarding the New Lanark Establishment*, Edinburgh, 1812.
A New View of Society, 1817 (third ed.).

Parker, F. *George Peabody 1795–1869*, Nashville, Tennessee, 1955.

Parkes, E. A. *Public Health*, 1876.

Parsons, J. *Housing by Voluntary Enterprise*, 1903.

Perkins, H. *The Origins of Modern English Society 1780–1880*, 1969.

Pevsner, N. The Buildings of England series generally, and particularly:
London, Volume One, *the Cities of London and Westminster*, 2nd ed. 1962.
London (except the Cities of London & Westminster), 1952.

Pilcher, D. *The Regency Style*, 1948.

Price, J. *Homes of the Poor*, ?1874.

Price, S. *Building Societies, Their Origin and History*, 1958.

Price's of Bromborough, 1854–1954, 1954.

Patterson, C. B. *Angela Burdett Coutts and the Victorians*, 1953.

Purdom, C. B. *The Garden City*, 1913.
Town Theory and Practice, 1921.
The Building of Satellite Towns, 1925.

Quennell, C. H. B. *Modern Suburban Housing*, 1906.

Quickley, H. *Housing and Slum Clearance in London*, 1934 (with I. Goldie).

Rasmussen, S. E. *London: The Unique City*, 1937.
Towns and Buildings, 1951.

Richardson, A. E. *The Smaller English house of the late rennaissance 1660–1830* (with H. D. Eberlein), 1925.
London Houses from 1660–1820 (with C. L. Gill), 1911.

Richardson, B. W. *Hygeia: A City of Health*, 1876.
The Health of Nations. A Review of the Works of Edwin Chadwick, 2 vols., 1887.

Roberts, D. *Victorian Origins of the British Welfare State*, New Haven, 1960.

Roberts, H. *The Dwellings of the Labouring Classes*, 1850.
Home Reform, 1852.
The Improvement of the Dwellings of the Labouring Classes, 1859.
Essentials of a Healthy Dwelling, 1862.

Rosenau, H. *The Ideal City*, 1959.

Rowntree, A. (ed.) *The History of Scarborough*, 1931.

Rowntree, B. S. *Poverty: A Study of Town Life*, 2nd ed. 1902.
Lectures on Housing, Manchester, 1914 (with A. C. Pigou).

Rowntree, J. *The Temperance Problem and Social Reform* (with H. Sherwell).

Rowntree, *The Joseph Rowntree Village Trust, One Man's Vision*, 1954.

Royal Institute of British Architects, The *Town Planning Conference, London 10–15 October, 1910*, 1911.

Rumsey, H. W. *On Sanitary Legislation and Administration in England*, 1858.

Saarinen, E. *The City, its Growth, its Decay, its Future*, New York, 1943.

Salmon, J. *Ten Years' Growth of the City of London*, 1891.

Scott, G. G. *Personal and Professional Recollections*, 1879.

Self, P. *Cities in Flood: The Problem of Urban Growth*, 1957.

Sennett, A. R. *Garden Cities in Theory and Practice*, 2 vols. 1905.

Sharp, T. *Town and Countryside*, 1932.
English Panorama, 1936.

Simon, E. D. *How to Abolish the Slums*, 1929.
The Rebuilding of Manchester, 1935 (with J. Inman).

Simon, Sir J. *English Sanitary Institutions*, 1890.
Public Health Reports, 2 vols., 1887 (ed. E. Seaton).

Sitte, C. *The Art of Building Cities*, 1945.

Smalley, G. *Life of Sir Sydney Waterlow*, 1909.

Smirke, S. *Suggestions for the Improvement of the Western Parts of London*, 1834.

Smith, S. *Results of Sanitary Improvements Illustrated by the Operation of the Metropolitan Societies*, 1854.

Solly, H. *Industrial Villages, a Remedy for Crowded Towns and Deserted Fields*, 1884.
Rehousing of the Industrial Classes, or Village Communities v. Town Rookeries, 1884.

Stewart, C. *A Prospect of Cities*, 1952.

Strange, R. (ed.) *Lodging Houses Acts*, 1851.

Strickland, C. W. *On Cottage Design*, 1864.

Summerson, Sir J. *John Nash, Architect to George IV*, 1935.
Georgian London, 1947.
Heavenly Mansions, 1949.
Architecture in Britain 1530–1830, 1953.

Sykes, J. F. J. *Public Health and Housing*, 1901.

Tarn, J. N. *Working-class Housing in 19th Century Britain*, 1971.

Teale, T. P. *Dangers to Health*, 1879.

Thompson, E. P. *The Making of the English Working Class*, 1963.

Thompson, W. *Housing Handbook up to date*, 1903.
Housing up to date, 1907.
Town Planning in Practice. With an Account of the Ruislip (Middlesex) Town Planning Scheme, 1911.

Thomson, D. *England in the Nineteenth Century (1815–1914)*, 1950.

Tims, M. *Ealing Tenants, Ltd., Pioneers of Co-partnership*, Ealing, 1966.

Tremenheere, G. B. *Dwellings of the Labouring Classes in the Metropolis*, 1856.

Trevelyan, G. M. *English Social History*, 1942 (Illustrated ed. 1952).

Tunnard, C. *The City of Man*, 1953.

Turner, R. E. *James Silk Buckingham, A Social Biography*, 1934.

Turnor, R. *The Smaller English House, 1500–1939*, 1952.

Unwin, G. (ed.) *Samuel Oldknow and the Arkwrights*, Manchester, 1924.

Unwin, R. *The Art of Building a Home*, 1901 (with B. Parker).
Town Planning Practice, 2nd ed. 1911.
Nothing Gained by Overcrowding, 1912.
Greater London Regional Planning Report, 1929 and 1933.

Vivian, H. *Co-partnership in Housing in its Health Relationship*, 1908.

Wells, H. B. *Swindon in the 19th and 20th Centuries (Studies in the History of Swindon)*, 1950.

Williams, R. *London Rookeries and Colliers Slums*, 1893.

Willmott, P. *Family and Kinship in East London*, 1957 (with M. Young).

Woodward, E. L. *The Age of Reform, 1815–70*, 2nd ed. 1962.

Worthington, T. L. *Dwellings of the People*, 1893.

Wylson, J. *Remarks on Workmen's Houses in Town Districts* n.d. [1849].

Young, G. M. *Early Victorian England*, 2 vols., 1934.
Victorian England, Portrait of an Age, 2nd ed., 1953.

Young, M. *Family and Kinship in East London*, 1957 (with P. Willmott).

Zoond, V. *Housing Legislation in England, 1851–1867, with special reference to London* [unpublished University of London M.A. thesis, 1931].

OTHER SOURCES:

Information about the history of the various societies, trusts and companies is also taken from private papers, records and drawings.

There is an excellent bibliographical article by Dyos, H. J., 'The Slums of Victorian London', *Victorian Studies*, XI (Sept., 1967).

Information about the bye-laws and building regulations is drawn from the published documents of the towns concerned.

Population information is taken from:

Census of Great Britain, Decennially, 1801–1851
Census of England and Wales, Decennially, 1861–
Census of Scotland, Decennially, 1861–

Index

Figures in **bold type** indicate whole chapters or sections; 'L' means London, '*p*' means *passim*.